The Karl Muck Scandal

The Karl Muck Scandal

Classical Music and Xenophobia in World War I America

Melissa D. Burrage

UNIVERSITY OF ROCHESTER PRESS

The author and the University of Rochester Press gratefully acknowledge generous support from the AMS 75 PAYS Endowment of the American Musicological Society, funded in part by the National Endowment for the Humanities and the Andrew W. Mellon Foundation.

First published 2019

University of Rochester Press
668 Mt. Hope Avenue, Rochester, NY 14620, USA
www.urpress.com
and Boydell & Brewer Limited
PO Box 9, Woodbridge, Suffolk IP12 3DF, UK
www.boydellandbrewer.com

ISBN-13: 978-1-58046-950-0
ISSN: 1071-9989

Library of Congress Cataloging-in-Publication Data

Names: Burrage, Melissa D., 1962– author.
Title: The Karl Muck scandal : classical music and xenophobia in World War I America / Melissa D. Burrage.
Other titles: Eastman studies in music ; v. 157.
Description: Rochester : University of Rochester Press, 2019. | Series: Eastman studies in music ; v. 157 | Includes bibliographical references and index.
Identifiers: LCCN 2019003206 | ISBN 9781580469500 (hardcover : alk. paper)
Subjects: LCSH: Muck, Karl. | Germans—Massachusetts—Boston—History—20th century. | Conductors (Music)—Biography. | Xenophobia—United States—History—20th century. | World War, 1914–1918—Massachusetts—Boston.
Classification: LCC ML422.M83 B87 2019 | DDC 784.2092 [B] —dc23 LC record available at https://lccn.loc.gov/2019003206

This publication is printed on acid-free paper.

Printed in the United States of America.

This book is dedicated to my late son, Zachary Burrage-Goodwin, a twenty-two-year-old music education major at the University of South Carolina who died tragically on August 25, 2015, in a motor vehicle accident in the first week of his final year of school. Zach was a gentle-hearted, intelligent, and funny young man. He was a talented cellist, bass vocalist, educator, and sound engineer with an enormously promising future ahead of him.

❧ ❧ ❧

Zach was a part of this project from the very beginning, and, in fact, he inspired it. As a boy, he found a large collection of World War I letters in a rusty basement trunk belonging to my grandfather, Philip Burrage. Philip had attended Boston University and then enlisted with the 101st Engineers in 1917, training at Boston's Wentworth Institute of Technology on Huntington Avenue, just down the road from Symphony Hall. Each day, his unit marched through the city streets to the Boston Cadet Armory and encamped in tents on the lawn of the institute each night. Through this source, I had a very personal window into 1917 Boston, as military men took over the city and prepared for war. I treasure the moments that I had with my precious son, who was so eager to read these interesting letters aloud to my family, particularly to my father, Philip Jr. Each note vividly captures home-front excitement, as well as my grandfather's experience with trench warfare in France, and together they sparked a desire on my part to learn more. Through this correspondence, it dawned on me that the peaceful and contented world that Karl Muck had enjoyed in Boston before the war became a very different place in 1917 and 1918.

It would be an understatement to say that Zach supported me throughout the research and writing phase of this project. He was involved throughout his brief life. When he and his sisters, Lydia and Miranda, were quite young, they helped me print drafts of my work, standing bright eyed beneath the printer to catch the pages as they fell. They helped in so many small and large ways. Zach rebuilt my computer when it crashed and, in the midst of his own homework assignments, saved my manuscript when I was in danger of losing it. He and his sisters accompanied me on research trips that became a routine part of our family vacations. In 2007, he traveled with me to meet Warren Cutler, the current owner of Karl Muck's house in Boston. In 2009, Zach and his siblings hiked with me through the site of Karl Muck's internment camp in Oglethorpe, Georgia, and, in December of 2014, our family traveled Down East to find Muck's summer cottage in Seal Harbor, Maine.

In 2008, Zach assisted me in preparing two conference talks on Muck, in England and San Francisco, designing PowerPoint slides and adding audio samples of the conductor's performances to make my presentations more interesting. He attended the January of 2015 American Historical Association meeting in New York City and the August of 2015 Cape Cod Writer's Conference just two weeks before he died. We would often find ourselves having great conversations about the topics covered at these events.

Zach and his sisters studied violin and cello with Boston Symphony musicians Bo Hwang and Ron Lowry, respectively, occasionally taking lessons in the basement of Symphony Hall. They performed on Symphony Hall's stage several times, giving me a window into my topic through this very personal source. I could walk the halls of Muck's workplace, peek into the conductor's office, and watch my children practice and perform there, allowing me to reconstruct Muck's physical world, as both audience member and musician.

Not long before Zach's death, I shared a news article with him about Steinert Hall in Boston, the boarded-up subterranean concert facility once liberally utilized during Muck's time. Zach was so fascinated to learn of this place that he wrote a letter to Steinert's management to see what was needed to make it concert worthy again. He could imagine the vibrancy of pre–World War I Boston, and he wanted to help in some way to revive this space to its former glory. Unfortunately, he did not live long enough to see that developers have purchased the structure and plan to make it useful again, but I will always wonder whether his letter somehow inspired Steinert's survival.

Zach was a wonderful young man, a bright light, a caring friend, and a loving son. He was an unshakable supporter of my life's work, as I was, and continue to be, of his. It is to him that this book is dedicated.

CONTENTS

INTRODUCTION

On March 25, 1918, at the height of American involvement in World War I, United States Bureau of Investigation agents and Boston Police Department officials interrupted eminent German-born conductor Dr. Karl Muck during a private Boston Symphony Orchestra (BSO) rehearsal of Bach's *Saint Matthew Passion* on the eve of its premier Easter performance in the city, demanding that he step down from the podium.[1] Symphony manager Charles Adams Ellis convinced the men to hold off until the rehearsal had concluded, which they agreed to do, strategically positioning themselves throughout the hall, impatiently waiting until the conductor had finished his work. Following the rehearsal, Muck was escorted to a nearby office where he was asked a series of questions before being removed from the hall and transported to Boston's Back Bay Police Station for a more intense interrogation. On April 6, 1918, after spending more than a week in the "iron cage" of the East Cambridge Jail, he was arrested as a "dangerous enemy alien" and accompanied by armed US Marshals onboard the westbound train to Fort Oglethorpe Internment Camp in Georgia, where he remained under surveillance for a year and a half. His Boston property and his savings were confiscated, and he lost his income, his position in society, and his freedom, before being deported in August of 1919. Muck was a very well-known figure in the United States at that time. He had been conductor of the BSO from 1906 to 1908 and again from 1912 to 1918. His musical pedigree was impressive. Action taken against him by the United States federal government seemed very shocking.

Karl Muck's life and legacy in America was entirely reshaped by World War I. His rise and fall occurred so quickly that little is known about him historically. One rarely hears his name today, and most Americans are unacquainted with this musical giant of the Romantic era. Muck was no spy, however, and patriotism represents only a fraction of the intrigue surrounding his treatment. Authors have occasionally written about Muck as a high-profile international musician who, in 1917, refused to conduct "The Star-Spangled Banner" at a Providence, Rhode Island, concert and therefore became a victim of anti-foreign sentiment. These accounts explain Muck's punishment in the United States as having something to do with dissent—that he had done something wrong, that this musical omission was an act of insubordination during wartime. These explanations are inaccurate.

While Karl Muck's treatment in America lies at the core of this project, this is not a biography. It is not a birth-to-death narrative of a famous conductor, although this is part of the story. As a historian, I am primarily interested in the theme of cultural change during the war. I use Muck and his difficulties in America as a prism into this topic. Through this lens, he becomes an example of vulnerability at a particularly turbulent time in American history. He represents cosmopolitan Boston in the years before the war, when German ethnicity and neighborhood vitality thrived, not unlike in today's Italian North End community, the Chinatown district, or the Irish American region of South Boston. During the war, however, immigrants like Muck became caught in the middle of a national debate over immigrant restriction, over whom the country would welcome and whom it would reject. In 1918, America manufactured munitions along with hatred for its German population. The tolerant prewar society became oppressive during the war. A country that had relied heavily on German culture cast it off during the conflict. I am interested in the social response to America's national security apparatus, the impact on human lives, and the effect of wartime pressure on democracy and society. I am concerned with power structures, how they are created and then sometimes utilized to harm innocent citizens, and how one's privacy can be exploited as a tool of compliance. I explore these themes through the lens of Karl Muck.

When the famed conductor arrived in fin-de-siècle America, he was lionized as "the uncrowned king of Boston and the idol of the whole nation."[2] Muck's 1906 appointment in the city came at the peak of a collaboration between Boston and Germany in a period of great creative energy in America. From the Civil War to World War I, Boston was the center of high culture in the United States, thriving in great part because of a transnational exchange between German intellectuals and musicians who had crossed the Atlantic and helped to shape American national identity. Muck was one of those influential immigrant musicians. He developed an emotional attachment to his new city and established a life there that allowed him to thrive. As John Higham points out, public opinion looked favorably on Germans as the most "reputable of immigrant groups." The nation's 8.6 million German immigrants were praised as "law abiding" and "speedily assimilated," and, in 1903, a Boston sociologist pronounced them the "best ethnic type in the city."[3] Muck reveled in his identity as an upper-class

German musician and intellectual, and he settled quite effortlessly into Boston's cosmopolitan world, a world that I reconstruct in this study.

Muck's acceptance was precipitated by great changes in American society more generally. By the turn of the twentieth century, the United States had become a wealthy nation, transitioning from a regional agricultural economy to an industrial powerhouse based in urban cities, transforming from a Victorian culture based on thrift to one ready to spend. With more money and extra leisure time, Americans invested in entertainment. Symphony orchestras in metropolitan Boston, New York, Chicago, and Philadelphia came into existence and professionalized their operations, actively recruiting European musicians, who had trained at the best conservatories there.[4] In 1881, financier and philanthropist Henry Lee Higginson founded the Boston Symphony Orchestra, which became a world-class ensemble by the turn of the century, inspiring the expansion of permanent symphony orchestras in other cities, like Cincinnati, Pittsburgh, Minneapolis, St. Louis, and San Francisco. Orchestras, like regional baseball teams, appealed to civic pride. The development of musical culture in America, and symphonic music more specifically, could not have occurred without the participation of German Americans and German nationals. Muck played an important role in that innovative period of cultural achievement.

Muck's elevated status in America seemed assured. With World War I on the horizon, however, cities like Boston changed, developing a paramilitary environment as soldiers prepared for war. Muck had yet to see how fragile his position would become and how rising American nationalism in the first decade of the new century would lead to changing conditions for US residents of German ancestry. The federal government's mobilization campaign, led by George Creel and the Committee on Public Information, utilized propaganda to alter public opinion. The German population was especially susceptible to discrimination by the state. The war dismantled the vibrant German cultural community that had existed in Boston. Anti-German hysteria forced people to assimilate and take their cultural traditions underground.

In the field of music, in which Karl Muck was involved, times were changing too. America was developing its musical identity, building and professionalizing its cultural institutions. National emergency conditions presented opportunities within these institutions to victimize competitors. Muck became caught in a rivalry for cultural dominance between the Boston Symphony Orchestra and the New York Philharmonic that affected his personal experience in America. He was essentially trapped on the battleground of high culture in America, and he had little hope of escaping unharmed.

Muck's story is indicative of the experience of numerous German immigrants who were targeted and destroyed during World War I for reasons other than national security. His personal life was mined for evidence of wrongdoing by an overzealous board member of the New York Philharmonic and by the capitalists of New York City who fomented negative sentiment against him. He was relentlessly pursued by the Bureau of Investigation (BOI), a division of the Department of Justice, that acted as a national police force, spying on him until evidence was found to arrest, intern, and deport him as a "dangerous" foreign national.

World War I provided the US federal government fertile opportunity to expand its powers, and Karl Muck was adversely affected by that power. He can be included as a victim in this period of American oppression, made vulnerable by a government charged with protecting civil rights, thus highlighting the consequences imposed upon individuals when the guarantees of the Constitution are suspended. Muck's immigrant experience in the United States provides one example of mistreatment in a narrowing definition of citizenship.

While Karl Muck is the focus of this study, he was also not the only musician on the American home front victimized during World War I. Following Muck's arrest and subsequent internment, BSO management dismissed eighteen German members of the orchestra, including assistant conductor Ernst Schmidt.[5] Arthur Fiedler, first-generation Austrian American and BSO violinist hired by Karl Muck, who would go on to become the celebrated conductor of the Boston Pops Orchestra from 1930 to 1979, miraculously managed to hold onto his job throughout this turbulent period. He was not interned, deported, or fired, as other German players had been, but he was also not spared harassment. In the spring of 1918, young Fiedler rented a home he called Villa Pagan in the fishing village of Rockport, Massachusetts, just forty miles north of Boston. He was frequently interrogated by federal agents, who "would come and show their badges and search the house." Baked goods that Fiedler ordered from a German delicatessen in Boston arrived with pinholes, as if they had been probed for secret messages. Fiedler's mail was tampered with, and he recorded that "even little kids around Rockport started to taunt [me], calling [me] a spy." Local and federal agents believed Fiedler's waterfront balcony, strung with Japanese lanterns, was a signaling station for German U-boats. When Fiedler took the train to Boston for concerts, he wrote, "There'd be some secretive-looking guy following [me]!"[6]

Other prominent conductors and musicians in America were affected by the war. On January 12, 1918, Austrian-born Ernst Kunwald, conductor of the Cincinnati Symphony Orchestra, was arrested under orders of J. Edgar Hoover and interned at Fort Oglethorpe, Georgia. He would become Karl Muck's good friend there.[7] German-born Frederick Stock, conductor of the Chicago Symphony Orchestra, was forced to step down from his position, spending the rest of the war proving his patriotism to America and enduring rounds of investigations by federal authorities.[8] Stock had lived in the United States for two decades but had not completed his naturalization process when the war broke out. Consequently, he became a target. Alfred Hertz, conductor of the San Francisco Orchestra, was accused of running a spy ring there. The accusation was never proven, and thus he was able to maintain his position throughout the war. The Philadelphia Orchestra, organized in 1912 under British-born Leopold Stokowski, dismissed eight German string and woodwind players during the war. The Daughters of the Republic, a patriotic organization, protested famed Austrian violinist Fritz Kreisler's concerts, and thus he was forced into obscurity during the war, living in a New York City hotel room.[9] *Musical America* magazine estimated that Kreisler lost $85,000 in concert fees during this period.[10] In August of 1918, federal officials announced that they would publish a list of suspicious orchestra members whose "dedication to the United States remained doubtful."[11]

Musicians were targeted by the federal government in World War I much the same way that 320 authors, screenwriters, directors, actors, musicians, and artists were accused of communist sympathies during the 1940s and 1950s by Senator Joseph McCarthy and the House Un-American Activities Committee in a repeating pattern of abuse. During the McCarthy era, celebrated composer Aaron Copland was classified as a Communist.[12] For two decades, the Federal Bureau of Investigation (FBI) kept a file on Copland, recording his travels, his associations, and his statements. In his memoir, he wrote, "I spend my days writing symphonies, concertos, ballets. . . . I became a victim of a political situation. I tried to carry on as usual. But I lost a great deal of time and energy (not to mention lawyer's fees) preparing myself against fictitious charges."[13] The experiences of Copland and others during the 1940s and 1950s, and German Americans during World War I, illustrate the rising authoritarian nature of the federal government, capable of crushing individual rights with the impunity enabled by war emergency powers.

This case study of Karl Muck during World War I brings to light the complexity and depth of his difficulties in Boston and suggests that he represents one of many people in America unjustly victimized as a perceived threat to the nation. His story needs to be placed in the context of other discrimination cases that are an inglorious part of American history. Going beneath the historiography on Muck, I endeavored to understand and demonstrate why he was targeted in the first place, not simply to document what had happened to him. I assert that he was one of many who suffered because of economic, political, and personal motivations, including jealousy, greed, rivalry, and power. I show that Muck did not refuse to conduct the "Star-Spangled Banner." He was not a dangerous enemy alien. Rather, he was framed by the robber barons of New York as a means of securing cultural and economic supremacy for their city. Anti-German hysteria was utilized to achieve their competitive goals. Moreover, Muck represented something that would allow the federal government to secure its larger mission of protecting the country during a national emergency.

When Muck was found innocent of crimes against the state, federal agents unlawfully mined his private sexual life to find inculpatory evidence against him. Authorities' knowledge of his relationships with women, particularly his involvement with soprano Rosamond Young, was used to embarrass, blackmail, and threaten him with a public scandal, to force his compliance. Given Boston's conservative sexual climate, Muck accepted his arrest as a "dangerous enemy alien" with internment in Georgia, rather than face public ridicule as a sex criminal with punishment in a Massachusetts prison. It was through this process that they removed him from American society for a year and a half to "eliminate the threat" during wartime.

It is difficult to overstate the extent of Muck's fame in America in the 1910s or the scandal that followed his downfall. Later, deported as a common criminal under US law, he was cast out of the country as a German troublemaker and decried as "anti-American" by the media and federal authorities. In a private letter written by Muck in 1916 and published without his permission in 1919, Muck said, "America, the country of [the] free, human rights. Never in the history of the world was there a greater parody."[14] Muck's story is an example of how America has treated (and continues to treat) its immigrants and minority populations, with sometimes unjust and inhumane punishments. It is an account that reveals that the US government conspired to violate, rather than safeguard, the civil liberties of noncitizens and citizens alike, failing to preserve and uphold the promise of the Constitution.

Following Muck's deportation, his ultraconservative German nationalism and anti-Semitism became more pronounced, and he developed close relationships with the Richard Wagner family and with Adolf Hitler in the years leading up to World War II. Despite the complexity of his personality and his actions in Germany, this book focuses primarily on his American (Boston) experience, arguing that he and other German nationals and German Americans were victims in the

United States during World War I, mistreated by the federal government that was charged with protecting their civil rights.

America's centennial of the Great War provides an opportunity to look at this historical moment more deeply and to reflect upon its significance. This account of one prominent Boston resident, Dr. Karl Muck, reflects the anxieties of the time, highlights the country's changing conditions, and provides a window into the difficulties of being a German in America during World War I. Muck's particular point of view, his ethnic identity, his elite social class, his status as a privileged male, and his sexual behavior stood at the very heart of America's tensions. Muck was on the periphery of total war, not on the European battlefield itself but on the American home front, and yet his limits were tested. Like a soldier in the trenches, he was in a perilous situation, in a "cultural battlefield." He had to suffer hardship and humiliation, to overcome the trauma of his circumstances, and to survive. His story reflects a sad and overlooked episode in American history.

Chapter One

HERE ON FOREIGN SHORES

Dr. Karl Muck's Acclaim in Boston (1906–1918)

Incredibly, here on foreign shores,
The fame of our fathers' blooms anew,
An all-Germanic holy place,
Rises up with supernatural speed.

—Kuno Francke, 1903

On October 2, 1906, just twenty days shy of his forty-seventh birthday, Dr. Karl Muck and his wife, Anita, boarded the first-class section of the North German Lloyd *Kaiser Wilhelm der Große* in Bremen bound for the United States.[1] This was the couple's first voyage across the Atlantic. Muck had been hired as conductor of the Boston Symphony Orchestra, where he would remain until 1908, ultimately returning to Boston in 1912 for a second term until 1918.

The Mucks arrived in Boston to find a vibrant and cosmopolitan city. Its small yet vital German population enriched the community by its presence. Boston's upper classes had been working for decades to make the city a leader in academic and cultural affairs, and German Americans and German institutions abroad inspired this endeavor. In the last half of the nineteenth century, German immigrants had established music businesses and amateur musical organizations in Boston, and, because of their efforts, a growing, musically literate middle-class population developed an insatiable appetite for high-quality classical music. Entrepreneur and BSO founder Henry Lee Higginson saw an opportunity to form a professional orchestra, supported by an enthusiastic community of educated listeners, eager for excellent performances, the sort that Karl Muck and the Boston Symphony Orchestra would offer. Higginson dreamed of replicating in Boston the kind of musical setting that he had enjoyed during his college years in Germany and Austria, recreating a German-style hall, hiring European musicians (most especially Germans), and presenting musical compositions from European masters, creating a world-class orchestra that was part of a single transnational music culture within a European framework.[2]

Karl and Anita Muck lived in Boston during this creative period, when Anglo- and German Bostonians alike were producing high-quality cultural "products" for a welcoming market, when the flow of personnel, artistic talent, and intellectual ideas traveled by ocean liner back and forth between Europe and the United States, and when permanent symphony orchestras on both sides of the Atlantic became a ubiquitous part of public life. German immigrants like Muck, who had trained and performed in Europe, decided to "try their luck in America," bringing the culture of orchestral music that they had known in Europe to the United States.[3] Muck was well received in the city precisely because he fulfilled Higginson's agenda in the United States, of bringing European culture with him. The city was not simply "tolerant" of its German population, it embraced it. As John Spitzer makes clear, "American society was international before it became national."[4] Muck's conductorship in the city came to fruition because he exemplified elite society's cosmopolitan identity. The Mucks were privileged Europeans, and their lifestyle, education, and values dovetailed nicely with Boston's exclusive (and sometimes snobbish) domain. Muck's celebrity status as a famed conductor added to the city's prestige.

By studying Karl Muck in Boston and reconstructing the world that he lived in, we can uncover the international nature of the city before World War I that drew on influences from Germany and Continental Europe to enhance its own Anglo-Saxon traditions. Germanophilia was widespread among the middle and upper-middle classes, ultimately laying the foundation for Muck's overwhelming acceptance in the city. During those halcyon years for Germans in Boston, Muck was prized because he was one of the most sought-after conductors in all of Europe and the United States. His talents, heritage, background, and worldview, as we shall see below, ensured his positive reception among Boston's upper classes, making his integration into the new city a smooth experience. Integration, however, did not imply that Muck had fully assimilated as an American. He was a man who loved and felt great loyalty for Germany. As we shall see in Muck's evolving story, his status in his new home became increasingly unstable during the war, as the country emphasized the importance of Americanization. In those prewar years, however, Muck was perhaps the most celebrated resident of Boston.

The Making of a German Master Conductor

Albert Anselm Karl Muck was born on October 22, 1859, in Darmstadt, Germany, to Jacob Alois Muck and Anna Sybille Hofmann Muck. Karl, as he was called, was raised with every possible advantage of education available to him. Karl's nurturing and protective mother passed away when he was just ten years old, and Karl and his brother, August, were raised by their father, a music-obsessed, "fanatical reactionary," an accomplished amateur choral conductor who insisted upon strict discipline regarding music and lessons.[5] As the son of a public figure, Karl became very aware of the political climate around him. In 1871, Germany unified. Karl was just eleven years old and not too young to sense the country's swelling nationalistic pride as it sought its place on the world stage, as the British Empire was in decline and the United States was on the rise. Many changes were taking place in Germany during Muck's adolescent years. The economy prospered with the Industrial Revolution. Its output of coal, steel, chemicals, pharmaceuticals, fertilizers, and electricity helped to make Germany prosperous.[6]

Muck brought an enormous sense of pride for his homeland to Boston, and he came to the city with all of the cultural prejudices from his upbringing as well. Anti-Semitism in Germany was rampant during Muck's youth. Jews had been valued for their entrepreneurial and financial skills during the country's economic boom. By 1873, they fell out of favor, however, when the German stock market crashed. Jews were blamed for the recession, and, in the 1880s, leading German intellectuals such as Heinrich von Treitschke, Wilhelm Marr, and Adolf Stocker exacerbated the hostility against Jews by utilizing racial pseudo-science to rationalize their arguments against them. Scores of agitators and writers joined in, creating a climate of fear pervasive throughout the country.[7] Young Karl was exposed to racism by the adults around him. He learned how to discriminate just as he learned how to study academic subjects and how to play musical instruments.

In 1874, when Muck was fifteen, he enrolled in the Würzburg Humanistic High School, where he studied piano, violin, and music theory. He was a piano soloist with a local chamber music ensemble and a violinist with the municipal symphony orchestra. Karl's father influenced and guided his son's career. The elder Muck's connections made it possible to secure performances and appointments that Karl may not have been able to obtain otherwise. In 1875, sixteen-year-old Muck entered the University of Heidelberg, where he studied philosophy, classical philology, and the history of music.[8] Heidelberg was a school for privileged students. In the 1870s, the university's Society of

German Students was at the forefront of radical nationalism and anti-Semitic thinking.[9] The college atmosphere during Muck's time there was political and patriotic. Students were subjected to compulsory military training, and their peers judged them by the number of dueling scars on their cheeks. Dueling scars represented "badges of honor" for the Heidelberg elite. They were visible signs of courage and bravery, signifying victory and the ability to walk away from danger with barely a scratch.[10] Karl Muck boasted two parallel scars acquired during his time there that blended into one mark over time. Years later, under the Nazi regime, the University of Heidelberg, like many other institutions in Germany, dismissed Jewish students and staff, researched and wrote treatises on eugenics, and practiced forced sterilizations on Jews at its clinics.[11]

In 1877, Muck acquired additional musical training at Leipzig Conservatory under Ernest Friedrich Richter and Karl Reinecke, and he completed a PhD in classical philology at the University of Leipzig in 1880.[12] Muck began his professional musical career with a formal debut on February 19, 1880, performing the Piano Concerto no. 1 in B-flat of Franz Xaver Scharwenka under Arthur Nikisch at the Leipzig Gewandhaus. The Gewandhaus performance was a catalyst for a career that took off shortly thereafter. Karl was engaged as choirmaster and theater conductor in the municipal opera houses of Zurich (1880), Salzburg (1881), Brunn (1882), and Graz (1884), before becoming the first conductor at the Deutsches Landestheater of Prague (1886). Under the authority of the czar, Muck conducted sold-out performances of Wagner's *Ring* in St. Petersburg and Moscow (1889) with Angelo Neumann's touring company, impacting audience members such as composers Nikolai Rimsky-Korsakov and Alexander Glazunov, philosopher Nikolay Strakhov, ballet impresario Sergei Diaghilev, artist Alexandre Benois, and painter Nicholas Roerich.[13] At the Hamburg State Opera (1890) under theater director Bernhard Pollini, he attracted widespread attention for his style and, together with Hans Richter and Felix Weingaertner, became known as "one of the three most outstanding conductors" in all of Germany.[14] Muck went on to become principal conductor of the Berlin Court Opera (1892) and was appointed musical director (1908), fulfilling his duties in that position for four years.[15] These opera houses and music halls were not simply random performance locations for Muck but places of long-standing musical tradition. Muck brought German musical culture to each of his concert engagements, just as he would when he conducted in Boston.

Muck's choice of marital partner, and the family that she came from, would also affect his way of thinking, and he would bring these

Figure 1.1. Portrait of Karl Muck in 1906 with a prominent dueling scar on his cheek. Courtesy of the Library of Congress. Copyright entry November 12, 1906, Class H. Number 85591. Accession Number A43074. Division of Fine Arts.

predilections to America as well. Anna Katharina Portugall, or Anita, was the twenty-one-year-old daughter of Anna Ott and Dr. Ferdinand Portugall, the mayor of Graz, Austria's second-largest city.[16] The couple were married on February 3, 1887, and Muck became exposed to his new father-in-law's viewpoints about ethnicity and nation. In 1885 in his inaugural speech, two years before Karl and Anita's wedding, Portugall proclaimed his administration's objectives: to defend the city's character as "German through and through," to terminate "each and every act of national agitation by foreign elements," thereby preserving Graz as a "refuge of German nature and custom," the "southeastern most bastion of German culture."[17] Portugall subscribed to the political philosophy of the Pan-German Movement, a political organization that promoted German nationalism. He held strong racial views, believing that Germans were a "superior race" that needed protection from Jews.[18] His opposition to Jews stemmed from the economic and cultural realities of refugees fleeing Russian pogroms in the 1880s and pouring into Austria and Germany.

In 1888, when Muck was twenty-nine years old, Kaiser Wilhelm II succeeded to the throne. Muck became the kaiser's favorite conductor. Muck's affection for the kaiser and his family was mutual: Muck routinely wore pearl buttons that he received from the kaiserin at the wedding of the crown prince "as a memento of a little experience I had with the Crown Prince when he was nine years old." Muck wore diamond-studded cuff links with the initial *W* for Wilhelm and an imperial crown stickpin with *A* and *V* for Kaiserin Augusta Victoria embossed in gold.[19] Muck kept a picture of the kaiser on his piano.[20] The kaiser's belief in Germany's greatness would come to influence Muck's worldview, giving him a nationalistic sense of German racial and cultural superiority.

In 1903, Karl Muck propelled his career to greater heights by accepting a position as principal conductor of the Bayreuth Festival Orchestra, where he conducted Richard Wagner's *Parsifal, Lohengrin,* and *Die Meistersinger.*[21] Wagner (1813–83) is considered one of the most influential and controversial German composers of all time.[22] His grand operas explore themes of honor, heroism, and passionate love, but they are also tainted with overtones of racism and elitism. Muck's appointment at Bayreuth places him in this environment and links him to Wagner's conservative and anti-Semitic world. Just three years after his appointment at Bayreuth, in 1906, Muck would bring his biases to Boston and the BSO, perhaps influencing Higginson's (and other Boston elites') views or affecting the way the elder patron conceptualized his enterprise in the city. Twenty-five years before Muck conducted at Bayreuth, Wagner had built Festspielhaus in southern Germany for

Figure 1.2. The Bühnen Festspielhaus (Bayreuth) Bavaria, Germany. In 1903, Muck propelled his career to greater heights by accepting a position as principal conductor of the Bayreuth Festival Orchestra, a position he maintained until 1930. Reproduction Number LC-DIG-ppmsca-00042 (digital file from original). Courtesy of the Library of Congress, Prints and Photographs Division.

the purpose of performing his operas each summer. Wagner disliked Europe's ostentatious grand opera houses with their gilded ornamentation. He designed a state-of-the-art classical theater with simple wooden floors and chairs to accentuate the acoustics. His goal was excellence in performance and production. Each summer's festival was a massive community undertaking. Wagner brought together hundreds of Germany's best instrumentalists, singers, actors, artists, dancers, writers, costumers, designers, and engineers. The librettos for the operas provided the newly unified Germany with heroic legends drawn from Germanic mythology.[23] In writing about his travels to Bayreuth, American author Mark Twain referred to this celebrated destination as a "temple" of German music.[24] After Wagner's death in 1883, the opera house was managed by his widow, Cosima Wagner, the brilliant businesswoman and daughter of composer Franz Liszt. Cosima developed the festival further until her death in 1930 and turned Bayreuth into a shrine for her husband. She and a "band of dedicated followers" cultivated "the dead master's sacred memory."[25]

American dancer Isadora Duncan described the atmosphere of Bayreuth in her autobiography, *My Life*:

> Every day I received a little word from Frau Cosima, asking me to lunch or dinner, or to spend the evening at Villa Wahnfried, where hospitality was dispensed in a regal manner. Each day there were at least, fifteen or more people to lunch. Frau Cosima, at the head of the table, presided with dignity, and with equal tact, for among her guests were included the greatest minds in Germany, artists and musicians, often Grand Dukes and Duchesses or Royal personages from all countries. The tomb of Richard Wagner is in the garden of Villa Wahnfried and can be seen from the Library windows. After lunch Frau Wagner took my arm and we walked out into the garden, around the tomb. It was a promenade in which Frau Cosima conversed in tones of sweet melancholy and mystic hope. In the evening, there were often quartettes, in which each instrument was played by a celebrated virtuoso. The great figure of Hans Richter, the slight silhouette of Karl Muck, the charming Mottel, Humperdinck, and Heinrich Thode, every artist of that time was received at Villa Wahnfried with equal kindness. I was very proud that I should be admitted, in my little white tunic, to a galaxy of such distinguished and brilliant personages.[26]

From 1901 to 1930, Karl Muck was part of Cosima Wagner's exclusive "family." She welcomed him into her private world and made him feel at home. She promoted his career as a preeminent conductor.[27] A fervent anti-Semite, she exposed Muck to the latest theories on race, which ultimately affected his own views. Karl Muck became part of the Wagners' inner circle. He was their summer festival conductor of choice for almost thirty years and was considered the greatest interpreter of Wagner's music. He viewed his role at Bayreuth in spiritual and historical terms as the "keeper of the grail," as if to protect Wagner's legacy and keep German cultural nationalism alive.[28] Rumors even circulated that Muck was the illegitimate son of Richard Wagner because the men looked so similar.[29] Bayreuth was a popular destination for German aristocracy at the turn of the twentieth century. The opera house featured an upper gallery where the audience could gaze upon them.[30] Muck was well known among elite classes of Germany. It would be an understatement to simply call him a court musician. Muck was one of the most recognized conductors and celebrity figures in all of Germany besides the kaiser himself. Souvenir postcards were available for purchase at Bayreuth with Muck's picture on them. Muck's performances were so lauded that he received letters of praise from Kaiser Wilhelm. Cosima requested that Muck conduct *Parsifal* at Bayreuth while Cosima's son Siegfried was alive. Muck wrote in 1908, "I gave Frau Cosima Wagner my word to help Siegfried with the Bayreuth work as long as it was possible to me. I have kept this word not only because I pledged it to Frau Cosima but because I felt myself bound to Siegfried by ties of true friendship."[31] Muck was part of the German aristocracy. He embodied German culture, with an air of superiority and chauvinism. He conducted at Bayreuth during the same years that he was contracted to the BSO. Muck's illiberal persona would eventually prove distasteful and threatening to some New Yorkers, who sought national conformity and Americanization during the war years.

A decade before the war, however, in 1906, at the height of his success in Germany, the forty-seven-year-old Muck found himself in great demand in the United States. In early January of that year, Henry Lee Higginson, founding director of the Boston Symphony, began scouting for an excellent conductor for his orchestra, looking for a "really top flight choice!"[32] Charles Ellis, Higginson's Boston Symphony manager, made various visits to Europe and sought out possible conductors. Ellis learned that Karl Muck had an excellent reputation, and thus Boston musician Charles Loeffler used his contacts to acquire Muck's Berlin address.[33] From that point on, Higginson vigorously pursued Muck. Higginson utilized Boston's best German-speaking musicians as well as federal assistance to help with his recruitment process. He asked New England Conservatory director George Chadwick, who was in London, to go to Berlin and pursue negotiations with Muck.[34] Charles Ellis then reported the difficulties in securing Muck, as he was engaged at the Berlin State Opera and the Vienna Philharmonic, so tearing him away from his scheduled assignments was problematic. On February 6, 1906, Higginson sent a letter to Agnes Braun, his wife's cousin in Berlin, and asked her whether she would visit Muck and encourage him to sign the contracts. She was also advised to persuade Pauline Strauss, the wife of conductor Richard Strauss, who had the social prestige to voice her opinion regarding Muck's possible opportunities.[35] Ellis cabled Higginson from Berlin on May 19, 1906, informing him that Muck was undecided. Growing impatient with Muck's uncertainty, Higginson replied that he did not want this appointment to slip away and described Muck as "weaker than an 11-year-old child," unable to make resolutions or plans.[36] Higginson initially viewed Muck as effeminate. After additional correspondence, however, Higginson's opinion changed, later describing the conductor as strong and warm. Now convinced, he wrote to Ellis that "my own belief is that we are better with Muck than with anyone."[37] Higginson suppressed any reservations he may have had about Muck, and developed a strong relationship with him that would last for many years. Only after the United States declared war, and after pressure mounted against the conductor, did their relationship begin to fracture, raising these old concerns again in Higginson's mind.

On May 24, 1906, Higginson contacted his cousin Henry Cabot Lodge, a senator from Massachusetts, and his cousin by marriage President Theodore Roosevelt, in Washington, DC, requesting that they intercede with the German emperor Wilhelm II, "who is of a very generous disposition."[38] Muck was in great demand in the United States, as evidenced by such high-level diplomatic negotiations to acquire him.[39] On June 4, 1906, Muck agreed to come to Boston for the 1906–7 season. Higginson was full of praise for Roosevelt's efforts and expressed "kindness and interest" toward Wilhelm for "agreeing" to let Muck leave Germany.[40] Higginson wrote, "It seemed doubtful for many weeks whether he could come; but at last the Emperor of Germany, who had a particular liking for Dr. Muck, agreed that he should come to us for a year."[41] In an interview soon after his arrival in the United States, Dr. Muck attributed this consent entirely to Wilhelm's regard for Americans, especially for Harvard University, which Mr. Higginson had attended and with which he was known to be closely associated.[42] In this stage of the negotiation, Muck was viewed as a goodwill ambassador and a symbol of good relations between the two countries.

Boston's Fin-de-Siècle German Community

From the first moment of the Mucks' arrival in Boston, the city must have felt oddly familiar, with its vibrant German American middle class and thriving immigrant business community.[43] As historian Edwin Bacon described, "There is scarcely a trade or occupation that has not Germans among its representatives. Many German-born citizens attained prominent and influential positions among Boston's business and professional men, and in the social and cultivated life of the city."[44] The Mucks felt comfortable in Boston because Germanic presence had made a strong and lasting impression on the region and helped to define public life. Germans had settled in Boston's South End along Shawmut and Tremont Streets, and in Roxbury and Roslindale.[45] They lived on Centre Street in Jamaica Plain's Hyde Square, around Washington Street in Egleston Square, and on Boylston Street in Brookside. They lived with their families in mansard cottages on Amory Street, and they settled on streets with names such as Germania, Bismarck, Beethoven, Mozart, and Schiller.[46] One could walk down the street and find German bookstores, butcher shops, bakeries, drinking establishments, cafes, furniture shops, tobacco shops, and outdoor sidewalk markets.[47]

There were several reasons why Germans came to the United States: A small number of German Puritans had come to Boston as early as 1634 for religious reasons.[48] Many Germans, however, left their homeland beginning in 1848 because of undemocratic political policies, a failed revolution, and an agricultural downturn. In the United States, the economy was booming, and business leaders required foreign workers. Germans came to America seeking economic opportunity, a decent standard of living, and the possibility of acquiring land.[49]

Like German communities in other US cities, middle-class Germans in Boston did not leave their identities or their pastimes behind them when they came to the New World. They utilized their leisure time to establish a wide variety of clubs for the enjoyment of their members. They had shooting and sports clubs and a gymnastics society that offered fencing, boxing, chess, billiards, and card games. The German National American Alliance promoted the preservation of German culture and helped immigrants transition to their new country. The Boylston Schul-Verein (school-society) in Jamaica Plain taught language classes, literature, drama, sports, and music and generally provided recreation for German people in the city.[50] The German author Karl Heinzin brought the concept of physical education to Boston through the Turner Movement, which taught that a sound mind and body go hand-in-hand. Thus, the Boston Turnverein, organized in the 1850s, erected an elaborate building on Middlesex Street in 1876 called the Turnhalle (later called the German Casino Club), boasting several hundred members. The facility contained a well-equipped gymnasium that "graduated some of the best athletes in the city," a billiards room, a bowling alley, a theater where musical and dramatic performances were given, a dancehall, smoking and reading parlors with a thousand-volume library, and a restaurant and refreshment room.[51] The German Music Club in Jamaica Plain provided a renaissance revival clubhouse and a concert and social space for German musicians and community members.[52]

Like most ethnic groups, Germans stayed connected with one another, assisted new immigrants, and maintained a connection to their homeland. Muck benefited indirectly from this energy, reading about their efforts in the local German-language newspapers. Boston had seven German-language presses in the prewar period, including the popular *Neue Englander Zeitung*, so Karl and Anita could keep abreast of news from home and in their new community. These papers provided a link to the old country, advertisements for housing and employment, and instruction for assimilating in the United States.[53] Historian Carl Wittke remarked that the "reasons for the development of a foreign language press are obvious . . . the newcomer wants to

Turnhalle, Middlesex Street.

Figure 1.3. Turnhalle, Middlesex Street, Boston. Image from Moses King, *King's Handbook of Boston* (Cambridge, MA: Moses King, 1883), 249. Drawn by F. A. Strauss.

know what is going on in the strange neighborhood in which he has decided to make his home, and he can learn about this more easily" in his native language.[54]

German churches also thrived in Boston in the years the Mucks lived there, serving as "central locations for the maintenance of ethnic identity."[55] While German immigrants may have had their quarrels with each other, in Boston, they were able to cut loose from the religious and political tensions they faced in the old country. Whether Bavarian or Prussian, Protestant or Catholic, German immigrants found relative tolerance and peace in pre–World War I Boston.[56] Anti-Catholic nativism thrived in Boston from 1840 to 1890, but intolerance of Catholics abated in the last decade of the century, as Jews became the frightening new "other" and as that small German population built Temple Ohabei Shalom and Temple Israel for the benefit of its members.[57] Catholic and Protestant Germans settled into their respective churches and built robust religious communities. The German Lutheran Church on Parker Hill, Immanuel German Evangelical Lutheran Church on Bennington Street, First German Methodist Church on Shawmut Avenue, German Methodist Church on Atherton and Amory, First German Baptist Church on Centre Street, German Reformed Christ Church on Chestnut Avenue, and Holy Trinity German Catholic Church on Shawmut Avenue all had strong memberships.[58] Each of these churches performed important charitable work: education and daycare for children, medical help for the sick, care for the elderly, financial aid to the destitute, and food and shelter for the orphaned. On May 10, 1914, the German Ladies Aid Society established the Deutsches Altenheim Home for the Aged. The Boston Symphony Orchestra, with the All German Men Singing Group of Greater Boston, performed at the grand opening.[59] Architecturally, German churches in Boston were beautiful visual reminders of the homeland and assertions of ownership over a corner of America. Holy Trinity, for example, recreated the appearance of a German gothic cathedral.[60] The main and side altars, the crèche, and other religious statuary were intricately hand carved by master carpenters from western Germany. The colorful stained-glass windows and painted murals reminded parishioners of home. Robert Sauer wrote, "Here, in an edifice of solid design and serious interior, they love to hear the precious accents of the mother tongue and listen to the music."[61] The Mucks were Christian, and yet they never mentioned attending church services in their correspondence with Boston friends.[62] During these years, Karl was absorbed in his musical endeavors, as well as the study of philology, linguistics, and the religious philosophies of Eastern cultures. He spent time with his friend Hugo Münsterberg, a renowned psychologist at

Harvard, studying rats in Münsterberg's laboratory. Because the Mucks' religious roots appear to have come out of the Catholic Church, Holy Trinity may have given the couple a level of support in the city, for records indicate that Boston Symphony members provided music for church services and German social clubs, loosely connecting the arts community with its German religious and social institutions.

German Influence in Boston before World War I

Despite having migrated to a new country, the Mucks were living in a world that had many of the social and cultural characteristics of a typical German town. Many middle-class German Americans owned successful businesses in Boston built on German traditions and values, and these businesses offered employment to a thriving ethnic community. In the prewar years, 50 percent of Germans in Boston worked in the restaurant industry or in the service sector.[63] Bavarian-born Adam Mock, for example, established the German Café, on Essex Street, one of many small German eateries in Boston.[64] According to an article in the 1916 *Boston Globe*, there were forty-three German restaurants, lunchrooms, or delicatessens in Boston.[65] Many Germans worked as waiters, relying on tips rather than fixed wages and developing reputations for neatness and civility. Bakers prepared pretzels, apple strudel, and pumpernickel bread in small shops. Anglo-owned establishments such as the Parker House on Tremont Street sold Parker rolls, prepared from a German recipe, which were delivered around New England and across the country.

Butcher shops and meat markets sold a wide variety of traditional German products, including pork knuckle, *Wiener Schnitzel* (veal cutlets), frankfurters, hamburger, meatloaf, sauerkraut, potato salads, and pickles.[66] Germans had rural dairy farms producing milk and cheese.[67] A chocolate industry developed in Boston, as sugar refining and chocolate production were highly skilled crafts carried on for centuries by German artisans. One such German American, W. F. Schrafft, began a candy-making business in Boston in 1859 with six employees, and by the turn of the century their chocolate was being sold all over the country. The Baker Chocolate Company employed German confectioners in their Dorchester factory. Sam German, master chocolatier for the company, transformed national baking norms by publishing his German chocolate cake recipe on the labels of Baker's products.[68] The Mucks were easily able to obtain German foods because this fare was widely available in Boston and had become a defining part of the "American" diet.

Figure 1.4. Parker House Hotel and Restaurant. Courtesy of the Library of Congress, Prints and Photographs Division, Reproduction number LC-DIG-det-4a22177.

In a letter to her Boston friend Ida May Chadwick, Anita Muck expressed thanks for "the delicious sauerkraut and sausages" and a Christmas *Nürnberger Lebkuchen,* a traditional German soft bread.[69] The Mucks and their friends, including a large community of Anglo-Bostonians, routinely consumed German food and contributed to the market demand for these products. German ethnic identity was viewed by many in Boston in these years as something exciting and exotic, becoming increasingly part of the mainstream palate.

In addition to food, pilsner-style beer was an appealing beverage to Boston's German and Anglo communities. The city had thirty-one German breweries prior to World War I. Starting in the mid-nineteenth century, German lager eventually replaced English ale as the beverage of choice among German and Anglo-Bostonians. Beginning with Michael Ludwig, who in 1846 had established his brewery in the Stony Brook region of Roxbury–Jamaica Plain, dozens of other German brewmasters followed, including John Roessle, Henry and Jacob Pfaff, Matthias Kramer, and Gottlieb Burkhardt. The most successful brewer in Boston was Rudolph Haffenreffer, who began his operation in 1870, intent on employing and housing German immigrants and suppling a spigot in his beer garden courtyard from which employees could fill their pails at lunchtime.[70] His beer and others were sold in hundreds of pubs and restaurants across the city.[71] Scholars have argued that many upper-class Anglo-Americans disapproved of beer drinking among working-class Germans, and while this may be true, in Boston, the practice eventually gained acceptance among all social classes. The Jacob Wirth Restaurant was the most popular eatery and bar in the city, frequented by German and Anglo-Bostonians and particularly beloved by Harvard students and faculty.[72] In 1917, the Wursthaus Restaurant, known for its German food and lager, opened in Harvard Square. Selg's Palm Garden near Scollay Square was furnished with German decor and stained-glass windows depicting German scenes. An advertisement for its rooftop beer garden suggested that one "forgets that he is in Puritanical Boston, for the Palm Garden is really a bit of old Germany."[73] Cosmopolitan Bostonians of all classes consumed German beer, and with the invention and subsequent improvement of refrigeration by German engineer Carl von Linde in the final decades of the nineteenth century, cold lager could be transported more easily without spoiling, making beer a hugely popular beverage in America before World War I. Acceptance would unravel in 1920 with Prohibition, however, which, in addition to its broader impact, would prove to be another severe blow to German traditions.

Figure 1.5. Henry and Jacob Pfaff Brewery advertisement. Boston had thirty-one German breweries in the city prior to World War I. As this image shows, Pfaff Brewery occupied several buildings at its Arch Street address. Courtesy of the Boston Public Library, Boston Brewery Posters Collection.

Germans also helped to shape American middle-class notions of etiquette, tradition, and taste. A visitor to Boston before 1850 complained that Americans ate their food with the "greatest rapidity and in total silence . . . bolting down their food (on bare wood tables) with knives instead of forks, or even worse, using their fingers."[74] German hotels and restaurants such as the Fritz Carlton and the German Room at the Hotel Touraine offered a level of sophistication not found in most American hotels and restaurants. Certainly, Muck and his compatriots socialized in these establishments, bringing German elegance to Boston's upper-class society. These restaurants offered a "European" or "Cosmopolitan Plan" whereby food was served on linen tablecloths with silverware, and where good manners and polite behavior was expected. Bostonians adopted the manners of German Americans, who became the tastemakers for the city. When Austrian composer Johann Strauss Jr. visited Boston for the 1872 World Peace Jubilee,

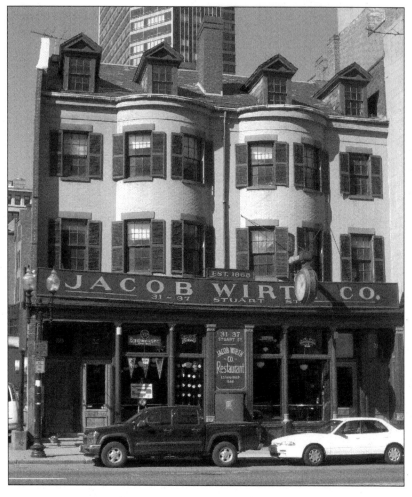

Figure 1.6. Jacob Wirth Restaurant. In 1868, Jacob Wirth opened a highly popular German restaurant and bar in the Theater District of Boston serving beer produced in the local area. Wikimedia Commons.

he commented that Boston was dull, lacking in elegance and luxury, and that the city's women did not dress well.[75] Anita Muck echoed Strauss's sentiments more than thirty years later when she complained about Boston fashion: "In daylight those skirts look awfully poor, yet they are by no means cheap. I think I shall . . . have one made for me by a dressmaker."[76] Anita Muck believed that Boston's style needed improvement. By having her clothing designed to her own German upper-class specifications, she was setting herself apart from those

Figure 1.7. German Room, Hotel Touraine, Boston. Melissa D. Burrage Collection.

Bostonians wearing locally made garments, and displaying a new fashion originating from the Continent. The Mucks, like many other German elites, were social role models who shaped Boston society with their own elegant European appearance and social etiquette.

German Americans also enriched Boston with their holiday traditions. As late as 1857, most Bostonians celebrated Thanksgiving only.[77] German Bostonians brought merriment to the Christmas season. Harvard language professor Karl "Charles" Follen, from Muck's hometown of Darmstadt, Germany, is credited as early as 1829 as the first person in America to display a Christmas tree decorated with fruit in the window of his Cambridge home.[78] Caricaturist Thomas Nast's 1860s magazine illustrations of Sinter Klaus popularized the tradition of Santa, who brought toys to "good" girls and boys.[79] With the introduction of this tradition, German toy shops thrived in Boston. Schwarz Toy Emporium and the Louis Wolf Company Toy Shop regularly purchased items made in Nuremburg, which were delivered to Boston by the Holland America Shipping Line.[80] The Advent calendar, a German tradition that begins with the opening of the first door of the calendar and ends on the twelfth night, extended the length of the Christmas celebration. Germans served goose, fruitcake, and spiced cider. They sang carols, rang bells, and delivered Christmas cards, all uniquely German traditions. Louis Prang's greeting card company became another incredibly successful German-owned business that specialized in furthering this

Figure 1.8. Invitation to the Christmas Exhibition, Richard Schwarz's Toy Emporium, 497 and 499 Washington Street, Boston. Germans brought their holiday traditions to the United States. This card announces Schwarz's grand opening and the sale of German toys. No date is listed. Courtesy of Historic New England.

tradition. Bostonians adopted German Christmas rituals, and they also embraced their other traditions as well. German Americans celebrated Easter with the Oschter Haws, or Easter Hare, who delivered colored eggs and specialty candies made by local confectioners. Germans brought the tradition of the summer barbeque to Boston, gathering in the local pine groves on Sundays to play music and feast on grilled foods and salads. German Americans confidently insisted on maintaining their amusements and traditions, which helped to relax America's Puritan habits. John Higham writes, "The German notion that it is a good thing to have a good time has found a lodgment in the American mind."[81]

In addition to shaping Boston's holiday customs, German literature also influenced American style. Perhaps a tradition most associated with Boston, the Swan Boat Rides in the Public Garden is based on a medieval German story in which Lohengrin, a knight, crosses a river in a boat drawn by a swan to defend Princess Elsa. This ride offered Boston children, young and old, an element of joy not seen

Figure 1.9. Swan Boat Ride. Robert Paget created the Swan Boat Ride for the Public Garden pond in 1877 after seeing Wagner's *Lohengrin*. The swan boats became a popular Boston attraction, continuing to provide joy for city visitors to this day. Courtesy of the Library of Congress, Prints and Photographs Division, Reproduction number LC DIG-det-4a13558.

in the city before. Germans played a key part in shaping Boston culture and what middle- and upper-middle-class Bostonians associated with good taste. German literary traditions with fantastic characters, enchanted castles, and dramatic romances became a popular part of the culture. Parents read their children *Rip Van Winkle*, by Washington Irving, who was influenced by Johann Wolfgang Goethe and Johann Christoph Friedrich Schiller. Young girls read Louisa May Alcott's *Little Women*, with the character of kindly professor Friedrich Bhaer from Germany.[82] Germans helped to define the very customs, manners, and styles that are now thought of as ultimately American. The Mucks fit perfectly in Boston society at a time when the city was embracing these new traditions.

Muck's appointment in Boston came when German culture was at its zenith. The city's academics had been going overseas for one hundred years in a transatlantic exchange of ideas.[83] There was much to absorb from Germany, as that country had experienced a cultural renaissance in the nineteenth century. Boston hoped to learn from it and create an "epoch" of its own.

In 1832, Goethe died, and the German reading public expanded dramatically after his death. In that decade, Bavaria had one hundred bookshops, Prussia had three hundred, sixty of which were in Berlin alone.[84] The German school system had expanded, the primary schools, or *Volksschule,* offered literacy and vocational training for children, and the "gymnasium" prepared young men for universities.[85] German scholars pioneered disciplines such as philology and archaeology. Noted German scholars, including Karl Marx, Max Weber, Sigmund Freud, and Immanuel Kant expressed new German philosophies, and these ideas were carried to the United States.

Many Boston intellectuals mined Germany's past for knowledge and inspiration, hoping to learn all that they could of German educational methods. They established alliances with German teachers to enhance American schools and institutions, borrowing German educational frameworks to guide them.[86] Among the first to make the pilgrimage, Germanicist George Ticknor, Harvard theologian Edward Everett, and philologist George Bancroft sailed to Germany in 1815 to study at the University of Göttingen and returned to America so enamored with Germany's postgraduate educational model that they publicized it to others.[87] Horace Mann returned to Boston after studying state education in Germany and opened the first public normal school, leading to a national public school system.[88] As a professor at Harvard College, Ticknor proposed a variety of reforms to improve teaching methods. He wanted classes divided by ability, and he fought for school vacations in the summer rather than the winter months, defining the American academic calendar to this day.[89]

In 1834, distraught over the death of his only son, Ticknor retired from Harvard and made a second trip with his family to Germany, returning to Boston with new educational ideas and proposing a large public library for the benefit of all citizens.[90] In the mid-nineteenth century, Boston had two of the largest libraries in the country—Harvard College Library with thirty thousand books and the Boston Athenaeum with eighteen thousand books. Neither of these institutions, however, was open to the general public, and Ticknor sought to remedy this.[91] In 1854, the Boston Public Library was founded, bringing "education to the masses." Ticknor believed that well-educated citizens with means had a responsibility to edify the rest of society. He imagined a democratic institution where patrons of all social classes could obtain a library card and borrow a book. By the turn of the century, the Boston Public Library was the largest free library in America.[92] Receiving his inspiration from Germany, Ticknor's important institutional creation brought enlightenment to the entire population, becoming a model for the rest of the country.

To fill the shelves of the Boston Public Library, publisher James T. Fields stocked the works of American authors such as Emerson, Hawthorne, Holmes, Howe, Howells, Jewett, Longfellow, Lowell, Stowe,

Thoreau, and Whittier. The Boston Public Library acquired books from Europe and hosted important literary figures such as Charles Dickens and Mark Twain, becoming a center of literary life in its own right. Bostonian bookishness was unsurpassed. The Lyceum Movement became an extremely popular pastime as audiences swarmed to attend lectures throughout the region in a quest for knowledge.[93] Thirteen thousand people attended a lecture series given by Emerson and Thoreau. Bostonians consumed three times the number of magazines, newspapers, and journals as any other city in the country. The poet and literary critic Bayard Taylor commented that "the people of Boston are full blooded readers, appreciative, trained." Because authors were so valued by the population, "the humble man of letters has a position here which he doesn't have in New York."[94]

Before his death in 1882, Ralph Waldo Emerson remarked, "I think the Germans have an integrity of mind which sets their science above all others." Emerson believed that Germany was "the embodiment of academic ideals," which Americans could learn from.[95] Many people at the time viewed Germans as "the most learned, patient, industrious, civilized people on the face of the globe, [attaining] the highest distinction in arts, in science, in arms, in literature, in everything."[96]

At the turn of the twentieth century, Germans had firmly embedded themselves into Boston's academic domain. A significant number found employment as bilingual governesses and teachers in Boston homes and schools. Germans were hired as professors at Harvard and other urban colleges. Karl Follen, mentioned earlier, taught the German language at Harvard, and Hugo Münsterberg, also mentioned earlier, taught clinical psychology. These men shared new intellectual discoveries, and enthusiasm for German culture exploded. The Germanic Museum was established at Harvard in 1903. The idea came from Kuno Francke, chair of Harvard's Germanic Civilization Department, who wanted to expose Bostonians to Germany's rich cultural heritage. In a spirit of goodwill, Kaiser Wilhelm made a gift of sculpture casts to the museum. The building opened to the public on the anniversary of poet Johann Schiller's birthday in November of 1903. The Museum of Fine Arts was so enamored of the idea of teaching classical European art that it sold local American oil paintings from its collection to fund the purchase of plaster sculptures, a collection that became the third largest in the world.[97] In 1910, Adolph and Lilly Busch, the German American brewing aristocrats from St. Louis, Missouri, donated $550,000 to Harvard to build a grand, new Germanic Museum building to replace the old one, which shared its space with a local gymnasium.[98]

Figure 1.10. Germanic Museum (Adolphus Busch Hall Courtyard, Harvard University). The Germanic Museum, or Busch-Reisinger Museum, is dedicated to art of German-speaking countries of Europe. The museum's Adolphus Busch Hall is named for German brewer Adolphus Busch, husband of Lilly Busch. Wikimedia Commons.

Around the corner from the Germanic Museum, Harvard's Botanical Museum acquired its most popular exhibit of glass flowers from glassmakers Leopold and Rudolf Blaschka of Dresden, who duplicated plants in three dimensions for students of botany. German educational philosophies inspired Boston to create professional schools, specialty fields at universities, bilingual education, kindergarten programs, the concept of free textbooks in the public schools, and adult and parochial education. The Prince School on Newbury Street was the first educational building in New England designed using the German model, with classrooms located on only one side of the corridor. Boston adopted German culture and ideas, and this presence was obvious throughout the city.

Boston worked hard to create an identity for itself as a highly educated and intellectual society dedicated to high standards of culture.[99] The life of the mind was given an important and dignified place in the total culture, and the city's intelligentsia relied heavily upon German opinions and institutions to achieve their goals. Thus, given Karl

Muck's keen mind and academic background, it is not surprising that he would come to find happiness in his adopted city.

The Prominence of European Art Music in Boston

Boston was also finding its musical footing in the decades before Muck's arrival. During those years, audiences were treated to a mix of sacred, secular, amateur, and commercial entertainment.[100] Boston gained enormous prestige as a preeminent musical and cultural center in great part through the contributions of Germans who brought their talent, knowledge, and skills to the urban marketplace. European immigration to America provided a new pool of European-born musicians as well as an insatiable demand for classical music.[101] In 1798, Johann Christian Gottlieb Graupner left Germany and made his home in Boston, where he opened a music shop, sold instruments and sheet music, published his own scores, and offered lessons and concerts.[102] In 1810, he organized the Philharmonic Society, made up of amateur instrumentalists, and he conducted the Federal Street Theatre Orchestra, which included many of these same musicians. His endeavors to fill the musical (and economic) vacuum in Boston inspired many other musicians and entrepreneurs to follow his lead.

Music publishing in Boston got its start when musicians became dissatisfied with the availability of sheet music and musical scores. Only sacred or patriotic music existed in printed form before Graupner's arrival in the United States.[103] After Graupner, particularly with improved print technology, the city's music industry blossomed. Music became the number one pastime for many Bostonians. There was a creative effort to find, publish, and disseminate music for a growing amateur demand. By the mid-nineteenth century, there were roughly forty music publishers in the city.[104] These companies published a wide variety of music, including art songs and choral music, secular and sacred works, solo instrumental compositions, violin and piano repertoire, brass band music, march and military selections, orchestral scores, minstrelsy, jigs and reels, theater accompaniment, and masonic music. Publishers distributed German, American, and other European compositions locally and abroad.[105] Toward the end of the nineteenth century, many of the smaller companies were absorbed by the Oliver Ditson and Vega Company during the "Great Merger Movement." Ditson alone published a hundred thousand titles in 1890, including forty-five thousand vocal selections and forty-eight thousand pieces of instrumental music, extending Boston's influence to markets throughout the world.[106]

The music publishing industry also supported music education in the city. In 1833, Lowell Mason founded the Boston Academy of Music, the first music school in the country promoting secular instrumental music. The academy offered the first extensive performance of Beethoven symphonies in America, five years after the composer's death.[107] In 1869, under German-born composer Julius Eichberg's supervision, music was first taught in Boston's public high schools for recreation and to relieve fatigue from other studies, evolving into a school-system requirement that trained every child to read musical notation, interpret music, and appreciate it.[108] Educational music publishers fostered a taste for "finer music" from abroad.[109] Ginn and Company published the *National Music Course*, and the *Mason Music Course* provided textbooks and manuals for teachers. Silver Burdett and Company published secondary school music pedagogy that orchestrated European symphonic works for beginning school ensembles. D. C. Heath and Company and the American Book Company also offered music books with their own versions of European-style pedagogy for the public-school market. In addition, many of these music publishers offered summer schools for students and teachers using their published materials in summer camps, creating a tradition still prevalent today. In 1884, Burdett started the first formal summer school in Lexington, Massachusetts, offering diplomas to music teachers who completed the fifteen-hundred-hour course, requiring that graduates master everything from ear training, sight singing, music history, theory, and private and classroom teaching methods. These courses paved the way for a host of other summer training programs at colleges and universities in even more exotic locations, like coastal Cape Cod and Maine.[110]

The publishing industry in Boston thrived because of the artistry and technological advances of the German-dominated music engraving and printing industry. In 1753, Christopher Sower of Germantown, Pennsylvania, printed what was probably the first book in the United States using musical type on copper plates.[111] Schlimper Company and Manicke and Dellmuth Company were noted in Boston for their fine music engraving work, using special hammers and stamps and imprinting clefs, accidentals, rests, and other dynamic notations on their sheet music, servicing the major music publishers in the city.[112] The quality of their work was not only functional but beautiful, shaping Boston's and the country's musical intellect and taste.

Boston was also home to several music journals from the pre–Civil War period through World War I that promoted a cosmopolitan musical agenda. Boston-based George W. Stratton edited a music journal that sold twenty thousand copies nationwide. His efforts were followed by Germanophile John Sullivan Dwight's *Journal of Music* (1852–81), which contained biographical sketches of European and American musicians and composers, translated musical essays from European languages into English, and critically reviewed concerts, "copiously covering the Boston scene."[113] The spread and dissemination of published essays, sheet music, and instructional materials helped to create a musically literate community—one that canonized German composers and musicians—ultimately helping Karl Muck to feel accepted.

With the massive output of published music came an effort by local craftsmen to manufacture quality instruments. Massachusetts businesses produced 30 percent of all pianos purchased in the country, generating a $5 million a year industry for the state.[114] Bostonian Jonas Chickering was perhaps the most well-known manufacturer. In 1855, he purchased a European piano and, in the prepatent era, copied the design and constructed a huge factory in Boston that was said to be the largest building in the United States, producing five thousand pianos a year.[115] The company sold so many pianos that Chickering sent sales representatives to almost every city in the United States while also shipping pianos to all parts of the world, from Finland to India. Franz Liszt's favorite piano was a Chickering, and Napoleon III of France had one as well.[116] Chickering put Boston on the map as a music manufacturing center.[117]

With an ever-increasing interest in music among the middle classes, violin makers also established businesses in the city. Initially, local companies, such as Weeman, Beal and Holmberg, and Jacob Thoma & Sons, imported violins and accessories from Europe because costs were relatively low. Demand increased so much that American craftsmen began their own domestic businesses. Ira Johnson, for example, purchased a Stradivarius violin for $1,000 in Europe, which he reproduced and sold inexpensively in his Boston shop. Many violin makers worked in this manner, copying European models and offering them for sale.[118] These companies duplicated, or attempted to duplicate, European products to meet the needs of the local economy.

Boston also became a leading flute manufacturing center in the nineteenth century. August Damm emigrated from Halle, Germany, in 1872, playing the flute with the Theodore Thomas Orchestra before eventually joining the Boston Symphony Orchestra. Without a local flute manufacturer, and out of necessity, Damm began making instruments himself, finding that traditional African Blackwood used in German flutes warped in New England's moist climate. He experimented with sterling silver as a more durable alternative.[119]

Boston families acquired numerous music products, whether through the purchase of an instrument or the procurement of a musical

Figure 1.11. Advertisement for Chickering and Sons' Piano-Forte Manufactory, Tremont Street, Boston, Massachusetts, 1854. Pianos and other musical instruments were manufactured and sold in Boston filling an insatiable demand for music in almost every facet of daily life. Courtesy of Historic New England.

score. The implicit message that the urban music community sent out was that it was entirely appropriate to purchase American reprints of German sheet music or to buy instruments copied from European models. If not for the wholesale "borrowing" of instrument designs and music, the industry in the United States would have collapsed.[120] Schoolchildren and parents learned through print media that, to succeed, a student needed to master music appreciation using books that contained important European works. The import of German music— from compositions to instruments—played a prominent role in Boston's cultural success and led directly to the city's warm reception for Muck in the first decade of the twentieth century.[121]

Someone in virtually every middle- and upper-class household took up an instrument and attempted to learn how to play it.[122] Lessons and daily practice were commonplace. Family members performed in home recitals. Children played their instruments for appreciative family and friends. Amateur chamber ensembles performed in brownstone parlors throughout the city. *Hausmusik*, the German word that describes this in-home musical movement, inspired an extraordinary enthusiasm for music seemingly everywhere.

Musical Life and Institutions in Boston

In Boston's public sphere, as in most American cities, amateur and semiprofessional music experimentation thrived.[123] Music was made "night after night" by composers, conductors, impresarios, virtuosos, and orchestra musicians in a climate of "shifting demographics and financial conditions in a rapidly urbanizing environment."[124] Orchestras provided entertainment in theaters, concert halls, opera houses, restaurants, bars, minstrel shows, amusement parks, burlesque houses, parades, summer resorts, dance halls, and at private functions.[125] Musicians who staffed these various venues were often German immigrants.[126] Music historian John Spitzer speaks of the ubiquity of orchestras in American life and the dynamism and diversity of entertainment in general. This certainly was the case in Boston.

The Handel and Haydn Society orchestra was founded in 1815 by local theater musicians.[127] In 1854, German-born flautist Carl Zerrahn became its conductor. The ensemble is known to this day for making Handel's *Messiah* a Boston Christmas tradition. In 1833, the Academy of Music Orchestra was formed, drawing its membership from Protestant ministers and church musicians. Boston's Puritan roots and religious idealism provided a basis for music in the city and influenced the trajectory of musical development of Boston's musical life well into the future.

In 1843, Gottlieb Graupner's Philharmonic Society got its start as a community amateur orchestra, hiring professional players in 1848 and giving concerts until 1855.[128] Carl Zerrahn also started a professional ensemble called the Philharmonic Orchestra (also called the Orchestral Union), which became the focus of orchestral music in the city for almost a decade, offering classical pieces and opera selections. In 1847, the Musical Fund Society, under George Webb, formed an orchestra of fifty professional musicians who served the broader community by raising funds for elderly and sick musicians.[129] The Germania Musical Society, made up of twenty-five young Germans who had fled the failed revolutions of 1848, established an orchestra in 1851, setting a new standard for symphonic performance in the United States, providing European symphonic masterworks and excellent musicianship.[130] In 1853, their premiere performance of Beethoven's Ninth Symphony drew thousands of Bostonians. Henry Wadsworth Longfellow describes in his journal a "pleasant" Germania performance that he enjoyed with

Figure 1.12. A popular ensemble in Boston in the mid-nineteenth century, the Germania Musical Society whetted audience appetites for classical music and helped to pave the way for the development of the Boston Symphony Orchestra. Photo from M. A. DeWolfe Howe, *The Boston Symphony Orchestra: An Historical Sketch* (Boston: Houghton Mifflin, 1914), 9.

his young sister-in-law Hattie Appleton, where the audience was full of zealous listeners.[131] Historian Jessica Gienow-Hecht compares the Germania's attraction for young female audience members as like today's "boy band, replete with solidarity, friendship, and sex appeal."[132] When the Germania disbanded in 1854, individual members became musical leaders in the city.[133]

In 1866, the Harvard Musical Association officially organized, offering "compositions of a high order" and leaving its imprint on musical organizations in the city.[134] Many of the association's members were of German descent, with a few having studied in Europe before emigrating to Boston. Some of the founding members went to Harvard Divinity School, and several taught music in local colleges and conservatories in the city. Their initial organizational mission involved creating Harvard's music department (which took thirty years) and developing a music library. The ensemble performed a series of public chamber music concerts and raised money to build the Boston Music Hall.[135] John Sullivan Dwight, who trained for the ministry and who managed the Harvard Musical Association from 1865 to 1882, worked to improve the quality and variety of HMA orchestral concerts by advocating "pure" and "serious" music. He introduced European composers such as Bach, Beethoven, Schubert, Schumann, and Mendelssohn to HMA audiences.[136] He worked to increase concert attendance, called for evening and Sunday concerts, proposed a summer season of light music, and established a permanent fund of $100,000.[137] He offered suggestions for his own orchestra that paved the way for developmental growth in Boston's orchestral and concert life. Dwight helped to set standards for orchestras for the next generation and "never lost his optimism and almost blind persistence about what could be (and eventually was) accomplished in Boston."[138]

In the years before Muck's arrival, performances were in high demand, and audiences flocked to the Boston Music Hall with its German-made organ, and to Faelton, Mechanics, and the subterranean Steinert Hall to hear concerts of all kinds. People bought tickets to hear German singing societies, like the Cecilia Society, and chamber ensembles, like the Mendelssohn Quintet and the Kneisel Quartet. They went to hear the Fadettes Ladies' Orchestra of Boston and the Marion Osgood Orchestra.[139] Small German bands played throughout the city and at summer resorts nearby.[140] Reporter John Brenon of the *New York Telegraph* noted on a visit to Boston that the audience there "listens seriously, equably, giving the artist the same courteous, careful hearing it would extend to a Huxley speaking on a problem of biology." He remarked that audiences in Boston absorb what they hear "earnestly, seasoning its admiration with a concentration of intellectual curiosity."[141] The German conductor Hans von Bulow told the *Chicago Times* that Boston was the most musically cultivated city in the United States.[142] The sheer volume of music making going on there, from *Hausmusik* to public performances, led to a demand for more, better-quality music, inspiring cultural entrepreneurs to envision the development of professional level musical institutions in the city.

In 1870, Boston experienced its first highly polished, professional ensemble when the Theodore Thomas Touring Orchestra came to town, made up primarily of German immigrants. Thomas was born in Germany in 1835, emigrating with his family to New York ten years later. He was a violinist with a love of Wagner, who had performed at the city's beer gardens and concert halls before establishing an orchestra of his own. Thomas would go on to lead the Brooklyn Philharmonic Society (1866–91), the New York Philharmonic (1877–91), and the Chicago Symphony Orchestra (1891–1905). He was considered one of America's most influential conductors and orchestra builders, raising the country's musical standards and elevating public taste.[143] Historian Howard Shanet believed that Thomas did

more than anyone else to establish German serious music in America.[144] In the final decades of the nineteenth century, the Thomas
Orchestra traveled throughout the country on the transcontinental
railroad, on a route that came to be called the "Thomas Highway."
A Pittsburgh newspaper claimed that "wherever Theodore Thomas
and his orchestra go they will sow seeds that will bring forth good
fruit[,] . . . inspire a love for a high order of music[, and] promote
local organization."[145] The Thomas orchestra gave men like Boston
financier Henry Lee Higginson ideas for what was possible in Boston.
The Thomas Orchestra premiered the Second New England School
composer John Knowles Paine's First Symphony (1875), upsetting
many in the audience who believed that the work should have been
debuted by a Boston orchestra, demonstrating that the Harvard
Musical Association was not up to the task. The Thomas Orchestra
represented a wake-up call that Boston needed to establish its own
highly polished full-time professional orchestra, and it stripped the
HMA of its prestige and usefulness.[146]

Henry Lee Higginson and the Creation of Symphony Hall

Contemplating the state of Boston's musical world, the wealthy Henry
Lee Higginson imagined that he could solve some of the problems
plaguing prior orchestral endeavors in the city. Boston had all the
makings of a more structured orchestral life. Throughout most of the
nineteenth century, ensembles had been loosely formed utilizing available amateur or professional talent in town.[147] Higginson would give
Boston the nation's first permanent, full-season symphony orchestra
devoted to fine arts music, and he would point a way toward a system of
philanthropic support for American orchestras in general that would
become "the cornerstone of America's musical culture in the twentieth
century."[148]

Higginson would build a sophisticated venue as a focal point of
musical culture in Boston, recreating a German concert hall and utilizing local engineers to design its acoustics. He would hire a small
professional staff to assist with day-to-day affairs and train a coterie of
volunteers to work behind the scenes to keep his operation running
smoothly. He would import full-time musicians, many of them from
Germany, and pay them a yearly salary, and he would recruit world-
class European conductors to lead his new orchestra. This would be a
stable ensemble that would perform twenty-four concerts a year, offering high-quality music on a regular basis.[149]

Figure 1.13. Philanthropist and Boston Symphony Orchestra founder Henry Lee Higginson. Portrait by Notman. Courtesy of the Boston Symphony Orchestra Archives.

Building on the foundations of German urban culture and musical amateurism prevalent in Boston for half a century, Higginson dreamed that the Boston Symphony Orchestra would "cure parochial habits at home."[150] His new establishment would create cultural traditions in Boston that would link to the old world and "provide some form of structure when none existed before."[151] Most performing opportunities at that time were gig based, where musicians cobbled together a living as orchestral musicians in theaters, minstrel shows, beer gardens, or summer resorts.[152] There were many more musical opportunities in New York than in Boston. It behooved Higginson to offer full-time work at Symphony Hall to entice excellent musicians and to avoid competing for part-time theater musicians.[153] The BSO, he envisioned, would set high standards for music in America.

While Higginson reached overseas in his quest for a new Boston enterprise, he also looked in his own backyard, particularly to Boston's German American community, for cultural direction. He became increasingly open-minded toward German immigrants, whom Boston intellectuals described as their "Teutonic cousins" or their "equals," by the standards of the ethnic hierarchy of the day. Higginson and others ransacked the past for a common genealogical connection, happy to have an ally in German Americans, who shared a similar work ethic and cultural outlook.[154] Influential Bostonians clearly welcomed German influences in building their cultural institutions.

Higginson was a Boston Brahmin, a word first applied by Oliver Wendell Holmes in his 1861 novel *Elsie Venner: A Romance of Destiny* to members of New England's small aristocratic status group.[155] This privileged group of Anglo-Saxon Protestants descended from Plymouth and Massachusetts Bay Colonies, having acquired their wealth in maritime ventures, textile manufacturing, and copper mining.[156] Holmes compared the priestly Hindu Brahmin leaders who defined moral standards in India with the Brahmins who became the economic leaders of Boston, and who in turn defined social, cultural, and moral values for the city. Boston Brahmins made it their mission to cultivate the arts, support charities, fund colleges, and assume leadership roles, further expanding their economic and social reach.

Paul DiMaggio has argued that, because of Boston's tightly knit, cohesive community, high culture developed at a faster rate than in other cities. Boston was successful because its elite social network funded and supported its creative institutions. The city was considered by many to be "the hub of America's cultural life," and the unity of Boston's economic and arts organizations made it unique in that regard.[157] Brahmins secured control over the city's social life and artistic output, forming organizations that were reinforced through marriages, Harvard educations, joint business ventures, social clubs, and charitable work. The strength of this integration gave Boston a cultural head start over other cities.[158]

The Boston Symphony was Higginson's way of demonstrating and preserving Brahmin social rank and preeminence. Wealthy citizens, like Higginson, took pride in creating artistic organizations to maintain elite ideals.[159] They looked to construct important and profitable identities for themselves by creating institutions like the Boston

Athenaeum and the Museum of Fine Arts as strongholds of Brahmin cultural eminence. DiMaggio writes, "Though Higginson created the BSO out of love for music, he nevertheless had a vested interest in the success of his institution within the Brahmin community," and Karl Muck was employed by him in part to achieve those social goals.[160]

Upper-class leaders of cultural establishments were also inspired by fear of the immigrant population. Brahmins built institutions to create boundaries between themselves and the immigrants, "against the intrusion of the unpleasant."[161] In the 1850s, the city's Brahmin families had witnessed mass immigration by the Irish and in the 1890s by the "new immigrants," including Italians and Jews from eastern Poland, Russia, and the Ukraine. They struggled to adjust to this new population that took hold of "their" city.[162] Boston transformed seemingly overnight from a recognizable place to one entirely unfamiliar and foreign. The city's Jewish population multiplied approximately sixteenfold between 1880 and 1920, growing from five thousand in 1880 to eighty thousand by 1920, bringing "strange new traditions" to their new home. Immigrants became linked to every urban problem, including poverty, hunger, disease, alcoholism, crime, vice, socialism, and communism.[163] Changes in the social fabric gave rise to anti-Semitism among the city's established families, although never on the scale endemic to Europe during the same period.[164] Much of what Higginson and other Brahmin elites were trying to do culturally was in response to the presence of Irish, Italian, and Jewish immigrants in the city.

As Joseph Sarna and Ellen Smith point out, "That Boston Jews were long the objects of genteel Brahmin anti-Semitism was commonly known."[165] They struggled to reconcile the historically stereotyped "mythical Jew" found in their books with the real Jew that they met on the street or in the workplace who seemed altogether different.[166] As Alton Gal articulates, "On the one hand, there was the traditional Puritan veneration of the Bible and the 'chosen people' of the Bible; on the other was the attitude of the Boston Brahmins, who felt themselves threatened by new fortunes and immigrant hordes."[167] The poet Oliver Wendell Holmes Jr. expressed this traditional admiration of Jews, while simultaneously arguing that they were "a race lying under a curse for their obstinacy in refusing the gospel."[168] The poet James Russell Lowell had a contradictory view of Jews: "He sought them out and avoided them, defended them and attacked them, admired them and feared them."[169] Many leading Bostonians insulated themselves from these newcomers and looked for ways to keep them out. They created a book called the *Social Register* to identify who were favored in high society and who were not.[170] Anti-Semitism and intolerance was commonplace in Boston.

Henry Lee Higginson's racial thinking was similarly flawed. While he was a Democrat and a Progressive known for his generosity and paternalism toward foreign musicians and members of his own social class, he was also a leading member of the Immigrant Restriction League, a semisecretive racist organization established in 1894 by upper-class Bostonians to restrict further immigration and disenfranchise immigrants already in the United States.[171] In part, Higginson's prejudice against Jews came out of economic difficulties he had endured in his banking enterprise, Lee, Higginson and Company. In the 1870s, Higginson had financed a railroad merger between the Boston and Maine and New Haven Railroads, pushing New England in the direction of the national trend toward consolidation and large-scale capitalism. As legal counsel for the Massachusetts Anti-Merger League, Louis Brandeis, a Harvard educated Jew, argued against monopoly. He saw Higginson's efforts as a "weakening of free competition and democracy by finance capital."[172] Years later, on April 24, 1908, Higginson wrote to Senator Henry Cabot Lodge, saying that Brandeis "has endeavored to throw the New Haven securities from the saving banks and to push the New Haven railroad out of the state. . . . I should consider him a most dangerous man."[173] In 1911, Brandeis was once again in a legal battle with Higginson. Brandeis was hired to represent Charles H. Jones of the New England Shoe and Leather Association in another anti-monopoly suit against the United Shoe Machinery Company—a firm underwritten by Lee, Higginson and Company.[174] Higginson assembled an "anti-Brandeis coalition" against the Jewish lawyer, made up of Boston's wealthiest and most powerful Brahmin business leaders. In 1916, fifty Bostonians signed a petition seeking to prevent Brandeis from winning Senate confirmation to the US Supreme Court.[175] As Gal points out, "Anti-Semitism in Brahmin circles clearly affected Brandeis's political prospects. Henry Lee Higginson spoke not only for State Street but for a good part of Boston."[176]

Higginson's opinion of Brandeis affected his views on Jews in general. In 1907, Higginson intensified his activity on the Immigrant Restriction League to keep "undesirable" immigrants out of the country.[177] Five years later, in February of 1912, he became an officer in that organization, and in 1913 he agreed to serve on the National Advisory Committee.[178] The league was "determined to mount a counteroffensive against the strange invaders who seemed so grave a threat to their class, their region, their country, and their race."[179] It agitated for a national literacy test that would restrict immigration to those privileged enough to be able to read and write English. The league sent speakers to address local groups, distributed propaganda leaflets, and lobbied Washington. Its work asserted that the United States had become a dumping ground for "illiterates, paupers, criminals, and madmen" who were endangering the country.[180]

The league also used pseudo-scientific dogma to divide European white men into biological categories, classifying eastern Europeans into the most inferior type to justify their arguments.[181] Its view of nationalism was built on an "ideology of kinship to enthrone their own tribe and oppress others."[182] It justified discrimination, arguing that America could "improve its race" by selecting immigrants based on "appropriate national origins."[183] The league was influenced by eugenicist Madison Grant, who wrote *The Passing of the Great Race* (1916), which promoted a theory of "Nordic" racial supremacy and advocated the separation or removal of all "worthless" and "unfit" types.[184] It was inspired by scientist Robert DeCourcy Ward, who publicized his view that "science decrees restrictions on the new immigration for the conservation of the 'American race.'"[185] Higginson's father-in-law, Harvard professor Louis Agassiz, was a prolific writer and teacher on the topic of scientific racism, believing that races were distinct and unequal and could be classified based on climatic zones.[186] Boston's upper classes feared that foreigners would replace their own native stock, and they worried about "biological defeat."[187] Immigration restriction was a "phase of national defense" against "the strange invaders who seemed so grave a threat to their class, their region, their country, and their race."[188]

The Republican Party provided the main platform for restrictionist sentiment.[189] In 1906, Senator Henry Cabot Lodge and his son-in-law Congressman Augustus Gardner pushed league measures through the Senate and the House of Representatives.[190] In 1907, the US Immigration Commission was formed, led by Vermont senator William Dillingham, who wrote a report in 1911 stating that immigration from southern and eastern Europe posed a serious national threat to American society. Immigrant Restriction League efforts led directly to the Emergency Quota Act of 1921 and the Johnson Reed Act of 1924 that severely restricted immigration to the United States.[191] Although the acts did not specifically target Jews, émigrés allowed to enter were primarily from northern European countries, diminishing the flow of immigrants from eastern Europe. In the 1930s, federal immigration restrictions excluded thousands of Jewish refugees from Nazi Europe, playing a complicit role the Holocaust.

Along with their work to restrict immigrants, the league labored to Americanize foreigners and educate the middle classes.[192] It published and distributed countless pamphlets in its attempt to make immigrants in the United States less foreign. Brahmin philanthropists like Higginson imagined ways they could teach the newcomer Anglo-Saxon

values and preserve cultural hegemony.[193] They sought to create new
cultural institutions or to improve old ones, hoping that their wealth
and leadership would transform and uplift social attitudes throughout the population. Many philanthropists funneled money into cultural endeavors.[194] As Frederic Cople Jaher points out, "Institutions
organized by the elite to instill in the masses the virtue of established
social arrangements were directed primarily to the out-group for the
purposes of maintaining patrician predominance . . . mass education
devices served to protect ascendancy in the larger community."[195]

Higginson hired Karl Muck to ensure that upper-class values were
passed on to new Americans. For Brahmins like Higginson, Symphony
Hall was not simply an entertainment venue but an educational facility. In a letter to his father, he wrote, "Education is the object of man,
and it seems to me the duty of all of us to help in it." Higginson greatly
admired Harvard president and art history professor Charles Eliot Norton, whose 1896 essay "Some Aspects of Civilization in America" called
upon the educated upper classes to elevate standards of taste in society
by creating and maintaining institutions such as museums, libraries,
orchestras, colleges, and parks.[196] Higginson was afraid of the impact
immigrants would have on his city and country. The BSO was Higginson's response to the immigrant problem. He wrote, "Democracy has
got fast hold of the world and will rule. Let us see that she does it more
wisely. . . . Educate, and save ourselves and our families and our money
from mobs!"[197] Henry Lee Higginson and Karl Muck would come to
learn that they had much in common. Higginson and his conductor
held snobbish and ultraconservative views regarding Jews. Both men
were highly privileged and had little understanding of other social
classes. They shared a view of themselves as racially superior to other
ethnic groups. Muck had been schooled in prejudice before his arrival
in Boston, and Higginson was deeply xenophobic, particularly toward
Boston's latest wave of eastern European immigrants. In Boston, Muck
found that he shared with Higginson and other Brahmin elites a
similarly flawed worldview with some of the same anti-Semitic racial
thinking.

When Karl Muck arrived in 1906, the BSO organization was
twenty-five years old, and its new performance venue, Boston Symphony Hall, was only six years old. Higginson had formed a corporation to build the hall, modeled after the Gewandhaus in Leipzig, at an
exorbitant cost of $750,000.[198] He wrote to architect C. F. McKim in
New York years before that "there isn't a day that I don't dream about
that Music Hall."[199] To develop his enterprise and make it successful,
Higginson broadened the orchestra's financial base by acquiring private funding from influential local families and giving them a stake

in the operation.[200] Harvard president Charles W. Eliot and other prominent Bostonians, including Elizabeth Cabot and Georgina Lowell, pledged money to build the facility.[201] In 1893, during a particularly difficult year, Higginson called on his constituency in an appeal for funds. He received pledges of support from a wide cross section of the city's elite, including Agassiz, Brimmer, Lodge, Lee, Gardner, Norton, Longfellow, Shattuck, Paine, Parkman, Peabody, Endicott, Forbes, and Perkins. Present on the list were at least four Museum of Fine Arts trustees, as well as other Boston financiers from competing banks and brokerage houses. The group raised more than $400,000.[202] It mortgaged the property and leased it to Higginson, who agreed to "meet costs of administration, taxes, and all charges, and to pay to the stockholders the rest of the receipts."[203] That Higginson was so successful in his efforts was a consequence of his solid business plan, his organizational vision, his commitment, and his centrality to Boston's economic and social elite.[204]

Higginson hired McKim's junior architect, George Gersdorff, and Boston artist Theodore Otto Langerfeldt to design the building, along with Harvard engineer Wallace Sabine for his acoustical expertise. The hall had a simple plan that Anglo-Bostonians would approve of. Sabine improved the acoustics of the hall by limiting the amount of upholstery on the chairs and experimenting with wood varieties on the floor.[205] The balconies were adorned with plaster sculptures from Europe, and the name Beethoven was embossed in gilt on the proscenium medallion above the stage, in tribute to Higginson's favorite composer and as a symbol of musical idealism that the BSO exemplified.[206] Muck had played his first solo piano concert as a young man in the Gewandhaus in Leipzig, and, since Symphony Hall was a copy of that facility, it is probable that he felt at home there. Muck, no doubt, was pleased with the quality of sound that his orchestra could produce in the new facility, but his musical mission was part of Higginson's larger social and political agenda.

Higginson was a Germanophile who had spent years in Austria and Germany as a young man studying piano, and he loved the musical culture of those places. He had learned the German language, and he could speak with Muck in his native tongue. Higginson had immersed himself in his musical studies in Europe. He had practiced piano eight hours a day and attended composition and musicianship classes. Ultimately, however, he could not make a living as a musician, and so he returned to Boston and became a junior partner in his father's brokerage house. In 1861, he married Ida Olympe Frederika Agassiz, who was born in 1837 in Karlsruhe, in the state of Baden Wurttemberg, in southwest Germany to Swiss-born Jean Louis Agassiz, the well-known

Figure 1.14. Boston Symphony Hall, Dadmun Co., Boston, 1909. Courtesy of the Library of Congress, Prints and Photographs Division, Reproduction number LC-DIG-det-4a11361.

Harvard zoologist and geologist, and German Cecile Braun. The Higginsons had two children, Cecile and Alexander, named after Ida's relatives.[207] It is probable that Higginson wanted his wife and family to feel at home in Boston, and he knew Bostonians would enjoy and appreciate German culture as much as he did.[208] In 1846, Higginson had visited Germany and was inspired by music that was performed in concert halls, in restaurants, in theaters, and on the streets. He later wrote of the influence that German music and culture would have on his future:

> Sixty years ago, I wished to be a musician, and therefore went to Vienna, where I studied two years and a half diligently, learned something of music, something about musicians, and one other thing—that I had no talent for music. I heard there and in other European cities the best orchestras, and much wished that our own country should have such fine orchestras. Coming home . . . [a]ll these years I watched the musical conditions in Boston, hoping to make them better. I believed that an orchestra of excellent musicians under one head and devoted to a single purpose could produce fine results, and wished for the ability to support such an undertaking. . . . After consulting with some European friends, I laid out a plan, and at the end of two very good years of business, began.[209]

In 1881, when Higginson organized the orchestra, he contacted Julius Epstein, his old schoolmate in Vienna, who had become a prominent professor at the Vienna Conservatory and who knew the foremost musicians in Austria and Germany. Julius became Higginson's European recruiter, helping him to acquire the best musicians, conductors, and musical scores available for his orchestra.[210] Higginson knew that there was an available pool of trained musicians in Europe and he took advantage of that market. As Karen Ahlquist points out, "Germans were expert at creating demand for musical performance and an interest in music study among both the immigrant and the native-born populations. . . . Putting together performances of difficult 'classic' works and the latest music from Europe piqued the curiosity of potential listeners and inspired pride among economic and civic leaders sensitive to culture as a source of prestige."[211] Higginson hired full-time musicians, giving a level of security to his performers. He took enormous financial risks to offer this benefit to his musicians, who normally earned their pay job-by-job.[212] Paul DiMaggio referred to Higginson as a "Cultural Capitalist," who vowed to manage and maintain the orchestra and raise the necessary money to pay the orchestra players each week.[213] He corporatized music making in the city, combining the income-generating aspirations of a profitable business with the social service aspects of a charitable organization. The nonprofit corporate structure was better able to withstand leadership and economic crises, becoming the primary institutional vehicle for orchestral performance in the twentieth century.[214] As DiMaggio makes clear, the corporation was a "successful tool by which nineteenth century elites organized their affairs." Borrowing business methods taken from the for-profit arena and using them in the nonprofit charitable sector enabled Higginson to rule without interference. This structure was one of the reasons for the BSO's enormous success.[215]

Higginson wrote of the financial risks in creating his venture: "Pray remember that I must go to my office daily, in order to earn money enough to carry on this enterprise yearly and to accumulate $1,000,000 on the interest of which the Orchestra will depend after my death."[216] Higginson was able to fund the BSO in great part by his lucrative investments in the copper mining industry, particularly the Calumet and Hecla mines of the Upper Peninsula in Michigan, as well as successful investments in western railroads, the telephone industry, and General Electric. He was a capitalist whose wealth came from the management of industrial enterprises from which he extracted a profit.[217] Consequently, he always carefully monitored market fluctuations and acted accordingly. To his father he wrote, "I was going to ask you to sell some of your Calumet shares; 2300 is a great many, and good as they are, how can anyone tell to what price copper will go? I fear the market always, don't you?"[218] In addition to the burden of providing his musicians a full-time salary, in 1903 he also established a pension fund for orchestra members that Higginson hoped would "be a comfort to you gentlemen of the Orchestra today as something to look forward to when you leave off work."[219] He established a model for the BSO based on his business acumen, organizational skills, and his economic investments.[220] Critic John Sullivan Dwight called Higginson's plan a "coup d'état" that would "take the wind out of the sails" of any existing efforts.[221] Higginson's Boston Symphony Orchestra became the standard of America's high cultural experience, providing the nation with its first permanent, full-season orchestra.[222] Boston set the tone for musical development to come.[223] Many American symphony orchestras that emerged in the twentieth century looked to Boston to establish their organizational structures.[224]

Higginson offered spring and summer "Pops" concerts to give orchestra players additional income and to satisfy the demands of an ever-expanding, musically knowledgeable middle-class population. He envisioned that Symphony Hall could transform into a German-style beer garden in springtime, with the orchestra playing lighter garden pieces such as Johann Strauss waltzes. To convert the hall into an informal beer garden, he made sure that the formal seating in rows could be removed and replaced with tables and greenery, such as trees and shrubs, to embellish the venue for the seventy-five-concert season. Audiences were offered light fare such as sandwiches, pretzels, and beer while the orchestra played.

This taxing, almost year-round orchestra schedule made more work for the musicians and the management and left little time for summer rejuvenation, and yet Higginson was acutely aware of the financial needs of his players and made it his mission to offer additional performance opportunities for them in the off season whenever he could. By taking on this financial responsibility for his players, he gave them stability, which allowed them to focus on making exceptional music. Music historian Joseph Horowitz has noted that "a symphony orchestra pure and simple does not exist in all of Europe. That is to say, that in no city in Germany, Italy, France, or Russia is there an orchestra which is made up of players whose only business it is to perform such music as is to be found on programmes of symphony concerts."[225] Because players were permanent employees, they had time to polish and perfect their work. Before the Boston Symphony, the Harvard Musical Association and the Boston Philharmonic rehearsed under "casual conditions—lax rehearsals, changing membership,

[and] provincial leadership." Higginson was determined to change this situation by offering comfortable salaries and providing a level of musicianship unparalleled in Europe or the United States that would allow him to entice the best musicians from Germany and Austria.[226] Muck reported to a German newspaper that Higginson's enterprise "deserves the highest praise and the best of reputations. . . . The management spares no expense to secure the best talent. Boston is the American Athens, and it possesses an art-loving and musically cultured public."[227]

To maintain his investment and his reputation, Higginson demanded perfection from his musicians. He sought out conductors who knew how to bring out the very best from their ensembles. Because Karl Muck was an upper-class German and a favorite of the kaiser, Higginson offered him a substantial annual salary of $20,000 plus investment securities.[228] Higginson's generosity was part of his business plan, providing financial incentives to keep Muck happy, offering him a lifestyle in keeping with what he had left behind in Germany. Free from the burden of having to manage his own finances, Muck could focus on the challenge of building an excellent orchestra.

Muck's Role in the Development of Music in Boston and America

Muck threw himself into the professional challenges of conducting the Boston Symphony, for Higginson gave complete artistic control to his conductor. In Germany, Muck had received state patronage under the watchful eyes of Kaiser Wilhelm and the Royal Superintendent Reichsgraf Boklo von Hochberg, who had restricted his independence and limited his repertoire. Furthermore, he was in the shadow of his more famous friend and colleague, Richard Strauss.[229] With the Boston Symphony, Muck managed his own schedule, his players, his programs, and his musical choices. He had a level of power and freedom unparalleled in his life before. As Higginson described it, "In my eyes the requisites about the Orchestra were these: to leave the choice and care of the musicians, the choice and care of the music, the rehearsals and direction of the Orchestra, to the conductor, giving him every power possible."[230] Higginson sought perfection, and yet his goal was to leave each person to his expertise. He said, "Dr. Muck chooses the music, prepares everything for the public, conducts the rehearsals and the concerts. Each of you gentlemen does his part excellently, and each of you is as well treated as lies in my power."[231]

Figure 1.15. Karl Muck conducting the Boston Symphony Orchestra on Symphony Hall stage. Courtesy of the Boston Symphony Orchestra Archives.

Muck did not have to start from scratch with his orchestra, for his ensemble was already well trained. Higginson had employed several excellent conductors before Muck, so the orchestra was prepared when he commenced his work. In 1888, the BSO's first conductor, Bohemian-born Georg Henschel, organized a mostly American orchestra with musicians taken from the Harvard Musical Association and a few musicians from Europe. Henschel remained with the orchestra for only three years before Higginson hired Austrian conductor Wilhelm Gericke, who brought many excellent musicians from Germany and Austria with him. He raised the standard of the orchestra by demanding more practice times per week and increasing the number of weekly performances to three. Gericke also educated and disciplined his audience. Late arrivals were not permitted into the hall until the orchestra had stopped performing. Concertgoers were taught rituals of applause, such as not to clap between movements and not to call out, demanding encores following performances. As John Spitzer points out, "Musicians tried to 'educate' their audiences to appreciate and patronize symphonic music."[232] Gericke initially served for five years; followed by Arthur Nikisch for four years; Emil Paur for five years; and then Gericke, who returned for another eight years until 1906. At the conclusion of Gericke's appointment, he called Boston audiences "one of the most cultivated and best understanding musical publics I know."[233]

Muck carried on the work of the prior conductors. He rehearsed his musicians very hard, conducting with small baton strokes, appearing to exert minimal effort. Muck attempted to master every detail of the musical score, requiring that his orchestra play with precision. While other conductors of the day interpreted classical pieces in a romantic and embellished style with exaggerated tempos, Muck maintained strict fidelity to the score.[234] Composer and conductor Felix

Weingartner said that Muck was a "punctilious workman" who was "without a doubt the most conscientious, hard-working conductor he ever had known, a conductor who took prodigious pains in his editing, preparation, corrections, and rehearsals."[235] In a time when recorded music was a new invention, a live presentation of Beethoven, Haydn, or Mendelssohn was a spiritual awakening for many. Bostonians worshiped German musicians, composers, and conductors in cultlike fashion, giving Muck a feeling of belonging in a city that had welcomed so many German musicians before him.

To get results during rehearsals, Muck was not always pleasant. In fact, he was explosive and impatient.[236] He would often "grumble, complain, and curse."[237] David Ewen described him as an "arrogant" man with a "stinging tongue" who "treated his men with the merciless severity of a Junker officer."[238] He impulsively called rehearsals without notice, at any time of day or night. His racial views also affected his actions and judgment. When composer Ernest Bloch presented his *Three Jewish Poems* for inclusion on the Boston Symphony program, Muck was reluctant to debut the work if Bloch did not change the title.[239] Bloch supposedly responded, "Dr. M[uck] you speak exactly like my Jewish friends, who advised me to change the title for obvious reasons." Bloch defended the title of his piece, to which Muck replied, "If there were more Jews like you, there would be less anti-Semitism."[240] In a letter to his wife about the episode, Bloch felt obvious animosity toward Muck, referring to him as a "Pangermanist" and a "fierce anti-Semite, nourished in Bayreuth." Bloch victoriously told his wife that Muck was "happy to see how my aggressive Jewishness confronted him."[241] Muck agreed to leave the title alone and told Bloch that he would defend the decision with the BSO and the Boston press if necessary, highlighting the obvious racism throughout Boston's upper echelons. Muck paid a backhanded compliment to Bloch, however, by suggesting that he was a unique Jew, and that if there were more Jews like Bloch, perhaps there would be less hatred. The dialogue lays bare Muck's obvious bigotry.[242]

When famed Jewish violinist Fritz Kreisler visited Boston before the war, Muck invited him to join the violin section during a rehearsal only to stop the practice session several times to criticize Kreisler for his "inadequate playing." A premeditated joke, Muck purposely created an "uneasy embarrassment" throughout the orchestra pit. The "stone-faced musicians" stared at Kreisler with "condescending compassion," leaving him entirely mortified and confused. "Then suddenly, the orchestra shook with laughter. Instantly grasping the joke that had been played on him, Kreisler joined in the hilarity."[243] Did Muck instigate this "joke" because Kreisler was a Jew and he wanted to intimidate him or because Muck liked to balance discipline with humor in his orchestra? Perhaps we will never know. What we do know is that Muck was a taskmaster who drove his musicians very hard during rehearsals. In response, they became very skilled at knowing exactly what he demanded at all times. On opening night, October 16, 1906, Higginson commented to his wife that Muck stopped conducting "for some minutes, tho' the Orchestra felt him all the time. The men and he are mutually content—and happy over it. It was a very fine, delicate, artistic concert."[244]

Muck's concerts were often structured thematically according to historical periods, performing classical music in one program and baroque in another. He took the art of performance to a new level by making this type of programmatic change. He made assumptions that his audiences were knowledgeable enough to understand his intent. Although he was not a huge fan of new music, he stretched his audiences' sensibilities by offering contemporary works by Sibelius, Mahler, and Schoenberg.[245] Muck experimented with the length of programs, too. He routinely repeated compositions that he believed needed to be heard and understood. After audience members left Symphony Hall in protest because they disliked the music of Brahms, Muck insisted on conducting the same piece during the next evening's program. Muck imposed repetition, forcing audiences to hear and adopt the German composer's music as part of the American concert repertoire.[246]

Muck was able to impose his will on his audience as a leader and educator in great part because he was charismatic. He was a thin man with high cheekbones and angular features. He dressed impeccably in a dark tailcoat and starched high collared shirt, carrying himself with the elegance and grace of a European gentleman. He had a tanned complexion that he acquired on daily walks around the city. Self-possessed, disciplined, and physically fit, he embodied all the ideals of manliness defined by Theodore Roosevelt's "strenuous life."[247] Muck was an early twentieth-century celebrity, and his fame satisfied an "exaggerated expectation of human greatness." As Daniel Boorstin puts it, "The celebrity develops their capacity for fame, not by achieving great things, but by differentiating their own personality from those of their competitors in the public arena."[248] Muck's Germanness and his perfectionism accentuated that celebrity status, affording him the reverence of Boston audiences. He was incredibly popular throughout the city.[249]

Higginson took full advantage of Muck's charisma to promote the orchestra at a national level, traveling with him on cross-country touring engagements. While on tour, the press photographed and interviewed Muck, and his picture appeared on venue billboards. As Graeme Turner points out, "the dissemination of the face" added to the "dissemination of ideas," exciting "new forms of desire" among audiences that attended his concerts.[250] Muck endorsed Boston's Gillette Razor Company, Mason and Hamlin Piano Company, and Steinway Piano Company in city newspapers around the country, and his image appeared in their advertisements as well.[251] He sat on the boards of directors of major musical institutions that promoted the BSO. Moreover, in 1917, Muck became one of the first orchestra conductors in the country to make an acoustical recording for the Victor Talking Machine Company in Camden, New Jersey. All of these efforts assisted in spreading his fame and gave his identity symbolic and psychological meaning over time.[252]

Boston's leading newspapers, funded by a network of Brahmin businessmen, published critical reviews and positive impressions of Muck almost daily. These laudatory depictions appeared in syndicated newspapers disseminated throughout the country, enhancing Muck's stature and the Boston Symphony's national reputation as a leader in the hierarchy of musical culture in America.[253] *Boston Herald* critic Philip Hale, a former pianist who had trained in Germany, praised Muck's accomplishments with the orchestra: "These concerts in Boston . . . have been so remarkable under the leadership of Dr. Muck that they are now taken by too many as a matter of course. For the Boston Symphony Orchestra is not merely one that contains certain accomplished virtuosos; the orchestra is a virtuoso. It is an instrument which, having been brought to a state of perfect mechanism by Dr. Muck, responds to his imaginative and poetic wishes."[254] Hale described Muck as "calm, undemonstrative, graceful, elegant, aristocratic; a man of singularly commanding and magnetic personality even in repose. The orchestra is his speech, the expression of the composer's music as it appeals to the conductor's brain, heart, and soul."[255] Hale viewed Muck in almost magical terms, with foresighted "vision" and as the supreme "interpreter of beauty and brilliance." Hale defined him as the "superb interpreter of composers as he understands them, as he shares in their own emotions, confessions, declarations, griefs, and longings."[256] *Transcript* music critic Henry Taylor Parker raved about Muck's "technique and tonal perfections," referring to Muck and the Boston Symphony as the most "incomparable orchestra of the world," at the highest level of attainment. In 1922 he wrote that "no living conductor has assembled in himself more of the attributes of a great conductor or held them in juster balance than Dr. Muck."[257] The *Atlanta Constitution* echoed Boston's reviews by praising Muck in their regional press, declaring that "Dr. Muck and the Boston Symphony Orchestra has [*sic*] brought to this country a man of all men fitted to be at its head."[258] These incredible reviews validated Muck's position in the city (and nation) and made him feel at home.

Karl Muck's reputation meshed so nicely with Higginson's cultural agenda that the BSO director took great pains to make a permanent position for him. On November 20, 1906, Higginson wrote to Senator Henry Cabot Lodge in Washington, DC, to ask for help in extending Muck's stay.[259] Higginson also contacted Secretary of State Elihu Root, who pressed the American ambassador in Berlin, Charlemagne Tower, to use his influence to procure an extension for Muck.[260] These multipronged efforts paid off. Tower wrote on March 7, 1907, to Lodge:

> I have pleasure in informing you that I have had a conversation with the Emperor in which he announced to me that he has decided to grant to Dr. Muck a leave of absence for one year more, in order that he may remain during that time in Boston. The Emperor said that he cannot well dispense with the services of Dr. Muck as director of his own orchestra here, though he recognizes the great service which Colonel Higginson has rendered in maintaining the standard of good music in America, and he is willing to assist him in his efforts in that direction by complying with his request that Dr. Muck may remain one more year. The Emperor added, however, that he cannot extend Dr. Muck's leave of absence beyond that period, but that, if he should decide to remain for a longer time absent from Germany, he would have to resign his position as director here.[261]

Regardless of what the kaiser requested, Higginson commented on July 11, 1907, that he hoped "Muck will be here as long as I am alive."[262] Higginson believed he had acquired the finest conductor in the world, and he wanted to secure his investment. A week later, clearly aware of Boston's love affair with Muck, he repeated his hope that the talented European conductor would permanently join the Boston Symphony.[263]

Muck's Sense of Place in Boston

Outside the bounds of work, the Higginsons included the Mucks in their Brahmin social circle, inviting them to their home at 191 Commonwealth Avenue. As a gesture of hospitality, Higginson and his wife spoke German at these gatherings for the comfort of the Mucks. In the summer months, Higginson invited them to his vacation home in Manchester by the Sea, Massachusetts.[264] In a 1906 letter, Higginson commented as if talking to Muck that "we all hold the creed that our ... home is what we make it, and that by joint work we can make it beautiful and happy."[265] Higginson devotedly assisted Muck in finding contentment in Boston's upper-class society in part because his own cultural success depended upon it.

During Muck's years in Boston, he developed a close collegial association with a group of composers known as the Second New England School or the New England Romantics, whose collective professional pedigree was deeply influenced by German music. These musicians had either acquired their training at the conservatories of Germany or had received instruction from others who had studied there.[266] These composers sought to create uniquely American works, believing that close observation and "adherence to the historical forms as developed by Bach, Handel, Mozart, and Beethoven" would provide a necessary first step in that process.[267]

Muck developed relationships with these artists, whose musical compositions had graced Boston's concert and recital halls.[268] Of this collective, John Knowles Paine, George Chadwick, Arthur Foote, Edward MacDowell, Amy Beach, Horatio Parker, and Margaret (Burrage) Ruthven Lang, were the most well known.[269] Idealistic and full of energy, their works were widely performed and disseminated to the public by the Arthur Schmidt Publishing Company, which had printing houses in Boston and Berlin.[270] The Second New England School musicians' agenda paralleled Higginson's, embracing German culture and all that Europe could teach them. They were hailed at the time as "America's composers."

Muck not only cultivated a professional relationship with the Second New England School musicians, he and Anita established close friendships with them, thus anchoring the Mucks to the city's musical elites. They formed a particularly close relationship with George and Ida May Chadwick, sharing correspondence on a regular basis. George and Karl had been classmates under composer and organist Josef Rheinberger in Munich, and Chadwick was the director of the New England Conservatory of Music during Muck's years in Boston.[271] The Mucks and Chadwicks shared "family dinners," and the Mucks made sure that the Chadwicks had tickets for BSO concerts.[272] When Ida May was sick, Anita comforted her. When Anita needed help planning a formal tea with Boston ladies, Ida May assisted her. The correspondence between the two women was on intimate terms: Anita confided to Ida May that Karl suffered from dyspepsia and was "living only on milk." More intimately she wrote, "I am so sorry that you shall have the trouble of returning the underwear. . . . I hope to see you at the concert on Saturday this week!" or "This was a lovely visit. I hope we will soon have another cozy talk together." The relationship between these ladies, and presumably their husbands, was close indeed. Mrs. Chadwick oversaw the Mucks' property in Boston when the couple returned to Germany. In one letter, Anita writes, "Dearest Chaddie, Will you ask Cosileu if he does not think this bill outrageous? If we take off the $48.

of which the basins cost, the man charges just $100 for fixing them. I think we ought not to pay him this, especially as he mentioned first something of the price for mounting the basins being $18. . . . What do you think? For greatest hurry and with much love, Yours, Anita." The Mucks had developed an important bond with their close Boston friends. Anita confessed to a news reporter that she "has no desire to return to Berlin and that she had never been more content than in the time she has spent in Boston."[273]

In addition to socializing with the musical community, Karl Muck befriended members of the local intellectual establishment. Anita attended classes at Radcliffe College where she enjoyed the companionship and scholarly stimulation of other women and was welcomed into the city's exclusive Ivy League society. Frederic Cople Jaher suggested, "Brahmins created New England private schools to seclude proper Bostonians from the urban multitudes," and through these associations the Mucks could avoid any contact with the immigrant masses they seemed to fear.[274]

Karl also joined three exclusive, by-invitation-only clubs. The St. Botolph Club was a gathering place for Boston's upper-class men in the arts, sciences, and humanities that boasted a membership of talented creative professionals, such as artist John Singer Sargent, sculptor Daniel Chester French, architect H. H. Richardson, historian Francis Parkman, publishers Henry Houghton and George Mifflin, and writers John Bartlett and Edward Henry Clement. Muck expanded his social network by becoming involved in all facets of upper-class life. The St. Botolph entertained its guests with Sunday quartet concerts by members of the Boston Symphony Orchestra, and attendees enjoyed lunches, dinners, and intellectual conversation.[275] Muck's second association, the Tavern Club of Boston, included luminaries such as authors William Dean Howells, Henry James, Charles Eliot Norton, and politician Henry Cabot Lodge.[276] On January 28, 1907, Tavern Club members hosted a dinner in Muck's honor, recreating a German festival of the sixteenth century "with all the gorgeous costumes of that period— the interior of an old German hall [forming] a splendid background for all sorts of picturesque dances and playful revel."[277] Muck enjoyed this festival and was emotionally moved by Boston elites' acceptance of and heavy reliance on German culture. Muck also became a member of the Phi Mu Alpha Sinfonia music fraternity, first established in 1886 at the New England Conservatory. Members included prominent men such as Henry Lee Higginson, George Chadwick, Arthur Foote, and Horatio Parker, eventually expanding to include male musicians in chapters throughout the country.[278]

Not only did Muck's friendships flourish, but his physical environment was conducive to pleasant living as well. In 1899, Thorstein Veblen wrote a popular thesis on material consumption patterns of the rich, suggesting that "to gain and to hold the esteem of men it is not sufficient merely to possess wealth or power. The wealth or power must be put in evidence, for esteem is awarded only on evidence. . . . [W]ealth serves to impress one's importance on others and to keep their sense of importance alive and alert." For Muck and the Boston Brahmins to maintain their social position and power, the city's upper classes needed to present their opulence in a public way.[279] The Mucks made their wealth evident with their initial home, the Tuileries, on Commonwealth Avenue, which was a fashionable and luxurious hotel and apartment facility ten minutes from Symphony Hall.[280] Commonwealth Avenue was a new boulevard designed to resemble the Champs Elysees in Paris, a wide, tree-lined thoroughfare. Residing in the most expensive section of the city, the Mucks could enjoy Sunday strolls to the park, or mall, located just across from their home, or enjoy the statues and grand homes along the way. They lived just down the road from Henry and Ida Higginson; next door to the Harvard Club, where they were invited for social gatherings; Harvard president Charles W. Eliot's house was two doors away, and he, too, engaged the Mucks in social activities. The elegant German-owned Fritz Carlton Hotel was located just around the corner, on Boylston Street. In 1915, the Mucks purchased a grand home at 50 Fenway, a four-story brick brownstone minutes from their former property, facing the lovely Emerald Necklace, the expansive park designed by Frederick Law Olmsted that circles the city.[281] The Mucks could enjoy an upscale lifestyle in a fine home and purchase the highest standard of material possessions.

From this location, they could walk through the nearby fens or observe plant species and bird life from their wrought-iron balcony. For more exotic plant specimens, they could visit Horticultural Hall across the street from Symphony Hall.[282] They could spend afternoons at the Museum of Fine Arts or take out a German novel from the new Boston Public Library McKim building in Copley Square, with the names of composers such as Bach, Beethoven, Gluck, Handel, Haydn, Mendelssohn, Meyerbeer, Mozart, Wagner, and Weber engraved on its Dartmouth Street facade. The Mucks were in the heart of Boston's Cultural Mile. They could walk down tree-lined Westland Avenue and be at the Symphony Hall stage door within one minute. Their house was located next to Boston Conservatory, founded by Julius Eichberg of Düsseldorf in 1867 and sustained by other German musicians during Muck's time. They could walk to the New England Conservatory,

Figure 1.16. Karl and Anita's house at 50 Fenway within Boston's Cultural Mile district, where the Mucks could enjoy the arts and academic interests within minutes of their home. Photo by Zachary Burrage-Goodwin.

built in 1902, where George Chadwick and the other Second New England School musicians practiced and performed. Eben Jordan, second-generation German and son of the retail giant who owned the Jordan Marsh Department Store, donated money to the New England Conservatory to build Jordan Hall in 1903, across the street from Symphony Hall. Jordan also constructed the Boston Opera House in 1909, which he located within a block of Symphony Hall and NEC.[283] The Opera House shared Symphony Hall's simple design and likewise utilized the talents of Wallace Sabine for the design of its acoustics.[284] Boston socialite and patron of the arts Isabella Stewart Gardner, who became a loyal friend and supporter of Karl and Anita Muck, opened her Fenway Court museum in 1903 almost across the street from the Mucks' Fenway house.[285] At the museum's grand opening, she provided entertainment in her three-hundred-seat concert hall by fifty members of the Boston Symphony Orchestra under Wilhelm Gericke.[286] She consistently cultivated a European salon-style environment, nurturing musical culture by bringing in musicians who performed in her lovely courtyard setting surrounded by collections featuring artists such as Rembrandt, Vermeer, and Holbein, as well as medieval German wood carvings and Meissen porcelains from King Ludwig II of Bavaria.[287] The Mucks were entirely surrounded within their immediate community by representations of Germany. Musicians, many of them German, filled these institutions and lived in row houses throughout this vibrant area. Karl could hear them practicing their instruments through the cracks in the open windows as he walked down the cobblestone street to Symphony Hall each day.

In the winter months, Karl and Anita enjoyed escaping to the country, pursuing upscale diversions at the Brae-Burn Country Club in Newton, Massachusetts, an elegant facility with sweeping landscapes, an eighteen-hole golf course, tennis courts, pool room, and elegant dining room. Anita commented to Mrs. Chadwick, "We are still here and like it immensely. I don't think one could have found any place that would have suited us better; wasn't that lucky! Dr. Muck . . . feels much rested. He will begin his work next Tuesday and we want to [see if it] will be possible for him to stay here and go into Boston every morning and come back after the rehearsal."[288]

The couple also spent their leisure time traveling together to the far reaches of the United States and sent glowing postcards to George Chadwick from Yosemite National Park reflecting on the beauty and majesty of the place.[289] In the 1907 season alone, the Mucks traveled on tour with the Boston Symphony to Rochester, New York; Cleveland, Columbus, and Cincinnati, Ohio; Indianapolis, Indiana; and Detroit, Michigan, so they were able to sample the culture in a variety of regions

Figure 1.17. New England Conservatory. Courtesy of the Library of Congress, Prints and Photographs Division, Reproduction number LC-DIG-det-4a11362.

Figure 1.18. Boston Opera House. Melissa D. Burrage Collection.

Figure 1.19. Boston Public Library. Courtesy of the Library of Congress, Prints and Photographs Division, Reproduction number LC-DIG-det-4a07108.

Figure 1.20. Boston Museum of Fine Arts. Courtesy of the Library of Congress, Prints and Photographs Division, Reproduction number LC-DIG-det-4a23424.

throughout the country.[290] In May of 1915, Muck conducted the BSO in thirteen performances at the Panama-Pacific International Exhibition in San Francisco.[291] Ultimately, their cross-country road trips were a testament to their ability to travel in the prewar years without difficulty, as Germans and as foreign nationals, to all parts of the United States.

Muck was a German in America and a vital part of the fabric of Boston. As the BSO publicity manager later recalled, Muck was a "good and patriotic German" who had "become greatly attached to this country."[292] A Stuttgart, Germany, newspaper reported, Muck's "precise genius [was] admirably suited to the quiet Boston culture."[293] He could eat German food and read German newspapers. He could express opinions about Germany and about America's relationship with his homeland without fear or worry. He could speak the German language in public, during symphony rehearsals, or with colleagues and friends. He could travel back and forth each summer to Germany or Austria and return to Boston prepared for the next musical season.[294] He could bring the latest musical compositions or the best instrumentalists from Europe for the orchestra. He could communicate by letter with family members he had left behind in Germany. He could mail money if they needed it. He could share news of home with his Boston colleagues. Muck was comfortable in his new environment precisely because Boston accepted his German identity. His experience as a new immigrant in a foreign place began very well. He adapted and integrated into Boston, and he came to love the city.

In 1908, Kaiser Wilhelm called Muck back to Germany, and the conductor felt obliged to return. The Harvard Union Club threw Muck a farewell dinner, and many people within Boston's intellectual and musical communities were there to see him off.[295] Higginson, however, lamented his departure and immediately began to persuade Muck to return to Boston. Unrelenting, Higginson used whatever excuse he could to maintain the relationship. On July 7, 1908, he wrote to Muck in Berlin asking for help recruiting instrumentalists. By having Muck pick out the musicians for the orchestra, Higginson guaranteed that Muck would be satisfied with the quality of players should he decide to return as conductor. On December 14, 1908, Higginson wrote to Muck in Berlin offering him a five-year engagement and an $8,000 increase on $20,000 annual salary and throughout 1909 made repeated attempts to bring Muck back to Boston. The following year, Higginson continued to court the renowned German conductor, proposing an even more lucrative package.[296] Because of Higginson's persuasiveness, and with fond memories of Boston in mind, Karl Muck finally relented, resigning his post in Berlin after four years and agreeing in 1912 to another five-year assignment as the BSO conductor.[297]

Over the course of the next five years, Karl Muck's reputation in Boston flourished, reaching its zenith in 1917. By then, America's entry into the war was imminent even though President Wilson had won reelection the year before having boasted that he had kept America out of the conflict raging in Europe. As the United States was increasingly set on a war footing, readying its sons for battle against the foreign enemy, Muck continued to conduct the orchestra. Following one performance, the *Boston Transcript* reported that he received thunderous applause and was presented with a wreath of gratitude, representing the high watermark for German culture in Boston.[298] Bostonians had not yet made the connection between the "Hun" in Europe and German personnel in their orchestra, and, as a consequence, the Mucks continued to feel welcome in their adopted city.[299] They felt a cultural connection to the German population that lived in the South End, a neighborhood where they enjoyed German food, much as they had in the old country. They were well received by the Boston Symphony Orchestra membership, by the local press, and by enthusiastic audiences at Symphony Hall. The couple developed a supportive network of like-minded musicians and their families, and they enjoyed their home in the heart of the cultural district.[300] They developed affection for the natural space there and appreciated the property's proximity to cultural institutions, shops, and museums.[301] The Mucks assimilated very easily (or so they thought) into Boston's upper-class society, having come from Germany's upper classes themselves. Karl Muck shared

Figure 1.21. Karl and Anita Muck with their dog looking content and happy outside of their home. Courtesy of the Boston Symphony Archives.

the same racial and elitist worldview as his colleague, Henry Lee Higginson. The people the Mucks associated with, be they Anglo-American or German, revered German culture, and, in many ways, their life in Boston was an extension of the one they had left behind, perhaps even better. Karl Muck had the best of all worlds—the adopted pleasures that he was familiar with, the comfort and love of music, collegial friendships, and a social network of like-minded people. The excitement and variety of new pleasures and new landscapes created an amalgam of energy and creativity within Muck's own character and within this cosmopolitan community as a whole.

The city embraced German culture, placed it under glass in its museums, put it on shelves in its libraries, played it on its phonographs, performed it in its concert halls, packaged it for sale in journals and sheet music, and then widely distributed it for the American masses to consume. Muck, himself, was like a prized German artifact on the public stage that eager audiences came to see. He was highly valued in Boston precisely because he helped to define Boston's musical identity for America, assisting Higginson and other conservative patriarchs in their mission to fashion a cultural "city upon the hill" with the BSO as its centerpiece.[302] Boston's musical dominance would soon be challenged, however, by New York City and other metropolitan communities in the United States that were equally committed to forging a position of cultural supremacy on the national stage.

Chapter Two

MOBILIZATION

A Changing Environment
for Boston (1917)

International Tensions and the Road to War

On June 28, 1914, news of the assassination of heir to the Austro-Hungarian throne Archduke Franz Ferdinand and his wife Sophie Chotek by Bosnian Serb Gravrilo Princip, ended peace in Continental Europe and led to the start of the world's first global war thirty-seven days later. With the death of one world leader, a veritable perfect storm of circumstances was unleashed, including a deadly series of political alliances arranged in the policy-making centers in Germany, Austro-Hungary, France, Russia, Britain, Italy, the Ottoman Empire, and the Balkan states, involving complex interactions between kings, emperors, foreign ministers, presidents, ambassadors, and military commanders who viewed the world through fearful and paranoid eyes. The world became embroiled in battle, pitting heavily armed country against country and neighbor against neighbor, changing history irrevocably.[1]

World War I scholars continue to debate the origin of the conflict, giving rise to an enormous body of historical literature with a wide array of hypotheses and interpretations. With an overabundance of sources, or missing archival materials, and with so many factors shaping the decisions that led to war, historians are perhaps no closer to understanding how this worldwide catastrophe came to be.[2]

The events that unfolded in Boston, and for Karl Muck more specifically, were the local consequences of a vast, global struggle for power taking place at the dawn of the twentieth century, as empires rose and fell, and as political tensions increased.[3] The German Empire was one of those rising nations officially unifying following its victory in the Franco-Prussian War in 1871. Under the leadership of Minister President of Prussia Otto von Bismarck (1862–90), who had been appointed by Kaiser Wilhelm I, Germany rapidly emerged as an industrial powerhouse, and the nation soon became a byword for

Figure 2.1. The assassination of Archduke Franz Ferdinand and Sophie von Hohenberg, on June 28, 1914, that led to the start of the world's first global war. Süddeutsche Zeitung / Alamy Stock Photo. Used with permission.

remarkable productivity and economic expansion. Ultimately, Germany would eclipse the British Empire to become the leading economic force in Europe.

Changing power relations throughout the continent caused diplomatic instability in the final decades of the twentieth century. Under Bismarck's leadership, Germany had remained at peace. When Wilhelm I died in 1888, however, and his successor, Wilhelm II, ascended to the throne, Bismarck was dismissed, and the intricate web of peace-building alliances with neighboring nations that he had negotiated fell apart.[4] Wilhelm II was nationalistic, wanting Germany to be large, strong, and unbeatable. In 1897, inspired by the teachings of historian Heinrich von Treitschke, Wilhelm II established a strategy of *Weltpolitik*, or world politics, to replace Bismarck's *Realpolitik*, or practical diplomacy.[5] This new assertive dogma threatened the traditional balance of power and led to diplomatic crises before World War I.[6] Using the philosophy of social Darwinism and the idea of "survival of the fittest," Germany sought to find its "place in the sun" by establishing colonial empires that rivaled those of other leading powers, believing that if Germany did not expand, it would become weak or would collapse.

Numerous developments took place in the years leading up to World War I, increasing tensions between the major powers. For example, Germany did not renew its Reinsurance Treaty with Russia, convincing Russia to look elsewhere to eliminate its own perceived isolation. France and Russia entered into secret negotiations in 1894, leading to a military pact called the Dual Alliance. Great Britain, feeling isolated, pursued diplomatic partnerships with Japan, France, and Russia when Germany refused to develop an Anglo-German alliance, resulting in the Anglo-Japanese Alliance in 1902, the Anglo-French Entente in 1904, and the Anglo-Russian Entente in 1907. The Anglo-Japanese Alliance resulted in the two powers agreeing to adopt a position of support in the event that the other member was involved in war. The Anglo-French Entente settled long-standing colonial disputes between Britain and France over North African territories. Egypt and the Anglo-Egyptian Sudan would become a British protectorate, and northwest Africa, specifically Morocco, would become a French province. Consequently, Anglo-French relations improved, leading to the Moroccan Crises of 1906 and 1911. Thus, by 1907, Germany and its two allies, Austria-Hungary and Italy, were pitted in the Triple Alliance against France, Britain, and Russia, countries that had formed the Triple Entente.

Austria-Hungary's reaction to the death of its heir took three weeks to materialize. Arguing that the Serbian government was at fault, it issued an ultimatum fully expecting Serbia to reject its terms, thereby giving Austria-Hungary the pretext for launching a limited war against the small nation. Serbia, however, sought out Russia, its Slavic ally, for support. Fearful of Russian intervention, the Austro-Hungarians sought assurances from its ally, Germany, that if Russia declared war on their nation, the Germans would join on their side. In part, paranoia and fear motivated policy-making decisions in Europe, as each imperial government took careful measures to protect itself from imposing threats. Like a horrible domino effect, each country, distrustful of every other, sought out alliances, until Europe was hopelessly locked in a series of binding agreements that made peace impossible and war inevitable. Austria-Hungary declared war on Serbia on July 28, 1914. Russia, bound by its treaty to Serbia, mobilized its army in defense, a process that took six more weeks. Germany, allied to Austria-Hungary by treaty, viewed Russia's mobilization as an act of war against Austria-Hungary and declared war on Russia on August 1, 1914. France, bound by an alliance to Russia, declared war on Germany on August 3, 1914. Germany immediately implemented its Schlieffen Plan and swiftly invaded Belgium with the goal of reaching Paris by the shortest possible route.[7] Consequently, Britain, allied to France and obliged to defend Belgium by treaty, declared war against Germany on August 4, 1914. With Britain's entry into the war, its colonies offered military and financial assistance, thus involving Australia, Canada, India, New Zealand, and South Africa in the conflict. Japan, honoring a military agreement with Britain, declared war on Germany on August 23, 1914. Two days later, Austria-Hungary responded by declaring war on Japan.

American and German Imperialistic Aspirations

The relationship between Germany and the United States grew increasingly competitive as well, as both powers sought to expand their economic and imperial influence, after most other major world powers of the time had already established their empires. Germany had begun naval production, developing its High Seas Fleet to surpass the British Royal Navy, producing thirty-eight new German battleships by 1920 and increasing submarine production, which proved to be a mighty force against British and American shipping interests.[8] In the decades before World War I, the US Navy built up its Great White Fleet to make possible American imperial ambitions in the Western Hemisphere. The two emerging nations rivaled each other most especially in Southeast Asia and South America, where they vied for control of the markets of developing nations like the Philippines and Venezuela. Initially, Germany and the United States pursued their colonial interests without a substantial conflict of interest. By the turn of the century, however, each nation's aggressive economic and diplomatic actions elevated their relationship to a confrontational level.[9] US officials became increasingly concerned with Germany's imperialistic aspirations during the Spanish American War in 1898, after the American navy destroyed the Spanish fleet in the Philippines and set up a blockade around the Port of Manila. During this conflict, British, French, and Japanese warships appeared in the harbor and respected blockade protocol, yielding to the US Navy, while German warships broke protocol and interfered in a Philippine rebel operation against the Spanish.[10] American officials justified their own colonization of the islands as part of their military strategy against the Spanish, under the guise of protecting the Philippines from a German takeover. Both empires were greatly influenced by naval theorists such as Captain Alfred Thayer Mahan, an American historian and president of the Naval War College, who argued in *The Influence of Sea Power upon History, 1660–1783* (1890) that command of the sea decided conflicts between great powers.[11] Each nation sought new territory to serve as a fueling station for its naval vessels, to provide private shipping merchants with a safe haven, and to satisfy its broader diplomatic and economic interests in China, Japan, and elsewhere in the Far East. Germany and the United States coveted the Philippines for these reasons, and Germany refused to leave. In addition, the kaiser purchased all of Spain's remaining Pacific colonies except for Guam, which the United States had already seized.[12] In December of 1902, in fact, when Venezuela was unable to repay its large foreign debts, Britain and Germany sent naval officials to collect their respective shares, blockading the port of Caracas, seizing several Venezuelan gunboats, and firing on the forts at Puerto Cabello. Dictator Cipriano Castro sought American intervention to solve the problem. Theodore Roosevelt utilized what would become known as his Roosevelt Corollary to the Monroe Doctrine which declared, "We cannot afford to let Europe get a foothold in our backyard, so we'll have to act as policemen for the West." In 1902, the United States was testing its new "police power" stratagem (to be proclaimed by Roosevelt as official American policy in 1904) during British, German, and Italian debt negotiations with Venezuela. The British and Italians cooperated, while the Germans refused to compromise, destroying a fort at San Carlos.[13] Germany did not abide by US diplomacy, bullied Venezuela, and created a greater divide between Germany and the United States, ultimately strengthening the relationship between the Americans and the British.[14] Imperial contests on the world stage and high-risk actions taken by leading decision-makers led to a series of events that would have dire consequences for millions of people worldwide, as well as for Karl Muck, more specifically. The personal tragedy of his persecution in Boston would be inextricably bound up with the confrontation between the two emerging global powers: Germany and the United States of America.

America (and Boston) Becomes Enmeshed in War against Germany

In 1914, when the First World War broke out in Europe, Bostonians followed the overseas drama from a safe distance. News reports of front-line battles barely penetrated the city's consciousness. It was not inevitable that the United States would come to face Germany in the twentieth century's first great global war. Nonetheless, while American military planners did not seek war, their contingency plans envisaged the possibility. Boston's Fore River Shipbuilding Company, located six miles south of the city, in Braintree and Quincy Point, Massachusetts, played a pivotal role in this arms race. From 1905 to 1910, 2,500 workers built torpedo boat destroyers for the US Navy, launching fifty-three in this five-year period. Fore River built many of the early classes of submarines, ammunition lighters, minesweepers, tugboats, cruisers, and battleships. In 1906, Fore River delivered its first battleships, the *Rhode Island* and the *New Jersey* to the navy, with a steady supply delivered after that, in the years before the war. War ships were in such demand that in 1907 the shipyard established an apprentice school to train young men to be shipbuilders.[15]

In 1913, Bethlehem Shipbuilding Corporation, a division of Bethlehem Steel Corporation of Pennsylvania, purchased the Fore River Shipbuilding Company. One year later, at the outset of World War I, the British Royal Navy contracted Fore River to build ten submarines. Because of US neutrality laws, however, Fore River was not allowed to deliver its products directly to Great Britain, so the company prefabricated submarines and shipped them to Canada. From there, Canadians assembled them and then shipped them across the Atlantic. The company employed fifteen thousand workers to handle additional war requisitions. To facilitate the buildup of naval ships for the American fleet, Fore River expanded to the north, to an area called Squantum, Massachusetts, at the Squantum Victory Yard, where seventy additional acres were appropriated and eight thousand additional employees were hired to handle the production.[16] The Fore River Shipbuilding community was conscious of increasing political and diplomatic turbulence between the United States and Europe. With the huge numbers of employees working at the shipyard, it was impossible for Bostonians to be unaware that the US government was involved in an arms race, aggressively building up its naval fleet.

The German invasion of Belgium in August of 1914 was a world away from Boston, but the city was nonetheless touched by that event. At first, the outbreak of war in Europe stirred Boston to compassionate acts of charity. More than six thousand Belgian civilians were killed by machine guns in a ten-day period the US newspapers called the "Rape of Belgium."

Whole villages were destroyed. In the town of Louvain alone, 250 of its citizens were killed, and the village was burned to the ground. Bostonians were horrified, and they responded by sending care packages to Belgium. Schoolchildren in Boston and Lowell used their recesses to make shoes for Belgian children.[17] Boston began a "tin box campaign" to raise money for the beleaguered country.[18] The war, however, still seemed too far away from New England to cause serious concern.

War became altogether more palpable as it began to threaten the safety of America's seafaring passengers and exposed shorelines.[19] On May 7, 1915, the British passenger liner *Lusitania* was sunk by a single

Figure 2.2. Fore River Plant / Bethlehem Shipbuilding Corp, Quincy, Massachusetts (1896–1980). Massachusetts playing a pivotal role in the war, supplying battleships and destroyers for the effort. Courtesy of the Thomas Crane Public Library, Fore River Shipyard Postcard Collection.

German torpedo blast off the coast of Ireland, killing 1,200 civilians, including 128 Americans. Every ship in the Atlantic was vulnerable to attack, particularly as Germany attempted to cut supply lines. Three months later, in August of 1915, the British passenger ship SS *Arabic* was sunk by Germany without warning, killing forty people, including two Americans.

Diplomatic pressure escalated, and soon, Americans were thrown into the hostilities as combatants. The final straw for President Wilson came with the German attack on the ferry *Sussex*, killing eighty passengers, including twenty-five Americans. On April 19, 1916, unable to maintain tactful relations with Germany, Wilson read an ultimatum before a special session of Congress. "Unless the [German] Imperial Government should now immediately declare and effect an abandonment of its present methods of U-boat warfare against passenger and freight carrying vessels, the Government of the United States can have no other choice but to sever diplomatic relations with the German empire altogether."[20] Five days later, on April 24, 1916, the kaiser issued the Sussex Pledge, vowing not to sink ships without warning; however, German U-boat attacks persisted.

Of concern in New England was the presence in the autumn of 1916 of the German commercial long-distance U-boat *Deutschland*, which made several transatlantic crossings from July to November.

THE OCTOPUS

Figure 2.3. Cesare, "The Octopus." American ships were vulnerable to attack by German U-boats. Cesare, *One Hundred Cartoons by Cesare* (Boston: Small, Maynard, 1916), 71, reflects that fear. Philip A. Burrage Collection.

Anchored along New England's shoreline on October 7, 1916, crewmen visited with Americans and even allowed visitors onboard. Although friendly to their guests during their ship-to-shore visit, the sailors sank seven European merchant ships the next day near Nantucket Island. Perhaps most disturbing was that the underwater ship had traveled almost eight thousand miles without refueling. This long-distance attack made Germany a very real threat to America and to New England, in particular. U-boat sailors were cunningly capable of being friendly one minute and deadly the next. Their duplicitous behavior as well as this specific U-boat episode, followed by Ambassador Johann Heinrich Graf von Bernstorff's February 1917 announcement that Germany would implement a new policy of unrestricted submarine warfare, shook New Englanders, who had viewed Germany as a far-off danger.[21]

Pressured by New England politicians to do something about Germany, President Wilson was in a conundrum. Trying to abide by his promise of neutrality, he was hopelessly unable to keep his word. His breaking point came that cold February with news of the Zimmerman Telegram, a coded message from Arthur Zimmerman, the German foreign secretary, to Heinrich von Eckardt, German ambassador in Mexico. The communiqué instructed von Eckardt to approach the Mexican government and offer them the territory they had lost in the Mexican American War—New Mexico, Arizona, and parts of California, Nevada, and Colorado—in exchange for a Mexican-German alliance. The Zimmerman Telegram was intercepted and decoded in mid-January by the British, who revealed it to the Wilson administration on February 19. It was then released to the press on February 28, 1917.[22] The telegram exposed Germany's plan, and American politicians began to believe a declaration of war was inevitable.[23] Henry Cabot Lodge, senior US senator from Massachusetts, played a significant role in convincing Wilson to declare war. He delivered a petition from three thousand Bostonians who urged Wilson to act.[24] On April 2, 1917, after careful consideration, Wilson went before Congress and asked it to accept the state of war "thrust upon it" by the German Empire.[25] Congress was convinced that war was the appropriate path to safeguard the nation and secure imperialistic opportunities for the future. Four days later the United States declared war on Germany.[26]

On that same day, newspapers reported that 1,200 horses bound for Liverpool on the SS *Canadian* were killed when a German U-boat torpedoed the ship.[27] This headline tugged at the heartstrings of readers, who found German actions against innocent animals an unforgiveable cruelty. One day later, a German vessel was sighted off Nantucket Island, and the deputy collector of customs warned New England sailors not to leave port.[28] For many people in New England, Wilson's declaration was long overdue.

In addition to securing the country and preventing attacks, as well as diplomatic reasons for declaring war, the United States had a financial stake in the conflict. In 1916, during the country's neutral period, American companies made $3.2 billion producing products for the war. J. P. Morgan had loaned the Allied governments more than $500 million, and it became critical for the United States to protect its foreign investments. Potential profits offered an economic incentive for joining the belligerents, which eased the path to conflict. In Boston as well, World War I offered economic leaders lucrative opportunities to amass enormous wealth. Massachusetts industries supplied railcars, picks and shovels, cloth for uniforms, shoes and boots, coffee, frozen meat and fish, and munitions in large quantities, transforming factories throughout the city into war manufacturing facilities. In the prewar years, the city had suffered with an inferiority complex in relation to New York over its economic situation, which had been in decline since the Civil War because of the collapse of the cotton industry. Thus, Boston had been extending its reach into the mining regions of the American West and, likewise, looked to profit from World War I.[29] Historian Joseph Garland describes city elites during World War I sipping port wine with presidents and diplomats in their elegant summer homes along the Gold Coast of Massachusetts, just north of Boston. Many of these individuals were "war mad," gloating over their financial windfall made during the war.[30] For many upper-class Bostonians, the bloodshed of war was secondary to war profits.

American magazine publishers capitalized on the national mobilization effort, turning patriotism into profit. One Boston publication, the *Youth's Companion Magazine* created a new American patriotic tradition. In 1892, Daniel Ford and his nephew, James Bailey Upham, began production of the magazine, which offered young male readers a mix of serials, short stories, and articles by famous personalities. The magazine was extremely popular during the war. In 1893, the magazine launched the School Flag Movement, advocating the placement of the American flag in front of all municipal buildings and classrooms nationwide. This plan was supported in the publication with patriotic instructions, encouraging all citizens to memorize and recite the Pledge of Allegiance while facing the American flag each morning with arm outstretched and palm upward, much like the Nazi salute.[31] The magazine also mass-produced American flags of every size, shape, and price, resulting in about twenty-five thousand sales to schools in one year alone.[32] The *Youth's Companion Magazine* office was located at 142 Berkeley Street in Boston, and it was called the Pledge of Allegiance

Building. The magazine's nationalistic campaign played a pivotal role in creating new patriotic traditions in the United States, including the daily recitation of the Pledge of Allegiance in schools and standardizing flag rituals in public parks and clubs across the country. These soon-to-be universal practices became important symbols of national unity, loyalty, patriotism (and profit) during World War I.[33]

When President Wilson declared war on Germany in April of 1917, the federal government expanded its bureaucratic authority over the population as it prepared the country for total war.[34] Government and businesses worked together on an unprecedented scale to meet wartime demands. The War Industries Board systematized registration for the draft. The Food Administration, the American Farm Bureau Administration, the Fuel Administration, and the Railroad Administration were all established during this time to control production for the war effort. The Federal Reserve System was implemented to control the banking industry and to raise public money for the war through Liberty Bond drives. As David M. Kennedy tells us, when Wilson summoned the American people to arms, "he strained even his large talents for swaying men's minds."[35] He had to convince the American people to join the army, to pay for the war, and to make personal sacrifices for it. "Every business man was shorn of dominion over his factory or store, every housewife surrendered control of her table, every farmer was forbidden to sell his wheat except at the price the government fixed."[36] The federal government had an interest in local affairs to a greater extent than at any time since the Civil War because of the need to mobilize the nation.

Boston's Military Infrastructure and Paramilitary Environment

Boston's physical environment changed dramatically during this period, as the city became a military center and supply depot. Troops trained everywhere. Public spaces were transformed to accommodate martial activity. The sight of weapons and the sound of marching boots became commonplace. City inhabitants changed their daily routines: Civilian department-store employees undertook paramilitary exercises on store rooftops. Thousands of people went to work in local factories making weapons and war materiel. The lurking threat of a German attack darkened the city—as the golden dome of the State House was painted black and the colorful flowers of the public gardens were covered with khaki tents advertising Liberty Bonds or food conservation.[37] The city's character changed, virtually overnight, and Karl Muck could not escape these changes.

In preparation for war, cities required new military infrastructure, such as training camps and shipping ports. In February of 1918, Congress appropriated $8 million to improve Boston Harbor.[38] The city became the military and naval headquarters of New England and the principal shipping port for Europe. Workers filled the South Boston mudflats and created the Boston Navy Base. The army constructed an allocation depot from which to ship supplies to Europe. A new dry dock was constructed along Commonwealth Pier, and the navy turned it into a shipping annex, housing one thousand men from the naval militia.[39] The Charlestown Navy Base was overhauled to repair and outfit ships. To protect the revamped wartime port, the harbor was mined, and a wire net was stretched across the channel to keep German submarines out and to upgrade overall defense along the coastline.[40] In 1917, merchant marines trained in East Boston and at a navigation school in Gloucester. Thousands trained on Boston's Harbor Islands, which became a military extension of the city used as a fortification and to house prisoners of war. Peddocks Island became a mock battlefield where, in 2011, archaeologists uncovered World War I–style trenches. Lovell's Island was defended during the war, and German merchant sailors were interned on Gallops Island.[41] The US Navy maintained a camp on Bumpkin Island, training elite yacht owners to patrol the New England coastline in search of German submarines.[42] War industry and military preparation became a visible part of city life.

Thousands of eager men volunteered for overseas service, even before America's declaration. When the United States entered the war on April 6, 1917, President Wilson was informed of the dangers of modern technological warfare and understood that massive casualties lay ahead, consequently enacting the Selective Service Act on May 18, 1917, registering twenty-four million men and successfully mobilizing almost five million Americans by war's end.[43] World War I marked the first time in US history that a mass army, the American Expeditionary Force, was conscripted early in its involvement. In prior wars, the draft was enacted only after voluntary enlistments dropped off. In 1917, the United States was ill prepared for the enormity of the undertaking. Training was rudimentary. Soldiers needed weapons. They had to learn marksmanship and the technical aspects of trench warfare. They required food, uniforms, and places to sleep. The government had to transport them overseas and supply them once they got there. This was a massive financial and bureaucratic effort that required immense coordination.

Massachusetts men represented volunteers who had rushed to serve under British and French command, and those who were conscripted after America declared war. Four thousand New Englanders

Figure 2.4. Commonwealth Pier. In February 1918, Congress appropriated $8 million to improve Boston's military infrastructure and shipping port. Melissa D. Burrage Collection.

attended officers training camp in Plattsburgh, New York, under General Leonard Wood.[44] An Army Reserve Officers Training Corp, the Flight Training School, and the Shipping Board Engineering School were established at Massachusetts Institute of Technology, educating airplane pilots, telephone and radio engineers, and communications specialists for war service. The college organized a summer camp on Gardner Lake in East Machias, Maine, to ready a "patrol squadron" for duty. This speed boat unit displayed its expertise by parading up and down the Charles River during "Preparedness Demonstrations."[45] Harvard University offered cadet training, enrolling almost one thousand students in "Military Science I." Harvard president Lawrence Lowell issued orders to convert Harvard Yard dormitories into military barracks.[46] The university lost nearly all its leading physics professors to governmental war work.[47] Nine Harvard men joined the American volunteer airplane unit called the Lafayette Escadrille.[48] General John "Black Jack" Pershing, major general of the American Expeditionary Force, visited Boston University and several other area colleges to inspire young men to volunteer.[49] He traveled across the country for eighteen months recruiting his army of almost five million. Former US president and vaunted hero of the Spanish American War Theodore Roosevelt, visited the city and stood on the steps of the Boston Public Library, calling young men who did not sign up to fight effeminate

Figure 2.5. Recruiting on State Street. Voluntary Committee of the Regiment, *History of the 101st United States Engineers, American Expeditionary Forces, 1917–1918–1919* (Cambridge, MA: University Press, 1926), 11. Philip A. Burrage Collection.

cowards. His message, questioning the manhood of New England males who did not enlist, was distributed to local newspapers.[50]

New England excitement was widespread, no doubt due in great part to the US propaganda campaign that pressured citizens to "do their part." That campaign effort inspired civilians, who in turn pressured their neighbors to serve. Cynthia Hollis of Brookline, for example, gave the mayor $100 to hire buglers to tour Boston in automobiles to recruit new soldiers.[51] Mildred Aldrich, a Boston author living in Paris, wrote a series of books encouraging Americans to get involved in the war.

Perhaps one Bostonian above all others had the greatest posthumous impact on recruiting men to fight in the war. Harvard graduate Alan Seeger had enlisted in the French Foreign Legion in August of 1914.[52] He wrote to his mother in very romantic terms about his adventures: "Just imagine how thrilling it will be tomorrow and the following days marching toward the front with the noise of battle growing continually louder before us. . . . You have no idea how beautiful it is to see the troops undulating along the road in front of one in colonies along the road." On October 23, 1914, he wrote, "I am feeling fine, in my element, for I have always thirsted for this kind of thing, to be present where the pulsations are liveliest. Every minute here is worth weeks of ordinary experience. . . . This will spoil one for any other kind of life." Killed in battle on July 4, 1916, Seeger instantly became a war hero and a beloved martyr for the patriotic Boston community. His poems were published under the title of *Letters and Diary of Alan Seeger* and his most famous poem, "Rendezvous with Death," inspired countless New England men to "do their part."[53]

In June of 1917, those men who had not yet volunteered, crowded in city recruiting offices to register for the draft.[54] In total, almost two hundred thousand Massachusetts residents enlisted and served.[55] The Boston-based Fourteenth Engineer Regiment went to France in August of 1917, serving under British command in Arras. Boston's Twenty-Sixth Yankee Division was the first National Guard unit deployed from the United States.[56] The 101st Engineers, an elite New England regiment with historical roots dating back to the country's founding, trained at the Armory of the First Corps of Cadets and at Wentworth Institute of Technology, encamping in tents on the lawn.[57] Before deploying overseas, these men trained and oversaw the construction of a new military facility at Camp Devens in Ayer, Massachusetts.[58] Under French supervision, they practiced assembling rail lines and constructing bridges in Boston, and dug trenches at French Pond Reservoir in Cambridge that they then blew up. The 101st Infantry, made up of soldiers from South Boston, trained to operate artillery for front-line action.[59] The African American Ninety-Third Infantry heavily guarded the Watertown Arsenal before its deployment to France.[60] The Seventy-Sixth Division trained at Camp Devens before shipping overseas in July of 1918. The Twelfth "Plymouth" Division, drafted just before the armistice from Boston's immigrant communities, remained "ever-ready" in the United States, waiting for the call to serve. Recruits from the "Brickbottom" Greek community in Somerville and Boston's North End Italian communities were eager to fight and show their loyalty to the United States for the war became a means for upward mobility.[61] Tony Pierro, a World War I veteran and immigrant from Florence, Italy, recalled being eager and proud to serve in the war, believing that Boston offered him opportunities he did not have in his home country. Consequently, when promised citizenship for serving, he went gladly.[62]

In addition to providing fighting men for the war, medical personnel throughout the country volunteered their services in France to care for wounded soldiers. In Boston, Dr. Harvey Cushing, a neurosurgeon at Peter Bent Brigham Hospital, and his medical team of sixty nurses were one of the first American units sent to the front lines during the war.[63] Anna Colemann Ladd, a Boston sculptor, utilized her artistic talent to make prosthetic casts for soldiers whose faces had been shot away by German bullets and shells.[64]

Artists and architects in Boston proudly commemorated the war by adorning the city's public spaces with murals, plaques, and monuments to demonstrate the region's heroic contributions. John Singer Sargent, for example, painted two huge murals entitled *Death* and *Victory* for the Widener Library at Harvard University.[65] The college also commissioned a large stone monument in Memorial Church in honor of the war dead.[66] Frederick Law Olmsted transformed the East Boston mudflats into the World War I Memorial Park. Boston's Logan Airport was constructed in 1923, named for Edward Lawrence Logan, the commander of the Twenty-Sixth Infantry. Liberty Mall was constructed on the Boston Common during the early months of the war. It is located behind the Civil War Memorial dedicated to Robert Gould Shaw and the Massachusetts Fifty-Fourth African American Regiment. Dedicated on October 27, 1917, its engraving reads, "To our soldiers and sailors in the Great War," and it leads visitors up a staircase to the Massachusetts State House where the Hall of Flags features World War I color guard flags and a massive mural dedicated to Boston's contributions to the war.[67]

Homefront Enthusiasm and Civilian Participation

The nation's social climate had certainly changed from its prewar days, and this was no different in Boston. Residents went about their war

Figure 2.6. 101st Engineers, Twenty-Sixth Division, marching down Park Street. The atmosphere in Boston changed during the war as soldiers marched on city streets. The gold dome of the Massachusetts State House (pictured in the background) was painted black in case of German attack. *Albert E. George and Captain Edwin H. Cooper, Pictorial History of the Twenty-Sixth Division United States Army: With Official Government Pictures Made by United States Signal Corps Unit Under Command of Captain Edwin H. Cooper* (Boston: Ball, 1920), 301. Philip A. Burrage Collection.

work very seriously. Mobilization, militarism, and patriotism became the city's common denominators. On every street, one could see American flags and buntings on buildings and soldiers carrying weapons. Civilians could hear klaxons sounding, military leaders on megaphones, and pedestrians cheering.

To fund a total war, the US Treasury issued a series of Liberty Bonds and orchestrated a number of Liberty Bond drives. Military leaders and clergymen gave emotional pleas in theaters, motion picture houses, hotels, restaurants, and churches explaining the urgent need for money, linking financial need directly to the safety and well-being of American soldiers and, by extension, the health of the nation as a whole. As a competitive game, these drives maintained fund-raising quotas, and towns received prizes for contributing the most money.[68] Henry Lee Higginson became treasurer of the Boston fundraising committee, urging citizens to give "a Million a Day." Boston exceeded its Liberty Loan quota by $40 million.[69] Citizens wore Liberty Bond buttons to show their patriotism.[70] Most of the Liberty Bond advertisements made civilians feel emotionally obligated out of guilt to purchase war bonds to fund the war: "What have you done to support and encourage our boys across the water? Are you doing your best today? Here, three thousand miles from the actual battle-front, you ought to do everything you can. Every extra stroke you do today helps save a soldier—don't lag on your job—don't lay down—just grit your teeth and do your 'durndest' and buy a bond."[71]

Most cities held rallies in public parks to excite the population for the war. These rallies, promoted by the federal government, bolstered morale and encouraged patriotism. During an April 1917 rally, Boston mayor James Michael Curley drew thousands of spectators to the Boston Common, where participants sang, listened to military speakers, and watched patriotic motion pictures in the chilly spring air. Curley announced that the meeting was intended to "aid the great move of democracy that was sweeping over the world. The most pleasing news will be when we hear that . . . the Kaiser is on the road to Siberia." Curley led three cheers for the United States, honoring Woodrow Wilson and the American flag, and the Navy Yard band played John Philip Sousa marches to conclude the event.[72] Every day following this spirited event, the *Boston Herald* announced new patriotic demonstrations, flag raisings, and national anthem sing-alongs throughout the city. On April 23 alone, twenty thousand people congregated to watch a flag ceremony, hear the cannon roar, and to sing patriotic airs.[73] This romantic scene was repeated in towns and cities across the state and nation.

Perhaps the biggest patriotic display in Boston occurred on May 11, 1917, just three weeks after President Wilson declared war, with a huge Memorial Day Parade.[74] Popular French military general Marshal Joseph Joffre was the guest of honor for the parade, sitting with Mayor Curley and his wife in the reviewing stand on Boston Common behind a banner which read, "Boston Welcomes Joffre with Ringing Cheers." Ardent patriotic support for American involvement in World War I was demonstrated by the number and variety of organizations that marched in the parade. There were six thousand military men from active duty army and navy units as well as from veterans of previous US wars, including the Civil War and the Spanish American War. Humanitarian organizations were also well represented, including the American Red Cross and nurses and staff from numerous Boston hospitals. There were also dozens of social organizations marching in the parade, ranging from historical and charitable societies, to Boy and Girl Scout troops, to rifle clubs. The Sunday Tabernacle Choir, which included 1,200 singers, performed for Boston's honored guest. Thirty thousand children lined the parade route from Commonwealth Avenue to Arlington Street to Boylston Street and on to the Common.[75] Mayor Curley's daughter gave Joffre a large sum of money from New England children for French orphans, moving the seasoned general to tears. More than 350,000 spectators enjoyed the parade, an event that was carefully designed to demonstrate the city's solidarity for the war effort.

For Karl Muck, however, the climate in Boston must have felt particularly oppressive. He was expected to support the war and attend the parades and yet, like most Germans living in America, his loyalties were conflicted. For his own safety, he had to keep his fondness for Germany to himself. Simply going about his daily business would have been difficult. Patriotic civilians took wartime preparation very seriously. Fearing a home-front attack, many civilians in Boston undertook their own version of military instruction. The Jordan Marsh Department Store trained nine hundred male and female employees (with a wait list of three hundred) on the rooftop of their downtown store. It was reported that "some drill with curtain poles; One woman's rifle team are expert shots." Jordan Marsh was not alone. R. H. Stearns, Gilchrist's, F. B. Leavitt, and Filene's Department Store all trained their employees in case of attack.[76] Five thousand Boy Scouts drilled at Harvard Stadium, and two thousand Girl Scouts practiced military maneuvers and first aid at the Boston Arena.[77] Boston even hosted a Fighting Tank Parade with the famed steel-sided *Britannia*, known for "bearing the dents of German shells," inciting fear on the city streets.[78]

While there was a heightened tension created by an overly eager civilian militia and a disturbingly strange and quasi-martial-law state in Boston, there was also a sense of community camaraderie and fun that marked the early months of the war. To prepare the nation for total war, Herbert Hoover established the Food Conservation Program, as a home-front effort to encourage Americans to manage food consumption by growing their own fruits and vegetables at home. His campaign slogan was "Food Will Win the War!" Eager to set an example, the mayor of Cambridge planted potatoes on the Cambridge Common. Tufts University divided its sports fields into food gardens, creating sixty-two 50 × 100–foot sites.[79] Women's clubs erected the Little City of Cottages on the Boston Common to grow produce and teach the art of food preparation. These cottages were described romantically as "Model Gardens that Seem a part of the World of Verse and Fairy Dreams, but are in fact severely practical." They came to be called "Victory Gardens" and they were enormously popular throughout the war and beyond.[80]

Boston women raised vast amounts of money for the Red Cross, the YMCA, and the Salvation Army. They knitted hats, socks, and gloves; baked and canned foods; and created recipes using whatever ingredients were available. They rolled bandages and planned festivals to raise funds for the war. They put on patriotic plays and musicals and opened canteens and clubs for traveling soldiers. They mailed "Black Cat Boxes," which included chocolate bars, stationary, candles, and pajamas to service personnel.

Women were seen in the public sphere more than ever before. There was an unprecedented level of excitement and energy. They worked on military assembly lines producing weapons, naval ships, uniforms, shovels, and shoes. Women at W. S. Wiunby and Company on Atlantic Avenue in Boston roasted seventy-five thousand pounds of coffee per day for soldiers overseas. Women processed fourteen million pounds of canned fish at the Bay State Fish Company in South Boston.[81] As one newspaper pointed out, "Who fashions the shoes that encase their (soldier's) feet?—the women of Massachusetts. Who makes their uniforms, their overcoats?—in large measure the women of Massachusetts! Who packs their food, their comforts, their little luxuries?—largely the women of Massachusetts. Who makes munitions . . . the women of Massachusetts." Women took on important manufacturing roles, and, as sentimental advertisements made clear, "amid the whirr of their machines, a multitude of Massachusetts women hear the music of these marching feet—the feet of their husbands, their brothers and their sons. No effort of theirs is too great to bring victory, peace, freedom—for America, for democracy, for all the world."

Figure 2.7. War Garden entrance on Boston Common (1918). The Boston Common was utilized during the war in a variety of ways, including tank demonstrations, parades, recruitment, Liberty Bond sales, and Victory Gardens. Courtesy of the Boston Public Library, Leslie Jones Collection.

Women achieved political and economic agency during wartime, and their roles in the war effort altered (and improved) the environment of the city.

Certainly in 1917 Boston was not the same place that it had been when Karl Muck first arrived. Global events and rising national tensions affected residents of the city. Wartime activities were visible in every public and private space. Home-front excitement filled the air. Community members went about their tasks with enthusiasm. Many soldiers sent to war were eager for the adventure of it. They had never experienced total warfare. They had no concept of modern weaponry or the devastation that war could produce. People in Boston were caught up in the romance of it all, blindly unaware of the heartache that would come. Karl Muck managed to survive in Boston in 1917. Uncomfortable yet not personally threatened. He, too, was unaware that the weight of war would arrive like an ominous cloud resting heavily over the horizon.

Chapter Three

SELLING THE WAR

Demonizing the Enemy (1918)

Hardships Increase in Boston

On the morning of December 6, 1917, the French ship *Mont Blanc* approached Halifax Harbor in Nova Scotia and collided with the SS *Imo*, a six-thousand-ton Norwegian ship on route to Belgium to deliver relief supplies. The day was just beginning. Children were walking to school along the waterfront. Workers made their way to factories, offices, rail and dockyards. Hearing the commotion, those still inside their homes ran to their waterfront windows to witness the crash. The *Mont Blanc*, bound for France and filled with six million pounds of high explosives, erupted in a fiery blaze that heated its volatile cargo to nine thousand degrees Fahrenheit, turning the ship into a "monstrous hand-grenade," sending chunks of metal projectiles from the disintegrating vessel outward in all directions at 3,400 miles per hour, puncturing nearby ships, slicing open rooftops, and vaporizing those in its path. The force of the blast caused a ground wave, or earthquake, penetrating the bedrock at 13,000 miles per hour, shaking homes off their foundations. The ferocious detonation produced a mushroom cloud, a giant gas fireball filled with vaporized particles, metal and human, that rose two miles in the air and threw into the atmosphere tons of dark oil that rained down on its victims, blackening their faces with a slimy tar. Air waves followed, traveling at 21,000 miles per hour and shattering almost every window in Halifax, shooting pieces of glass like knives into the eyes and bodies of those who stood watching. Within a second, onlookers were blind, riddled with glass shrapnel, or dead.[1] Most buildings within a two mile radius were obliterated. The shock from the blast violently parted the harbor waters, forming a tidal wave, or tsunami, that engulfed inland streets, drowned inhabitants, and flooded buildings nearly sixty feet above sea level. In the final accounting, the explosion killed almost two thousand people and wounded nine thousand more. Twenty-five thousand people, almost

Figure 3.1. Postcard captioned "Great Halifax Explosion—utter desolation and devastation so complete that this picture might have been taken on the battlefields of France / Montreal, Quebec." Novelty Mfg. & Art Co., Limited. Courtesy of Mt. Allison University Archives—2012.26/5/2/2.

half the population, were suddenly homeless. The thickly settled waterfront community that occupied more than three hundred acres looked like no-man's land—a war zone. Ruptured gas lines blew up additional structures, trapping many survivors in the rubble of their flattened homes. Trees and telephone poles were snapped at their bases. Cement and masonry structures were obliterated. Fires started everywhere, as wooden buildings acted like kindling fuel. This horror was followed by a blizzard that dropped sixteen inches of snow on the frozen ground, making search and rescue almost impossible. Many survivors, waiting for first aid and food, died of exposure and hunger.[2]

The Halifax Explosion is recorded as one of the largest human-made disasters in world history. By nightfall on December 7, Boston had heard the grim news and responded by organizing an entire field hospital to assist the victims.[3] The Massachusetts Relief Committee sent surgeons, nurses, Red Cross workers, social workers, medicine, X-ray equipment, and supplies; money, food, trucks, and ambulances; building supplies including glass, putty, lumber, stoves, bathtubs, and beds; and laborers including engineers, carpenters, and plumbers via train and ship to Nova Scotia. More than 120 doctors from New England turned the Bellevue Building in Halifax into an emergency hospital, while Massachusetts workers aided residents by building more than three hundred homes and repairing three thousand others in the newly constructed Hydrostone neighborhood. The Bay State provided more than $750,000 in aid, equivalent to $15 million today. For weeks to come, Boston newspaper reporters, who accompanied the relief trains, wrote emotionally charged stories with heart-wrenching details about the disaster. As they made clear, most victims were convinced that Germany was responsible for the explosion and that additional attacks were imminent. The truth of the matter, that Germany was not responsible, would be revealed only months and years later.

Bostonians who were reading these stories in their local newspapers were horrified. The Halifax Explosion snapped Americans out of their romanticized complacency and a fervent patriotism, last witnessed when the United States declared war, burst back onto the scene. The disaster marked a turning point on the home front, heightening tensions toward German Americans (particularly in New England) in the final month of the year. By the end of 1917, enthusiasm for the war had begun to wane as hardships hit home. The Halifax Explosion, food and coal shortages, labor discontent, Allied losses, including casualty reports in the American newspapers, and German American service exemptions, gave rise to feelings of American vulnerability that made the population more susceptible to wartime propaganda demonizing German Americans and foreign nationals. Hostility and persecution intensified in the early months of 1918, and, according to John Higham, the "fury that broke" upon this ethnic community "represented the most spectacular reversal of judgment" in American history.[4] Boston serves as a microcosm of the broader tensions in America at this time.

The first signs of unrest in Boston occurred in January of 1918, just weeks after the Halifax Explosion, with a sudden shortage of sugar. Thousands of tons of this favorite sweetener were locked up in Java warehouses, and, because of U-boat fears, ships were unable to transport their cargo to Boston. Sugar was said to be "no more available than un-mined gold." At first, Bostonians gladly accepted the shortages and searched for alternative treats. Newspaper headlines read, "Use Less Sugar in Cake: Patriotism Requires Economy and Benefit to Health Results." City food administrator Henry B. Endicott told a mass meeting at Tremont Temple that if the people of America selfishly neglected to conserve their food supplies, the war would be lost and that "if the Germans win, your lives and more will not be worth living."[5] Food experts encouraged homemakers to use dried fruit, beets, maple syrup, or nuts.[6] As the war continued, however, the matter became more pressing. In one report, 40,000 pounds of sugar had been hidden away in a furniture warehouse in Boston's Back Bay, not available for distribution.[7] Perhaps the worst case of civil unrest

Figure 3.2. US Food Administration poster, World War I. "Save Wheat, Meat, Fats, Sugar, and Serve the Cause of Freedom" (1917). Courtesy of the Samuel P. Hayes Research Library, Perkins School for the Blind, War Blind and Propaganda Collection.

occurred when a mob of fifteen thousand women stormed the City Hall in Brockton, Massachusetts, just twenty-five miles south of Boston, to acquire a share of the 8,600 pounds of sugar advertised in a lottery there. Thirty women were trampled as the crowd rushed through the doors of the building. City physicians and all available police throughout Plymouth County were called in to calm the mob.[8]

The sugar crisis in New England was part of a larger food supply problem brought about by the war. As mentioned in chapter 2, people initially enjoyed growing Victory Gardens and taking part in conservation programs, but over time the country became frustrated with federal authorities who controlled the supply. By early 1918, New Englanders were eager to cast off their short-lived depravations and enjoy the meals they loved.[9] Delegates from the Boston Mothers League boycotted chicken, potato, onions, and beans sold by merchants at inflated costs. League member Mrs. Godfrey Cabot advocated that women raise their own chickens, but such ideas only temporarily solved the larger food crisis, as the war brought wheatless, meatless, and fat-saving days.[10] Housekeepers were told that waste was bad, and yet they were at wit's end to come up with hearty meals with few ingredients. Certainly, shortages in America were not as extreme as the hardships endured in Europe, but they did bring the reality of total war a bit closer to home.

To make matters worse, much of the nation suffered through blizzard conditions in the early months of 1918. At the beginning of January, with frigid temperatures, it became clear that there was not enough coal for the entire country, and the federal government severely controlled and rationed its supply.[11] Civilians were instructed to bundle up and to suffer the cold for the good of the nation. President Wilson appointed Harry A. Garfield, the former US president's son, head of the Fuel Administration, instructing him to put a fuel order into effect, shutting down all nonessential businesses and making fuel provisions for railroads, public utilities, and war manufacturing. Consequently, the Fore River Shipyard and other governmental work facilities received their ration of coal, but average homeowners and most nonessential factories and office buildings did not.[12]

Many business owners in Boston protested the fuel order, as it cost millions in lost productivity. Garfield disregarded the pleas from economic leaders who had been instrumental in pushing for war in the first place. Rather than yield to the protests, the federal government instead enforced police protection to maintain the war agenda. This was an unpopular measure with many Boston leaders, who resented this increasing presence of state power and thus began taking a different view of their government and of the war. Adding insult to injury, the

Fuel Administration asked the owners of closed businesses to put up posters in store windows stressing the necessity of fuel conservation.[13]

In addition to impacting employers, the fuel order caused labor hardships and increasing discontent among civilians, many of whom were put out of work. Hundreds of plants were shut down. People were forced to take pay cuts, reduce work hours, or give up their jobs altogether. Boston's Central Labor Union proclaimed that Garfield was incompetent and adopted a resolution at its meeting that placed responsibility for the coal shortage directly on the shoulders of the federal government.[14]

Labor unrest was yet another side effect of total war. Many company employees in Boston organized to strike. Irish municipal workers, Boston Elevated Railway employees, Western Union workers, Lowell mill workers, Boston shipyard workers, and New England telephone workers all sought wage increases to meet the skyrocketing cost of living and voted to strike.[15]

Female telephone operators joined the Women's Trade Union League and fought for better working conditions. Rose Norwood recalled, "The telephone company enforced a military discipline. We couldn't whisper, we had to sit all day. They'd fire a woman if she were five minutes late. They made her stay in a retiring room a half hour, until she lost her pay. They punished us."[16] Boston police officers were talking about striking as well, which created an unstable atmosphere in the city.[17] In most cases, labor troubles were put down by Massachusetts governor Calvin Coolidge. Samuel Gompers, president of the American Federation of Labor, was enlisted by the War Industries Board to quiet the unions. He told workers not to strike and that it was unpatriotic to walk off the job during wartime.[18] Some Massachusetts economic leaders placed full-page advertisements in Boston newspapers illustrating the virtues of living and working in New England and the importance of carrying on despite hardship.

Hardships went beyond the city's businesses, however. The government was controlling almost every aspect of civilian life. This was new. The fuel shortage put a halt to daily community activities: Public schools were shut down. Colleges and universities around Boston reduced their hours or sent their students home. Grocery stores closed. Transportation, like the elevated subway, was shut down or operated with reduced hours. Bars could stay open, but without heat, and buildings were very uncomfortable, particularly in January and February of 1918, one of the coldest winters on record in Boston. Brewers were required to close their doors three days a week. Clubs and restaurants shut down, and theaters operated only at specified times.[19]

Figure 3.3. Daylight Savings Time poster. In 1918, the country was suffering with fuel shortages and labor problems, forcing many businesses to shut down. Consequently, the federal government adopted Daylight Savings Time as a solution. Courtesy of the Library of Congress.

The state even interfered with mother nature by determining the time of day. As a possible solution to the coal shortage, Congress passed the Standard Time Act on March 19, 1918, a daylight savings bill, which pushed the clock forward by one hour to take advantage of natural light during productive working hours. Since daylight is shorter during the winter months, shifting working hours seemed like a good idea. The act, however, did not solve the general malaise and depression caused by the war.[20]

The Costs of War Become Known

Even worse than the coal shortage was a more serious concern: American men were fighting and dying on the front lines in France. Artists, photographers, reporters, and filmmakers captured stories and footage of warfare, and, for the first time, home-front Americans saw the devastation, which was quite a contrast to the candy-coated romanticism of previous government propaganda.[21] This knowledge brought the grotesque reality of the battlefield home to New England. Regardless of the government's attempts to control the reports of deadly battles, the horror of war poignantly found its way into the American consciousness. Soldiers' letters home told of confusion, noise, fear, illness, boredom, rain, cold, and cramped conditions. Parents worried about their children, and the innocence of war and the idealism that came with their lack of awareness was swept away.[22]

Not only were parents worried about their children, they were angry that German Americans were not fighting (and dying) too. The Selective Service Act (1917) exempted immigrants from the draft because many could not read or speak English and therefore, it was feared, they could not follow orders. American citizens resented German immigrants, who enjoyed their freedom in America while citizen soldiers filled military quotas.[23]

By early 1918, Boston had lost its patience with the war. Families felt great anxiety as they waited for news from their loved ones. The *Boston Herald* published a page-long casualty report called the Roll of Honor in the weekly paper.[24] The list included categories such as youngest yet to die, wounded severely, wounded slightly, missing, killed in action, died of accident, prisoner of war, gassed, or died of disease. Almost five million American men mobilized for war, 117,000 died, and 300,000 were wounded.[25] Worldwide, twenty million military and civilians lost their lives, and twenty-one million more were wounded.[26] Modern warfare made 50 percent of those who perished unrecognizable. Wounds obliterated facial features, and, because most had been blown to bits, their body parts were mixed with those of their comrades and their foes. Condolence letters to families were often fraudulent, as officers did not always know the soldiers or the details of their deaths, and cemeteries with carefully ordered crosses in tidy rows belied the fact that soldiers were often buried in groups without nametags in mass graves. Many who were wounded suffered from "hysteria," a malady that Freud and other contemporary psychologists defined in sexist terms as the "classic female response to stress, applied to the symptom of stressed soldiers—paralysis, muteness, blandness, debilitating anxiety."[27] Medical personnel had yet to understand the condition that we call post-traumatic stress disorder today.[28] Soldiers and citizens alike suffered from extreme anxiety, and, whether on the battlefield or the home front, the conditions of war led to emotional extremes. The government exploited civilian suffering to acquire more money to keep the war machine alive, hosting a fifty-thousand-person memorial mass and military service in Boston's Fenway Park.[29] Relatives of the deceased gave emotional speeches to rally the troops and keep civilian morale high. Cape Codders complained that life was being devalued during the war. They compared fishing industry mortality to the conflict: "In the old days, a great storm at sea would take eight or ten men and boys out of one long village street; there is not a graveyard from Buzzard's Bay to Provincetown without the marking stones for lads and grown men never buried there, but 'lost at sea.' Today . . . the war's taking of young men has been hungrier than ever was the sea's."[30]

Even though American soldiers had served in the war for a shorter duration than their European counterparts, they had still experienced the reality and bloodshed of war. In the Meuse-Argonne Offensive alone, the American Expeditionary Force lost more than twenty-six thousand men and almost a hundred thousand wounded in a six-week campaign. The United States witnessed its share of ugliness. In the cold winter months of 1918, most people wanted the war to end, and yet soldiers were still needed at the front, and laborers were required in American munitions factories.

A Federal Government Campaign of Anti-Germanism

The Halifax Explosion became a convenient rallying cry for the war. The US government took full advantage of American fear over the disaster to intimate that Germany was to blame. The shock of the explosion and the psychological trauma that ensued fanned the flames of anger toward "the enemy" and heightened hostility toward all people of German descent.[31] The Halifax Explosion raised suspicions about German Americans and German nationals living in America and revived patriotic enthusiasm once again. As intellectual Walter Lippman put it, to maintain morale and support for the conflict, the federal government "manufactured consent," when natural support for the war declined.[32] "Selling" the war through Liberty Bond drives and patriotic parades had become far less effective as hardships mounted. With home-front food and fuel shortages and rising death tolls, the federal government needed a new approach to reignite emotions in favor of war. Anti-Germanism became a key method for maintaining war momentum at home. Through a well-orchestrated propaganda campaign, the federal government successfully demonized the enemy and increased the level of bigotry and paranoia against Germans and people of German descent in America.

President Wilson hired George Creel to develop a propaganda campaign to sell the war to the American people. Creel, head of the Committee on Public Information (CPI), an enormous public relations apparatus of the federal government, promoted the viewpoint that Germans in America endangered American society and were not to be trusted. The CPI produced seventy-five million brochures, six thousand press releases, sponsored war exhibitions and parades, trained seventy-five thousand "Four Minute Men" to give speeches around the country promoting the war, and employed 150,000 people to mobilize hearts and minds against a common enemy.[33] Scapegoating Germans became the most effective way to keep Americans from hating their government when hardship and death became a reality in the early months of 1918. Trading upon negative German stereotypes, the CPI manipulated the media and articulated an ideology of racial nationalism, portraying America as a homogenous population infiltrated by an evil German enemy.

Many national newspapers ran sensational stories, further fueling the climate of fear among the general population. Often, these fabricated accounts came from anonymous federal sources. In February of 1918, a report claimed that crushed glass was found in peanut butter jars. Another in the same month claimed that the enemy added ground glass to chocolate candy bars sent to Camp Dix, New Jersey, and a March 1918 federal food board report warned the public: "Be most careful in the future when eating bread, rolls, cakes, and pastry because jagged bits of glass have been found in flour, bread, and bread wrappers."[34] Americans were scared that Germans had made their food supply dangerous to eat, at a time when food was scarce to begin with.

Figure 3.4. Portrait of George Creel, 1917. President Wilson hired George Creel to develop a propaganda campaign to sell the war to the American people. Courtesy of the Library of Congress.

The CPI worked with newspaper publishers across the country, inflating local noteworthy stories to fit the government's national agenda to demonize Germans. When dynamite was found near the Cordage Park Rope Factory in Plymouth, Massachusetts, just forty miles south of Boston, the *Boston Herald* reported that it was an attack by German Americans in the United States.[35] Newspapers reported that two Germans were found wandering around a Holbrook, Massachusetts, munitions factory, and they were brought in for questioning.[36] The press reported on a German plot to blow up the Commonwealth Pier in Boston. The article claimed that telephone operators overheard a conversation between two German men, they contacted authorities, and military patrols were doubled.[37] The *Boston Herald* reported that a bomb was placed on Brahmin Bostonian Dr. Hugh Cabot's Marlboro Street vestibule, and that a German had attempted to assassinate him because of his strong anti-German leanings.[38] When an explosion occurred under a Cambridge trolley, the press reported that Germans were responsible.[39]

In 1918, CPI propaganda posters increasingly portrayed Germans as depraved, brutal aggressors.[40] Artwork served as a carrier of both overt and covert messages that tapped into the emotions of the viewer. The posters were harbingers of fear on the home front and on the front lines. America printed more than twenty million copies of an estimated 2,500 posters in support of the war effort. In an era preceding radio and television, the poster was the principal medium for mass publicity, appealing to the ideals of unity, patriotism, service, and sacrifice.[41] Anti-German propaganda during World War I contributed to ethnic intolerance on a massive scale.

Creel also established the Division of Films on September 25, 1917, thereafter issuing a steady stream of "hate-the-Hun" movies.[42] Films became an effective means of manufacturing fear and prejudice. In *Over Secret Wires* (1915), German spies operate on the US coastline, making contact with German submarines; in *Paying the Price* (1917), foreign agents in Washington, DC, attempt to steal a secret formula for explosives; in *The Road to France* (1918), Germans dismantle the American shipbuilding industry; and, in *Claws of the Hun* (1918), Germans invade American munitions plants.[43] All these films made Americans more fearful of their German American neighbors and increased paranoia around the country.

At the Majestic Theatre in Boston, film viewers watched *Hearts of the World* (1918), which offered this caveat in its advertising campaign: "To the People of New England. If Anyone Within Your Hearing Makes Uncomplimentary Remarks about D. W. Griffith's Supreme Triumph, 'Hearts of the World' You Can Safely Believe That Such Remarks Are

Figure 3.5. "Halt the Hun! Buy U.S. Government Bonds, Third Liberty Loan" (1918), by artist Henry Raleigh. This poster implies that Germans hurt women and children and that American men must protect them. Courtesy of Library of Congress, Prints and Photographs Division.

Figure 3.6. "Destroy This Mad Brute Enlist—U.S. Army" (1918). Propaganda poster created to incite fear of Germans and rally support for the war. Courtesy of the Library of Congress, Prints and Photographs Division, Reproduction number LC DIG-ds-03216 Digital file from original item number 457.

Inspired by Germany, and the Persons Speaking German Are Acting
Against the United States Government. ... Denounce the Spies!!!"
Any failure of the film was blamed on German Americans, and the
advertisements encouraged hatred for anyone in America of German
ancestry. The Majestic Theatre was not the only Boston theater to show
this film. Louis B. Mayer, of Haverhill, Massachusetts (and later of
MGM Films), had purchased six theaters in 1910 in the Boston area.
He refurbished them elegantly with grand marble lobbies and stair-
cases and provided seating for 1,500 people. Unlike the opera or the
ballet, his theaters were affordable for every social class, and they were
the ideal place to watch the propaganda films produced by the CPI.[44]
These films and others spread the stereotype of Germans in America
as "dirty Huns," calling into question their loyalties and actions and
perpetuating harsh treatment by civilians and authorities against them.
Karl Muck would have seen advertisements for these films in the local
papers and would have been very aware of America's demonization of
his ethnic and national identity.

Perhaps the most harmful anti-German sentiments came from
the most prominent political figures in the nation. President Woodrow Wilson and former president Theodore Roosevelt gave a series
of emotional speeches attacking Germans in America and the "Hun
within" for having divided loyalties.[45] Roosevelt had told the Knights
of Columbus in New York as early as 1915 that "there is no room in
this country for hyphenated Americanism."[46] Wilson expressed a high
level of distrust and animosity toward German Americans from the
outset of war. He referred to them as "infinitely malignant" and "creatures of passion" that "preach and practice disloyalty." In a December
7, 1915, speech, he claimed that they "destroy our industries" and
"poured the poison of disloyalty into the very arteries of our national
life." He argued that the "hands of our power should close over them
at once."[47] Wilson was referring to a select few individuals who had
committed acts of sabotage, and yet his message targeted the entire
German population in America. In his June 14, 1917, Flag Day speech,
Wilson accused "the military masters of Germany" of infiltrating
"unsuspecting communities with vicious spies and conspirators" seeking to "undermine the Government with false professions of loyalty to
its principles." Such talk made clear Wilson's lack of trust in the German community in the United States and created a volatile environment for people of German ancestry in the United States.[48]

In addition to Wilson's propaganda campaign and his inflam-
matory rhetoric, the president also enacted several national security
measures under war powers that targeted German Americans and
negated basic civil liberties provided by the Constitution. The October

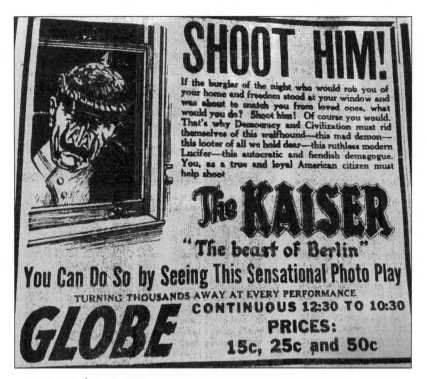

Figure 3.7. "Shoot Him! The Kaiser." The propaganda film *The Beast of Berlin* was released as enthusiasm for war waned. This advertisement appeared in the *Boston Herald* on March 9, 1918, playing a role in the demonization of Germans so prevalent at that time.

1918 Alien Enemies Act gave federal authorities the right to "detain, expel or otherwise restrict the freedom of any citizen fourteen years or older of the country with which we are at war." Suspending the writ of habeas corpus, and without offering any judicial review, the new law took away the right of a legal hearing under the irrefutable "presumption that enemy aliens are dangerous, based solely on their national identity."[49] The act applied to virtually any foreign resident the government deemed undesirable. The motivation for the act was to establish control over immigrants (or labor radicals) who disagreed with government policies and who were deemed dangerous to the security of the nation.

The United States has a long tradition of suspicion toward its immigrant residents: the Alien Enemies Act had initially been utilized in 1798 by the Federalists, who feared the French and distrusted anyone with French ancestry in the country. The act was used again in

Figure 3.8. "Guarding the Waterfront: Sentry Patrolling Atlantic Avenue Boston Looking for German Spies." Surveillance of Germans in America increased during the war, with a pervasive paranoia and fear of "enemy" attack. Courtesy of the Boston Public Library, Leslie Jones Collection.

the War of 1812 to target individuals from Great Britain who lived in America.[50] In the 1850s, the Know-Nothing Party worked to prevent the immigration of the Irish, and, in 1882, the Chinese Exclusion Act utilized the restrictive language of the Alien Enemies Act to block Chinese laborers from becoming naturalized citizens. In 1941, the day after Pearl Harbor was attacked, President Roosevelt would invoke the act to intern seventy thousand US Japanese citizens and forty thousand Japanese nationals.[51] Following the September 11, 2001, terrorist attacks against the United States, Arab and Muslim citizens and foreign nationals would be targeted as well. During World War I, the Alien Enemies Act involved wholesale ethnic discrimination against Germanic people. The unjust law banned their use of weapons, prevented them from coming within a half mile of any military base or airport, and forced these individuals to endure mass arrests and untold suffering, simply because of their ancestry. Such a law proved particularly problematic in Boston and other waterfront communities. Germans there were prevented from walking in areas where they lived and worked, and, in spite of the hot summer weather, they were not permitted to be near the ocean, the only source of respite from the heat.[52]

Laws were enacted to control and suppress free speech. The US Congress enacted the Espionage Act of 1917, which prohibited any attempt to interfere with military operations, to support US enemies during wartime, to foster insubordination in the military, or to impede recruitment. This law was further amended to include the Sedition Act of 1918, which prohibited "disloyal, profane, scurrilous, or abusive language" toward the country, the American flag, or military uniforms. Essentially, this censorship law prohibited any negative opinion about the war. It demanded complete and total support for the war effort and the government's anti-German campaign. When labor leader Eugene V. Debs gave a speech in Canton, Ohio, criticizing the Espionage Act and the war in general and voicing his lack of animosity toward people of German ancestry, he was promptly arrested and sentenced to ten years in prison.[53] Implicitly, the law required that Americans hate Germans.

Clearly, Woodrow Wilson had anti-foreign tendencies, fearing the growing and ever-more-powerful immigrant population in the country. Only fifteen years earlier, in 1901, the Polish anarchist Leon Czolgosz had assassinated President William McKinley, and, for decades following the murder, the federal government clamped down on foreign nationals with a series of increasingly restrictive immigration laws.

What is remarkable about this World War I story is that German Americans were anything but the stereotype of an embattled, marginalized immigrant community before the war. In 1917, Germans represented the largest minority in the United States, numbering more than 2.3 million. And yet, as John Higham tells us, during World War I they faced a swift and sudden reversal of fortune in America.[54] When the United States declared war in April of 1917, the Department of Justice made a list of "German citizens in this country who are dangerous and are plotting trouble, men from whom we must necessarily expect trouble promptly of a sinister sort."[55] More than two thousand people were prosecuted for speaking out against the war, and half of those were sentenced to prison terms of up to twenty years.[56] On November 6, 1917, seven months after the declaration of war, Wilson ordered all German alien males fourteen and older to register with the government. Austro-Hungarian men registered three weeks later. Women from both countries faced registration beginning April 19, 1918. In total, 480,000 people registered at their local post offices. They were required to carry their registration cards at all times and report any change of address or employment to the federal government. Two hundred thousand permits were issued allowing people to leave their homes for work or travel. Historian Jorg Nagler estimated that between 8,500 and 10,000 German Americans or foreign nationals were interrogated and arrested during World War I across the country.[57] Many were held without warrants or formal charges and were interrogated without the benefit of legal counsel. Their convictions were not eligible for appeal. German Americans were accused of all sorts of crimes, and 2,300 civilian German Americans and German nationals were interned (along with several thousand German merchant marines, military personnel, and German nationals from other countries) based on imagined fears of sabotage or for supporting the German war effort, and yet there were only five proven acts of sabotage during World War I in the United States.[58] Even native-born citizens accused of ties to Germany were threatened with the loss of their citizenship, suggesting that the civil liberties afforded to citizens were almost as fragile as those for immigrant aliens.

As Christopher Capozzola points out, "When Americans talked about wartime bureaucracy, they called it 'Government' and they gave it a capital 'G.'" The government grew exponentially from World War I forward, first with its standing army and then its bureaucratic apparatus of surveillance policing.[59] With the enforcement of these acts came restrictions on individual freedom and civil liberties, and demands for loyalty and obedience, in a narrowing definition of citizenship. World War I marked a pivotal moment in American history with respect to the wholesale mistreatment of citizen foreigners. The government whipped up patriotic passion among the civilian population that would have long-lasting implications for the future treatment of "others" in American society.

The biggest helpmates of the federal campaign against German Americans were the muckrakers, who were suspicious of Germans in America and convinced of their guilt. They did not simply report the news or even inflate it; rather, they incited violence among the population. Jingoistic newspapers printed anti-foreign opinions, like that of Walter Hines Page, US ambassador to Great Britain, who argued, "We Americans have got to . . . shoot our hyphenates and bring up our children with reverence for English history and . . . English literature."[60] The *Chicago Tribune* offered, "Let us hope that before long our government will stop dilly-dallying with these so called German-Americans and put them into concentration camps until the end of the war."[61] The *Saturday Evening Post* argued that the time had come to remove "the scum of the melting pot."[62] Isaac Marcosson, editor of the *Saturday Evening Post*, spoke at Boston's City Club in March of 1918, arguing that German spies who infiltrated Boston should be shot. He said,

"If we were to shoot a few German spies and conduct a publicity campaign to let every citizen know what we had done about it that would be worth more than years of agitation and protest."[63]

While English-language newspapers and magazines in America were allowed to speak harshly about German Americans, German-language newspapers were suppressed. They were required to supply the US Post Office with English translations of "any comments respecting the government of the United States . . . its policies, international relations [or] the state and conduct of the war."[64] The cost of providing these documents put many German language newspapers out of business and had a profound effect on the editorial policies of those that survived.

Anti-German Hysteria: Suspicion, Accusations, Restrictions, and Physical Assaults

Many Americans were fearful of German attacks and were happy when the government took a harder stand against perceived "spies" among them. Dr. B. W. Swain, for example, a black minister who visited Boston in April of 1917, suggested that President Wilson should take serious action against German spies in the country. He advised having Secret Service agents "run them down and shoot them for treason."[65] Swain was likely responding to intellectual and activist Dr. W. E. B Du Bois's call for black unity during the war. Du Bois encouraged black soldiers to enlist, saying, "Our country is at war. . . . If this is *our* country, then this is our war."[66]

The fear of German attack and the rage toward German nationals and German Americans manifested with a commercial response in Boston. An effigy of Kaiser Wilhelm was hung from Gilchrist's Department Store: "The shiny tin helmet which adorned the head of the effigy bore many dents, each one of which represented an additional Liberty Bond purchased by a patriotic American to overthrow Prussian rule."[67] As a reward for contributing money to the war effort and demonstrating their patriotism, citizens were invited to commit violent acts against the German effigy. People escalated their response from verbal threat to action, carrying out their intimidations and not just paying lip service anymore.

Pacifists who spoke out against violence in the city at a public peace parade were no longer tolerated as they had been in earlier years. Even the police, who were assigned to protect demonstrators, turned against them. Many people, regardless of ethnicity, were arrested or beaten. The ranks of the marchers were broken up by self-organized squads of uniformed soldiers and sailors. Several marines forced a demonstrator to kneel and kiss the flag, and others were attacked for failing to remove their hats during the playing of "The Star-Spangled Banner."[68] It took federal officials four hours to quell the riot that ensued and disperse the twenty thousand people who assembled. Intolerance and ethnic discrimination gripped the city. Some members of the press, so outraged by pacifism and dissent, incited violence by arguing that protesters should be sent to the front line in cages so they could be subjected to poison gas.[69]

On April 4, 1918, in the most infamous case of anti-German hysteria in America, Robert Prager, a German American coal miner, was lynched in Collinsville, Illinois, before a crowd of two hundred people. Led blindfolded through town with his clothes and shoes removed, the mob crushed beer bottles and required that Prager walk over the broken glass while being forced to sing "The Star-Spangled Banner." His body was draped with an American flag, a noose was placed around his neck, and he was hoisted ten feet in the air.[70] With the evening papers, millions of Americans heard of the murder.[71] Thomas Williamson, defense attorney in the Prager case, justified the lynching by arguing that laws pertaining to murder were written before the country went to war. He stated that there were five hundred thousand reservists of the German army living in the United States and there were five hundred thousand lampposts to hang them on.[72] No justice was served during the trial, for all the accused were acquitted of the crime. Senator Henry Cabot Lodge of Massachusetts responded to this news by validating the mob's behavior and suggesting that disloyal German Americans should be shot. These extremist attitudes led to additional mob activity throughout the country.

In Oklahoma, German-speaking Mennonite Henry Reimer was hung by a mob on April 19, 1918, for his pacifism and refusal on religious grounds to accept military service. Police convinced the crowd to cut him down before he died, with the promise that he would be tried the next day. Daniel Diener and his son Charles, Mennonite ministers in Canton, Kansas, were whipped and tarred and feathered. They were also robbed, and their homes were ransacked for refusing to purchase Liberty Bonds.[73] Four Hutterite farmers from South Dakota, Jacob Wipf and brothers Michael, David, and Joseph Hofer were sent to a dark basement dungeon at the US Disciplinary Prison at Alcatraz Island for refusing military service. For eight hours each day, they were handcuffed and chained to the ceiling with their toes barely touching the concrete floor. Youngest brothers Joseph and Michael Hofer later died.[74] More than 1,500 Mennonites, Hutterites, and other pacifist sects from the Midwest and Great Plains fled their homes following

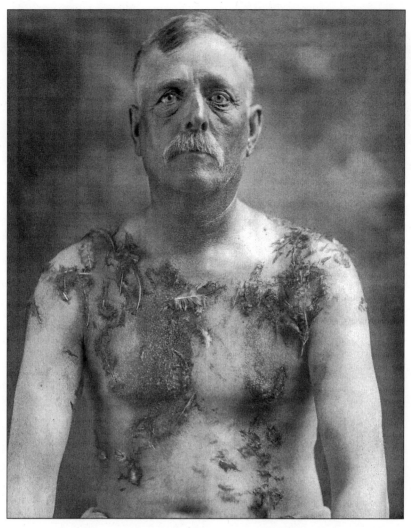

Figure 3.9. In August 1918, John Meintz, a Minnesota farmer, was whipped and tarred and feathered for being a German American. Courtesy of the National Archives Records Administration. US District Court for the Second (Mankato) Division of the District of Minnesota (04/26/1890-ca. 1951).

vigilante night raids, beatings, and prison torture, resettling in the Canadian provinces of Alberta, Saskatchewan, and Manitoba.[75]

In Luverne, Minnesota, John Meintz, a farmer, was forcibly taken from his home by local vigilantes and whipped and tarred and feathered. Meintz was transported to the border of South Dakota and threatened with death by hanging if he ever returned to his former home.[76]

In Portland, Maine, one hundred miles north of Boston, Charles A. Miller, a German restaurateur, was attacked and threatened with hanging for speaking his mind about the war. Engaged in a political debate with a patron, Miller responded to the comment, "The allies will lick them before they [the Germans] get through," with, "The Germans are too strong and too smart for the allies." For this, Miller was punched in the jaw and knocked to the ground. A crowd gathered and upon hearing about the fight shouted to get a rope to hang him. Miller escaped to safety through a rear doorway. Perhaps worse than the incident itself, however, was the *Boston Herald*'s report that Miller was "knocked down by a true patriot," encouraging further violence toward German Americans with dissenting views.[77] Clearly, anti-German hysteria had reached a fever pitch, and Americans were practicing their own overexaggerated forms of vigilante justice.

New England anti-German hysteria did not end with the Miller incident. Germans and German Americans were the targets of additional abuse, as fourteen hundred Italian reservists preparing to sail for Italy on board the *Canopic* at the Commonwealth Pier spotted three uniformed Germans from the Hamburg steamships the *Amerika* and *Cincinnati*, both ships having been interned in Boston since the war began. Italy had been a part of the Triple Alliance with Germany and Austria-Hungary but had switched sides to become a part of the Triple Entente with France, Great Britain, and Russia in 1915. Italian reservists in Boston demonstrated their loyalty to the Allies by humiliating the German sailors and having them swear allegiance to the American flag. When they objected and would not be bullied further, they were booed and severely beaten before the police arrived to rescue them. The Italian reservists were so angered that the police had assisted the men that they began throwing rocks at the ships, breaking porthole glass and ship fittings and striking several men on board. The unruly mob carried its violent demonstration to the US Customs Office nearby, before the police suppressed the crowd.[78] And, in East Boston, a group of Italian immigrants attacked a man for making anti-patriotic statements, forcing him to "drop to his knees, kiss the flag, and swear allegiance to [it]."[79]

Many cases of anti-German hysteria were not violent outbreaks perpetrated by angry mobs but quiet affairs behind closed doors by officials charged with protecting against injustice. In the field of art in Boston, Lilly Busch, patroness of the Harvard Germanic Museum, faced the most egregious violations of her civil liberties. She was vacationing in Germany in 1914 when the war broke out and, feeling concern for her married daughters who lived there, stayed on until the spring of 1918, when she was informed that the US federal government planned to take control of her entire estate on the grounds that her vacation home in Germany made her an alien of the United States.[80] It did not matter that she had lived in the United States for all of her seventy-four years and that her parents had been naturalized citizens. Lilly Busch urgently returned home to correct the situation. When she reached American soil, she was detained. Her baggage was taken from her, and she was escorted to a nearby hotel. Marines positioned themselves outside of her room, where she was interrogated at length for several hours. When the US Marshals were unable to acquire the information they were looking for, they escorted Mrs. Busch and her maid, Mrs. Baumann, into a different room where they "laid the old lady on a bed and examined her private parts, making a very thorough examination of her vagina and womb."[81] Authorities completely stripped Mrs. Busch of her civil rights in this case, committing a physical violation that by law could be considered rape. The government's search and seizure policies were expanded beyond the usual inspections of material possessions, to include sexual assault as a tool of war. This example suggests that even German Americans of high class status were liable to degrading treatment and abuse. A pervasive attitude existed that all Germans, regardless of economic status, were subhuman, thereby justifying violence and sexual exploitation against them.

Not only was Mrs. Busch physically and emotionally violated but her property was threatened as well. Anti-German extremists in Boston pressured Harvard College to halt construction and tear down the half-completed Germanic Museum, which Lilly Busch had endowed. The kaiser's gifts of German statuary to the museum were hidden away in an unknown location to prevent destruction. Level-headed Harvard students and faculty suppressed the controversy and saved the project by saying, "Some day we will be glad to have a collection of German things. That day may not come for years, at least not until a new generation has grown up. . . . Above all things, let us not get fanatical." Fortunately, because of these enlightened peoples' actions, the building was completed to specification, and the museum opened in 1921 after anger over the project cooled down.[82]

Simply having German ancestry was reason enough for many to fear that their homes or businesses would be vandalized, burned, or destroyed, and such was the case for Arthur Volkmann.[83]

Figure 3.10. A youthful picture of philanthropist Lilly Busch, who, during World War I, was physically violated by federal authorities. Photograph by C .M. Bell Company, Washington, DC. Courtesy of the Library of Congress, Prints and Photographs Division.

Figure 3.11. Arthur Volkmann, founder and headmaster of the prestigious Volkmann School of Boston, was forced to shut down his institution when newspapers falsely accused him of being a German spy. Courtesy of Noble and Greenough School Archives.

Founder and headmaster of the prestigious Volkmann School, a pre-
paratory school on Newbury Street in Boston for boys bound for the
Ivy League, he was forced to shut down his institute when newspapers
falsely reported that he was a German spy. Volkmann was a man with an
unmistakable German accent, whose success in educating young men
was well known and praised. His school was a model that other private
schools followed and yet, with the war and the attacks on his character, parents quickly pulled their children from his school.[84] On May
26, 1918, the Volkmann School Locker Building, a one-story wooden
structure in the Boston suburb of Allston, was destroyed by fire. The
cause of the fire was never explained, but the damage amounted to
$1,500, which only added to the mounting financial difficulties Volk-
mann faced.[85] To prevent outright loss, the Volkmann School merged
with its rival, Noble and Greenough, combining students and staff.
Arthur Volkmann, the committed founder and headmaster of the Volkmann School and one of Boston's most upstanding citizens, retreated
to a fishing village in northern Maine and died a broken man shortly
thereafter.[86]

Like Arthur Volkmann, many people in Boston were victimized
simply because of their German names. Boston bookstore owner and
small-press publisher Theodor J. Ritter was arrested and charged with
circulating German propaganda at his Boylston Street bookshop. Hans
Miller, Heinrich Kox, and Alfred Wittig were rounded up and arrested
as German agents.[87] Their "crimes" involved the transfer of a large
sum of money. A fair investigation would have revealed that Wittig was
about to be married and Miller and Kox were catering the wedding.

Suspicion abounded. German waiters at the Jacob Wirth Restaurant were taunted by local patrons who accused them of being German
spies. Fritz Fruh, headwaiter of the famous German restaurant challenged his accusers by saying, "I am a loyal citizen of America. I have
one son in the army and one in the navy. I forbid you to call me that
name."[88] Fruh escorted the bullies to the nearest police station, where
they were arrested and detained for twelve hours. Fruh was given protection by the Boston police, a testament to the relatively positive attitude many Bostonians had toward Germans, as compared with other
regions of the country.[89]

Minor acts of violence or verbal cruelty were quietly condoned
in Boston, and citizens learned to conform to the oppressive climate.
A typical act of vandalism involved applying yellow paint to German
monuments, churches, schools, and homes. On average, members of
the German American community responded to these random acts by
becoming intensely patriotic, submerging their German identity out
of fear for their safety and livelihood. Martha Engler, a young German

girl living in Boston during the war, reported walking to school with a small American flag to prove her patriotism. Her German Catholic parochial school held weekly loyalty ceremonies. The German language had been banned from her school.[90] Martha's father, who had lost his job with the French consulate during the war, gave her German-language lessons quietly in their home.[91] Most German parents, however, erased the ethno-cultural marks that identified them. Author Kurt Vonnegut, who settled in Barnstable, Massachusetts, recorded that anti-Germanism "so shamed and dismayed my parents that they resolved to raise me without acquainting me with the language or the literature or the music or the oral family histories which my ancestors had loved. They volunteered to make me ignorant and rootless as proof of their patriotism."[92] Forgetting the past was the price many Germans paid to become American citizens. Father William Schmidt, a visiting priest at Holy Trinity German Catholic Church in Boston, reported that his uncle was so fearful during the war that his family changed its name to Smith, trading their identity for safety.[93] Steinweg, the piano manufacturer, became Steinway for this reason as well. Street signs, parks, and school names were Anglicized.[94] Traditions that were obviously German became American. Scores of secular clubs disappeared. Anglo-German clubs, such as Saint Boltoph's, carefully limited their membership. Several German singing societies in Boston merged into one, the Saengerchor. Surviving German social clubs transformed themselves by opening their membership to all ethnic groups.[95] German books were either stowed away in attics, sold as scrap paper, or burned in patriotic ceremonies. German food was renamed. Universities removed Germanic subjects from their curriculum. All but one German newspaper, the *Germania*, had gone out of business by war's end. German Bostonian businesses suffered. Sales slumped at German candy companies because of public accusations that they added glass shards to their products. German toy manufacturers were no longer permitted to ship their products to America. In November of 1918, Congress passed the Wartime Prohibition Act, which banned the manufacture of wine and beer. This law targeted German beer manufacturers and local pubs, forcing many to close. The German communities of Boston's South End and nearby Jamaica Plain, intimately connected to the beer industry, gradually disappeared after the war. Their residents scattered farther from the city center, blending in and assimilating into their new neighborhoods.[96]

World War I placed civilians on the American home front in the thick of a foreign conflict, thousands of miles away from the European battlefield.[97] When popular support for the war declined at the end of 1917, the federal government "manufactured consent" and created policies that demonized the enemy and harmed innocent immigrants in America.[98] As Frederick Luebke makes clear, "On every hand the American people were encouraged to make war on German language and culture and to watch persons and institutions carefully for signs of subversion. The persecution of innocent American citizens was a natural and understandable result."[99] Total war demanded vigilance from the entire population, sanctioning the public pursuit of adversaries, even if they existed in one's own neighborhood. Tension seeped into everyday society and influenced how people responded to one another. Paranoia and fear prevailed over rational thought, and the country expressed fickleness and cruelty toward its once favored ethnic group. The formerly multicultural city of Boston cooled its reception of its German friends. Anti-German hysteria tragically claimed its victims. Respect for human dignity disappeared in the wind. Most German Americans conformed to the ruling orthodoxy, demonstrating their loyalty to America and homogenizing into the national culture.[100] In protecting themselves from hate crimes and violations of their civil liberties, many German Americans erased their old identities and became invisible threads in the fabric of everyday life.[101] As we shall see in the chapters to follow, Karl Muck and the German music community were not immune from the difficulties.

Chapter Four

"LOOKING FOR THE TRUMP CARD"

Mrs. William Jay's Attacks on Karl Muck in Wartime America (1915–1918)

Not only was Karl Muck dealing with oppressive changes in Boston's public spaces as the country prepared for war, but he was living in a hostile period, as animosity increased toward people of German ancestry in the United States. Trying to do his job and not attract negative attention, Muck hoped that he would get through the war unscathed. His luck would not hold out, however. He became caught in the middle of a rivalry between Boston and New York that would have grave consequences for his future, bringing him into the spotlight at a time when Germans in America needed to keep a low profile. For many decades before the war, Boston's upper classes had embraced German high culture. During the war, however, certain members of New York's elite society railed against that German foundational basis in Boston. Muck found himself in the middle of that conflict. His downfall can tell us something about the way American culture was changing during World War I. History turned on this moment.

Karl Muck and the Boston Symphony Orchestra, the Envy of New York

Muck was considered one of the finest conductors in the world by the European musical community. He was highly prized by symphonies in US cities, especially New York, that wanted to advance their reputations on the global stage.[1] In 1898, while still in Germany and prior to his initial assignment in Boston, Muck had been offered the lucrative position of conductor of the New York Metropolitan Opera Company for a yearly salary of $27,000, a substantial sum that Muck refused.[2] Opera in New York was a fashionable entertainment form backed by wealthy patrons. German dramatic works, composed by Wagner and conducted by members of the Wagner family's inner circle that included Karl Muck, were particularly coveted. Between 1893 and 1918, the Met gave 3,500 performances of Wagner operas.[3] Despite the Met's persistence, the illustrious conductor was drawn to the relatively quiet and intellectual city of Boston.

There are several reasons why Muck chose Boston over New York at the turn of the twentieth century. High culture at that time was more established in Boston. Perhaps in part because of its small size, Boston was committed to classical music and took it very seriously. New York's cultural ascendancy came later, following a different trajectory. Boston's arts community was more cohesive, making it the envy of New York.[4] Civic enterprises were created and supported by a tight-knit social network of upper-class individuals with relatively uncontested cultural authority. New York's cultural world was defined by a "fragmented collection of plutocrats" who competed with one another, ultimately delaying the organization and professionalization of cultural institutions there, which it was trying to establish in the years before and during Muck's arrival in America.[5]

Boston's musical intimacy allowed artists to thrive. In 1894, Otto Florsheim of the *New York Musical Courier* wrote, "Boston is more musical than any other city in the United States. . . . Take a concert like Saturday's twentieth symphony concert and its preceding public rehearsal. It rained all Friday and it snowed all Saturday. In New York on such unpropitious occasions all concert attendance, even that at our six Philharmonic concerts, decreases in number most materially and the atmosphere puts a damper on all musical enthusiasm in listeners and performers alike. Not so in Boston."[6]

New York's privileged classes, particularly the capitalists associated with the New York Philharmonic, sought the cultural preeminence their rival city had developed over time.[7] They wanted the prestige of having the best orchestra in the country. During the 1906 BSO tour, the *New York Times* reported that Karl Muck's appointment "is a matter of much interest to the New York musical public for the Boston Symphony Orchestra's ten concerts are among the most important features of the New York musical season, and none of its audiences are more jealous of its perfection than its New York audiences."[8] As Howard Shanet points out, "Boston provided for its orchestra, in a single step, conditions that New York could not begin to match. Every time the secure, well-drilled, permanently organized BSO came to New York on its concert visits, the New York Philharmonic winced under the inevitable comparison."[9] News even reached Atlanta, Georgia, as the *World of Music* reported, "Interest in the orchestra in Boston is greater this year than it's ever been before. . . . The conviction steadily grows that in securing Dr. Muck the BSO has brought to this country a man of all men fit to be at its head."[10]

New York also wanted Muck as its conductor because of his public notoriety and for how he elevated the performance level and status of the organizations he worked with. New York cultural elites were eager to create excellent, highly organized, permanent cultural institutions. The city sought a prestigious national identity with a premier orchestra of its own. Elites in Manhattan wanted the world to view it as a cultural mecca with the nation's best music.

The Rise of New York as a Center for American Capitalism, Tourism, and Culture

This quest for cultural supremacy came in tandem with the city's rise as a world financial leader, as it became a hub for transportation and trade. New York was the center of American capitalism and a thriving market city for the nation.[11] Immigration and industrialization accelerated the pace of change. Between 1880 and 1919, New York was the point of entry for European immigration. It was "America's public face."[12] Steamships brought large numbers of immigrant workers to America through the port of New York to feed the country's industrial machine. The railroads brought settlers from New York to the interior American West, and businesses subsidized steamships and railway companies to transport laborers to farms, mines, and factories across the country. These workers, in turn, produced goods for new markets. The collective factors of the Industrial Revolution; corporate exploitation of vast, mostly untapped natural resources; and a massive influx of new laborers made the country's capitalists, many of them centered in New York City, enormously wealthy. American industry had grown rapidly, funneling massive profits into Manhattan, the Stock Exchange, and the "House of Morgan." J. P. Morgan was the director of hundreds of railroads, mining, electrical, telegraph, and steel companies. Almost all of the leading American capitalists were associated with him at his Wall Street address.

Not only was New York becoming the center of American capitalism, it was also fashioning itself as an important tourist destination. The same railroads that had delivered immigrants to the hinterlands of America now brought them back to the city as tourists.[13] Businessmen and their wives came in pursuit of middle class pleasures. They visited Bloomingdale's, Wanamaker's, and Macy's Department Stores.

Figure 4.1. Macy's Department Store and Herald Square. Melissa Burrage Collection.

They explored the shopping district of the Ladies Mile on Sixth Avenue. Visitors could explore Central Park, or take a ferry to Staten Island or Liberty Island to see the Statue of Liberty, or wander the halls of the American Museum of Natural History or the Metropolitan Museum of Art. They could walk down Fifth Avenue and see the famous mansions of the rich. They could dine at Delmonico's, Rector's, Sherry's, Shanley's, Churchill's, Maxim's, or Murray's Roman Gardens, all opened between the mid-1890s and 1910. They could stay at one of more than two hundred hotels that opened in New York by 1912, including the Waldorf, the most expensive and luxurious in the city.[14]

City promoters, or boosters, made up of entrepreneurs and businesspeople—owners of newspapers, department stores, restaurants, hotels, museums and performance venues, manufacturing enterprises, financial establishments, railroads and steamship lines—endorsed New York's various pleasures because tourism benefitted their enterprises. Public relations experts promoted Manhattan's architecture as a showcase of American power, ingenuity, and modernity. Skyscrapers were marketed as distinct representations of American national identity.[15] They were tall, modern, and unique. Promotional material convinced tourists that if they visited New York City, they could "see America." The Flatiron Building and the Brooklyn Bridge, it was argued, were emblematic of American power and inventiveness.[16] New York's

Figure 4.2. Flat Iron Building, New York. Manhattan's architecture was promoted as representations of American power and modernity. Melissa Burrage Collection.

commercial buildings were the tallest in the world. Joseph Pulitzer's World Building was described in advertisements as "The Central and Highest Point of New World Civilization."[17] In contrast, Boston's highest structure, the Ames Building, was thirteen floors high, small in comparison to the World Building's twenty. No other city had such skyscrapers. Promoters described the New York skyline and the mountains of the West as uniquely American.[18]

New York was also more culturally dynamic and audacious than Boston. The latter city was a stable, old mercantile city with a focus on history, tradition, and religious idealism. Boston had a conservative and aristocratic bearing. New York, on the contrary, took risks. It led the nation in publishing popular music and novelty songs in an area of the city that came to be known as "Tin Pan Alley." This music district mass-produced new songs at an unparalleled rate and distributed them to theaters and vaudeville syndicates around the country. One publisher, M. Witmark and Sons, hired song pluggers to sing from their sheet music catalog in pursuit of commercial advantage. African American composer and pianist Scott Joplin lived in this area and published music such as the *Maple Leaf Rag* in the years before World War I. Irving Berlin, a Russian Jew from the Lower East Side of New York, composed ragtime music such as *Alexander's Ragtime Band* between shifts as a singing waiter at the Pelham Cafe.[19] New York City drew tourists to its vaudeville and Broadway playhouses, and by 1910 there were thirty-four theaters in the Times Square area alone. Its first Broadway musical, *Lady Be Good*, was composed by first-generation Russian immigrants from Brooklyn Ira and George Gershwin.

By the early 1920s, New York City was a magnet for jazz and blues musicians, including Duke Ellington, James "Bubber" Miley, and Fats Waller. Jazz musicians staged "rent parties" in parlors and living rooms, and they performed on millionaires' yachts, in hotels, and at resorts. They played at the Hollywood Club, the Apollo Theater, and other cabaret venues in Harlem, the creative heart of the city. West Fifty-Third Street was the social hub for New York's most prominent black citizens. Jazz musicians mixed with Broadway performers, theater producers, black and white writers, Yiddish actors, black showgirls, Armenian belly dancers, Hungarian escapologists, and vaudevillians.

Out of this vibrant ethnic blend came the Harlem Renaissance, one of the most vibrant and important periods in American history. Poets, authors, and artists, such as Langston Hughes, Zora Neale Hurston, Jean Toomer, Countee Cullen, Charles Chestnutt, Rudolph Fisher, James Weldon Johnson, and Alfred Stieglitz enjoyed a bohemian lifestyle, visiting the same dive bars, dingy restaurants, and bookshops and living in ramshackle tenements along with the latest Ellis Island immigrants.[20]

Figure 4.3. Upper Broadway New York. New York City was a dynamic cultural destination, drawing tourists to its Broadway playhouses, of which there were thirty-four by 1910. Melissa D. Burrage Collection.

The city was alive with ethnic spectacle. Heavyweight boxer Jack Johnson's Club De Lux, later the Cotton Club on 142nd Street, was a "temple of primitivism." Patrons were made to feel as if they stepped into a jungle with wild vegetation, tribal sculptures, and African drumming. Log cabins and picket fences greeted patrons inside the Plantation Club on 126th Street. African American "mammies" cooked waffles and flapjacks for hungry customers. Every possible sensation, it seemed, could inspire creativity in New York.

Throughout the nineteenth century, Klein Deutschland, or Little Germany, on the Lower East Side, attracted German immigrants and provided ethnic spaces that fostered sociability through music, theater, and drink.[21] In the one-hundred-year period between 1840 and 1940, some fifty thousand separate events including operas, operettas, classical concerts, folk plays, serious drama, musical revues, comedies, minstrel shows, and vaudeville acts were performed by and for the German American community in Manhattan. New York was the third-largest German city in the world after Berlin and Vienna, and this ethnic population had a powerful influence on New York's cultural direction.[22] From the 1850s to the 1870s, people flocked to the Stadt Theatre in the Bowery neighborhood to drink beer, meet friends, and listen to German comic and romantic operas.[23] The first performances in the United States of Wagner's *Tannhäuser* and *Lohengrin* were given at the Stadt Theater starting in 1859, with beer and cakes served between acts.[24] From the 1870s to the 1880s, audiences enjoyed large-scale operetta and opera productions at the Germania Theater next to Tammany Hall in Union Square.[25] The Atlantic Garden, in the Bowery, was in operation from 1858 to 1911, seating two thousand people in its Thalia Theater and offering a variety of entertainment, including the Vienna Elite Ladies Orchestra, dramatic performances, and operettas.[26] From 1866 to 1925, the Terrace Garden, also called the Lexington Avenue Opera House, was a social gathering place for the German American community. Audiences enjoyed fine food and entertainment under one roof. The Terrace Garden included an elegant restaurant; an "old German Bierstube," or alehouse; a bowling alley; an outdoor garden, and a ballroom.[27] High-quality musical performances were given there, including German-language operettas. The Theodore Thomas Orchestra led a series of summer orchestral concerts at the Terrace Garden in the first two years of its operation, and Thomas also conducted more than a thousand classical performances at the Central Park Garden on Seventh Avenue between 1868 and 1875.[28]

German American theaters and beer gardens played an important role in the eventual acceptance of classical music in America, leading to a greater demand for more permanent orchestral development in the United States.[29] Musicians, including members of the New York Philharmonic, performed at these venues, as orchestras were a necessity in these establishments. Large audiences supplied the base support of people eager to enjoy this entertainment.[30] The *New York Times* recorded that these German theaters were successful and profitable, resulting in a "willingness to pay for it [which was a] good deal more general among the German population than among the more fashionable persons," who occasionally purchased tickets to musical events.[31]

And while there was widespread and growing support for orchestral music in New York City, attracting an ethnically diverse and dynamic population, cultural elites sought to wrest competitive control from popular commercial entertainment and elevate orchestral music as a high art form.[32] For fifty years, from 1880 to 1930, an abundance of commercial ensembles competed in New York, with tension between high art institutions and popular entertainment venues.[33] Elites in the pre–World War I years played an active role (along with musicians themselves) to forge a niche market for symphony music, offering "enjoyment of the highest intellectual character," where classical music was perfected and audience appreciation was cultivated.[34] For competitive reasons, the New York Philharmonic took longer to achieve the level of success that the BSO had acquired during Muck's tenure. New York audiences had been supporting three orchestras: the New York Philharmonic, the Theodore Thomas Orchestra, and the New York Symphony Orchestra founded by Leopold Damrosch. The population was large, the city was economically strong, and its audiences familiar enough with symphony repertory to support a variety of orchestras that played serious music.[35] Each ensemble added vitality to New York's concert scene, and audience participation continued to increase, but the rivalry between these city orchestras held the New York Philharmonic back from achieving the level of fame and prominence that the BSO had achieved by the turn of the century, and it was not until 1929, when the New York Philharmonic and the New York Symphony Orchestra merged, that the former orchestra escaped intercity symphonic rivalry.[36]

Moreover, symphonic music in New York took a back seat to opera, which was hugely popular.[37] Old commercial elites, like the Belmonts, Stuyvesants, Roosevelts, and Astors, supported opera at the Academy of Music (1854–85). The social elites of the Manhattan Opera Company (1906–10) also backed opera performances. The Metropolitan Opera Company, which began in 1883, was endowed by the Goulds, Vanderbilts, Morgans, Whitneys, and Rockefellers. The Met drew enormous crowds during Muck's time in America.[38]

Wealthy New York capitalists worked hard at the turn of the century to develop and fund cultural institutions and make their city a destination for high culture. They made significant contributions to Carnegie Hall, the Metropolitan Museum of Art, and the Museum of Natural History, dwarfing Boston elites' own philanthropic gifts to high culture. Wealth and economic power in this emerging musical competition was transitioning from Boston to New York, as city leaders there sought to ensure that it became a center for American culture as well, overtaking the former city's established position.[39] As Frederic Cople Jaher points out, by the end of the nineteenth century, "upper-class Bostonian altruism was . . . entering a twilight era. . . . Leading philanthropists, especially Gilded Age tycoons, did not limit their gifts. . . . New York donations doubled those from Boston."[40] Boston had built its fortune on the China trade, textiles, mining, and railroads.[41] By World War I, however, Brahmin elites were unable to equal the level of wealth generated by the Rockefeller, Guggenheim, and Morgan fortunes.[42] As Russell Adams points out, "As the nation's center of capital and enterprise had shifted relentlessly to New York, Boston had been eased into the role of financial spear carrier, upstaged by the bigger guns of Gotham."[43] While economically Boston ceded power to New York, Boston still reigned supreme as the nation's preeminent authority on high culture. Times were changing, however. New York began positioning itself as a world-class city and a cultural leader, utilizing its wealth to create fabulous new institutions where none had existed before. It began the process of developing a symphonic organization to rival (and surpass) the BSO.

The Reorganization of the New York Philharmonic

When Karl Muck began his position in Boston in 1906, the New York Philharmonic (NYP) was a cooperative society, having been established in 1842 by Connecticut-born Ureli Corelli Hill. The NYP was the oldest orchestra in the United States. In Europe, Hill had studied with German violinist and composer Louis Spohr and had returned from his experience eager to form a high-level ensemble in America like those he had heard in Europe.[44] Initially, the NYP was made up of fifty-three musicians, twenty-two of whom were German. Although German musicians were involved with the philharmonic's founding, English, French, and American musicians were also important participants. Many of the immigrant musicians in the orchestra were long-time residents of the United States, and their ensemble supported local composers and experimented with their programming choices. As Barbara Haws

Figure 4.4. New York Philharmonic Club pre-1923. Courtesy of the New York Philharmonic Archives.

makes clear in her study of Hill's diary, the philharmonic was not simply a transplanted European orchestra but a "hybrid of wide-ranging experiences and traditions, like the United States itself."[45] By 1855, the orchestra expanded to include sixty-seven members, including fifty-three Germans. Beginning with the appointment of the orchestra's first full-time conductor, Theodore Eisfeld, each subsequent conductor during the nineteenth century was German, and the majority-German orchestra began performing more traditional European works.[46] In the first decade of the twentieth century, NYP members, like the city's cultural elites, sought to modernize and lay the groundwork for a more permanent orchestra, like the BSO.[47] At that time, NYP members had an equal vote. They elected their conductor from within the orchestra itself. They paid initiation fees and annual dues, and shared the responsibilities, profits, and financial risks of their small concert series. Members performed a wide range of music in a variety of venues and concert settings. Performances were sophisticated, and members understood the importance of rehearsals to achieve exceptional performance quality.[48] Without a regular salary, however, most of the musicians in the orchestra required additional work, often taking part-time employment in theater or opera orchestras, or in nonmusical fields that offered steady, modest incomes.[49] The cooperative was vulnerable to market incentives, and the philharmonic was unable to secure the complete allegiance of its members.[50]

To professionalize the orchestra, the New York Philharmonic kept a watchful eye on the Boston Symphony. Under the direction of Henry Lee Higginson, the BSO had corporatized its business and provided full employment to its musicians, forbidding them from seeking additional employment outside of the orchestra. They were required to devote their full attention to the job of creating highly polished music for the benefit of their audiences. Theirs was a modern symphony and part of a new era in the development of orchestras in America. The NYP looked to Boston, for, as Paul DiMaggio points out, New York and other American cities were "to a large extent influenced by the Boston model."[51]

In 1909, the New York Philharmonic was officially reorganized by a powerful group of wealthy ladies, including Mary R. Sheldon, wife of banker George Sheldon; Minnie Untermyer, wife of Jewish lawyer and self-made millionaire Samuel Untermyer; and Dorothea Draper, whose family owned the *New York Sun* newspaper. These ladies formed the Guarantors Committee, assuming management of the philharmonic and changing the organizational form from a cooperative society to a professional full-time orchestra.[52] Their goal was to create a "first rank" permanent orchestra.[53] They undertook the necessary behind-the-scenes tasks to bring performances to New York—assessing the market, booking artists, speaking with agents, and negotiating contracts. They secured concert venues, met with building facility owners, acted as community liaisons to the public, and promoted shows through media publicity, fund-raising, and ticket sales. They often went out on a financial limb to secure the needed arrangements.[54] With their energy and ability, "they knew how to make a committee system work." They did not have one man, like Henry Lee Higginson, providing patronage and making decisions. Theirs was a collective effort. Shanet says, "The Society has been blessed with an unfailing supply of rich, hardworking, intelligent, loyal, and public spirited women who have been willing to give their time and money for the good of the city's musical life."[55] The female patrons of the NYP took on ambitious projects, creating leadership roles for themselves in the arts that they helped to define.[56] The philharmonic "was being strengthened at just the time when prosperity was beginning to smile upon the society."[57]

NYP guarantors were powerful agents in the process of elevating the status of high culture in New York, as well as in shaping the development of symphonic music in the United States. While they retained Vice President Richard Arnold and Secretary Felix Leifels from the earlier cooperative, the guarantors led a successful drive to secure financial backing, adding a large number of affluent people from social and business circles to expand their operation.[58] The list of wealthy

New Yorkers who pledged money included J. P. Morgan, Thomas Fortune Ryan, Joseph Pulitzer, John D. Rockefeller, and Mrs. Harry Payne Whitney.[59] With their financial and social support, the New York Philharmonic was able to hire an excellent conductor and offer musicians steady employment. The NYP hoped that with consistent rehearsal time it could achieve a high musical standard and develop its reputation as one of the best orchestras in the country.

In 1909, the New York Philharmonic guarantors hired Jewish Bohemian Gustav Mahler, the respected forty-nine-year-old composer and conductor who captivated audiences with his performances.[60] Before this appointment, he had conducted at the Met for two years and had been the director of the Vienna Court Opera (1897–1907), where he was a victim of anti-Semitic abuse from the Viennese press. Mahler had a reputation in Europe as a "fierce and uncompromising taskmaster," and the guarantors hoped that his artistic passion would inspire and guide the orchestra.[61] Born into a humble family, Mahler was not the upper-class man that Muck was, yet his reputation as a conductor equaled that of the Boston conductor, and he was eminent in his own right. Mahler viewed himself as Czech and Austrian, Jewish and Christian, having converted to Catholicism in his later life. He was neither a conservative elite nor particularly nationalistic toward his place of birth. Unlike Muck, who preferred Germans in his orchestra, Mahler reorganized the New York Philharmonic, making it "much less German in its personnel," hiring French and Italians musicians, and Jewish immigrant instrumentalists from Russia and central Europe.[62] He appointed American-born Theodore Spiering as concertmaster. Looking for a lighter sound and a better balance, he cut down the number of bass players and added more violins and cellists. The New York Philharmonic was ideologically different from Boston, and yet, under Mahler, the NYP began to have the same level of excellence.

During the Mahler years, the New York Philharmonic guaranteed full employment to its musicians, just like the BSO. He held regular rehearsals and required a full orchestra when touring.[63] He insisted on educating the public by giving historical lectures before concerts. Like Muck, he performed classical compositions and debuted new works.[64] Mahler polished the orchestra and made it competitive with its rival city. His goal was to make it "the best orchestra in the United States and the equal of any in the world."[65] There is no question that he began to succeed. In the first year of his conductorship, he increased the number of concerts from eighteen to forty-six. According to Shanet, "The force of the revitalized New York Philharmonic under Mahler was felt even outside New York."[66] In 1911, however, after two years suffering with management difficulties, nervous disorders, and a heart condition, Mahler resigned his post and went back to Europe, and within the year he had passed away from cardiac arrest. New York had lost one of the greatest composers and conductors of all time. The philharmonic needed a new conductor with a strong international reputation to keep the momentum of the earlier two years going. Management sought to continue its quest for excellence, to compete with Boston, and to define its identity as something very different from conservative upper-class Boston.

Mahler's successor in the fall of 1911 was thirty-nine-year-old Bohemian Josef Stransky.[67] Stransky had been an opera and concert conductor in Berlin, Hamburg, Dresden, and Prague. In New York, he "conducted more concerts in one season than a typical European orchestra gave in five years."[68] He offered a wide variety of music and he brought in big crowds. An attractive and friendly man, he was less a conductor for connoisseurs and more of a "people's conductor."[69] With Stransky, the New York Philharmonic was attempting to appeal to all social classes and ethnic groups. Stransky offered regular subscription concerts, which included a Thursday evening, Friday afternoon, Saturday evening, and Sunday afternoon series, as well as young people's concerts. He gave lectures and special performances at Columbia University, at Cooper Union, and at US Army camps. Stransky maintained a competitive touring schedule, traveling to New Jersey, New England, the South, the Midwest, the Pacific coast, and Canada. As Shanet points out, "There was a satisfaction in being the grand New York Philharmonic . . . representing New York City in the style that lesser communities expected of it. . . . The Philharmonic was now of more than local interest . . . it would seem to be as much a national as a metropolitan institution."[70] In January of 1917, Stransky and the New York Philharmonic performed twenty-five favorite classical pieces, expanding the orchestra's reach even further.[71] Stransky attempted to make classical music available to a broad spectrum of people from all walks of life but always with management's larger goal in mind of national competitive excellence.

While prospects seemed hopeful, the orchestra faced financial challenges, and the guarantors discussed how to bring more money into the organization. They continually worried about expenses, such as renting halls, paying salaries, buying music, paying soloists, and covering touring costs. In 1911, Joseph Pulitzer had bequeathed $800,000 to the philharmonic, with the stipulation that the guarantors recruit a thousand new sustaining members and that the orchestra continue to perform Pulitzer's favorite music, such as Wagner, Beethoven, and Liszt.[72] The philharmonic needed more benefactors like Pulitzer.[73] In December of 1914, the guarantors made a concerted effort to bring

Figure 4.5. Portrait of young Mrs. Jay from the John Jay Homestead State Historic Site, Katonah, New York. Melissa D. Burrage Collection.

wealthy individuals onto their newly formed board of directors, including banking and mining mogul Louis Rothschild and Louisine Havemeyer, the wife of sugar millionaire Henry O. Havemeyer.[74] At this same meeting, New York socialite Mrs. William (Lucie) Jay was unanimously accepted as a member of the board.

Mrs. Jay began her work for the NYP when the organization was trying to improve its reputation and professionalize the orchestra by building a permanent hall, like the one Boston had completed in 1900. The philharmonic equated national excellence with having its own home, appealing to regional, civic pride and separating itself from other popular forms of entertainment.[75] The directors were aware that audiences wanted superb experiences and that a concert venue with excellent acoustics was a necessary part of any orchestra's greatness.[76] The Chicago Symphony had built Orchestra Hall in 1904, which served as a performance facility and movie theater before World War I. Prior to that time, the orchestra had occupied the much larger five-thousand-seat Auditorium Theater, which served a variety of performing groups but challenged efforts to secure season subscriptions. The new hall eased this burden by cutting seating capacity in half, creating an artificial demand for tickets.[77] An NYP concert hall would provide a similar vitality to the orchestra and the community and propel it to greater national importance.[78] Moreover, experts reported that "inexperienced concertgoers tend to react enthusiastically to the sound of a great hall, even when they may not be aware of what makes them feel the way they do. Similarly, they often feel less enthusiastic about concerts in mediocre halls even if they are not aware that acoustics play a factor."[79] Consequently, the New York Philharmonic board hired experts to teach them about acoustics, hall design, and fundraising.[80] They created an endowment fund, embarked on a subscription campaign to bring in new members, and sought to expand their touring schedule, hoping to bring much-needed income (and prestige) to the organization. They issued a letter to subscribers justifying their idea for a hall:

> The possession of a permanent visible and monumental building devoted to the uses of the Orchestra has been found in Boston. . . . There is a feeling of dignity and stability which does not attach to temporary quarters or to a mere series of fine concerts in a hired hall. Public-spirited men or women like to associate their names with such institutions, and to become active supporters during their lives. The Philharmonic Society of New York is a great public institution, whose history and dignity and standing in the community make the possession of its own home a practical necessity for the worthy accomplishment of its allotted work. New York is fast becoming the lead-

ing musical centre of the world, and it is entitled to have, and ought to have, the assurance of the continuance of the finest Orchestra in the world. Such an Orchestra will itself help to give to New York its proper recognition and in its permanent establishment its supporters will feel justifiable pride.[81]

Just as the philharmonic began moving ahead with its plans for a hall, World War I broke out, making more fundraising seem inappropriate, if not unpatriotic. Therefore, the directors "temporarily abandoned [their plans] on account of existing conditions caused by the European war," with intentions to renew their efforts when conditions were acceptable.[82] Impatient to move forward, the board resumed its work to secure funds for building the hall at the December 16, 1915, meeting. Perhaps the NYP was energized by William Sloane Coffin Sr., president of the trustees of the Metropolitan Museum of Art, who argued that "the Great War in Europe gives New York an opportunity to become the Great Art Center of the world." New York musicians claimed in the press that "musical supremacy" could be achieved and that "now is the time to place our imprint upon art."[83] The New York Philharmonic continued to strategize ways to secure large amounts of money and discussed how to compete with other symphonies for national recognition.

Part of the philharmonic's hopes for a new hall rested on the income supplied by concert tours, particularly those in Baltimore and Washington, DC. Touring was lucrative, bringing the orchestra into the national consciousness and providing a prestigious reputation over time. In February of 1915, however, attendance at its Baltimore concerts had dropped off, and a new committee was formed to study how to increase attendance in that city.[84] The committee decided to change the dates of the concerts so that they did not conflict with the BSO's touring schedule.[85] The board mailed a letter to all the philharmonic subscribers in Baltimore seeking support: "The concerts, which have been of unquestioned success artistically, have proven a financial failure hitherto, and in order to insure their continuance a practical guarantee has become necessary."[86] Touring expenses were high and the orchestra faced deficits. The board worked hard to fill seats and compete with other concerts offered at the same time. By April of 1916, the New York Philharmonic had discontinued subscription concerts in Baltimore and Washington, DC.[87]

While other board members worked on fundraising campaigns and strategized traditional ways to make money by adding concert dates or reaching out to subscribers in the community, Lucie Jay used competitive tactics to undermine Boston and elevate New York using methods that rival tycoons practiced in the business world. Symphony entertainment would become a multimillion-dollar industry in America, and orchestras would compete for revenues. In Boston, Karl Muck had continually improved the quality of the BSO to the envy of other orchestras. He was a perfectionist who demanded the very best from his musicians, and, because of the high quality of Boston Symphony performances, even New York's arts patrons were drawn to them, affecting the financial status of the philharmonic. If New York wanted to become a world-class musical city, it needed to outdistance Boston, its nearest competitor. If New York could not acquire the best of Boston for its city, as it had tried to do by offering Muck a position in 1898, then it would tarnish his reputation. Maneuvering from a position of power within the philharmonic establishment, Jay capitalized on conditions created by the war to weaken the NYP's biggest opponent. She sought to unseat Muck (and therefore the BSO) from national competition and draw attention back to her city. The *New York Times* reported that Mrs. William Jay was "looking for the trump card" that would remove Karl Muck as conductor of the Boston Symphony Orchestra.[88]

Mrs. Jay Works to Dethrone Muck from the Boston Symphony Orchestra

In 1915 and 1916, during Muck's second term in Boston, he received great acclaim for his accomplishments with the BSO, and the orchestra was seen as the country's premier symphony. Mrs. Jay made repeated attempts during these years to sabotage his position. She took full advantage of America's changing views on Germany to target the German nature of the BSO, knowing that, without a German conductor, German musicians, or German compositions, Higginson's enterprise would be compromised. The first major incident occurred long before the United States entered World War I. On March 29, 1915, Jay, a newly christened board member of the NYP, arrived in Boston to "begin a campaign to abolish the use of all German music."[89] She told the Boston press, "I want to make a statement concerning my plans in Boston because this city is considered a stronghold of German musical influence."[90] She traveled to Blue Hill, Maine, where Muck, the Kneisel Quartet, and members of the Boston Symphony Orchestra vacationed and performed, making the same point that Germans in America should abandon the music of their heritage.[91] The *Boston Herald* reported that upon "reaching Bar Harbor she will organize committees made up of persons preeminent in the musical world. These committees will begin at once a campaign to educate the people against

German music, which she terms the 'last stronghold of German propaganda in the United States.'"[92] Jay targeted German musical influence in Boston, and yet music programming at the New York Philharmonic, which also performed German works, remained relatively untouched. On January 28, just two months earlier, thousands of people of German birth descended on Boston Common and to the city's waterfront to celebrate Kaiser Wilhelm's birthday. German vessels docked in the harbor were "a flutter with bunting from stem to stern," and those in attendance "made merry" by singing patriotic German songs accompanied by ship musicians, wishing health and long life to the kaiser.[93] Karl Muck took part in these festivities.[94] Perhaps Mrs. Jay's attack against German music stemmed from this event. Her activism in Maine in March, just two months later, surprised the German musicians there, that this New York woman would have the nerve to enter their musical domain and demand the discontinuance of German music. Her insistence must have seemed preposterous to them. They had the complete support of the Boston Brahmin and musical communities. Not surprisingly, Mrs. Jay did not achieve her desired outcome, and the incredulous artists continued to perform German pieces.

On January 17, 1916, when the Boston Symphony Orchestra was making a tour of New York City, Muck became ill with influenza and was unable to conduct a concert there. He returned to Boston and convalesced at home for a week, missing concerts in both cities.[95] Shortly thereafter, in an effort to discredit him, Mrs. Jay reported to the New York press that Muck had feigned illness to purposely avoid conducting Nellie Melba, the famed British opera singer.[96] Jay asserted that because Muck was German, he would take a political position against England. Her accusation was false, for Muck had gained global acclaim in the United Kingdom, having conducted The Henry Wood Promenade Concerts, or The Proms, before his arrival in the United States. Henry Taylor Parker, music critic for the *Boston Transcript*, came to Muck's defense, arguing that Mrs. Jay's accusation was fabricated, that Muck "takes no thought to partisanship in all that concerns the Symphony Concerts," and that he "thought of Mme. Melba only as an eminent singer."[97] In fact, Nellie Melba had settled in Australia in her teen years, followed by a move to the United States after a bitter divorce. Muck commented to the press that he was eager to work with her, and he got his chance almost two years later, on Sunday December 16, 1917, at a special benefit concert in Boston for the Halifax, Nova Scotia, explosion relief.[98] Mrs. Jay had misled the public, exploiting wartime anti-German hysteria to damage Muck's reputation. This accusation was just one of many to come from the New York socialite against the famed German conductor.

The next attack occurred almost four months later when the New York press reported on internal management conflicts between Higginson and Muck.[99] Parker, a Harvard dropout with little musical knowledge but full of adoration for Karl Muck, quickly and sharply denied the "preposterous" and "malicious" rumor—a rumor, given Jay's media manipulation skills and robust tenacity, that was designed to destroy Karl Muck and the BSO.[100] Boston arts patrons responded by supporting Higginson and Muck during their final concert of the 1916 season.[101] When Muck closed his score, the applause "was not stilled until the conductor had thrice returned to the stage." The Brahmin-owned *Boston Transcript* reported that the city's symphony goers admired Muck as a man who, in trying circumstances, "has borne himself so quietly and so impeccably that the mean insinuations of baseless gossip have fallen, not upon him but upon those that invented and repeated it."[102] Muck came out of the conflict at the end of the season with his reputation intact.

While trying to rid Boston of Karl Muck, Mrs. Jay also pushed the NYP to acquire a new conductor with an international reputation for excellence. New York's music connoisseurs did not believe Stransky maintained artistic standards that would "satisfy a self-conscious metropolis convinced that the eyes of Europe were fixed critically upon it."[103] New York Philharmonic board members debated whether his talent ranked as high as Karl Muck's in Boston. He got mixed reviews from board members and from the press. Henry T. Finck, music critic for the *New York Post*, a newspaper owned by Oswald Garrison Villard, president of the New York Philharmonic, was his strongest defender versus Richard Aldrich of the *New York Times*, who opposed Stransky in the 1916–17 season with "equal fervor." Aldrich complained that Stransky "catered to public taste" and performed the "most easily accessible music."[104] He believed that audiences enjoyed this friendly and fun-loving man and his "colorful array" of concerts but that he was taking the orchestra away from its mission to provide excellent music. Even Finck admitted that Stransky "was by no means always at his best at these concerts. Sometimes he conducted in a slovenly way that quite justified adverse criticism."[105] Not surprisingly, Jay had an opinion on the matter, and she wanted a perfectionist to lead the philharmonic.[106] Richard Fletcher, editor of the *Chronicle*, who served as the "mouthpiece of Mrs. William Jay in her effort to prevent Dr. Karl Muck from conducting the Boston Symphony Orchestra Concerts in Carnegie Hall and Brooklyn's Academy of Music," wrote a letter demanding Stransky's resignation or discharge. According to the *American* newspaper, a paper affiliated with Pulitzer's the *World*, the New York Philharmonic Board of Directors ignored Mrs. Jay's request.[107] Jay argued

Figure 4.6. Conductor Josef Stransky, circa 1919. Courtesy of the New York Philharmonic Leon Levy Digital Archives.

that Belgian Eugène Ysaÿe, who was hired by the Cincinnati Symphony in 1918, or Henri Verbruggen, who became the conductor of the Minneapolis Symphony in 1923, would be "highly acceptable substitute[s]" for Stransky, but the board did not take her opinion seriously.[108] While most of the board members seemed satisfied with Stransky, Mrs. Jay wanted to raise the standard of the philharmonic by acquiring a better conductor. She was trying to eliminate New York's biggest competition and help the New York Philharmonic surpass Boston as the leading American orchestra.

The Biography of Mrs. William Jay

Why was the New York Philharmonic so important to Mrs. Jay, and what provoked her obsession with Karl Muck and the Boston Symphony? Jay had a variety of personal motives behind her actions against the celebrated Boston conductor. Her background may reveal something of her interests and biases. Lucie Oelrichs Jay was a second-generation American of German ancestry. Her father, Charles (Henry) Oelrichs, was "a German gentleman" from Baltimore and New York City. Family members were the American agents for the North German Lloyd Steamship Company, one of the largest passenger shipping companies in the world. Mrs. Jay's brother Hermann Oelrichs was general agent of the company.[109] Their greatest high-speed luxury ship, the *Kaiser Wilhelm der Große*, was built in 1897, before the *Lusitania* (Cunard, 1907) and the *Titanic* (White Star Line, 1912). An enormous ship, at 655 feet long, it could transport two thousand passengers. Reports claimed that it was "rivaled only by the big city skyscrapers" and that it was "a sensation throughout the world."[110] Lucie's sister, Hildegard Oelrichs, was married to Richard Henderson, head of the Anchor Steamship Line of Great Britain. Anchor's passenger ships served the Mediterranean, European, Asian, and North American markets, and in 1911 the Cunard Steamship Company purchased Anchor "to gain access to Anchor's lucrative emigrant trade."[111]

Mrs. Jay's family had numerous links to Germany. Her sister-in-law, Mary Jay, had married into the prominent Schieffelin family of New York.[112] E. G. Oelrichs, Mrs. Jay's grandfather, had come to the United States from Bremen. Her brother Hermann was trained for military service in Germany and learned the steamship business there. In 1876, he began importing and exporting goods from Germany to Central America. Hermann was part of the US Democratic National Committee in 1888 and organized a German bureau during the 1888 campaign. Mrs. Jay's husband had been the minister to Austria. Her

Figure 4.7. The North Lloyd Steamship Pier in Hoboken, New Jersey, 1903. Their agents, the Oelrichs, coordinated travel of passenger ships between the United States and Europe, and South America, Asia, and Australia. Moses King, *King's Photographic Views of New York* (Boston: Moses King, 1895).

family's North German Lloyd Steamship Company held a majority interest in the Deutsche Ozean-Reederei, the manufacturer of German U-boats.[113] She deflected attention from her family by using her married name, Jay, connecting herself to her husband's Anglo-Norman heritage.

Jay's animosity toward Karl Muck may also have involved citizenship. While both were of German ancestry, Jay was an American citizen with Anglocentric leanings. Her family made their money in the United States. Karl Muck was not an American citizen, and he embraced a level of German elitism that Jay found distasteful.

Lucie Jay was intimately linked with Americans of German and Dutch ancestry, many of whom were members of families with deep roots in the United States. These self-made families, such as the (Jewish) Guggenheims, the Vanderbilts, and the Havemeyers, were among the wealthiest in the United States, having made their fortunes in mining, shipping, railroads, and sugar. Lucie's brother Hermann and his wife, née Theresa Alice "Tessie" Fair, hosted elaborate shipboard dinner parties and elegant "fairy tale" balls at their fourteen-acre Newport, Rhode Island, mansion, Rosecliff, which was designed by renowned architect Stanford White and based on the Grand Trianon Palace at

Versailles. The 1974 motion picture *The Great Gatsby* was filmed at the Oelrichs mansion. Tessie Fair's family made millions mining silver in the Nevada Comstock Lode. Her sister Virginia married William K. Vanderbilt II, whose family acquired their wealth in shipping and in the railroad industry. William Vanderbilt built Marble House and his father, Cornelius II, built the Breakers, both in Newport's elite summer resort.[114] The combined power and wealth of this group of people was enormous. These families owned economic resources on an unimaginable scale, and Lucie Jay was part of this community. Her family and friendship circle were part of Ward McAllister's "Four Hundred," a list of the most influential families in New York.[115] Mrs. Belmont, the famous aristocrat, was Lucie's best friend. Lucie socialized with the prominent Astor family and mixed with the city's most wealthy and famous citizens. Her brother Charles May Oelrichs Jr. married Miss De Loosy, sister-in-law to Theodore Havemeyer, broker with the sugar trust, connecting her directly to New York's captains of industry.[116] By focusing public attention on a prominent German in Boston, Mrs. Jay could foment anti-Germanism far away from her home while deflecting potential wartime persecution from her own upper-class community in New York City. She could also use her significant influence to assist the NYP in its quest for prominence.

While Mrs. Jay vehemently opposed German music and musicians in Boston, the same standards were not imposed on the New York Philharmonic. The philharmonic did reduce the percentage of German music it performed during the war, modestly increasing its French and Russian offerings, but very few changes were made overall. Wagner, for example, remained on the programs. On February 28, 1918, at the height of America's involvement in World War I, the philharmonic performed an all-Wagner concert.[117] On January 9, 1917, the philharmonic celebrated the seventieth anniversary of the Deutscher Liederkranz der Stadt New York, a German men's singing society, by performing a "Grand Concert." In that same year, patriotic philharmonic audience members were chastised for knitting for soldiers during concerts, as the needle clicking bothered the musicians.[118] The NYP Board of Directors lacked the level of patriotism that Jay was demanding of the Boston Symphony. In January of 1915, Austrian nationalist Fritz Kreisler was engaged as a violinist with the New York Philharmonic. In that same year, conductor Josef Stransky programmed Beethoven's Ninth Symphony, and the board had no objection. In November of 1915, German-born Oswald Villard was elected to the board of directors, with no opposition from Mrs. Jay. On March 2, 1916, philharmonic treasurer Rudolpf E. F. Flinsch sent a letter to orchestra secretary Felix Leifels offering his resignation until the war was over, because of his German ancestry. The board refused to accept his resignation. "It is the unanimous wish of the board that you be requested to withdraw your application of severance from The Society. The board expresses herewith, its entire confidence in you, and its grateful appreciation of the splendid work you have done in the interest of The Society. The board feels that in this precarious period of the organization's life it would be dangerous to lose the cooperation of one who has proven his devotion and unselfish interest in the cause of music and in the present and future of The Philharmonic Society." Lucie Jay signed the document.[119] On April 24, 1916, Josef Stransky requested and received twelve hundred dollars from the board for ship passage to and from Berlin after the concert season. In this same meeting, Oswald Villard was made president of the board of directors.[120] In February of 1917, steel magnate Charles M. Schwab, of German ancestry, paid for a New York Philharmonic dinner concert at the Waldorf Hotel. Mrs. Jay voiced no objections to the event. On May 7, 1917, Mrs. Hugo Reisinger gave $5,000 to the guarantee fund, and the orchestra loaned German Carl Stoecker its celeste for his spring music fest in Connecticut.[121] Life went on as usual for the philharmonic with very few signs that a war was going on.

The capitalists of New York were in positions of power. There were no financiers of equal stature in Boston capable of attacking the New York Philharmonic, and thus the NYP remained relatively unaffected during the war. To ensure this, on June 7, 1917, in anticipation of war pressures, the philharmonic engaged a press agent for $2,000 to protect its solid footing. The first sign of difficulty came on September 27, 1917, when subscriber Thomas Elder sent a letter to Secretary Felix Leifels complaining about the German "pacifist president, Mr. Oswald Garrison Villard."[122] On October 2, Leifels defended Villard, an American of German ancestry, saying that he hoped "Germany will get a good licking." The next day Elder replied, "I myself belong to the New York National Guard and have already done some military service during this war up-state. I do not question your patriotism aside from your attitude on the subject of programs of all German music." In response to this exchange, on October 15, 1917, the philharmonic hosted a patriotic concert at the Twenty-Third Regiment Armory where it was advertised that the "committee will spare no effort to insure the success of the performances."[123] Twelve days later, on October 27, 1917, the philharmonic gave a benefit performance for "the wives and families of Brooklyn soldiers at the front." In the fall, Flinsch once again offered his resignation, and again the board refused his resignation, stating that it "declines to recognize the existence of any emergency at the present time of sufficient importance to warrant the acceptance of his resignation."[124] By January of 1918, however, Flinsch's and Villard's resignations were "regretfully" accepted.[125] While this experience was likely uncomfortable and harrowing for those involved, other than these two voluntary resignations, the New York Philharmonic was left relatively unscathed.

On April 18, 1918, the board agreed unanimously to continue concerts "without interruption." Subscriber John D. Rockefeller Jr. expressed the following resolution, which was adopted by a standing vote:

> One, it would be a serious setback to the musical development of this city to discontinue the Philharmonic concerts even for the period of the war. Two, the concerts should be continued on the same high plane as before. Three, we pledge ourselves individually to use our best efforts through personal subscriptions and in other ways under the guidance of a committee to raise a guarantee fund to cover the estimated deficit for the coming year and the balance of the deficit for the year just closed.[126]

With the backing of its wealthy capitalists, the New York Philharmonic continued normally. Mrs. Jay focused her anti-German attacks on Boston.

Jay had even deeper motives for her persistent attacks on the Boston Symphony that cut to the heart of her own economic security. In September of 1906, her brother Hermann had passed away. Estranged from his wife, much of his estate was bequeathed to Mrs. Jay and her brother, Charles. Mrs. Jay acquired a large share in the North German Lloyd Steamship Line and presumably railroad stocks from the Vanderbilt interest as well.[127] It made logical sense to support her family's interests and further their progress within the United States, which was threatened, as we shall see, by political forces directly related to the BSO.

The principal business of the North German Lloyd German Steamship Line (as well as the Anchor Steamship Line and the Vanderbilt railroad business) was to transport passengers from one place to another by sea or by rail. The Oelrichs and Vanderbilt families became unspeakably wealthy in the steamship and railroad businesses, for at no time in history had so many immigrants crossed the Atlantic or moved across America. Between 1880 and 1919, more than twenty-three million immigrants arrived in the United States, seventeen million of whom entered through the Port of New York alone.[128] During this same period, high-speed steamships replaced old sailing vessels, shortening the crossing and making it safer, faster, and more economical to transport passengers.[129] Competition between steamship companies kept steerage rates low and made massive immigration possible. As John Higham points out, business leaders placed a dollar value on the heads of immigrants who arrived in America.[130] Capitalists needed laborers for their farms, factories, mines, and mills. The Oelrichs family relied on a steady stream of immigrants to keep their enterprise profitable.

Immigrants could reach their destination much more easily because of the development of railroads that snaked throughout the country.[131] Expansion of the railroad system opened up the country to its vast natural resources. As Higham made clear, "There seemed no end to what the country could produce with men enough to do the work."[132] Nearly everyone had something to sell or produce. Industry grew in great part because of immigrants, allowing capitalists who exploited them to become the driving force in American culture. Mrs. Jay's influential friends and family became wealthy because of immigration. The Oelrichs steamship line delivered people to America, and the Vanderbilts' railroad lines transported them across the country. Their combined fortunes were directly tied to the steady flow of immigrants to, and across, the United States. For Jay, and others like her, immigrants fueled the American economy.

Muck found himself caught in the middle of an ideological battle over immigration and a rivalry between Boston and New York regarding how they made their money, as well. From 1901 to 1913, one million foreigners had come each year into the United States, and, in the seventy-year period from 1850 to 1920, fifty-two million Europeans had emigrated.[133] The United States became highly diverse, as people of various nationalities and cultural backgrounds crowded together. Muck arrived in America as its urban residents struggled to respond to rising immigrant populations. Muck's patron, Henry Lee Higginson, and New York Philharmonic patron Mrs. William Jay responded to immigration in opposing ways. John Higham describes "crosscurrents of nationalism" that developed among Americans. There was great tension between those who welcomed immigrants and believed they were good for the country and those who viewed immigrants defensively or wanted to prevent their entry.[134] Muck was caught in a tug-of-war between these two competing ideological views of restrictive and liberal nationalism.

As mentioned in chapter 1, Higginson was an officer in the Immigrant Restriction League. He worked with his cousin Senator Henry Cabot Lodge to restrict immigration to the United States, considering these newcomers to be "un-American" and potentially unassimilable.[135] Between 1880 and World War I, more than two million Jews had arrived in America, fleeing poverty or displaced by pogroms in the Russian Empire. By 1920, almost 40 percent of New York City's population was foreign born, with 480,000 Russian Jews forming the largest ethnic group of that population. Immigration congestion at Ellis Island became so great that transportation officials diverted New York–bound ships to Boston.[136] Higginson and other Boston Brahmins pushed for tighter restrictions on steamship passage to America.[137] They worked to enact federal legislation that would quarantine immigrants in their home countries until they were "fit" for passage. They pushed for literacy tests that would prevent entry of anyone unable to read or write.[138] Higginson supported Germans and imported them for his orchestra, but he had great ambivalence about accepting huge numbers of other immigrants into the country. Restrictionists eventually succeeded in limiting steamship companies from transporting massive numbers of new citizens to America, thus affecting the profits of the captains of industry, including Mrs. Jay. Higginson wrote letters to influential people at Harvard College and the Navy Department encouraging them to "take and hold fast" any German ships delivering "merchandise," or immigrants, to American ports.[139] Several North German Lloyd steamships were interned by the federal government in Boston Harbor for the duration of the war in part because of Higginson's correspondence.[140]

Jay took a contrary view on immigration. She borrowed the rhetoric of the Americanization movement and Theodore Roosevelt's 1915 Columbus Day speech that railed against "hyphenated Americans" as morally treasonous, to denounce Muck as a man who clung to a divided loyalty.[141] If German immigrants could not offer full obedience to America, then, in her view, they should be interned or deported. She saw Americanization as a transformative event, a renunciation of or divorce from the immigrants' former home. Bring immigrants in line or remove them. She viewed Muck as a haughty elite in the Junker mold who maintained his associations, spoke the German language, and continued to perform German works. German musicians, especially BSO musicians, threatened the notion that all immigrants could fall in line. German Americans who would not Americanize imperiled her economic business of transporting massive numbers of immigrants to American shores. Mrs. Jay saw a way of eliminating the competition for the New York Philharmonic while also weeding out nonconforming German immigrants who endangered the steady flow of passengers to the United States. She specifically targeted Karl Muck, the most celebrated German musician in the country. Muck represented elite conservatism and German nationalism, values that clashed with the rising American nationalist sentiments that stressed patriotic conformity during World War I.

Not surprisingly, Jay sided with big business interests, which included German steamship companies and manufacturing lobbies that railed against the restrictionist movement. The *Commercial and Financial Chronicle*, the *Wall Street Journal*, the *New York Bulletin*, the *National Association of Manufacturers*, the *American Iron and Steel Institute*, leading Chambers of Commerce, Pulitzer's the *World* newspaper, and many others spoke out against immigrant restriction in the decade leading up to World War I and pressured the senate to maintain an open-door policy.[142] Their marketing brochures "cast off the nativist outlook." They attacked xenophobia and "celebrated the economic value of immigration."[143] Eastern Europeans and German Americans added their collective voice in support of capitalists, which "swelled into a mighty, insistent chorus."[144] They argued that America needed workers. "Deport and regulate if you must," they argued, "but don't restrict."[145] Mrs. Jay was an anti-restrictionist and an assimilationist who believed that America could absorb massive numbers of new immigrants, provided these newcomers learn American ways and transition into mainstream society. German musicians, particularly Jay's rivals in Boston, spoke German and played German music when Germany was at war with America and its allies. Jay saw a way of reducing the competition for the New York Philharmonic while also disenfranchising Germans like Muck, who she argued were disloyal and who endangered the steady flow of passengers to the United States.

Mrs. Jay had other motives behind her actions against the BSO and Karl Muck. She hoped to achieve greater social mobility and power. Long before the demonization of Muck, New York's upper-class community had taken on the role of social arbiter in the city's cultural affairs. It worked hard to "create a class segmented public sphere" that catered to its own needs.[146] As elite wealth expanded, so did the income gap between the "haves" and the "have-nots." With this growing economic and social chasm between industry leaders and wage earners, upper-class New Yorkers became increasingly class conscious. New York was on the move as a world financial giant, and its leaders wanted their social life to reflect their wealth and power.[147] They hosted elaborate society events at these institutions, and they dressed in expensive jewel-adorned gowns to display their wealth, setting a national standard in social and cultural affairs.[148]

Mrs. Jay was a high-society matron. Like Mrs. Astor in the decades before her, she embodied aristocratic New York and became a leader of note during the war.[149] She had the pedigree, money, connections, ambition, and organizational ability to take on this role.[150] Mrs. Jay was clever enough to utilize her elite position in cultural affairs to destabilize and challenge Boston's musical establishment. She exploited wartime patriotism in her campaign against Muck, elevating New York's cultural sphere by bringing different segments of the elite population together under one collective cause.[151] Mrs. Jay was not afraid of publicity. She knew how to use it to her advantage. She had no compunction pounding on the door of an adversary or picking up the telephone to call authorities in the federal government if it suited her purpose. Because she was so well connected in both the old Knickerbocker elite circles and among the nouveau riche, she had the power to communicate with anyone she desired to influence change in support of her objectives.[152]

And, like Caroline Astor, who demanded to be called "Mrs. Astor," Lucie Jay insisted on being addressed as "Mrs. Jay." This married name conferred on her a position of distinguished superiority over other elites and reminded the public of her husband's English and French heritage rather than alerting them to her German surname, Oelrichs.[153] Mrs. Jay's husband, William, was a member of the most prominent New York legal family. He was descended from John Jay, one of New York's earliest statesmen. He was a member of the Continental Congress, the country's first Supreme Court judge, and a signer of the 1783 Treaty of Paris. As a politician, he advocated for a national art museum, and, as president of the Union League Club, he organized the city's wealthiest men to lay the framework for the Metropolitan Museum of Art in New York.[154] William, too, was a lawyer with great political power. He was a member of the New York Knickerbocker Club and the Sons of the American Revolution. The Jays were members of many clubs and social organizations and sat on the boards of many city businesses. William Jay was the founder and president of the New York Coaching Club, and the couple regularly led the procession of carriage horses in the annual Coaching Club Parade on Fifth Avenue and into Central Park.[155] His prominence gave Mrs. Jay social legitimacy in an era when ancestral progenitors determined one's cultural place in society. Mrs. Jay's married, Anglo-Norman name gave her the authority to speak publicly regarding matters of war, and she used her name as a weapon against Muck.

Mrs. Jay, like Mrs. Astor, also presided over a large social enterprise. Her place in society held great influence. She had a huge number of names on her calling list. Rallying around issues of war, patriotism, and anti-German hysteria gave her topics that everyone in elite society could agree upon, buttressing her position and power within that community. Mrs. Jay wanted to shape the cultural landscape of her city. Muck was her vehicle for gaining greater power and prestige.

Just like Mrs. Astor, Mrs. Jay utilized a series of social controls to prevent individuals from entering her circle of influence. She was the

Figure 4.8. "The Coach of William Jay: At the Annual Meeting of the Coaching Club." This image shows William and Lucie Jay on their four-in-hand. W. S. Vanderbilt Allen, *Sporting Incidents: Being a Collection of Sixteen Plates Done in Color, with numerous Smaller Cuts, Representing the Most Important Events of the Track, Field and Road* (New York: Henry T. Thomas, 1893). Courtesy of Thomas J. Goodwin and the New York Public Library Rare Book Collection.

"center of the social mechanism which admitted or excluded individuals from society." She had "almost absolute power to make or mar the social destiny of those who sought her patronage."[156] Elite matrons like Mrs. Jay "set standards of behavior in public and private places." They created forms of entertainment and dictated appropriate dress, decorum, and other aspects of daily life. Mrs. Jay behaved like an overbearing parental figure, teaching arts patrons appropriate concert etiquette, as if they were children.[157] She attempted to influence musical taste, deciding which music or musicians were appropriate for concerts, and she was not shy about publicizing her opinions in the local newspapers.

Mrs. Jay's efforts elevated her own status, both as a woman and as an older grande dame of the New York elite set.[158] Mrs. Jay wrote newspaper editorials, which were highly effective tools for increasing her social position. She hosted meetings at her Fifth Avenue home, creating an artificial community that strategized ways to spread the word about Muck, organizing women within her circle to picket BSO events.

Younger woman within her sphere of influence looked up to her and obeyed her demands to boycott Boston Symphony concerts.[159]

Having a cause that she could throw herself into so fully may also have served as a tonic for Mrs. Jay. She had suffered three personal tragedies: first, the loss of her one-year-old daughter Dorothy from diphtheria in 1888; the death of her seventeen-year-old daughter Julia from the same disease in 1896; and the sudden death of her husband from a heart attack in 1915, the year she began to attack Muck in Boston.[160] Such catastrophic losses might have defeated her, and yet, to the contrary, Mrs. Jay had found a cause to absorb her time. She found sympathetic support from members within her privileged community. At a society horse show, just after the announcement of Julia's death, newspapers reported that "there were too many empty boxes and seats, however, and too much depression over the news of Miss Jay's death to make the afternoon session other than a dull one, and by 6 o'clock the Garden was virtually deserted by the society occupants."[161] In 1915, when William passed away, the *New York Times* reported that Trinity Church "was packed with socially prominent New Yorkers and representatives from his many clubs and businesses."[162] Mrs. Jay had the encouragement of her friendship circle. She would guard her own economic livelihood, and she would ensure the survival of the New York Philharmonic by harming its competition. She would help to expand New York's cultural position.

Jay's various motives fueled effective action against Karl Muck and the BSO. She leveraged anti-German hysteria and the expansion of federal powers to unseat him from his position and weaken the BSO's national dominance. While many people naively believed that music was a universal and emotional expression of mankind and therefore exempt from political strife, Jay (and many others) proved that this was not the case. Indeed, as Muck learned, music was not apolitical, and it served a very partisan purpose.

"The Star-Spangled Banner" Controversy: The Press, and Rising Populist Sentiment against Karl Muck

Lucie Jay was not the only one to attack Karl Muck and the Boston Symphony Orchestra. On the morning of October 30, 1917, Karl Muck and the members of the BSO boarded a passenger train bound for Providence, Rhode Island, for their evening concert at Infantry Hall. The musicians traveled fully equipped with their instruments and sheet music for the performance. Meanwhile, Symphony Hall management received a telegram representing several women's organizations, including the French, Chopin, Monday Morning, MacDowell, Schubert, Chaminade, and State Federation of Women's Clubs; as well as the Liberty Loan Company of Rhode Island, requesting that the orchestra perform "The Star-Spangled Banner" at the evening Providence concert.[163]

Higginson conferred with BSO manager Charles Ellis, publicist William E. Walter, and assistant manager William H. Brennan before collectively deciding to ignore the telegram. It was too late to make such a request, as programs were decided upon well in advance. In an age before fax machines, photocopiers, and computer printers, it was difficult to make changes at the last minute or to provide the musicians with a score quickly enough to be included for the concert. Moreover, "The Star-Spangled Banner" was not the national anthem during World War I and was not the familiar piece we know today. It would undergo many changes with a variety of arrangements before becoming the official national anthem in 1931.[164]

Ultimately, Higginson's unwillingness to adopt populist sentiment regarding patriotic music provided the primary reason the piece was not performed at the Providence concert, inspiring a backlash against the well-known conductor. As biographer Bliss Perry noted, Higginson had reservations about performing the work. This popular piece was included on summer Pops programs, which typically featured lighter music, and not during the more serious symphonic concerts by the symphony. Higginson held an elitist view that "persons of musical training" would find it "out of place" and that "people who have more zeal than judgment" should not be allowed to make the decisions about programming. "The Star-Spangled Banner," according to Higginson, was "not well-fitted for a full-stringed symphony orchestra, good as it is for a military band."[165] Years later, the *New York Times* argued that this episode could have been avoided if Higginson had appropriately judged the climate of the country and acted accordingly.[166] He held to his convictions for the Providence concert, however, and was not easily persuaded, seeing patriotic airs as popular works, not appropriate for institutions such as the BSO, for they were a "violation of artistic taste."[167]

Australian-born American John R. Rathom, editor and manager of the *Providence Journal* and one of the biggest promoters of anti-German hysteria in the United States, warned Providence on the day of the BSO concert that "the programme as announced is almost entirely German in character" and that "Professor Muck is a man of notoriously pro-German affiliations." He called for putting Muck "to the test."[168] Following the concert, Rathom fabricated a sensational story out of the BSO's omission of "The Star-Spangled Banner" from the Providence concert, reporting that Muck was a German nationalist who had intentionally refused on political grounds to play the anthem, an account that was echoed in newspapers around the country, propagating a myth that lasted throughout the war and is often repeated today.[169] "The Star-Spangled Banner" was used to attack Muck, an effective tactic because the episode occurred at a high point in the CPI's anti-German propaganda campaign. The zealous newspaperman spread reports among his readership that Muck was pro-German and a friend of Kaiser Wilhelm. Rathom distorted the facts, claiming to uncover foreign espionage plots that were later revealed to be fraudulent.[170] One such plot suggested that Muck intended to destroy American munitions factories. On November 21, 1917, the *New York Times* reported that Rathom "thrilled and enthused" seven hundred members of the Pilgrim Publicity Association at the Boston City Club with a story of "German spies in Boston" outlining his great campaign against them. He alluded to music people in Boston being part of the plot.[171]

Rathom was an Anglocentric muckraker who disliked Germans and advocated American involvement in World War I. In 1906, he worked as a reporter for the *Providence Journal*, becoming its managing editor six years later. British propaganda operatives purportedly utilized Rathom to distribute anti-German messages in the American press. Newspapers, including many in New York, reprinted *Providence Journal* exclusives. The national press turned Rathom into a hero. In 1919, he allied himself with Attorney General A. Mitchell Palmer to fight Bolshevism, and he became the director of the Associated Press.[172]

During Rathom's bitter attack of Muck in Providence, Higginson argued that "Dr. Muck had never heard anything about ["The Star-Spangled Banner" request]." Karl Muck was likewise upset by Rathom's reports, saying that "it was a miserable, cheap lie."[173] Higginson did not inform Muck about the "The Star-Spangled Banner" appeal until the concert was over, when the ensemble was on the train bound for Boston, and by then the trouble had already begun. Muck was upset that he had not been made aware before the concert, for, as he claimed in a later telling, he had no objection to playing the piece and, in fact, suggested that it was entirely appropriate as a guest to honor the request of his host.[174] Musicologist Matthew Mugmon correctly points out that there are inconsistencies in Muck's story and that the conductor likely shared Higginson's elitist view that the patriotic piece lacked musical value. But Muck was also fearful, and he wished to keep a low profile, certain that problems would escalate for him with the omission of the piece from the program.[175]

Following Rathom's newspaper campaign, the Rhode Island Council of Defense adopted resolutions condemning Muck, and the Rhode

Island police commissioner barred him from future concerts in the state. Higginson worked hard to defend Muck and accept responsibility for the problem, explaining that the omission of "The Star-Spangled Banner" had nothing to do with Muck or his patriotism. Higginson provided this comparison: "If these same people were to demand that, as a proof of loyalty, you should wear a star spangled blue waistcoat and a red-and-white-striped-trousers, you would refuse, not from lack of patriotism, but from a sense of what is appropriate."[176] Despairing of the sordid affair, Higginson lamented to a relative that "the chief people who attack [Muck and the BSO] are those who do not go to the concert, who aren't in the cities where the Orchestra has played."[177] John Rathom intentionally defamed Muck to sell more copies of his newspaper.[178]

It is possible that Mrs. Jay was in a questionable collaboration with Rathom, although the relationship between the two cannot be conclusively proven.[179] Perhaps it is enough to say that both John Rathom and Mrs. Jay worked in tandem. Both were equally effective in their war on Muck, and both benefitted from his downfall in their own unique ways. Rathom was a member and officer of the American Defense Society.[180] Richard Hurd, chairman of that organization, and W. T. Hornsday, trustee of the ADS, and "scores of other organizations and individuals," made known their attitude toward Muck and his backers.[181] As we shall see later in this chapter, Mrs. Jay worked with members of the ADS to criminalize Muck. While no primary source material exists to prove that Mrs. Jay specifically instructed John Rathom to falsely accuse Muck in his newspaper, given Mrs. Jay's prior and mounting conspiratorial actions against Muck, it is possible that she recruited the "unidentified ladies" who contacted Higginson about "The Star-Spangled Banner" and then enlisted Rathom to spearhead the public assault on Muck's alleged disloyalty. Even the short-lived *American* newspaper recounted that Mrs. Jay was the chairperson of a "body of women vigilantes" who reported to the press and the federal authorities "every doubtful phrase they hear in the high social circles to which they belong." The *American* claimed that Jay was "a sort of feminine Ku Klux Klan traveling in the best set" and that their "effectiveness lies in their secrecy. Their names appear on no list, and society does not know who they are. . . . Any seditious or treasonable or even questionable—from a standpoint of patriotism—phrase which may be spoken at a Fifth Avenue or Park Avenue tea is likely to be heard by one of these women, who are pledged to report it." The paper claimed, "Similar committees are said to be operating in Boston, Philadelphia, Washington, Chicago and other large cities. They are all associated with the parent body in New York."[182]

Interestingly, sources conflict regarding the New York Philharmonic's first performances of "The Star-Spangled Banner." One source suggests that the orchestra delayed playing it until national anti-German hysteria had reached its peak in the winter of 1918, and another source suggests that the orchestra performed the piece shortly before the *Providence Journal* attacked Karl Muck.[183] Other orchestras, such as the New York Orchestra Society, began performing the anthem in the autumn of 1917, feeling patriotic pressure, but the New York Philharmonic's omission of the piece at their performances until 1918 was not front page news.

Indifferent to the New York Philharmonic's patriotic programming choices, Mrs. Jay was relentless in her pursuit of Muck. She used the press as a device of persuasion against him. She knew that news reports about the well-known conductor would be incredibly popular and would reach millions of people "anonymously" and "simultaneously," having the power to radically alter public opinion.[184] In fact, her own relatives and friends had been prey to the public's thirst for stories and photographs of the rich.[185] Beginning in the 1880s, newspaper editors realized that Americans were fascinated by the lives of the wealthy class and eager to be entertained with gossip about them. The mansions along New York's Fifth Avenue became a tourist destination, and spectators "lined the sidewalks for a glimpse of well-dressed opera goers." At times, affluent New Yorkers welcomed the publicity, inviting journalists to society balls, the opera, and other public venues to report on their activities.[186] In these moments, America's aristocrats relished their celebrity status, for it heightened their visibility and prestige. At other times, they valued their privacy, acquiring railcars, yachts, and country estates to escape the public's gaze. Scandals of any kind could destroy those involved. The upper classes worked hard to maintain their private lives and prevent any sign of scandal or inappropriate behavior from leaking out.[187] Avoiding bad publicity was a "necessary survival skill" in a country hungry for celebrity news.[188] Mrs. Jay was aware that elites paid off gossip columnists, and she knew about weekly tabloids such as New Jersey's *Town Topics* or *Diversions and Achievements*. Gossip was no laughing matter, and a social matron like Mrs. Jay was a public relations expert. As well versed as she was in eluding victimization herself, she was entirely savvy when it came to attacking Muck in the media, feeding him to the press like meat to a hungry lion, hoping the press would devour him. Her goal was to paralyze the prominent Boston Symphony establishment so that the New York Philharmonic could gain advantage.

Muck was particularly vulnerable to publicity. In a pre-television, pre-radio era, he was a huge celebrity. Articles about him appeared in influential newspapers throughout the country. Muck endorsed the BSO and a variety of musical instrument manufacturers, and photographic images of his face routinely appeared in national newspaper advertisements. Personalities like Muck were even more popular than debutantes, precursors to modern-day movie stars or sports personalities. As New York historian Eric Homberger points out, "It does not seem to matter what the man is the very best at; so long as he has won out in competition over all others."[189] Muck was perceived by many to have surpassed all other conductors in Europe and America. Newspaper editors knew that stories about celebrities like Muck would sell papers.

On November 4, 1917, five days after the Providence concert, overtly nationalistic Edwin Warfield, ex-governor of Maryland, president of the Fidelity Trust Company, and one of Baltimore's foremost financiers, threatened to violently assault Muck if he appeared with the Boston Symphony Orchestra in his city for its scheduled November 7 concert. Warfield reported to the press:

> Karl Muck shall not lead an orchestra in Baltimore. I told the police board members that this man would not be allowed to insult the people of the birthplace of the *Star-Spangled Banner*. I told them that mob violence would prevent it, if necessary, and that I would gladly lead the mob to prevent the insult to my country and my flag. I told them that I know of a thousand others who would gladly aid in leading the throng . . . our people have only contempt for the man who utters a criticism of the demand to play our national anthem.[190]

Warfield, in fact, had arranged a large patriotic mass meeting at Baltimore's Lyric Theatre with two thousand angry protesters, including soldiers from Camp Meade, in attendance. When a resolution was read declaring that Dr. Muck should not be allowed to lead the orchestra in Baltimore, "the applause was deafening."[191] Warfield told the crowd that Muck was a Prussian who had said "to hell with your flag and your national anthem" and, therefore, "should be in an internment camp." The crowd cheered for almost a minute. A woman who had been waving the flag from a box near the stage shouted, "Muck should have been shot," to which the crowd chanted, "Kill Muck, Kill Muck," as the meeting concluded. Muck was an innocent man, attacked with threats of violence based on reports that he had not conducted the patriotic air.

"The Star-Spangled Banner" inspired great populist sentiment and civic pride in Baltimore, for it had been written in 1814 by Francis Scott Key after he witnessed the British bombardment of Fort McHenry during the War of 1812. The state of Maryland had been pressuring

Figure 4.9. Former governor of Maryland Edwin Warfield incited violence against Karl Muck during a patriotic rally in Baltimore. Courtesy of the Library of Congress, Prints and Photographs Division.

the federal government for a century to make the popular song the national anthem. Warfield's actions brought needed publicity to their cause and propelled "The Star-Spangled Banner" into the national spotlight. His attacks, however, alerted Muck and Boston Symphony management to the volatility of the public during wartime and, thus, led them to remove that city from the BSO concert tour schedule.[192] Interestingly, Mrs. Jay's father and grandfather had been prominent businessmen in Baltimore before moving to New York, raising suspicion that she may have influenced Warfield's actions. It made competitive sense to whip up animosity against the Boston Symphony in a city where the New York Philharmonic had hoped to tour again and gain a financial foothold.

Mrs. Jay Continues to Fan the Flames of Rage against the Boston Conductor

Even with the fear of mob violence, the Boston Symphony continued its concert schedule, intent on meeting its professional and financial obligations and refusing to be intimidated. On Sunday afternoon, December 16, 1917, Muck led the Boston Symphony in a benefit performance at Symphony Hall for victims of the Halifax Explosion. Responding to new wartime pressure for patriotic music, the program began with a rousing rendition of "The Star-Spangled Banner." The concert starred Fritz Kreisler, the famous Austrian violinist, and Nellie Melba, the well-known soprano that Muck had planned to work with the year before. As mentioned earlier, Mrs. Jay had accused Muck of refusing to perform with Melba because of her connection to Great Britain. Not only did this concert raise needed money for Halifax disaster relief, but it also implicitly suggested that Germans, British, and Americans could work together harmoniously and that music could bridge the political and national divide. Such idealism flew in the face of wartime realities in the United States, however, and the assault on Muck's character persisted, along with calls for his dismissal by Mrs. Jay and others.

Muck's life spiraled further out of his control. Three days after Boston had heard the news of the Halifax disaster, the US Department of Justice questioned him about his citizenship, assuming he was a German subject and attempting to classify him as an "enemy alien" under Section 4067 of the Alien Enemies Act. Muck, however, was a Swiss national, having summered in Switzerland with his family since the mid-1860s when he was seven years old, having lived there with his father for a brief period in the early 1870s after his mother's death, and having taken out citizenship papers there when he was twenty-one years old.[193] During World War I, the United States was at war with Germany and not Switzerland, so any claim of enemy alien status would be invalid.[194] Anita Muck worked diligently to prove Muck's Swiss citizenship before the BSO concert tour, and on January 7, 1918, confirmation arrived from Bern, Switzerland, in the form of an official yellowed document, number 644, issued on March 4, 1881, stating that Muck was a citizen of Neuheim in the canton of Zug. Muck's papers were authenticated by Paul Ritter, the Swiss ambassador to the United States.[195] Still suspicious, the US federal government placed Muck under surveillance, requiring that he inform authorities at all times of his whereabouts.[196] The country feared its foreign nationals, and Muck was no exception.

Mrs. Jay repeatedly called into question Muck's national status, continuing to do so even though he held Swiss citizenship, carried a Swiss passport, and was legally classified as a resident of Switzerland. Granted, he had lived in Germany and admired that nation, and yet federal agents reported that they had "found nothing to incriminate him as a German agent or as having performed any act which is prejudicial to the interests of our country."[197] The Bureau of Investigation knew that Muck could not be classified as an "enemy alien" under the terms of President Wilson's wartime proclamations, although he had been labelled a "denizen" of Germany. It simply did not have adequate evidence to prove that he was a dangerous threat to the United States. Regardless, they followed up on every lead, seeking some form of guilt.[198] Muck felt the full weight of the government's power upon him.

On January 22, 1918, Mrs. Jay protested by letter to Higginson expressing that she "couldn't stand seeing that hateful Dr. Muck" conduct the orchestra, although she had never met him and perhaps had never even attended a BSO concert.[199] Still, she demanded Muck's dismissal.[200] Higginson responded eight days later that "if your request was carried out, the orchestra would disband, and it would be owing to a small number of people who take your view. . . . These men . . . have behaved perfectly during the past three years—no easy matter, considering their temperaments. Do you wish the responsibility of throwing these men out of employ?"[201] Higginson understood the plight of home-front families waiting for news of their loved ones during the war, and he also sympathized with his musicians, who did not cause the war and deserved to be able to keep their jobs. But he had no tolerance for Mrs. Jay, who for competitive reasons wished an innocent conductor harm. He replied, "As to the women who have husbands and brothers and sons and grandsons at the front, and who are nervous about them or else deeply grieved, there is only one word to be said. We must pity them, sympathize with them to the utmost. . . . [I]f they are nervous or cannot bear to hear a German conduct the orchestra . . . I have nothing to say."[202] He wrote, "It is illogical and perhaps irrational; yet most of us, in our disgust and horror at Germany's conduct in the war, could not help transferring our dislike to any object that reminded us vividly of Germany. Now Dr. Muck, however innocent he might be, was certainly one of those objects."[203] Higginson supported his conductor and was convinced that Muck was not interested in political matters.

While the BSO attempted to remain politically neutral, the country was becoming increasingly xenophobic. The symphony's management maintained its scheduled routine, which included its yearly national tour. Newspapers had fomented such a threatening atmosphere around Karl Muck, however, that a scheduled concert tour of Midwestern cities was abandoned. Also, the Department of Justice ruled that because of the war emergency, the orchestra, made up of German musicians, could not enter or perform in the District of Columbia. Ever present for Muck and his orchestra was the fear that patriotic vigilantes would become violent and carry out what the Baltimore mob had chanted for—the execution of the Boston conductor.[204]

Developments in Europe did not help matters for Muck. The BSO's winter concert tour coincided with America's bloodiest and most extensive military involvement to date in the war. In March of 1918, Russia surrendered on the eastern front, freeing up fifty German units to fight on the western front. American casualties increased dramatically during this period as the US military played a crucial role in stopping the German advance toward Paris. Many patrons of the symphony could not bring themselves to attend the concerts. Higginson wrote of the situation to his friend, Charles Eliot, president of Harvard, "This morning I have been hearing the words of a wise, enthusiastic lover of music and of our Orchestra. She takes her tickets, but she does not go because she cannot bear to hear these Germans play. She tells me that many, many people feel the same way; and when I asked her why there were not many vacant seats, she said they give their seats away."[205] Many mothers and sisters of soldiers could not watch Muck conduct, although they continued to support the symphony.

While sadness over the war caused some formerly enthusiastic Bostonians to give up their concert seats, Mrs. Jay's reaction in New York was far more severe. She used her influence in an attempt to prevent the Boston Symphony from performing in her city. She took advantage of anti-Germanism, exploiting catastrophe to secure her own advantage by launching a media campaign to prevent the BSO from performing at Carnegie Hall and the Academy of Music. Her husband William Jay had been the vice president of the *New York Herald* until his death in 1915.[206] Founded by Democrat James Gordon Bennett, the *Herald* was perhaps the most important and damning influence against Muck. It was considered one of the most sensational leading circulation newspapers in the United States, appealing primarily to business interests.[207] As Joseph Horowitz points out, the newspaper "often relied on friction with conventional wisdom to ignite controversy."[208] Bennett died in 1918, made weak by William Randolph Hearst, publisher of the *Journal*, who accused Bennett of Comstock violations. Bennett never recovered. Jay was able to take advantage of her husband's influence and the *Herald*'s circumstance to say whatever she wanted, as long as her attacks on Muck sold papers.

In addition to the *New York Herald*, the New York Philharmonic was affiliated with a variety of newspapers that sought to build circulation. Many newspapers at the time used unscrupulous methods to bring in readers. As mentioned earlier, newspaper mogul Joseph Pulitzer had bequeathed a sizable contribution to the orchestra, funded through his liberal and pro-immigrant the *World* newspaper. The *World* reprinted many of the sensational stories that John Rathom, of the *Providence Journal*, first published and often reprinted Mrs. Jay's opinions running in other newspapers.[209] The *World* published scandals, crime stories, and dramatic exposes of tenement abuse, and it often came to the defense of immigrants. New York Philharmonic board member and one of the original guarantors, Dorothea Draper, was the granddaughter of Charles Dana, editor and founder of the conservative *New York Sun*. The president of the New York Philharmonic, Oswald Garrison Villard, was the German-American owner of the *New York Post* and the editor of the *Nation* magazine. He was the grandson of abolitionist William Lloyd Garrison. The *New York Post*'s music critic, Henry Frinck, was a committed Wagnerian who idolized Karl Muck.[210] The *Post* tried to stay neutral in its reporting during the war and reprinted only stories about Mrs. Jay and Karl Muck that other newspapers had published the day before. Historian Richard Wetzel suggests that Muck "became the victim of slanderous newspaper reports and malicious reviews by music critics" in New York.[211] It is true that many newspapers seemed eager to publish anything about Karl Muck that would promote their newspapers and bolster the city of New York, but not all of the New York papers were so quick to disparage him. Several newspapers, including those affiliated with the New York Philharmonic like the *Sun* and the *Post*, were measured in their response to the controversy.

Mrs. Jay knew which papers she could count on in her campaign to sabotage the BSO tour in New York City. In March, she hosted a meeting of society ladies and gentlemen at her home, in an attempt to arouse public interest in removing the "blotch upon the otherwise proud patriotic record" of her city.[212] She created a petition that read, "We the undersigned, protest Dr. Karl Muck coming to this town, as we regard him as a dangerous alien, having been a close friend of Von Bernstorff and is now a representative of the Kaiser, as he acknowledges in *Who is Who*, of 1916 and 1917."[213] One thousand men, women, and organizations signed the petition "in her fight against Muck."[214] On March 12, 1918, she traveled to the office of John Gilchrist, commissioner of licenses for Carnegie Hall, to have the Boston Symphony's performance contract rescinded, presenting her petition and asking Mr. Gilchrist whether he did not consider it sufficient reason to revoke the permit.[215] Gilchrist argued that the BSO did not need a special license for its concert and that "this department at present sees no reason why it should prevent Dr. Muck's appearance with his orchestra. There is no evidence that the law is being violated or the public peace or decency endangered."[216] Not satisfied with Gilchrist's response, Jay took the matter to Carnegie Hall's upper management and spoke with C. C. Smith, who echoed Gilchrist's sentiments that "the orchestra concerts would be handled just as any other orchestra concerts here."[217]

Mrs. Jay reported to the *New York Herald* that "this is a fight to a finish, and we will not stop until such disgraceful exhibitions have been stopped."[218] Several prominent New Yorkers submitted their opinion about Muck to the press, offering their views as to why he should not be allowed to perform in their city. The *New York Herald* reported that "patriotic organizations, preachers, artists, and patrons of music formed in one solid phalanx to oppose the Prussian orchestra leader."[219] Mrs. Henry Ashton Crosby, a city socialite and wife of a banking and railroad magnate, blamed Muck for the war, chastising him for being alive while so many American soldiers were dead. "Compare these musicians, able bodied, with their eyes, legs and arms, to the millions of innocent men who through Prussian frightfulness, can never earn a livelihood again."[220] American baritone David Bispham, known for his excellent diction and wonderful interpretations of art songs, expressed his opinion that "Muck is not tolerated in this country."[221] Miss Elizabeth Marbury, a well-known theatrical and literary agent in New York City, who was raised in one of the city's oldest and most influential society families, expressed her disapproval of Muck.[222] Mrs. August Belmont, the wife of New York financier and Belmont Park race track developer, wrote a letter in support of Jay.[223] George Gould, son of Jay Gould, one of New York's richest and most influential men, called the BSO the "Boston Alien Enemy Orchestra." He indignantly argued that Baltimore was "so much more patriotic than New York that it can have a mass meeting and arrange a tar and feather party ... while New York is perfectly indifferent is an insult to us and to our flag by a citizen of the most unspeakable nation of the world, is a matter of shame and a cause for humiliation upon the part of those whose ancestors have fought for this country."[224] Once again a capitalist praised Baltimore, the very city the New York Philharmonic needed on its concert tour schedule.

Even Walter Damrosch, the German American conductor of the New York Symphony Orchestra, who had supported Karl Muck at the outset of the war, publicly dismissed him, echoing comments made by other prominent New Yorkers.[225] Damrosch lashed out at Muck's "cynical disregard of the sanctity of our national air," protecting his own fragile reputation by attacking the Boston conductor. That he did not enjoy the task is evident by his chauvinistic remarks about Mrs. Jay, claiming that she had no place in the home-front cultural battle because of her gender: "Mrs. Jay's sex disbars her from wearing the khaki and shouldering a rifle."[226]

Jay inspired several prominent clergymen of the city's most endowed churches to make appeals in support of a Muck boycott. Dr. William T. Manning, rector of Old Trinity Church, said, "We are in the midst of the greatest conflict in all history. . . . While our boys, fighting at the front in our defense, are being assailed by liquid fire, poison gas, and other like inventions of German Kultur, it is not fitting nor decent for us at concerts or in any other places, to give our countenance and support to the avowed friends and upholders of the Kaiser."[227] One pastor wrote, "I am glad to see the stand the *Herald* has taken in the matter of the Boston Symphony Concerts. As a great lover of music, I have always patronized those concerts. But no man can do so now without proclaiming himself in sympathy with the German beasts." He called Muck and other Germans in America "hordes of swine."[228] Clergymen had great influence over the New York population, and their endorsement of Mrs. Jay's manipulative scheme greatly stoked anti-German sentiment against Karl Muck.

Richard Fletcher of the New York *Chronicle* published a full-page attack against Muck, praising Jay's efforts to have him removed:

> True to the tradition of patriotic achievement with which the name she bears is identified, Mrs. William Jay is performing a great public service. . . . It must be remembered in touching this question that the German Imperial Government has employed Germans and German musicians in their propaganda in the United States so that Doktor Muck, by his unchanging pro-Germanism, has become a storm centre no less than the fortified town of Cambrai. If the American people retain Doktor Muck, they are conniving at a German victory. If the American people insist on Doktor Muck's withdrawal from his place as head of the eminent orchestra, there will be an American victory.[229]

Jay filled the *New York Herald* with editorial opinions to discredit Muck, determined to keep him from touring in her city. She argued that "Doktor Muck is pro-German in his sympathies and there is no doubt that he still bears proudly the Teutonic title, 'Königlich Preußicher General Musikdirector,' or royally Prussian. The man who bears the German Emperor's decoration and whose sympathies are most palpably opposed to the United States should not be allowed to make musical choices. [If Muck had] less willingness to accept American dollars, he would not be here." She published another letter to Higginson, this time demanding Muck's resignation.[230] Chastising Higginson she wrote, "Isn't it cause for congratulations at Potsdam and in Wilhelmstrasse that a man so distinguished as yourself should support Doktor Muck against the aspersions of other Americans." Mrs. Jay argued, "Rather a thousand times that the orchestral traditions fade from our lives than one hour be added to the war's duration by clinging to this last tentacle of the German octopus!"[231] Jay clearly wanted the Boston Symphony to "fade from our lives." She used anti-Germanism as a competitive strategy to destroy a New York Philharmonic competitor.

Jay attacked the patriotism of those who planned to attend BSO concerts in New York, reminding them, "We are at war, and at war with the German nation and the German people." She described New York's soldiers returning from battle, poisoned by German gas, maimed, or disfigured by bombs and bullets, and she asked readers whether the city was going to tolerate public appearances by a German who "hates our flag and plays the *Star-Spangled Banner* only by compulsion?" Further, and more brutally, she argued that it was "Dr. Muck's fellow subjects of the Kaiser who cut a lot of American throats." She demanded that the doors to the city be closed to Muck and that any stage that allowed him access should be "at once taken over by the government, and converted into a storage house for munitions of war."[232]

Mrs. Jay visited the military commanders at Governors Island and the Brooklyn Navy Yard and protested their acceptance of BSO tickets, which were routinely offered to soldiers during New York tours. She argued in the *New York Times* that those who accepted the tickets were not loyal Americans: "The abominable use that is being made of our soldiers and sailors to support an enemy alien in his arrogant conduct could only have sprung from the modern German brain. To use these fine men to support German propaganda through a love of music should be condemned by every loyal American and lover of fair play."[233] Due mainly to efforts by Mrs. Jay, former justice of the Appellate Division of the New York Supreme Court George L. Ingraham ruled that servicemen would no longer be permitted to accept free tickets to BSO concerts.[234] She also pleaded with civilians to give up their seats and boycott the program. Jay urged New York Daughters of the American Revolution to "suppress the musical Prussian" by not attending symphony performances and by not selling tickets to others.[235] Mrs. William Cummings Story, honorary president of the National Society of the DAR, begged every woman "to do her part."[236] Private girls' schools in New York left their seats unoccupied to "attest to their patriotism."[237]

Mrs. Jay's assaults were so sensational that the *New York Sun*, the *New York Times*, and the *New York Tribune* repeated Mrs. Jay's call to prevent Muck from performing in her city. The *American* headlined, "Mrs. Jay Moves to Stop Muck's Concerts: Patronage of Boston Symphony Is Largely Pro-German." It reported that Jay sought a "force of public opinion" to stop the scheduled Carnegie Hall concerts, for New York was not an American city if it let the orchestra and its conductor perform there.[238]

On the afternoon of March 14, just hours before the concert, Mrs. Jay threatened the Boston Symphony in the *New York Tribune*, insisting that the orchestra answer questions concerning Karl Muck, or she "would take other measures."[239] She made Muck the subject of a public investigation of his personal life:

> As conductor of the Boston Symphony Orchestra, you are to appear in New York City on Thursday night in spite of a protest signed by a group of responsible American citizens. . . . Bear in mind that Dr. Muck is a Swiss citizen, born and brought up in Germany and of German parentage. He has lived in Germany all his years and has many friends there. The New York public has every right to receive from you enlightenment as to your nationality. Are you a Swiss Citizen? If so, when were you naturalized? Have you a passport issued by the Swiss Government? Have you ever served in the German army? Have you ever referred to the American flag in contempt? If you have papers attesting to your Swiss citizenship, will you show them to a representative of our group before you appear in Carnegie Hall? Will you agree to answer these questions through the press of New York, or else will you retire permanently from public musical life?[240]

Mrs. Jay demanded that private information about Muck be made public. When Muck's citizenship papers proved legitimate, Jay pleaded with the public, "Judge his heart, not the papers in his pocket."[241] Using the power of her position and of the press to vilify Karl Muck, she pressured him to conform to her own idea of America. That she was capable of calling attention to someone so eminent suggests how vulnerable immigrants were in America during the war.

All day on March 14, 1918, New York newspapers buzzed with speculation over whether Muck would perform. The *New York Herald* reported, "Whether the investigations will bear fruit before the curtain rises on his New York performance this evening was a matter of conjecture last night."[242] The *New York Herald* waited anxiously for "developments today, which will decide definitely whether Dr. Karl Muck will lead the Boston Symphony Orchestra tonight at Carnegie Hall, or will it be prevented by the authorities."[243] The orchestra, however, maintained its schedule. Higginson announced that the BSO would play that evening with Muck at the helm and that "those who object to Dr. Muck or the nationality of any of the players can stay away if they don't want to hear the music."[244]

During that evening's Carnegie Hall concert, Mrs. Jay kept up attacks in the press, protesting the "Kaiser's Direktor" and giving New York citizens a patriotic lashing for allowing Muck to come to their city. Once again, the *New York Herald* supported Mrs. Jay with the headline, "New York Bows Its Head in Shame as Muck Leads: Fifty Uniformed Policemen and a Horde of Government Secret Service Looked on the Teutonic Element in the House." The article berated Muck for playing "The Star-Spangled Banner" after "claiming it was not fit to play." Another *New York Herald* headline read, "Muck and His Enemy Aliens [Are] Here Tonight and Patriotic Societies and Loyal Citizens by the Thousands Protest in Vain."[245]

Newspapers stirred up emotions, and tempers ran so high that several "patriotic citizens" suggested tearing down Carnegie Hall.[246] The *New York Herald* editorial page was filled with overzealous opinions arguing that "the friends of the soldiers and sailors should tear down the building before they would let him play."[247] Friendship Gloucester, of Yonkers wrote, "If New Yorkers will tolerate the Muck foulness in Carnegie Hall this evening, then, alas, New York City is stigmatized for all time. Wake up, members of the American Defense Society! Stand to your guns. Where are our minute men? Stop it."[248] John Phillips, member of the East Orange Rifles and a participant of the Vigilance Committee that had prevented Fritz Kreisler from performing in New Jersey, expressed his indignation when he discovered that there was no militant demonstration before Carnegie Hall. "Why, I expected to see 5,000 people outside this hall ready to tear it down in order to prevent this enemy alien from appearing here. . . . What's the matter with New York patriotism?"[249]

In spite of the uproar, the Carnegie Hall concert was well received. Muck played the Brahms Third Symphony under police guard. Higginson began the program by expressing his support for his maligned conductor and by showing Muck's Swiss naturalization papers.[250]

A 66b. Carnegie Hall, N Y. City.

Figure 4.10. Carnegie Hall became a contentious touring location for the Boston Symphony Orchestra under Karl Muck. Mrs. Jay persistently attacked the conductor and stirred emotions against him in the New York press. Tempers ran so high that patriotic zealots suggested tearing down Carnegie Hall. Melissa Burrage Collection.

Regardless of Jay's bitter campaign against Muck, audiences came to hear the orchestra anyway. Jay complained about "plump Germans" who "roundly applauded" as Muck entered the hall, signaling her obvious animosity toward working- and middle-class German Americans who dismissed her boycotts.[251] She saw the event as a mass assembly of Germans in an "enemy alien" venue that was dangerous for the city.

Because of her media storm, Jay became a news sensation herself, and the press reported on her activities along with Karl Muck's. Upset by the first Carnegie concert, the *New York Herald* announced that Jay continued to "wrest Dr. Muck's baton from his hand" and that she had not as yet located the "trump card" that would remove him from the podium. The reporter expressed optimism that she would be successful eventually.[252]

Jay's orchestrated campaign roused so much public attention against the celebrated conductor that the BOI began investigating, actively seeking a pretext to arrest him, assuming he would be loyal to Germany and would eventually carry out criminal activity against America in the future. As US constitutional lawyer and author David Cole points out, "The Constitution prohibits detaining a person based on fear that he will do something dangerous." Authorities need reasonable grounds and specific leads to prove a threat. Consequently, "indirect methods—pretextual law enforcement" are used.[253]

Muck could not walk down the city street without being shadowed. He reported:

> Two men, one of whom I know positively to be a detective, walked back and forth in front of my house, one from right to left and the other in the opposite direction. At 5 o'clock I went out and had some fun with them, and when the one of them whom I knew to be a detective sneaked up again, I said to him: "You must be very tired and hungry; will you not take a seat in the hall and have something to eat and drink?" He stared at me, horribly embarrassed, muttered a few inaudible words and disappeared.[254]

Mrs. Jay's attacks on Muck excited the public to such a great degree that threats of physical violence against him seemed imminent and he feared being assassinated by an "American fanatic."[255] As an avid outdoorsman, he sarcastically wrote:

> It would be great sport to bar my house into a fortress, to lock the doors and windows. I have three guns—a rifle, a repeater, and a six shooter, and two Browning automatic pistols, each a seven shooter, and a bunch of ammunition. With the help of my German valet and my strong, Irish, rabid anti-English janitor I could easily

hold my house against a cowardly mob for a few hours until the police could come.[256]

Riots were expected at Boston Symphony concerts in New York, and many Secret Service agents were stationed throughout the building.[257] During the tour, Muck was guarded around the clock by armed police officers. As a safety measure during concerts, no patron was allowed to enter the hall during performances.[258]

On March 16, undaunted by her failure either to bar Dr. Muck from conducting the BSO at Carnegie Hall or to influence patrons to remain at home, Mrs. Jay worked to prevent the BSO from performing at the Brooklyn Academy of Music, which was also on the scheduled New York tour. The press reported that Mrs. Jay labored feverishly "in an eleventh hour" to "save Brooklyn" from "desecration and invasion." Her persistence never abated, and yet the concert occurred as planned. Six uniformed police officers were stationed at the doors with numerous plain-clothed detectives scattered throughout the hall. The New York *World* reported that the officers "had nothing to do, as the audience appeared more curious to see Muck than to take active part in a demonstration for or against him."[259]

While members of the New York Grand Army of the Republic, a veterans' group, protested Muck's appearance at the nearby Borough Hall in Brooklyn, the talented conductor thoroughly entertained the crowd inside the academy. A cordial audience greeted him, thus "enabling the conductor to score once more against the faction, which has sought to bar him from the stage of the city as pro-German."[260] Muck appeared over the protests of his antagonists and was heartily received by a house almost as crowded as Carnegie Hall. The *World* proclaimed, "There can be no doubt that the advantage was all with Dr. Muck and against Mrs. William Jay and her anti-Muck followers."[261] There are limits to press vilification campaigns, and the audience in this case did not respond as Mrs. Jay had hoped.

Before the first intermission, Muck received three curtain calls, and on the third had the entire orchestra rise and bow to the applause, eliciting a fresh outburst of clapping, which outdid what had come before.[262] The *World* reported, "Boston won this round but it would not be the last. Nor did the mild attempt at heckling that followed tend to oil the waters of a muddy troubled morning. . . . [I]t did have the effect of stiffening the belligerency that has marked Mrs. Jay's attitude since she started out to retire the Boston Symphony leader from semi-public life."[263]

Interestingly, the *World* had been attacking Muck since Rathom had sensationalized him in November, and yet by March the paper

Figure 4.11. Brooklyn Academy of Music, 1920. The New York Grand Army of the Republic protested Muck's appearance at the Brooklyn Academy of Music. Secret Service agents guarded Muck and the Academy of Music during the performance. Melissa Burrage Collection.

took an entirely different view, sarcastically reporting after the academy concert that nothing violent or threatening had occurred when Muck conducted the symphony there:

> Not a single national disaster was reported in the morning newspapers. . . . As Dr. Muck raised his baton 100,000,000 people with bated breath waited for the first note. Not a munitions plant from Connecticut to California blew up. . . . The suspense was nerve-wracking. When the orchestra stopped playing, nowhere was the horizon lighted by the dull-red glare from a ship-yard in flames. The concert closed with the Prelude from *Tristan und Isolde*. When the end came and the audience rose to go, no word had come over the wires about the destruction of the Brooklyn Navy Yard or the capture of Fort Wadsworth by hostile forces armed with fiddles and trombones. It was a fearful fiasco on Dr. Muck's part after all the elaborate preparations, the Boston Symphony Orchestra furnished the ticket holders with nothing more sensational than a concert of the usual excellence.[264]

The concert was a huge success. Mrs. Jay, however, was thoroughly disgusted that the performance had occurred in the first place. She badgered the directors of the academy to prevent Muck from conducting there in the future.[265] Charles D. Adkins, director of the academy, called a special meeting to discuss the problem: "Despite the warmth of his reception and the loyalty of the orchestra subscribers, who turned out in their sartorial best to all but fill the [hall] from footlight to high gallery," the Brooklyn Institute "has declined to renew its contract for the season ahead."[266] The conservative *New York Sun* weighed in, having been mysteriously absent from reporting on Muck, finally suggesting that his "sacrifice is hinted."[267] Adkins lamented, "It is too bad that a great artist should have to be sacrificed to patriotism, but that, I suppose, is what we must expect, at a time like this. 'Sincere people' are likely to be carried away by patriotism and after all it is higher than art."[268] Mrs. Jay had successfully influenced the academy to ban Muck from performing there in the future. Latching on to the *Sun*'s report, the *Providence Journal* and the *World* published the same information in the next day's newspaper. "Brooklyn wants no more of Muck. Brooklyn Institute of Arts and Sciences announced yesterday by the Board of Trustees that the contract with Major Henry Lee Higginson would not be renewed."[269]

The American Defense Society
Calls for Muck's Internment

Just after the Brooklyn Academy concert, the American Defense Society voiced its opinion on Muck. The ADS was a wartime watchdog group made up of business and professional men who self-funded the organization and received subsidies from large corporations.[270] They had an economic interest in the growth of the state and the war economy. This small grassroots organization grew to a multimillion member force in just a few years, becoming a formidable extension of the federal government.[271] Hundreds of members of the ADS were deputized as "home front police" to supplement the Justice Department's staff of three hundred investigators.[272] An improvisational period resulted, and coercion and vigilante justice was rampant, ranging from local gossip, newspaper reports, flag wrappings, lynchings, calls for internment, deportations, and executions.[273] The ADS raided private homes and arrested scores of suspected spies, many of them eastern European immigrants. It was not the only volunteer organization playing a threatening role on the home front. The American Protective League trained an army of twenty-five thousand amateur spies who conducted three million investigations during the war, setting up checkpoints across the country to inspect enemy alien registration cards. In 1919, the group was so militant in its efforts that it broke up a May Day Parade in Centralia, Washington, capturing Wesley Everett, an International Workers of the World leader, killing him and dragging his body

Figure 4.12. American Defense Society Vigilance Corps poster. The American Defense Society, a wartime watchdog group, called for Muck's internment. Courtesy of the New York State Library Manuscripts and Special Collections, Albany, New York. US GEN 591.

through the city streets. During the war, the Ku Klux Klan of Birmingham, Alabama, gained vigilante authority, reporting that it was "on the lookout for alien enemies" and disloyalty of all kinds.[274] The growth of the KKK after World War I was a Protestant response to immigration and ethnic diversity its members saw around them.[275]

In New York City, a powerful community of elites emerged under the pretense of patriotism and service, forming a regional ADS chapter. Members included some of the wealthiest people in the world—men like John D. Rockefeller Jr., George Gould, and William Guggenheim. Guggenheim was chairman of both the New York Vigilance Committee and the American Defense Society, and he took an active role in destroying Muck's career. John Rathom, the editor of the *Providence Journal* who had attacked Muck for not playing "The Star-Spangled Banner," was also a member. Theodore Roosevelt served on the ADS advisory board, later becoming the organization's honorary president. The society worked to preserve its big-business agenda. During the BSO tour in New York, ADS chairman William Guggenheim aggressively lashed out at Muck in the *New York Herald* and other papers: "We gave the Muck matter serious thought. We believe Dr. Muck should be interned. Naturally such a procedure is in the hands of the federal authorities and our society cannot do more than suggest internment and aggressively work for its enforcement."[276] Guggenheim was not the only high-powered member of the ADS arguing for internment. Teddy Roosevelt, who had communicated with the kaiser before the war to champion Muck's cause as conductor for the Boston Symphony, later proclaimed him to be an "alien menace" who should be "forced to pack up and return to the country he came from."[277] The ADS, an organization made up of some of the country's most commanding capitalists and politicians, defamed an innocent man and urged the federal government to take stronger action against Germans in the United States. They called for "increased vigor in the interning of aggressive pro-German sympathizers, whether German citizens or not." English authorities, they claimed, had foiled malicious plots and reduced German propaganda when they interned seventy thousand Germans and German sympathizers during the war. The American Defense Society authoritatively argued that the United States should follow England's lead and make Muck—even though investigations revealed him to be an innocent man—an example by interning him, too, for he posed a security threat to the United States.[278]

On March 19, 1918, the day after the Carnegie concert, Muck angrily wrote a private letter about the New York ADS:

This new patriotic society, National [American] Defense League has made it its special business to make a blacklist of all Americans who associate with Germans, and to discredit them publicly as "traitors." They go so far, that a short while ago a business man had all his bank connections cancelled, and he almost went into bankruptcy; only because he received in his house twice a harmless old German professor. And then I! Not at all harmless, but emissary and spy, etc., etc., pursued everywhere and suspected and boycotted! You still do not understand that the fanatics here in this country wish to make existence impossible to Germans by trying to persecute with never heard of terrorism those few remaining Americans whose thoughts are honorable. No means, no lies, no slander is too bad for them. A German—that is simply a Hun. But an American who means to be friendly with a German: he is a traitor to his country, a cad—the worst criminal in the land. . . . Did not these terrorists break even this stubborn head? By business—boycott, slander, lies. . . . The local "National Defense League" had the impertinence to send me a letter today with a number of questions for me to answer! Woe to the American who falls into the hands of these beasts today.[279]

Muck was understandably angry. He was no match for the powerful ADS and Mrs. Jay, who recorded, "Whatever the government may decide to do with Doktor Muck is its own affair, but . . . the fight . . . will be carried on until every one of their number has been put out where he can do no further harm."[280]

Mrs. Jay Finds the Trump Card

Department of Justice officials and local Boston authorities were pressured to remove Muck from his position in the orchestra. Despite two thorough investigations in 1917 and 1918, the Department of Justice reported to Higginson that "no objectionable conduct whatsoever on [Muck's] part has been discovered."[281] On March 25, 1918, days after the New York tour, Karl Muck was arrested without charge. The Boston branch of the *International News Bureau* reported, "Government officials proved themselves incapable of resisting popular clamor and adopted courses which would have been unthinkable in times of peace. This was one of the most conspicuous cases." The *Bureau* also published a statement from the US Attorney General's Office claiming that "Muck's presence at large was a danger to the public peace and safety to the United States [and was] now under [the] classification of enemy alien." That office stated that Muck was a "danger to public safety [and] will be moved to a hygienic place."[282]

Three days later, on March 28, 1918, Mrs. Jay presented her letter of resignation to the New York Philharmonic Board of Directors. Jay's four-year term was done at the end of March. Her letter was read before the board and was accepted.[283] She had met her own personal goal of destabilizing the Boston Symphony, leaving it up to the New York Philharmonic to ramp up its efforts and become a superior orchestra for the nation.

In summary, Mrs. Jay worked to destroy Karl Muck and remove him from his position as conductor of the Boston Symphony Orchestra. When her initial attacks in 1915–16 failed, Jay intensified her efforts when America declared war. In early 1918, she suggested that Muck was a dangerous foreigner, precisely when anti-German paranoia had reached an all-time high. Marshalling growing anti-German sentiment, she utilized the press to fabricate bogus stories about him. Jay organized New Yorkers throughout the city to demonize Muck and boycott BSO concerts. Unable to remove the celebrated conductor on her own, she was assisted by the ADS and other patriotic volunteer organizations given power by President Woodrow Wilson during wartime.[284] William Guggenheim and other members of the ADS argued that Karl Muck should be interned because he posed a security threat to the United States. Jay collaborated with a network of highly influential individuals in leadership positions who, in their "top command posts" had money, influence, and their own motivations, to mobilize against Muck.[285] It was through these connections, and her persistence, that she found the trump card that assisted the federal government in removing him from power. As we shall see in subsequent chapters, all these efforts gave Mrs. Jay the winning hand in destroying Karl Muck's personal and professional life and weakening, albeit temporarily, the Boston Symphony establishment.

Chapter Five

"A LEAF IN THE STORM"

Muck, Higginson, and the Boston Symphony Orchestra (1918–1919)

Oh, German melody, stand forth and sing
Thy meaning to these dull, unwilling ears
That listen now with me! So let it ring.
A Teuton truth, through mists of blood and tears.
To ignorance and prejudice, to hate.
To fear, to faltering hope and fecund lie,
Speak now thy classic word, and vindicate
A people's honor with serene reply.
They sit before thee, silent, unentranced,
And I among them silent—but my heart
Is thine with understanding, and each note
Blesses, my German heritage, enchanced
And glorified with pain that seems a part
Of this great song the German master wrote.

—Lady Speyer's Poem to Muck, 1919

Henry Lee Higginson, financier and founding director of the Boston Symphony Orchestra, who single-handedly established one of the most successful musical institutions in the United States, faced enormous social and economic pressure to maintain his orchestra during World War I. As mentioned in chapter 1, Higginson had established the BSO by adopting German traditions—building a German-style concert hall, gilding Beethoven's name above the stage, and hiring many German musicians to perform European compositions for his audiences. In the prewar years, Boston defined American cultural identity. German influence was inseparably intertwined with every facet of music making in the city.[1] By 1918, however, the nation's attitude toward Germany was changing. America was rejecting German cosmopolitan culture and a space was opening up for something new.

Figure 5.1. Henry Lee Higginson. *Bostonians: As Seen by Boston Newspaper Cartoonists* (Boston, 1906). Courtesy of the Massachusetts Historical Society.

Muck, too, was caught in these changing times. He was Higginson's most visible "company man." Actions taken against him occurred when America was at a crossroads, when workers pressed for greater justice in the workplace, when large-scale businesses came to dominate the market, when capitalists gained power using unscrupulous methods to defeat their competitors, and when the federal government became more bureaucratic and powerful. Higginson and Muck felt all of these pressures.

Higginson, the classic paternalist, attempted to meet the needs of his musicians and protect them in a fatherly way from outside forces. He viewed music in universal terms and assumed that political conflict would never penetrate Symphony Hall. During the war, however, his way of thinking was naïve, and he was unable to shield Muck and his German musicians from state pressures. Targeted by Mrs. Jay of the New York Philharmonic, who viewed music politically, Muck became fuel for a frightening nationalistic cultural battle exploding in Boston and New York. Higginson's biographer and *Atlantic Monthly* editor Bliss Perry wrote, "The nation was at war. The fate of the Orchestra was of course only a 'leaf in the storm' of wartime troubles."[2]

The Boston Musical Union Challenges the Boston Symphony Patrician

In the early decades of the twentieth century, the Boston Musical Union (BMU) took aim at the BSO, utilizing anti-German sentiment and the rising tide of union activism to demand that Higginson hire union musicians to Americanize his symphony. This pressure was integral to broader national developments among labor unions at the time. In the summer of 1915, a series of labor strikes in a variety of industries demanded an eight-hour workday. As unions became more popular and powerful, workers boldly revolted against injustices in the workplace. As James R. Green and Hugh Carter Donahue argue, "World War I created some favorable conditions for labor. One of the ironies of United States economic history is that wars create jobs for workers who stay at home. Wartime has usually been the occasion when the unemployment characteristic of capitalism has been reduced sufficiently to allow workers to bargain effectively with employers."[3]

As American workers became more vocal in their labor demands, BSO's musicians mirrored the nation as well. There was growing tension among American musicians who believed that they should be given preference for jobs over their German counterparts. In 1913, for example, William C. Gebhardt, a disgruntled Boston Symphony horn player from Jamaica Plain, Massachusetts, was angry with Muck for discharging him from the orchestra, complaining of Muck's favoritism toward foreign-born musicians.[4] Higginson had given Muck artistic authority to hire and fire orchestra players at will. As a result, during Muck's tenure, he hired more than thirty-eight new musicians from Europe, including twenty-seven Germans and eight Austrians, creating an orchestra with more than half of its members from Germany and Austria and the rest coming from fourteen other countries.[5]

As early as 1880, Higginson had been angering musicians in Boston more generally. At the founding of the BSO, two competing orchestras, the Harvard Musical Association and the Philharmonic Society, were struggling. Higginson indirectly put these orchestras out of business by hiring full-time musicians from Europe for his new organization, thus eliminating the practice of sharing local itinerant musicians among city orchestras.[6] The *Boston Transcript* reported that he "makes a corner" of orchestral players and monopolizes them for his own concerts. "Mr. Higginson's gift becomes an imposition, it is something that we must receive, or else we look musical starvation in the face."[7]

As mentioned in chapter 1, Higginson was a restrictionist who wanted to close the doors to immigration, but he took a very different view in terms of importing his own symphony players. From the outset, he had always selected musicians who he believed were the best for his business, even if it meant discriminating based on race, class, gender, and national origin. He had no faith in American musicians and was reluctant to recruit them, thus hiring almost exclusively from overseas. Both Higginson and Muck believed that European musicians were better trained than American players. The United States was still in its infancy in terms of musical training. American conservatories in the early decades of the twentieth century were not adequately equipped to turn out the level of performers that Muck demanded. In a letter to BSO manager Charles Ellis, Higginson describes his affinity for Muck's musical philosophy: "I have doubted whether he would care to play at all unless he got his best men. It isn't the lessened numbers but it is the lessened quality which I dread, and which may disturb Dr. Muck very much. . . . Dr. Muck will not try to live with the Union, nor will I. I have so great a respect for Dr. Muck and his qualities and his ideals that I wish him to know all these things."[8] Having seen excellent ensembles in Europe, Higginson believed he could create something more spectacular in his own hometown without union involvement. Boston historian Martin Green wrote that Higginson "cared more about quality than about equality."[9] Both Higginson's and Muck's views regarding unions became problematic as America entered the war, as German musicians in the nation's orchestras became the targets of public distrust.

As evidence of Muck's bias, when the Bureau of Investigation questioned BSO cornet player Gustav F. Heim in 1918, the German nationalist revealed that Muck had raised his salary two or three times. Furthermore, Heim arrogantly boasted that Germany would win the war. Muck and Heim seemed to share a special bond. Heim described Muck as a "great man—a wonderful man, and if he was put up against the wall for it he would say 'I love him.'"[10] And yet Muck did not feel such a high regard for BSO players of other nationalities. During the war, he wrote in a private letter, "I have daily letters concerning the orchestra members who have not renewed their contracts and desire higher salaries. I am very glad that among the people who seek shameless compensation there is not a single German. A Belgian, a Frenchman, and an Englishman have the doubtful honor to stand at the head. Mr. [Higginson] is a very zealous member of the most famous society for America and the allies, so he had better pay these allied musicians, and probably that is what these men think."[11] As Heim's statement suggests, Muck overcompensated his German players, while viewing musicians from America and Allied nations as "shameless" for requesting similar compensation.

Henry Higginson wanted complete jurisdiction over the business elements of the orchestra, such as setting hours, pay, and other terms.[12] He had witnessed lax rehearsals and poor leadership at the Boston Philharmonic and the Harvard Musical Association, and he wanted to have a higher level of professionalism and financial control within his own organization.[13] He wrote, "I refused to have anything to do with the musical union, because the union stipulates how many rehearsals shall be given and what the men shall do and what their pay shall be."[14] During these years, the unions were fighting for a forty-hour work week and overtime pay. Higginson believed he could not have achieved the performance level he sought if he had to limit rehearsals to forty hours. Given that he had borrowed money from his brother to manage financial shortfalls, it is likely that he would have struggled to pay his musicians overtime compensation. As he saw it, he needed to exploit his musicians by basically cheating them out of overtime wages. Meeting union demands threatened his ability to do that. Higginson was determined to create one of the finest orchestras in the world by hiring musicians and staff who shared his mission and values. He would not allow the union to influence these decisions.

Higginson's unwillingness to unionize enraged the Boston Musical Union, which sought basic worker rights. His autocratic and inflexible business style irritated American musicians, who asserted their

Figure 5.2. Cornetist Gustav Heim was a favorite of Karl Muck in the Boston Symphony. Courtesy of the Boston Symphony Orchestra Archives.

collective power and demanded more from their patriarchal employers. The BMU incessantly pressured Higginson and persistently attacked Muck, the most visible spokesman for the orchestra. Using the war to their advantage, they argued that they deserved preferential treatment, job opportunities, and higher wages over musicians from belligerent nations. This led to an escalation of tension within the orchestral community. Higginson's pattern, going back to the symphony's inception, had been to lay off weaker, local musicians and import stronger ones from Europe.[15] The New York publication *Music*, reported that "some of the oldest members of the Orchestra, men whose services to music in Boston had entitled them to deference and respect" were rejected by him. They were replaced by men without Boston connections, "mostly European, of greater technical accomplishment upon whose loyalty he could count."[16] On June 14, 1915, two years after the Gebhardt complaint, artist and musician Dodge MacKnight of East Sandwich, Massachusetts, a member of the BMU, wrote an angry letter to city socialite and longtime Boston Symphony supporter Isabella Stewart Gardner, complaining that the Boston Symphony management fired their American flutist and replaced him with a European player.[17]

Leveraging the opportunity of anti-German hysteria during World War I, MacKnight and others pursued a nationalistic agenda, arguing that German BSO players had "taken their jobs" and that the BSO was not a democratic organization. Union men also demanded to know why Higginson needed a German conductor when there were "perfectly good" conductors in the United States. They believed America lacked musical opportunities for local artists, and they began a campaign against the importation of foreign musicians.

Union complaints were understandable: Early twentieth-century transatlantic steam travel had connected the continents, making it easier for European musicians to take positions in the United States. This concerned union leaders who reasoned that local musicians were more practical and more readily available. When war broke out in the summer of 1914, twenty-five Boston Symphony musicians were stranded in Europe, having traveled overseas for their vacation after the spring symphony season. This trek to the continent was a routine occurrence, as musicians often visited with family or sought inspiration from European musical centers.[18] Suddenly, the war made it almost impossible for these performers to return to Boston for the start of the new season. Without musicians, there could be no concerts. If Henry Lee Higginson could not meet his expenses, the entire operation would be in danger of collapse. One could see why Boston's union men would be upset sitting idle while Higginson did everything in his power to assist German musicians to cross the Atlantic to return to their posts. Charles Ellis was in Europe when the war broke out. On August 20, 1914, he told Higginson that he had arranged a special train to Holland for Boston Symphony players struggling to arrange passage, but with U-boat attacks and immigration issues, it was too dangerous to travel, and Ellis could not guarantee that the musicians would arrive in Boston in time for the opening of the symphony season.[19]

Union men not only complained about transportation back to Boston, they also questioned the European musicians' commitment to Boston's orchestra, as well as their loyalty to the nation during wartime. Many European players had conflicting allegiances. Some were conscripted into war service.[20] On September 14, 1914, BSO oboist Pierre Fosse in Chatillon d'Azergues, France, informed Higginson that he was drafted into the French army but hoped to be released within a few months.[21] On September 15, cellist Otto Urack wrote a letter in German from Berlin, complaining that Muck accused him of breach of contract even though he was doing his military duty in the German army.[22] BSO clarinetist Georges Grisez wrote to Higginson on August 4 from Bordeaux explaining that he wished to do his military duty but hoped his position would be available after the war. He also admitted that he owed Higginson $400 and that if he was killed, Grisez's wife would pay Higginson out of his $5,000 life insurance policy.[23] There was much uncertainty within the orchestra itself, whether the men would serve their countries or attempt passage to America to resume or begin their musical positions. This uncertainty gave the union even more ammunition for complaint, for Higginson had built his entire musical enterprise on the backs of European musicians, some of whom could not fulfill their professional duties in Boston during the war.

Musical unions in the United States got their start in 1889, with the founding of the American Federation of Musicians (AFM), when musicians convinced Samuel Gompers, American Federation of Labor president, to create a comprehensive musicians' trade union. From then on, musical unions around the country and in Canada gained ground, with three thousand members applying that first year. By 1896 the United States had more than ten thousand unionized musicians.[24]

On March 20, 1897, Boston established Musicians Union No. 9, made up of the city's white musicians. Their mission involved finding stable employment. In a time before radio and television, live musical performances were popular, which gave the union a strong argument for legitimacy, and, consequently, it thrived. Members met each week at their St. Botolph Street clubhouse, located one street away from Symphony Hall, to find out about and acquire jobs in restaurants and dance halls for the following week.[25] In 1915, black musicians established the Musicians Union No. 535, finding employment in venues like the Crawford House Restaurant and the Savoy Cafe. Union leaders pressured BSO management to hire union members, claiming that the immigration of German musicians violated state labor laws, but Higginson remained stubborn.[26] The AFM leveraged wartime nationalism to build its membership, openly questioning Higginson's favoritism of European players. The *Musical Courier* trade journal, which was popular among union members, argued that Higginson was behaving in an unpatriotic manner by passing over local talent for imported musicians. The magazine bitterly griped, "We rehearse our orchestra in German because we import them instead of educating our own bright, and dashing, and joyous American boys to play."[27] Joseph Weber, AFM president from 1900 to 1914 and from 1915 to 1940, emphasized at the annual AMF convention that if "Americans gave their musicians a chance," their music would flourish.[28] The AFM did not permit union membership unless an individual obtained papers of intent to become an American citizen.[29] Higginson remarked at the end of the war that the union "warned me that they would hit us when they could," and he suspected that they were somehow involved in attacks against Karl Muck.[30]

Despite AFM pressure to unionize, Higginson planned a number of tricky maneuvers to escape its grasp. When conductor Arthur Nikisch arrived from Europe in 1889 to assume leadership of the BSO, he barely made it into the country before the Musicians Union accused him of violating the Control Labor Law. To sidestep the union, Nikisch traveled straight to Boston upon his arrival in New York. The grand public party that was planned for him in New York was a decoy for a smaller reception at Higginson's Boston home. Nikisch was secretly and speedily transported there in a closed carriage.[31] Higginson also contacted the Treasury Department about legal ways to import other foreign conductors.[32] He utilized his family connections with Teddy Roosevelt and Henry Cabot Lodge to obtain the necessary papers to release Karl Muck from the German government. Higginson used political connections that were too powerful for the union to overcome at that time. As the unions gained strength, however, it forced even the most powerful politicians to step carefully.

Labor tensions were not unique to Higginson or to the Musicians' Union. Difficulties in Boston's labor unions were echoed throughout the nation during the war. Military conscription disrupted working lives. Because immigrants were disproportionately disqualified from the draft, when American soldiers went off to war, immigrants filled their jobs, and animosity toward them increased. The greatest rise in immigration in American history took place between the 1880s and 1920, with more than a million people arriving annually. Anglo-Americans began to fear that they were losing economic opportunities to these newcomers, especially in light of unprecedented wartime inflation that rose to a staggering 77 percent at its height, making it difficult for most families to make ends meet.[33] The Communist and Socialist Parties gained footholds in the United States as well, and their collective numbers increased to a total of sixty thousand members in this period. The stage was set for radical syndicalism.

Union unrest and working-class militancy made American business leaders like Higginson nervous. By 1919, one-fifth of all US wage earners were on strike. The International Industrial Workers of the World, popularly known in the United States as the Wobblies, had a growing membership. The *Masses*, a left-leaning socialist newspaper in New York, sympathetically reported on labor strikes, eliciting public apprehension when some of its articles questioned the value of unfettered capitalism. Other factors may have substantiated these suspicions. In 1892, the charismatic activist Emma Goldman and her lover Alexander Berkman were behind a plot to assassinate Carnegie Steel plant manager Henry Clay Frick following a failed labor strike, and it became increasingly difficult for management to control its workers. As mentioned in chapter 3, labor discontent across Massachusetts in 1919 was rampant, with 396 strikes, among them the New England Telephone Company, the Boston Elevated Railway, the Lowell Mills, and the New England fisherman's strikes. In that same year, the Boston Police Department went on strike. Massachusetts governor Calvin Coolidge sent the National Guard to quell the unrest. His decisive action would help establish his reputation and ultimately propel him to the vice presidency in 1921 and, consequently, the presidency in 1923 upon Warren Harding's sudden death. The American Legion, founded by Teddy Roosevelt, got its start by beating up union organizers and "promoting" national conformity. Class wars were erupting all over the country.[34]

Around the world, ruling elites were losing power to the working classes, and Higginson, a wealthy Bostonian himself, was aware of these changes and afraid of union solidarity. Whether reading about the Russian Revolution and the overthrow of the czar, or factory-worker takeovers in Italy, or the rise of socialism in China, American capitalists grew uneasy as they watched events unfold and as the former domination of the old ruling order crumbled under the increasing power of the collective working classes. The business class feared a revolution in the United States as unions became empowered by what they saw overseas.

As a paternalist, Higginson believed he was treating his employees fairly, and yet he audaciously argued against union demands. Despite his belief that he was behaving as a benevolent fatherly figure, he had difficulty understanding his musicians' plight, for he was a product of an earlier time, when workers had virtually no say about their wages, hours, and working conditions. Martin Green wrote that Higginson's "stiff-backed autocracy and social frigidity seemed the epitome of old Boston manner."[35] Harry Ellis Dickson, violinist and assistant conductor of the Boston Pops from 1955 to 1999, wrote, "We were in the Boston Symphony, which was run by the Boston Brahmins who hated anything that had to do with unions. Remember that, when they heard 'union' they heard 'communism,' they heard rebellion."[36] Native-born paternalists like Higginson, who believed Brahmin philanthropy was a viable alternative to unions, shared a psychological need to control and influence the immigrant masses in their own "unique" ways.[37] He was falling increasingly out of fashion in the complex and rapidly transforming world that he was living in. Higginson's strict and ultra-conservative rule included making his orchestra members sign a contract that prevented them from performing with other ensembles and prohibited them from playing music for dancing.[38] Dance music was the sphere of the union musicians, and Higginson viewed his orchestra as a higher-class institution, separate from the dance hall. Higginson had autocratic power, and he made rules at his own discretion. He spent countless hours sitting in various seats in Symphony Hall listening to individual players and making lists regarding their status. He determined that Auguste Sautet, second oboist, "must go, and we want a man to take his place as extra oboe." To Muck he wrote, "We want also somebody to take Elmar's place as second clarinet, for I think he is rather dull." One can assume that players were fearful of their job security, for, at a whim, Higginson (or Muck) could fire them.[39]

Until World War I, Higginson had been able to "take care" of his conductor and musicians and protect them from the outside world, but, with mounting pressure from the musician's union, Mrs. Jay, the press, and federal investigators, it became harder for Higginson to sustain his support. This was not unlike Higginson's actions in a prior business venture. During Reconstruction, using money he had acquired as an agent for the Buckeye Oil Company, Higginson had become a carpetbagger, purchasing Cottenham, a five-thousand-acre Sea Island cotton plantation on Bryan Neck of Red Bird Creek, in Richmond Hill, Georgia.[40] He listened to lawyer and Union general Francis Channing Barlow, who told him, "Making money there is a simple question of being able to make the darkies work."[41] Higginson intended to make a profit while simultaneously employing former slaves. When they became disgruntled with low wages, however, Higginson refused to meet their demands and provided an all-or-nothing ultimatum

Figure 5.3. Cottenham Plantation, Richmond Hill, Georgia. Henry Lee
Higginson purchased the plantation after the Civil War, hiring freed slaves
to work his crops. Higginson abandoned the enterprise because of labor
difficulties. The property was later sold to car manufacturer Henry Ford.
Courtesy of the Benson Ford Research Center, The Henry Ford, Dearborn,
Michigan.

that "work or starvation is before them." Attempting to bully his workers without success, he abandoned the enterprise. Similarly, the BSO
presented challenges during World War I. Higginson was up against
historical forces greater than himself, and his employees became an
expendable means to a financial end.

Muck was two years into a five-year engagement with the Boston
Symphony when the war broke out. Having just completed the final
performance of Wagner's *Parsifal* at Bayreuth, Germany, on August 1,
1914, Muck was conflicted about returning to Boston for the start of
the fall season.[42] Two weeks later, Ellis wrote to Higginson that he had
been having difficulty arranging Muck's return to Boston.[43] Muck was
reluctant to sail, as he was torn by his own nationalist loyalties to Germany and physically fearful of submarine attacks. Moreover, as a German, Muck was not sure he would be welcomed back to Boston, and
he voiced those fears to Ellis.[44] Regardless, Higginson and Ellis convinced Muck to make the journey. Crossing the Atlantic under threat
of U-boat attack, Muck risked his life to fulfill his Boston obligation.
He returned because he trusted Higginson, who told him that everything would be alright. Muck had faith that his wealthy and powerful
sponsor could keep him safe.

Higginson believed that Symphony Hall would be a place of sanctuary and neutrality, untouched by the war. He convinced Muck that
he would remain unharmed by anti-German hysteria. On September
15, 1914, Ellis cabled Higginson from London excitedly reporting that

he had persuaded Muck to return. He wrote, "First quality concerts assured."[45] Ellis informed Higginson that Muck would sail on September 26 via Ryndam and that other Boston Symphony players would join him.[46]

At the first rehearsal of the 1914 season, Higginson expressed optimism regarding the orchestra, happy to have many of the players back in Boston. "We have lost only a few men, and have filled their places well," he assured them. "I have thought of you all as needing the work; I have thought of the beautiful concerts already given, and have thought of the people who wanted them; and, considering all these points, I wish to go on with the concerts. The conditions of this year were against us, and it was our part as men to overcome these conditions if we could."[47]

Higginson defended his musicians, in a genuine attempt to safeguard them from trouble. To counter the negative comments made by Boston's Musicians Union about his European players, for example, Higginson praised his orchestra routinely in the local press. On December 13, 1915, he wrote to the *Boston Transcript* applauding the respectful decorum maintained by the orchestra's multinational membership during wartime.[48] "We have a dozen nationalities in the Orchestra," he raved, "and the men have behaved perfectly well toward each other." Higginson commented that Muck "has been cordial to me since the war began, as before; and he has been most kindly received by audiences here and in other cities. . . . I trust him entirely as an artist and as a man, and he has worked as no other conductor has worked."[49] Higginson concurred with Harvard's president, Abbott Lawrence Lowell, who wrote on November 20, 1914, "that the continuance of the Symphony concerts, and the retention of Dr. Muck as Director is a very important matter for our community. Music is one of the things in which America is singularly backward, and the amount that the Symphony Orchestra has contributed to American education cannot be overestimated. I do not see how German music, or German musicians, can corrupt America, or Germanize us. Because we quarrel with a nation because their conduct is outrageous and requires to be suppressed by force, is no reason why we should deprive ourselves of their art." Higginson stressed what he believed was the necessary educational benefit Muck and the orchestra brought to the city, and he continued to tout a national cultural agenda that borrowed from Europe.[50]

In 1916, when news broke that Italians in East Boston were intent on harming Germans in the city, Higginson visited Muck at his home to discuss the crisis. Muck wrote, "At first he tried to draw out of the situation with a few stupid jokes. Then he admitted that he had heard of the nonsense, but that was quite out of the question that anything could happen—'We have the police, and in the extreme need, our militia.'"[51] In 1917, seeing danger ahead, Muck asked Higginson for permission to return to Germany. Higginson, once again, convinced Muck that he was safe in America, persuading him to sign a five-year contract. Higginson had delusions that his power, coming from one of the most influential aristocratic family networks in Boston, could insulate Muck and his orchestra from all the difficulties that the war created—threats from zealous patriots and struggles with the union, capitalists from New York, and federal authorities. Alas, Higginson would soon realize that the BSO was not invulnerable to political strife and that he could not protect his men from these adversaries.

Mrs. Jay Attacks Higginson Claiming Overdependence on German Music

Each clash took its toll on Higginson's resolve. The most zealous and persistent pressure came from Mrs. Jay, who had made it her mission to push for the removal of German music from BSO's symphony programs. Perhaps Mrs. Jay was influenced by New York music critic Carl Van Vechten who argued in his book *Music after the Great War* (1915) that the conflict gave Americans the opportunity to create their own musical identity separate from Europe. Clearly, Mrs. Jay espoused this idea, for Van Vechten's language was reflected in her attacks.[52] Over the course of seven essays, the American public was told that music was on the edge of revolution: the exalted canon of German Romanticism "has had its day." The tradition of Brahms, Bach, and Beethoven was to be "incinerated in the flames of war, clearing the way for an uncompromising movement."[53] For Van Vechten, the Great War offered America the opportunity to destroy "the spirit of imitation . . . through violence and death," to create something new.[54] With *Music and Bad Manners* (1916), Van Vechten restated his faith in a musical panacea with "up-to-the-minute connoisseurs if they only discarded their irrational attachment to the past." He encouraged them to look within their own sphere of influence for inspiration.[55]

On May 6, 1916, Mrs. Jay contacted Higginson, arguing that the BSO performed entirely too many German selections at their concerts, even though she had made no attempt to scrutinize the New York Philharmonic's selections.[56] She put the Boston Symphony organization on the defensive, as management scrambled to count German selections, to determine whether an adequate representation of music was chosen by the conductor or whether he overwhelmingly favored

Figure 5.4. Mrs. Jay in Wagnerian costume, 1911. Jay vigorously attacked Higginson and the Boston Symphony for performing too many German selections. Courtesy of the Library of Congress. January 16, 1911, Class J, ISO849 Prints Division 44189.

German music. Higginson intractably recorded that "the percentage of German works—as the patrons of music would call them—has been no higher than for many seasons past and lower than that of one and another year before."[57]

On March 22, 1917, Mrs. Jay reported to the *New York Herald* that she had established the Anti-German Music League to eliminate all German musical influence in Boston, to "remove the hunnish contamination." In a public appeal, she wrote:

> I would be glad of cooperation in the effort to bring a stop to this subtle and most appalling of all German propaganda, and for that purpose have decided to form a league to be called the Anti-German Music League. There will be no charge for admission to it, and I would be glad to have those who wish to join it communicate with me at my home. Public opinion alone can combat this evil.[58]

Mrs. Jay had brought up a valid point, that Boston, and America more generally, relied too heavily on German music and that the field of opportunity should expand. Music became a symbol for larger struggles in America, a vehicle for rejecting German influence and the elitism that accompanied it. People were tired of hearing only the "courtly muses of Europe."[59] Jay's campaign to "intern German music" and "break its spell" continued even after Muck's arrest and internment, and shook things up for Boston, forcing the BSO to reevaluate its concert programming.[60] "Just as we of the Allies use poisonous gasses to meet our savage foe," she reasoned, "so must we regretfully retaliate and suppress the works of her composers." Jay claimed that people like Higginson, who defended the use of "Teuton composers," did so "for economic and political advantage."[61] Her forceful crusade caused great anxiety for Higginson, for he had spent his life's earnings creating the BSO—a German-style hall, with a predominance of German music, and many German musicians. Mrs. Jay threatened to destroy everything he had built and stood for. The elder paternalist had naively viewed music as apolitical until the BSO became caught in the political maelstrom itself.

Mrs. Jay's attacks also had repercussions for Second New England School composers who lived and worked in the Boston area. These musicians had traveled to Europe and returned home to compose their own brand of music using German forms. Their music and their friendships were entirely interwoven with German culture. During the war, their relationships with Germans became a cause of suspicion, and with new nationalistic rules regarding musical composition, Second New England School musicians were in crisis. Many New England composers believed that their work was no longer significant, and they were labeled German clones.[62] Politics seemed inseparably entwined with art as the public cried out for musical selections that satisfied an American agenda.

Amy Beach, one of Boston's Second New England School composers and concert pianists, offers an example of this political link. Beach performed with the Boston Symphony Orchestra (1895, 1900), and her compositions were debuted with the Handel and Haydn Society (1891), the World Columbian Exposition in Chicago (1893), and the Boston Symphony Orchestra (1896, 1900, 1916). She had a fondness for German repertoire, having studied and toured in Europe. In 1911, one German critic had proclaimed her to be America's leading composer.[63] In March of 1916, Muck had conducted one of Beach's works. Musicologist Adrienne Fried Block records that "Karl Muck had brought the Boston orchestra to a point close to virtuosic perfection, and Beach, ever sensitive to the conductor's and player's responses to her interpretations, was doubly inspired."[64] Because of the war, however, Beach felt pressure to perform new works by Italian, French, English, and Russian composers. Unhappy with increasing nationalism, she reflected nostalgically on the past: "I belonged to a happy period that may never come again." Of her German friends in Munich and Boston, she wrote

> Who knows if we shall meet again?
> Behind each parting lurks a fear
> We smile to hide the haunting pain
> The rising tear."[65]

Beach declared her allegiance to "universal musical culture" in the Boston press, but the public treated her with contempt, viewing her statements as supportive of Germany. She said, "Understand, I am not pro-German, or pro anything except pro-American. . . . But I do wish that our German friends could be understood here." Her partisan attempt to foster understanding rather than fear did not go over well, and she was forced to join patriotic organizations to prove her loyalty. Beach became paralyzed musically during the war, curtailing her performance schedule until the armistice. A wealthy member of the Daughters of the American Revolution, and a woman with prejudices against Jews, Beach was typical of many upper-class Boston Brahmins who idolized German culture and harbored anti-Semitic feelings toward eastern Europeans.[66] Second New England School musicians like Beach never regained the popular and prominent position they had prior to the war, and their affiliations and friendships with

Figure 5.5. Second New England School composer and concert pianist Amy Beach was hugely popular before World War I. Fond of German repertoire and a supporter of Germans in America, she lost popularity during the war and retreated to her New Hampshire home for the duration of the conflict. Courtesy of the Library of Congress, George Grantham Bain Collection, Biography File, cph 3b04622. Reproduction Number LC-USZ62-56790.

German-Americans became a mark against them after the war.[67] Many Americans who supported Germans in America were marginalized, intimidated, and ostracized. Karl Muck was intimately linked to this community of musician composers.

By 1918, the high point of German Romanticism in music was coming to an end, for it was seen as emotional, syrupy, and appealing primarily to tea-drinking Victorian ladies. Gail Bederman's biographical case study of Teddy Roosevelt tracks this cultural shift in values in *Manliness and Civilization*.[68] As Roosevelt was calling for a greater reflection of masculinity in American society, composer Charles Ives was writing rugged and unconventional music, experimenting with polytonality and polyrhythms, pairing church hymns and patriotic marching tunes simultaneously in a mind-blowing combination of sounds.[69] For him, dissonance came to represent authenticity and modernity, mirroring, whether intentionally or not, postwar tension and trauma. American music became linked to a national obsession with manhood and strength, as well as social Darwinian notions of survival of the fittest.[70] Ives walked out of a Boston concert by the Kneisel Quartet because he could not stomach a "whole evening of mellifluous sounds, perfect cadences, perfect ladies, perfect programs, and not a dissonant cuss word to stop the anemia and beauty during the whole evening."[71] George Santayana of Harvard detested the "custodians of culture" with their roots in Germanic idealism. As Joseph Horowitz points out, "America's Germanic genteel tradition, with its emphasis on uplift, seemed musty and vague, anything but 'American.'"[72] During the war, the ideals of rugged manliness began to penetrate the social elite. Descriptions of Muck began to suggest that his attire was too perfect and pressed. Not a hair out of place, he became viewed as prissy, effete, and not masculine enough for America. He dressed in a style "prevalent at the turn of the century and never departed from it," as if belonging to "a bygone age."[73]

This national mission to break away from the prevailing German musical style placed Higginson in a difficult position. His inflexible adherence to German musical culture did not serve him well during this changing politicized climate. His difficulties, in fact, centered on the very definition of musical culture in America. In practice, "culture" referred to elite goods and activities such as museum-quality art and classical music, and being "cultured" referred to people who knew about and took part in these activities. Germany, however, had a slightly different word, *Kultur*, which referred to its own artistic identity coupled with its militaristic goals. Americans began to interpret the word *Kultur* more broadly in terms of German conquest and domination, and people began to fear that German *Kultur* had taken control of the country's artistic institutions as well. German music in the United States became controversial, and many believed that German musicians were tools of Germany's imperialistic mission.[74] The BSO, which naively believed itself free of any political agenda, was very much a part of the national debate. Muck and his musicians seemed to be a favorite target of attack by the press, which insisted that the Boston Symphony represented German *Kultur.* Following German unification in 1870, works by Beethoven, Schubert, Brahms, and Mendelssohn, with their perfected symphonic structural form, came to symbolize German pride.[75] Prior to World War I, American audiences had not viewed the symphony, the conductor, or Beethoven in any negative way. This perception changed during the war, however, as American audiences and critics reinterpreted music in the larger international and imperial context.

When Muck accepted his position as conductor of the BSO in 1906, many Germans believed that his mission in the United States was to represent Germany as a national ambassador for its "glorious" musical tradition. A Berlin newspaper, for instance, claimed that Muck wanted to elevate the status of German music in America while reducing the importance of French works.[76] Muck, however, made no public statements in the United States to back up such German reports. He was not employed by the German government at the BSO but as a private individual. He made clear that he was eager to escape state-supported conducting positions in Germany and had come to America where he would have more artistic freedom. He conducted the works of modern composers such as Sibelius and Debussy and "even composers he disliked, such as Tchaikovsky."[77] In 1914, he premiered Stravinsky's *Fireworks* and Schoenberg's *Five Pieces for Orchestra.*[78] He programmed French works and utilized members of the BSO to assist with their interpretation. Critic Louis C. Elson observed gleefully that Muck had "taken the American music under his special guardianship," and yet there were limits to his open-mindedness. George Chadwick noted that Muck prioritized "everything by a *great* composer" over "anything by a minor practitioner," calling into question the conductor's biases.[79] Muck, did, however, devote eight BSO rehearsals to Chadwick's student Henry Hadley's First Symphony, op. 18. Muck also promoted and conducted several of Chadwick's works with the Boston Symphony, including *Cleopatra* (1906, 1907), *Symphonic Sketches* (1908, 1915, 1918), *Aphrodite* (1913), and Symphony no. 3 (1914), but never premiered excerpts from *The Padrone,* an opera about Italian immigrants in Boston's North End.[80] It was not until 1995 that the Waterbury Symphony Orchestra in Connecticut debuted the piece, and while Chadwick's adult children were in attendance, the composer was

Figure 5.6. Second New England School composer and New England Conservatory director, George Whitefield Chadwick, was a colleague and friend of Karl Muck. Courtesy of the New England Conservatory.

long deceased. Regardless of the conflicting perception of Muck's role in the United States, he was viewed by many as a political proponent of German cultural imperialism who played a prominent diplomatic role (whether he wanted to or not) in international affairs.[81]

Muck's Associations with
High-Ranking Germans Inspire Suspicion

Despite Muck's seemingly diverse repertoire and his personal desire to conduct his orchestra without international political intrigue, as World War I progressed, he became a popular target of anti-German sentiment. Many viewed him as a token offering by the "benevolent" Kaiser Wilhelm, like a poisoned apple for innocent and unsuspecting Boston music lovers to bite. Goodwill gestures, like sending Muck to the United States as a guest conductor, were no longer received with the same level of enthusiasm as they had been before the war. Americans were becoming suspicious, and Muck came to be viewed as a corrupt and evil spy connected to a tyrant who murdered innocent people.

The American fear of German nationalism stemmed from actions taken before Muck's first appointment with the BSO. In 1902, Prince Heinrich of Prussia, Kaiser Wilhelm's brother, visited the United States to receive an honorary degree from Harvard. Harvard's president, Charles W. Eliot, described it as a "somewhat theatrical performance" intended as a publicity stunt contrived by the German monarch to maintain friendly relations. In 1904, Kaiser Wilhelm offered the United States a bronze statue of Frederick the Great. The kaiser meant this gift to be an expression of thanks for the kind reception of Prince Heinrich and as a sign of the close relations between the two great nations. Despite opposition from Congress and the press, Roosevelt had to accept the unsolicited gift, placing it on the Army War College esplanade. The *Washington Evening Star* suggested that the United States should return the favor with a statue of James Monroe to remind Germans of that president's famous doctrine.[82] The *Star* was referring to the Monroe Doctrine of 1823 that warns European powers that colonial expansion and interference into the Western Hemisphere is an act of aggression. Germany had ignored the doctrine by intervening into the affairs of several South American nations, namely Venezuela in 1902–3, resulting in President Theodore Roosevelt's amendment to the document, called the Roosevelt Corollary, which declared that the United States would be a "police power" of the Western Hemisphere. Increasing political tensions and territorial rivalries between the

United States and Germany besieged Muck, who unwillingly became caught up in the geopolitics of the time.

As mentioned in chapter 1, Muck had enjoyed his experience in the United States and was treated quite fairly before the war. He came to America fully intending to stay and to become a citizen. He had sold his property in Germany and had made the United States his home. In a private letter he wrote, "You see. I came back to the United States in 1912, and in 1914, I decided to settle down in Boston, and in March of that year I bought a house at 50 Fenway, intending to take out my citizenship papers. Then came the war, and, well, I intended to become a citizen and stay here."[83] Muck was able to live comfortably as a cosmopolitan man in Boston before the war broke out. At that time, it was acceptable to be a German in America and to love two countries. Muck thrived in Boston, and he befriended many of the city's leading American and German residents. As Panikos Panayi points out, first-generation immigrants like Muck understandably never give up thoughts of their home country. Two or three generations are required for immigrant families to feel fully assimilated. Muck held onto his associations with other Germans in America and stayed in contact with Germany, even though he loved America and planned to make it his permanent home.[84] Alvaro Vargas Llosa makes clear that many immigrants "look for comfort" with fellow nationals in their new communities.[85] He reports that "most immigrant associations are not enclaves removed from the host society, but actually a vehicle for engagement with, even assimilation into, the adopted country." Sentimental attachments are not incompatible with assimilation, rather, they help to navigate a new home. "Immigrants who maintain ties to their country of origin . . . also cultivate attitudes that show they are putting down psychological roots."[86] While it seems clear that Muck became emotionally attached to his new city, he never took out citizenship papers. That simple act, had he taken it, may have removed some of the doubts that the federal government had about him, and perhaps would have prevented his later arrest or internment, just as having naturalization papers helped Chicago Symphony Orchestra music director Frederick Stock during the war.

The BOI, as well as many other governmental agencies, demonstrated intolerance of "hyphenated Americans" with divided loyalties during wartime. Immigrant groups that shared and promoted foreign ideas were targeted because they were perceived as threats to American security. The anarchist clause of the Immigrant Act of 1903, for example, was expanded in two ways during World War I—to exclude from entry into the United States of advocates of violent revolution or sabotage and to deport aliens preaching radical doctrines. Thus, organizational memberships, or even social gatherings, were linked to anarchism and viewed as subversive, making innocent people associating collectively in groups targets for deportation.[87] Muck's German American friendships and affiliations were viewed in a negative light by federal officials, and he became guilty by association with them. These colleagues were viewed with suspicion because of assumptions that they were supporting the German war effort. Many of Muck's acquaintances were high-profile Germans living in the United States whom BOI officials placed under surveillance, hoping to catch committing unlawful acts. Looking at the details of Muck's associations with important German American intellectuals and diplomats gives us a window into Muck's views and actions during World War I. By studying their FBI records, autobiographies, biographies, and newspaper clippings, we can see that Muck and his associates were actively supporting the fatherland and that the federal government targeted them and used anti-Germanism to break up concentrations of German elite culture.

The BOI questioned Muck's association with Hugo Münsterberg, noted Harvard professor of psychology. Münsterberg offered Muck intellectual companionship separate from his musical acquaintances. He hosted Muck and other intellectuals at his Ware Street home in Cambridge, Massachusetts, and offered the conductor impromptu lessons in psychology using rats at his laboratory in Harvard's Emerson Hall. In 1910, Münsterberg established the Amerika-Institut in Berlin as an exchange program between American and German scholars. Given international conflicts and increasing tensions between the two countries, however, the program never developed a reputation as a high-level research institute.[88] The Harvard psychologist attempted for many years to mediate between America and Germany, and he became increasingly frustrated by diplomatic breakdowns between the countries. During those years, Münsterberg argued that the United States, Germany, and England needed to become stronger allies as a way to maintain a balance of power throughout the world. His ideas, however, became increasingly nationalistic as the war progressed and he openly supported the German cause. He assisted the German Information Service, a press office in New York established to repair Germany's image in America after the outbreak of the war.[89] In 1918, Münsterberg wrote an essay for the *Boston Herald* entitled "The Impeachment of the German-Americans" in which he argued that Europe was the mother country of the United States and that Americans of whatever descent should contribute "their special racial virtues" to their adopted home. He supported German imperial policies, becoming an apologist for Germany's questionable wartime actions.[90] His opinions appalled the increasingly patriotic American public, and he received a great

Figure 5.7. Harvard psychology professor Hugo Münsterberg was one of Karl Muck's intellectual companions. Courtesy of the National Archives Records Administration, 165-ww-157a-5. December 1918. Marshall Studio Photographer.

deal of hate mail. People who had formerly stopped to converse with him on the "serene streets of Cambridge, where he pleasantly walked for twenty-five years," began passing him "with a stiff bow, and still others passed without bowing at all."[91] His speeches and essays were often misconstrued by the press as more extremist than they actually were. As a result, Münsterberg, in his naïve attempt to create a bridge of understanding, became a convenient target of anti-German attacks. Hoping to escape the indignities of this persecution, Münsterberg enjoyed a pleasant visit in the summer of 1916 with Muck at his rented home in Seal Harbor, Maine. Despite the respite, just four months later, on December 16, Münsterberg collapsed and died of cardiac arrest while teaching a class at his beloved Emerson Hall. The strain was too much for the outspoken professor.[92]

Another of Muck's friends under investigation was Edmund von Mach, a German American writer and professor of fine arts at Harvard University and Wellesley College. In 1914, just after the outbreak of war, von Mach, like Münsterberg, attempted to improve Germany's image among Americans, writing a book entitled *What Germany Wants.* He also published a pamphlet called *Loyal American Citizenship Consists in Keeping Unsullied One's Allegiance to the Constitution and to the Principles of Which This Nation Was Founded—Humanity, Justice, and Good Will toward All.*[93] Hardly extremist documents, the US government nevertheless used these and other materials in its attempt to build a case against von Mach and other Germans in America.

Muck also associated with high-ranking German political figures such as ambassador to the United States Johann Heinrich Graf von Bernstorff (1908–17). During their college days, Muck was Bernstorff's "chum and crony" at Heidelberg in the Schwaben Corps, which was one of the oldest and most elite student organizations at the college.[94] On August 2, 1914, Bernstorff arrived in America to fulfill his duty as ambassador, with a multipurpose agenda: to aid in the German war effort, to forge a propaganda campaign that would foster American neutrality, to help Germans who wished to return home to enlist, acquire passports, obtain passage through the Allied blockade, and assist with war relief. Bernstorff's role was to be a visible diplomat and to speak to all audiences about the positive aspects of his home country. Authorities, no doubt, were concerned that Muck may have been complicit with Bernstorff, who, with Franz von Papen, allegedly headed the German intelligence efforts in the United States during the war, although the allegations were never proven and von Papen returned home in 1915. Muck's association with Bernstorff placed him on the BOI's radar in surveillance of illegal activity.

Muck was intimate with both ambassador and Mrs. Bernstorff, having visited them at every opportunity when in or near Washington, DC. Muck had also entertained them at his own home in Boston.[95] Muck and Bernstorff maintained a vigorous correspondence. When the BOI raided Muck's home in 1918, it found that most of Bernstorff's letters were of a social nature. If they had business relating to German propaganda, they spoke in person or by messenger, and they never left a paper trail concerning delicate matters.[96] Earlier in the war years, Muck was often frustrated that his mail with Bernstorff took too long to arrive and that perhaps it was being read by Department of Justice officials. On March 26, 1916, he wrote, "How is it possible that a special delivery letter—an absolutely innocent, private letter from Count Bernstorff—took four days to come from Washington to Boston?"[97] On July 12, 1916, he wrote, "A letter from Bernstorff addressed to me, sent on the 8th of July from Washington has not yet arrived and a registered letter I mailed to Bernstorff on the 28th of June was delivered at Washington on the 4th of July."[98] He believed that Wilson was not honoring his promise of neutrality. Muck became increasingly anxious as America sided with England as the war progressed. He wrote, "Isn't this a fine situation with this English-American mail? Yes, it is so: The United States of America has become [an] English colony again, nothing more."[99] Anita Muck's activities also cast suspicion on the conductor. In November of 1916, the conductor's wife was involved with war work, traveling to Washington for German Women's Society meetings. She ran a fundraising bazaar to assist Countess Bernstorff, who "has nearly all the work to do alone."[100]

When Woodrow Wilson severed diplomatic relations with Germany in February of 1917, Bernstorff and his wife returned to Germany. Muck wrote on February 13, "I have a very painful hour to go through tomorrow—the goodbye of Bernstorff and two other old acquaintances in the embassy, but it means shutting my teeth together." The next day he wrote, "I was one of the last four men to bid our ambassador goodbye."[101]

One of Muck's closest friends in Boston, Baron Ferdinand Otto von Scholley, was a member of the German military aristocracy, a former German army commander, and the director of the G. F. Burkhardt Brewery in Boston. Von Scholley had married Helene Dorothea Burkhardt, whose father established the well-known brewery in 1850 and ran it until his death in 1884. Von Scholley took control of the business after his father-in-law's passing. He was a Freemason and was "in with men higher up in Boston." He was a member of the Eastern Yacht Club and the Algonquin Club, strongholds of the Brahmin upper classes. His daughter attended the prestigious Winsor School and the

Figure 5.8. Ambassador Johann Bernstorff. Muck and Johann Bernstorff began their friendship at Heidelberg in the Schwaben Corps. Bernstorff went on to become a high-ranking German political figure and the ambassador to the United States. Courtesy of the Library of Congress, Prints and Photographs Division, Reproduction number hec. 05597.

Museum of Fine Arts School in Boston.[102] The Mucks were frequent visitors to the von Scholley's houses in Squantum and Brookline, Massachusetts.[103] According to von Scholley's secretary, Mrs. May, her boss talked every day on the telephone with Karl Muck.[104] The men shared many things in common. They both came from Germany's elite society. They both became increasingly nationalistic, especially after the US entry into the war. Furthermore, Muck shared his books and maps of World War I battlefields with his friend.[105]

Von Scholley's waterfront home in Squantum was near the Fore River Shipyard that built and launched US destroyers. From his residence, he could see German ships in Winthrop that had been confiscated by authorities during the war. Suspiciously, von Scholley took boat rides to the German ships, and he and Muck regularly socialized with the German naval officers, apparently sending a ship-to-shore message to the kaiser pledging loyalty.[106] Moreover, as BOI surveillance revealed, the naval officers visited von Scholley's house where he hosted clam bakes, which the Mucks also frequently attended.[107]

In the spring of 1917, von Scholley held private meetings at the Hotel Buckminster in Boston that were deemed suspicious by the BOI.[108] He had special locks placed on all the doors, windows, and closets of his hotel room. He met in private with several German men and was suspected of sabotage, although there was no evidence linking him to any crime.[109] Still, BOI officials arrested von Scholley on October 29, 1918, seven months after Muck's arrest, and, like the BSO conductor, he was sent to Fort Oglethorpe—in his case, just three days before the armistice, allowing him to return to Germany soon thereafter.[110]

Another member of Muck's friendship circle under close observation was German-born Sir Edgar Speyer. In 1899, Speyer first met Muck when he guest-conducted at the Royal Opera House, Covent Garden, in central London. Speyer was the chairman of Speyer Brothers, an international banking firm with branches in England, Germany, and the United States. He was a prosperous and successful financier. In 1892, Speyer had become a British citizen, befriending Prime Minister Herbert Henry Asquith, becoming a baronet in 1906, and joining the Privy Council of the British government in 1909. Speyer financed the London Underground subway system as well as Captain Robert Falcon Scott's Antarctic expedition. He also donated extraordinary amounts of money to hospitals and museums in Great Britain.[111]

Speyer was a patron of the arts in London, rescuing Sir Henry Wood's Promenade Concerts from bankruptcy. Speyer's wife Leonora (née Nona von Stosch) was not only a Pulitzer Prize–winning poet but also a distinguished American classical violinist who had studied in

Leipzig, Brussels, and Paris, under Arthur Nikisch and Anton Seidl.[112] Their friends included leading composers such as Edward Elgar, Edward Grieg, Richard Strauss, Percy Grainger, and Claude Debussy. The Speyers hosted many concerts at their London home and their country estate called Sea Marge on the Norfolk coast. The financier also funded the premieres of several Elgar works at Queen's Hall in the first decade of the century including *Cockaigne Overture* and Elgar's Second Symphony. Speyer financed the introduction of Strauss's *Symphonic Poems* to English audiences. Strauss dedicated his opera *Salome* to "my friend Sir Edgar Speyer."[113] Through his financing, Speyer helped to introduce to the public Sibelius's *Finlandia*, Debussy's *Ibéria*, Ravel's *Valses Nobles et Sentimentales*, Vaughan Williams's *The Wasps*, Frank Bridge's *The Sea*, Percy Grainger's *Mock Morris*, and Igor Stravinsky's *The Firebird*.

Like Karl Muck, Edgar Speyer first became acquainted with anti-German attacks through a competitor in the musical world. William Boosey was managing director of Chappell and Company, which owned the lease on the Queen's Hall and was Speyer's rival bidder in 1902 for the patronage of the Queen's Hall Orchestra. Over the next decade, Boosey conspired to remove Speyer from competition, and in 1914 pressed him to cancel a Wagner program he had funded.[114] Boosey targeted Speyer on "patriotic grounds," suggesting that he was a "notorious German" whose musical programs were "aggressively German" and his influence should be removed from the city. During the war, Speyer's American, Central American, and Cuban investments stagnated, and people who had invested with him were disappointed, adding to the controversy about him.[115] He was demonized in the British press. Sir Almeric Fitzroy, clerk of the Privy Council, called him "a most characteristic little Jew."[116] In January of 1915, author William Le Queux produced a book entitled *German Spies in England*.[117] This led Cecil Chesterton, editor of the weekly *New Witness*, to implicate Speyer in a "German-Jewish conspiracy."[118] The article stated that Speyer and others "should be sent to a concentration camp and put to some useful occupation, like wood chopping, so as to do for the first time in their lives an honest day's work."[119]

In 1915, Speyer was accused by the British government of using a wireless telegraph to signal German submarines at his waterfront home in Norfolk, England. The property was thoroughly searched and nothing was found.[120] The Speyer family was shunned during the war. Speyer's wife, Leonora, was blackballed from society clubs, and their children were prevented from attending school.[121] In June of 1915, with hostilities mounting against them and fearing internment or deportation to Germany, the Speyers moved to the United States,

Figure 5.9. Leonora Speyer, American Pulitzer Prize–winning poet and concert violinist, and one of Karl and Anita Muck's friends. Photo reads, "To Dr. and Mme. Edvard Grieg with kindest regards and affectionate greeting. Leonora Speyer." Wikimedia Commons and the Bergen Public Library, Norway. June 7, 1907. 5612279753.

settling in Boston because of its literary and musical life and, later, moved to New York.[122]

Edgar became part of the St. Botolph Club where Higginson and Muck were members.[123] In 1916, Speyer and Muck became good friends, sharing similar interests in music. Their mutual friendships with leading composers gave them much to talk about. The Mucks and Speyers regularly "received one another." At informal gatherings, they discussed music and performed together. Leonora played violin while Karl played the piano.[124]

The Speyers and the Mucks summered near each other on the Maine coastline. The Speyers rented the Birnam waterfront "cottage" in Bar Harbor, and the Mucks rented Lichen House, a waterfront property in Seal Harbor, just five miles away.[125] This region was a center for musicians in the summertime. They performed in the lovely neoclassical music hall in Blue Hill situated in a pine grove, and they dined and entertained one another each evening by gaslight. Walter Damrosch, the Kneisel Quartet, Fritz Kreisler, Paderewski, Leopold Stokowski, and his wife, pianist Olga Samaroff, among others, vacationed there.[126] Speyer wrote of the "tremendous difference to the life of the neighborhood" having the Mucks nearby. "We were very anxious that Dr. Muck should join the musical coterie there."[127] The Mucks often shared dinners or were "guests of honor" at the Speyers' cottage. On August 4, 1916, Muck wrote that "Sir Edgar Speyer came over this afternoon from Bar Harbor and spent the night with me and is taking me back in the morning in his car to lunch at Bar Harbor. Tomorrow afternoon his car is bringing me back again."[128]

The Speyers were exceptionally generous. They made substantial contributions to distressed friends and family back in Germany. When Justice Department agents raided Muck's Seal Harbor home in the summer of 1917, they found a financial contribution from Leonora Speyer to Anita Muck to "help defray expenses of getting a certain German woman back to the *Fatherland*."[129] Both women were assisting with German relief efforts. On December 21, 1915, before America entered the war, Anita Muck, Baroness von Scholley, Mrs. Münsterberg, and Lady Speyer sold homemade cakes and confections at Boston's Hotel Somerset to raise money for orphans of German soldiers fallen during the war; 12,000 marks were sent to Germany from this sale. Edgar Speyer paid John Koren, treasurer and friend of the St. Botolph Club, to travel to Berlin during the war to deliver aid for war relief and to check in on Speyer's sister and cousin.[130]

Muck was energetically involved with Speyer raising money for German relief. In the fall of 1916, Muck met with several men at Jacob Wirth's Restaurant to talk about creating a bank account for their

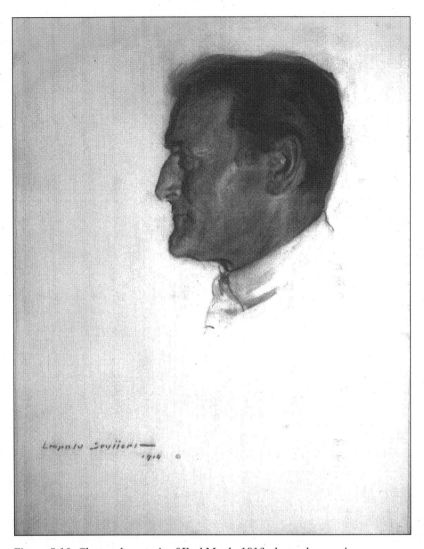

Figure 5.10. Charcoal portrait of Karl Muck, 1916, drawn by evening candlelight by Leopold Seyffert, a native of Seal Harbor, Maine, as celebrity musicians performed for one another in their summer cottages. Courtesy of Robert Seyffert, the artist's grandson.

efforts. Muck also met at the Hotel Tuileries Ballroom to interest Germans loyal to the fatherland in their work.[131] On March 27, 1916, Muck wrote, "It is a regular Sunday for me, as usual" meeting with these men at his house. "At 1 o'clock we had a little luncheon of three-quarters of an hour, the whole remaining time devoted to documents, reports, and records."[132] Muck received contributions for German war relief from prominent Boston Brahmins with whom he associated.[133] When Muck was arrested, the BOI found "in his possession" receipts from the Trans-Atlantic Trust Company and Deutsche Bank "for the purchase of 70,000 marks of the third German War Loan."[134]

When Muck was not performing at Symphony Hall, he was actively supporting his homeland in different ways. Muck recorded that he was "out at a concert for the German Red Cross."[135] In 1915, during a concert tour in San Francisco, he donated $300 to the German New York newspaper *Fatherland.* Muck had doubts regarding the salesman's authenticity and telegraphed the newspaper's headquarters to learn that he "was the victim of a swindler."[136] Muck brought the case to court, and Frederick Griesheimer of Chicago was promptly found guilty of obtaining money from Muck under false pretenses and sentenced to eighteen months in San Quentin Penitentiary.[137] Muck was given due process under the law. He was treated sympathetically by the court. Two and a half years later, however, at the height of America's involvement in the war, Muck was demonized by John Rathom of the *Providence Journal* for having contributed money to support a German national newspaper. On November 7, 1917, Rathom accused Muck of being "active in pro-German propaganda" and being "a most virulent and rabid supporter of Germany's cause."[138]

Muck and Speyer wrote of their desire to be left alone, to return to a level of contentment that they had enjoyed before the war began, when the United States was a neutral nation. They sought to live peacefully in America and hoped to support their German friends and family with money and with diplomacy. They believed that cooperative relations between England, Germany, and the United States was possible. Both men had divided loyalties. Speyer naïvely believed that international finance would bridge the divide, whereas Muck believed music had that power.[139] Lucie Jay, on the contrary, threw her full loyalty behind the United States and denounced her German heritage. Muck and Speyer hoped for ongoing good relations between their birth and adopted countries.

When Speyer came to America, he was still being watched. British and American intelligence offices worked in collaboration, "looking into Edgar's activities in America."[140] Detectives broke into the New York apartment of his confidential secretary. They spied on Speyer at his Bar Harbor home.[141] England was looking for evidence to revoke Speyer's certificate of naturalization. No evidence could be found.[142] In 1922, Speyer was stripped of his British citizenship in part because of his connection with Karl Muck.[143] The Naturalization Committee cited Rathom's *Providence Journal* story as fact—even though it was slanderous and full of false information. The judicial committee reported, "On the basis of such evidence . . . Edgar had shown himself disaffected and disloyal as charged under the Alien Act."[144] The reasons his citizenship was revoked included doing business in Germany, corresponding with his brother-in-law in Germany, and openly associating in America with Karl Muck, a known pro-German.[145] By 1922, the year Speyer was judged in the British courts, Muck had acquired an international reputation as a criminal in great part because of the syndication of the American press. To be linked in any way to Karl Muck, America's "dangerous enemy alien," added to the evidence against Speyer and helped to ensure certain guilt and hardship for him.

Association with these acquaintances raised suspicion that Muck was involved with spies and that he could have been involved in sabotaging America's efforts in the war.[146] He was "guilty by association" even though no evidence was ever found to prove that he had committed any crime. More likely, Muck relied on his friendships to vent his increasing upset over the war. He worked with them to provide aid to the German people, giving him a feeling of helping, even from a distance. In hindsight, we can see that Muck was nationalistic and loyal to Germany. A selection of his private letters published in the *Boston Post* after the war reveal his feelings as the war progressed. He attempted to assist Germany through club activities and social associations. Only after the war, by looking at his letters and reading the FBI transcripts of those he was associated with, can we piece together his changing attitude toward America as the war progressed. Clearly, the German conductor had become increasingly agitated and bitter.

Muck's Developing Anger toward America as the War Progresses

Muck had been worried about his family back in Germany. When the war broke out in 1914, the British implemented a naval blockade that prevented needed food and supplies from reaching Germany. Total war exacted a strain on civilians on the German home front, and relatives living abroad became deeply involved on an emotional level and worked to send needed relief. In private correspondence, Muck expressed his frustration and helplessness in not being able to assist his family: "Today a postcard came from my brother, dated March 12. My sister is slowly but surely getting worse, and the question of nourishment seems to be getting continually more unpleasant."[147] On April 12, 1915, Muck wrote, "There are so many things . . . claiming my thoughts and nerves. . . . I dare not speak with even my own brother. . . . I am overloaded with worry. . . . My head burns like an American cannon factory."[148]

Muck worried about German widows and orphans of soldiers killed in battle, and he was aggrieved by the hypocrisy of war. He wrote:

> Every single person there, every man, woman, and child sacrifices himself. We Germans here can only look on from a distance. That alone has been making me more and more miserable for the last two years. . . . Is it possible that this war has shortened my life just as it has taken hundreds of thousands of other lives; but that is only a matter of course. In Bloomfontain [South Africa] there is a monument in memory of 32,000 Boer women and children whom the English in the Boer war starved at Kitchener's orders. At that time the American papers were full of articles about the English brutality and bestiality and hundreds of protest meetings held. Today the English attempt the same starvation process with about forty million women and children but the cultivated Americans full of humanitarian consideration and the right of men, find this perfectly correct. They are only German women and children who are starving; and furthermore, America indeed is making these splendid millions of profits during this starvation process.[149]

Karl Muck was conflicted. On the one hand, he claimed he wanted to make Boston his home, and, indeed, he seemed to create a happy life there. On the other hand, he became disillusioned by America during the war. His letters show that he became increasingly acrimonious about Allied policies regarding Germany and angry over American munitions plants creating weapons intended to kill Germans. His private letters illustrate his agony over what he believed was the senseless violence perpetrated by America and Great Britain against his homeland. His nineteenth-century sensibility was shocked by the twentieth-century brutality of modern warfare involving soldiers and civilians: "Since November, 1914, when the first American shell was fired from an English cannon upon German soldiers, until Dec 1, 1915, 220,000 German soldiers have been killed and about 400,000 wounded and maimed through American ammunition. Is this not terrible? . . . These are terrible times, and sometimes I nearly perish from impotent bitterness . . . what terrible bloodshed this country is responsible for."[150] While giving a concert in Pittsburgh, in January of 1917,

Muck was unable to restrain his venom when he saw steel mills making cannon and munitions. He wrote privately, "May the devil take this Pittsburgh—a horrible day."[151] Muck's heightened political views paralleled his feelings about anti-German hysteria in Boston. In an October 15, 1915, letter to a friend, he wrote:

> I cannot tell you how cruel life appears to me here, surrounded by enemies, who hate me from the depths of their hearts because I am German. . . . It requires my whole capacity (my Kultur, the Kultur of barbarians) not to thrust ten times daily in the faces of these lying, hypocritical, corrupt, lip-artists—"Once the day will come" (*Einst wird kommen der Tag*)—that is my only comfort. Tomorrow I must step before the public again; it is hateful to me.

Less than six months later, before conducting the Boston Symphony at Harvard College, Muck wrote that the "fanatical nest of hypocrites" made it impossible "for a decent German to breathe in this country."[152] Muck expressed his rage and frustration regarding the mistreatment of the first officer of the *Cecilie*, a German ship docked in the Boston Harbor: "A splendid man, [with] wife and two children in Germany, has died. He lay in bed with bronchitis and a high fever when the brave officials plundered the ship. In spite of the doctor's protest and the captain, the sick man was obliged to get up and leave the ship in the bitter cold weather. He got pneumonia and died."[153] Muck was disgusted by such inhumane and senseless treatment. As the war progressed, he despaired that America might not be the international and cosmopolitan place that he had dreamed of, and he found himself torn between Germany and the United States, forced to choose sides.

Regardless of his rancorous feelings, Muck kept his emotions to himself. He voiced his opinions only within his intimate circle of friends, never in public. To the contrary, his public demeanor was quiet and respectful during the war. On November 1, 1917, under pressure to comply with the public's wishes, while also understanding Muck's German background, Higginson timidly asked Muck to begin playing "The Star-Spangled Banner" at the start of all concerts throughout the remainder of the war. Muck agreed, conducting the piece for every performance thereafter.[154] Muck remained utterly charming and polite and in no way wore his political opinions on his sleeve, although his concert programs continued to be filled with works by German masters. As Henry Lee Higginson expressed:

> For eighteen months past, no man could have striven more zealously than has Dr. Muck to keep the symphony concerts clear of any differences that the war and partisanship over it has provoked. . . . No

man in public and responsible place has been more careful than Dr. Muck not to obtrude his own loyalties and judgments between nation and nation upon those who knew him only in his public capacity. . . . And the reward of such sense of obligation steadfastly maintained has been the petty slander.[155]

Higginson's Patriotism, Naïve Paternalism, and Paranoia Lead to Problems at the BSO

Higginson attempted to keep Muck safe from attacks. He downplayed problems in the press. On October 22, 1917, he wrote a letter to Richard Fletcher, the editor of the New York *Chronicle* and Mrs. Jay's personal agent, stressing the BSO's neutrality and lack of political agenda.[156] Four days later, he echoed the same reassurance with his friend Miss Elizabeth G. Norton, in response to her concern that the federal government would treat the orchestra harshly: "Dear Lily, Your letter made me laugh. The government has nothing on Muck or anyone in the BSO."[157] Ignoring the warning signs from everyone around him that trouble was coming, Higginson laughed off all suggestions of future difficulty for the BSO and remained positive that the storm would pass.

Following the Providence "Star-Spangled Banner" incident, Higginson draped Symphony Hall, outside and in, with enormous American flags.[158] Muck conducted the BSO at the US Army's Camp Devens in central Massachusetts for the troops there. Like wearing a good-luck amulet to ward off evil, people within the musical community began performing "The Star-Spangled Banner" or displaying their American flag to keep trouble away. Public expressions of American national pride proved tantamount to eluding persecution.

Too many forces were pressuring Higginson, however, for these simple tactics to overcome the inevitable harassment. The Boston Symphony founder and musical patrician's thinking evolved from that of a man who would walk through fire for his musicians, to one who began to believe the demonic portrayals of Muck in the local press.[159] Higginson knew his players better than anyone, and yet even he began to have his doubts. Karl Muck would come to realize that he could no longer count on the protection that Higginson and Boston Symphony Hall afforded him, for this was like remaining on a sinking ship. In 1914 and 1915, Higginson had attracted German musicians to Boston with the promise of security—that his orchestra and Symphony Hall would remain untouched by politics or a nationalist agenda. He naïvely believed that musical culture was international and unchanging and, therefore, he and his musicians could transcend political difficulties. Over time, however, his idealism crumbled as public pressure and the economic realities of war penetrated the hallowed walls of Symphony Hall. Higginson became more nationalistic himself and less able to maintain his objectivity. He developed a split and contradictory personality regarding his musicians, wanting to protect them while simultaneously fomenting a climate of suspicion within the orchestra. His own ideological transformation rocked the former stability of the Boston Symphony and created a toxic environment there.

Before the war, Higginson had warm regard for his German musicians and for Muck: "You know my knowledge of, association with, and liking for the German people." Of Muck, he said, "We have at its head the man who seems to me the best musician in the world as conductor of an orchestra, and a man of the highest ideals as a musician and as a gentleman." Higginson was able to separate his opinions about German culture and its people from German imperial policies. "The feeling here with regard to this war is entirely against the German Emperor, and not against the German people."[160] Higginson assumed that the American public could do the same and distinguish between imperial policies and an innocent population. "Rightly or wrongly," he wrote, "our people believe that the Emperor could have stopped the war, even if he did not make it. They believe that he has prepared for this war during his whole lifetime."[161]

Higginson was out of touch with the popular sentiments of the day, foolishly believing that arts patrons were grateful for Muck. He recorded that "there is one feeling universally, and that is great admiration and gratitude for the beautiful concerts he [Muck] has given, and which the people hope he will continue to give."[162] Higginson believed that "nobody will take any attitude toward him but that of the kindest, most cordial appreciation of him and all his work."[163] Higginson underestimated how damaging attacks could be toward "his" musicians.

Higginson professed his genuine affection for his German players, and he often referred nostalgically to the Germany of his youth. Upon his retirement, on May 4, 1918, he said of his musicians:

> For many years, we—you and I—have been good comrades—an honor and a pleasure for me. In these years, we have worked hand and glove together, and have kept true to our rule, laid down at the outstart, of intelligent study under one conductor at a time; and we have reaped the reward of success sure to follow. We have played in many cities of the United States, and have won great applause and better still have deserved it. Each year has marked an advance in the quality of our music, and this year has seen our high point. I like to

think myself a member of our Orchestra, and have done my best to help you; and, on your side.[164]

Higginson's Symphony Hall was a replica of the Gewandhaus in Leipzig, where Higginson had spent many happy days in his youth. His hall and his musicians gave him daily reminders of those halcyon years. At the same time, Higginson was a loyal American. He was a Civil War veteran, with a prominent saber scar on his face from that conflict and with a patriotic personality that seemed to forget his German affiliations and obligations.[165] While he spoke affectionately to his orchestra and begged its members to keep their political opinions to themselves during the war, Higginson's own business and political activity suggests a far different agenda. He became more passionate about the war and more jingoistic himself.

Recalling his war service fifty years earlier, Higginson had marshaled home-front Bostonians to be prepared "no matter who knocks at the door." Then, eighty-year-old Higginson became the chairman of the World War I committee that arranged the Preparedness Parade, and on October 27, 1915, he marched proudly in this role along the entire parade route. Intensely spirited, Higginson argued, "If our American citizens are not going to look after our country, who will do it?" He went on, "Manhood suffrage requires manhood service, and this means service for every man and woman in the country."[166]

As an investment banker, Higginson realized he could profit from an Allied victory; thus, he floated war loans to the French. He had a lot to lose if Germany won the war. Moreover, Higginson invested heavily in the copper market, becoming a competitor with Germany.[167] While he complained "on high moral principles" about the way that "our people seem to have rigged the copper-market," he still greatly enjoyed watching the struggle. He wrote, "For two hundred years Europe has clubbed her capital to rig markets against us, and now comes a first class fight to see who has the biggest pile."[168] In a letter to President Woodrow Wilson and his foreign policy advisors, Higginson pushed for a suspension of trade with Germany: "We can refuse to let anything in the way of merchandise go to Germany, and we can refuse to let any of her merchandise come here." He also suggested that the United States should take control of German ships docked in American ports, "until ample money indemnification is given for all that she has done."[169]

As early as 1914, when newspapers in the United States reported that German soldiers were committing atrocities against Belgian citizens, Higginson could not resist writing to US senator from Massachusetts John W. Weeks, requesting that the US government publicly condemn the kaiser's behavior. Higginson, a man committed to

supporting German culture in Boston, grew hostile toward the imperial government's actions in the war. "My Dear Senator: In these horrible times, may I say a word? ... We ought to do everything that we
can for the good of the side opposed to the German Emperor, and I
see no reason why we should not express publicly our detestation of
his conduct." To New York financier J. P. Morgan, who had also floated
massive war loans to the French and British, Higginson wrote, "This
man [the kaiser] is an enemy to the world. . . . As I see it, if he succeeds
it is not a fit place to live in."[170]

As time went on, Higginson had difficulty maintaining the pact
with his orchestra to keep quiet and not take sides. A man who was
married to a German wife and who vacationed in Austria, Higginson
feared what the kaiser was capable of. He struggled in the throes of
war to make sense of his affection for Germany and its citizens. He
feared that Germany would invade the United States after conquer-
ing Europe; thus, he encouraged Americans to take preparation seriously: "If he [the kaiser] should succeed, we would come next. He will
be sure to order us about. He may take Canada by treaty; he may go
into South America; and we have no use for him nor his ideas this side
of the water. I think our Navy should be kept in first-class order." He
urged President Wilson to prompt action and supported his policy of
arming American ships against submarine attacks.[171]

Higginson was growing increasingly agitated with his "beloved"
Germany and proposed a series of punishments against the beleaguered nation that would result in hardship for Germans in America.
In a 1918 letter to President Charles Eliot of Harvard, and repeated in
correspondence to President Wilson, Higginson suggested cutting off
communication with Germany to make "it so unpleasant for the German Ambassador that he would like to go home."[172] Higginson did
not think through how his actions would ultimately impact the lives
of his musicians. Muck was friends with the German ambassador, and
he relied on him for news from Germany. The ambassador worked to
improve the relationship between Germany and the United States.
Sending him home would cut off a lifeline of communication and
support for many of the players within Higginson's orchestra. Further
undermining trust, Higginson and Eliot began gossiping about the
Germans in the orchestra, publicly vocalizing their animosity toward
German culture and its people in general. "Music is really the only
subject in which Germany can still claim superiority," they argued.
"Her philosophy and religion have failed to work; her education has
not developed in the people power to reason or good judgment; her
efficiency even in war is not greater than that of her adversaries; and
her ruling class is too stupid to see that their game of domination in

Europe is already lost."[173] It was becoming harder for Higginson to keep his opinions to himself.

The situation for German orchestra members became more volatile as Higginson's nationalism escalated. As a result, Boston Symphony musicians were disquietingly pulled into the political maelstrom. Bliss Perry describes this unsettled time and the fate of Muck and the orchestra members as "a leaf in the storm," for there was no security from the impending wartime dangers that they faced.[174]

Higginson began to empathize with Mrs. Jay's call to abandon German music and musicians. On December 7, 1917, one month after the *Providence Journal* attacked Muck for not playing "The Star-Spangled Banner," Higginson wrote to Eliot, "I sympathize with the people who cannot bear to hear German music or Dr. Muck or the men in the Orchestra."[175] Higginson became less willing to defend or protect Muck as he had originally promised, deferring to the government regarding Muck's care. He wrote, "The exact status of Dr. Muck will be settled presently by the Attorney General's office. . . . The whole question of citizenship [German or Swiss] is very mixed and must be left to the experts."[176]

Higginson seemed increasingly unable to draw a dividing line between German imperial policies and the German population in Boston: "I knew very well the stupidity and arrogance of the Germans, particularly in Prussia." Beginning in 1916 and throughout the following year, when German U-boats began sinking Massachusetts codfish boats off the coast of Newfoundland, Higginson was livid. He raged, "It is more than senseless for the Germans to sink those boats, for every boat sunk makes a thousand enemies."[177] Codfish was the backbone of the Massachusetts economy. The state had always venerated the fishing industry, so much so that it hung a large wooden codfish from the Massachusetts State House ceiling, where it still hangs today. Higginson, the ever-loyal Bostonian, could not bear an attack on the state's economy or maintain his objectivity toward German people in the United States.

As the war progressed, Higginson's conversations with Eliot involved questioning whether members of the orchestra were German agents or spies. External political pressures and increasing anti-German hysteria made Higginson more paranoid and fearful of the players he had formerly trusted. War-era propaganda reports and motion pictures that portrayed spies and agents bombing munitions plants added to Higginson's doubt. Eliot suggested that Higginson query his French players for information on Muck, and, shortly thereafter, Higginson met privately with non-German musicians and asked them, "Have you, or the French members of the Orchestra had any reason to believe that the German members, or some of them, were what may fairly be called German agents?"[178] Higginson tasked his French players with the duty of spying on his German players, creating discord within his formerly harmonious ensemble.

Even Muck's dear friend, composer George Chadwick, began to suspect that the BSO harbored traitors. He shared his fears in a letter to Frederick Stock, the German American conductor of the Chicago Symphony Orchestra, who had avoided trouble more successfully than Muck. "There are many members of the Boston Symphony," Chadwick wrote, "who are anything but loyal to this country, although they are legally naturalized."[179]

For several months, Higginson kept a watchful eye on his orchestra and on Muck. He admitted to the *Boston Herald*, "Sundry good and friendly people have told me to look out for Dr. Muck and his doings, and some of them are sure that he is making mischief."[180] Tension was mounting, and Higginson appeared to be waiting for authorities to bring him information on Muck's misconduct.[181] Eliot counseled Higginson that "unless Dr. Muck or some other members of the Orchestra commit real offenses against this country . . . until we get real proofs of misconduct on their part a safe conclusion then is to go on just as you have been." Before the war, Higginson had promised to protect Muck from anti-German hysteria. He had viewed his conductor positively, and yet, as the war progressed, Higginson became more doubtful and suspicious of Muck's activities. It was hard enough for Muck that Mrs. Jay and others were stirring up difficulty, but when his boss and mentor distrusted him and even solicited the French musicians to spy on him, it was clear to Muck that he had no safe harbor in America anymore.[182] The country he had come to love and enjoy was fast becoming an entirely different place.

Higginson, the founder of the BSO, who had counseled his musicians to think of their orchestra as an international body, exempt from the political fray, created tension within the ensemble by his own actions. In earlier times, members had been loyal to each other and to the institution. Higginson's orchestra had been friendly and productive, and it had maintained a cohesive esprit de corps. Diversity was genuinely accepted and appreciated, and all of the musicians believed in the universal quality of the music they performed. As World War I progressed, however, the musicians only pretended to get along with one another. Genuine mutual respect steadily degraded into mere tolerance and, eventually, into scorn and distrust. As a means of survival, the musicians suppressed their national identities and remained silent for the good of the organization and to honor their contracts. The one-hundred-man orchestra, which included fifty-one US citizens (and, of those, thirty-four foreign born) and twenty-two German nationals, were unable to ignore wartime pressures.[183]

Tension and Division among the Formerly Tight BSO Ensemble

A climate of negativity seeped into the confines of Symphony Hall, leading to internal difficulties among the personnel. Those who had been certain of Muck's innocence began to question him. Nationalism and anti-German hysteria created social divisions. Bureau of Investigation officials also began questioning orchestra members concerning their loyalties, first in March of 1918 and then in September, separating players into pro-American and pro-German camps, interviewing the American players, or "safe men to talk to," about those they viewed as suspicious.[184] Orchestra members Walter Piston, Ernest Major, Roy Kenfield, and Augustus Battles accused German players Gustav Heim, Charles Barth, Karl Rissland, and Louis Kloepfel of questionable behavior. They reported that "Heim bragged about efficiency of [the] German army and inefficiency of our own." Heim had a boat on Lake Winnipesaukee in New Hampshire called the *Hindenburg*, but during the war he changed the name to *Pershing*. The men wondered whether Kloepfel was a spy. Due to lack of evidence, BOI agents believed the men "to be as much Americanized as any other German in the Boston Symphony Orchestra," therefore closing the investigation against them.[185] After Muck's internment in April of 1918, no German members of the BSO were interned. The damage had been done, however. Fissures had been widened, and relationships (including the one between the conductor and his director) had deteriorated.

Higginson could no longer protect his conductor or his German musicians from the hysteria, and Muck felt betrayed and disposed of by his boss. On March 12, 1918, Muck wrote:

> I have long since lost faith in [Henry Lee Higginson]. . . . He explained to me on his word of honor that he would immediately disband the orchestra . . . that he would at my departure . . . disband the orchestra, and that he is now setting heaven and earth in motion to find a French man or a Belgian as my successor, and now the story goes calmly on only that my scalp shall hang on the belt of Mr. [Higginson] and his Boston friends.[186]

In April of 1918, just weeks after Muck's arrest, Higginson was heartbroken over the political turmoil within the BSO and resigned his position as patron after thirty-eight years of service. Higginson told his friends that "the joy of the concerts and the joy of music is gone for me."[187] The *Sunday Herald* reported that Higginson had originally expected the BSO to fold after Muck's arrest but that friends had persuaded him to appoint a board of trustees to take over the affairs of the orchestra, which is what he did. In his final farewell on May 4, 1918, Higginson told the audience, "Our Orchestra has always been heartily supported by you and by the public throughout our country, else it could not have lived. It must lie in all its strength and beauty, and now will be carried on by some friends who have taken it up, and for them I ask the same support which you have given me through all these years."[188] His new board included prominent Brahmins Judge Frederick P. Cabot, Ernest B. Dane, M. A. DeWolfe Howe, John Ellerton Lodge, Frederick E. Lowell, Arthur Lyman, Henry B. Sawyer, Galen L. Stone, and Bentley W. Warren.[189] The men filed papers to incorporate the organization and to guarantee the continuation of BSO concerts. Their first task involved dismissing eighteen German members of the orchestra, including assistant conductor Ernst Schmidt.[190] For a brief period, they appointed French composer and conductor Henri Rabaud for the fall 1918 season. Rabaud hired many new staff members, including a French military band. His appointment was quickly followed by conductor Pierre Monteux, making the orchestra very Parisian in character. Under Monteux, the BSO performed works by Ravel and Stravinsky for the first time. New England's composers now began going to France to study with Erik Satie and Nadia Boulanger, instead of to Germany.

While Karl Muck languished in a hot Georgia internment camp, the new BSO management distanced itself from him. Speaking on their behalf, the *Boston Post* reported that "there has been the mistaken impression on the part of some people that Dr. Muck made the BSO. Dr. Muck did not make the BSO. The BSO made Dr. Muck, made him a greater conductor than he ever was before he came here."[191]

Henry Lee Higginson was thoroughly exhausted from the ordeal. The BSO, his creation, had almost collapsed, but, with new management, it was revived again. Higginson died shortly after this transition, on November 5, 1919, just two and a half months after Muck's deportation and four days short of his eighty-fifth birthday. The *World* reported, "No doubt the [BSO] organization will survive as it deserves to survive, under the nine trustees who take over Major Higginson's support; but it will be 'the Symphony without its Maecenas.'"[192]

Chapter Six

MUCK'S ARREST

"Finding 'One Weak Spot'" (1918–1919)

Render, which are the whole art of music alike for him who
prisons it in notes and staves and for him who gives it wing.

—"Dr. Muck of the Wasting Years,
Yet Power of Prime," 1926

I start from the supposition that the world is topsy-turvy,
that things are all wrong, that the wrong people are in jail
and the wrong people are out of jail, that the wrong people
are in power and the wrong people are out of power.

—Howard Zinn, 1970

Muck Investigated for
His Relationship with Margaret Herter

In February of 1918, Francis Coffey, New York district attorney and
regional agent for the Bureau of Investigation, sent a report to Judd
Dewey, Massachusetts district attorney for Alien Matters and Boston's
BOI representative, regarding the renowned Dr. Karl Muck, for his
questionable relationship with Margaret Dows Herter, a twenty-two-
year-old musician from a wealthy New York family. It was Margaret's
mother, Susan, who had raised concerns about Muck's conduct with
her daughter. She had initially contacted the New York Police Department, and it soon became clear that this would be no ordinary complaint. The case was referred to Coffey, who opened an investigation
that would ultimately lead to the downfall of the celebrated Boston
Symphony Orchestra conductor.

Karl Muck's friend and colleague, Margaret Herter, was an accomplished violinist.[1] Federal authorities brought their private relationship into the spotlight. Although the BOI found nothing illegal about
the relationship, it led federal officials (and Mrs. Jay) on a quest to

find other questionable relationships that Muck was involved in. The *New York Sun* reported that "while government officials here refused to make any statement concerning Doktor Muck's case, it was understood that much of the evidence leading to his arrest came from the little band of patriotic women in New York, led by Mrs. William Jay."[2]

An accusation of sexual impropriety was the latest in a series of attempts to destroy Muck's musical career in Boston and extinguish German cultural influence there by linking it to moral indecency during wartime. Before this attempt, Muck's enemies struggled to destroy him with open allegations of disloyalty. Several New York newspapers had characterized the conductor as untrustworthy and devious, claiming that he had come to America to carry out espionage efforts on behalf of Germany. He was accused of being a dangerous spy, of blowing up munitions plants and tampering with guns used by American soldiers.[3] Anonymous letters in newspapers accused him of sending prostitutes with venereal diseases to American military bases and plotting to blow up Henry Wadsworth Longfellow's birthplace in Cambridge, Massachusetts.[4]

The government also badgered him, eager to find something to confirm these unfounded rumors. In a letter, Muck recounted the ignorance of the Department of Justice officials who believed that his orchestral scores were filled with coded messages.[5] Federal agents pored over his entire library, ransacking musical manuscripts that he had spent his entire career acquiring and notating.

Federal authorities also became suspicious of Muck's perceived activities at his Seal Harbor, Maine, rental home, located "on a high cliff commanding a wide view of the ocean." Often traveling there from Boston to "enjoy a bath in the ocean," Muck was accused of communicating by ham radio with German submarines at sea. BOI agents spied on him in the summer of 1917, leaving their car in town and approaching the house through the woods. The officials inspected the house "from garret to cellar" and "in an alcove just off his den," they found part of a radio transmitter. "The instruments had been removed, but the alcove was filled with wires." In that same room, the men found a "secret trap door" where a wire led to the cellar and ground. In Anita Muck's bedroom, a chest of drawers had been built into the wall "containing wires and dry cells." The press reported that "only a skilled operator with extreme cunning" could signal German submarines without being caught. They speculated that Muck had a man chop wood on the premises while he operated the wireless "in order that the noise of the wood chopping might drown or at least detract from the sound of the wireless."[6] The BOI authorities followed up on every imaginative and suspicious lead printed in the press, and

Figure 6.1. Lichen House, Karl and Anita Muck's Seal Harbor rental property. The land where the house once stood currently belongs to author and television celebrity Martha Stewart. Courtesy of the Maine Historic Preservation Commission and Robert Seyffert.

yet they found no evidence against Muck to back up such claims. It was later determined that the landlord, Dr. A. E. Lawrence, a New York science professor who studied electric magnetic currents, was responsible for the ham radio apparatus and that Muck knew nothing about it.[7]

Muck may have been unaware of the wireless radio, but he did know that Mrs. Jay was behind each allegation, and he referred to her and her followers as "a pack still more rabid."[8] Like animals seeking their prey, he claimed they had "lynx eyes" and they would "find one weak spot in our position, drag it into the open, before the public, and make it course, common, dirty." Frustrated and exhausted by their witch hunt, Muck said, "The whole situation is so degrading for me; I am like a shabby dog here in this country, whom every cutthroat may bombard with stones unpunished."[9]

It is true, in the early years of the war, Muck had, in fact, engaged in war-related work, such as aiding German relief and contributing financially to its cause. But, on this evidence alone, he was not unlike most German Americans or German nationals living abroad who showed concern for loved ones in Europe with financial contributions or political efforts to influence American war policy. His actions in the United States were far from threatening, certainly not illegal or "dangerous." There was no law in place in 1918 making Muck's war actions unlawful.[10] Attorney General Thomas W. Gregory was a Texas lawyer and political progressive who took his role as a "policeman to the nation" seriously. He sought to punish "disloyalty" and "dissension," and yet those words were so undefined that "German-Americans had no way of knowing where they stood in the eyes of the local communities that actually enforced these laws." As Christopher Capozzola points out, "Germans found little refuge in the nation's legal structure."[11]

Muck's personal relationships with young women seemed to provide the "one weak spot" that both Mrs. Jay and federal authorities had been searching for to prove some illegality on Muck's part. Resorting to allegations of sexual impropriety, they used their significant power to find Muck's vulnerability, to weaken his important social position, and to destroy his character.[12] The New York press, in fact, praised Mrs. Jay, who was pleased with her efforts in bringing new information surrounding Muck's female acquaintances to light, leading investigators to pursue the cases further.[13]

Francis Coffey's report on Muck's "inappropriate" relationship with Margaret Herter piqued his interest because the file went beyond the usual anti-German complaints reported during World War I. Officials typically investigated individuals who could become dangerous to American lives and institutions.[14] As mentioned earlier, President Wilson's wartime policies gave federal authorities expanded powers to invade privacy, search and seize at random, confine and interrogate without access to lawyers, inflict torture upon, detain, deport, or restrict the liberties of any "suspicious" person. Without US constitutional protection of these basic human rights, anyone in the country was vulnerable, most especially German Americans and German nationals.

Powerful authority figures were suspicious of immigrants, as so many had entered the country before the war. They feared anarchists setting off bombs, potential terrorists harming innocent civilians, and Germans distributing propaganda that would impact wartime morale. The BOI took a paranoid approach regarding even small instances of concern, exaggerating and elevating fear into a potential threat. Some politicians argued that it was better to punish and imprison "dangerous" individuals or groups than to let them grow into a real hazard to the country's security. Karl Muck was interned in April of 1918, the same month that German coal miner Robert Prager was lynched by an angry mob in Collinsville, Illinois. After that event, Senator William E. Borah of Idaho said, "Already the news comes over the wire that patriotic citizens are taking the law into their own hands. If we do not do our duty, the impulses of loyal men and women will seek justice in rougher ways."[15] Borah called for preemptive governmental intervention—internment—to keep people safe.

Coffey's report on Muck involved sexual allegations, which was something scintillatingly out of the ordinary. The Boston branch of the BOI, along with federal attorneys general Thomas W. Gregory and his successor A. Mitchell Palmer and their young assistant J. Edgar Hoover, were charged with pursuing them. Palmer was a patriotic American nationalist with a "bulldog jaw" who opposed the boss system and all forms of liquor sales. He hated "the Hun" and had huge political ambitions.[16] John Hoover, as he was called then, was a twenty-three-year-old law clerk who had just graduated from George Washington University having landed a job in the Justice Department, and he was eager to do a thorough job to please his supervisors.[17] As David Cole explains, Hoover would become the most powerful leader of the Bureau of Investigation (later the FBI), a post he would hold for nearly fifty years, from 1924 until his death in 1972. He made full use of the federal government's expansive powers during wartime to target, censure, and imprison "dangerous" German Americans, foreign nationals (and African Americans, socialists, and other "troublemakers") without criminal charges.[18] Hoover, Gregory, and Palmer treated Muck, the subject of one of the first cases of this kind, as a danger to the security of the nation, following through on Coffey's report with an investigation of their own.

Ironically, when Coffey's report arrived on Dewey's desk, Muck was preparing to leave the country for the duration of the war because of the worsening climate of anti-Germanism throughout the country. He had given his resignation to Henry Lee Higginson, who had accepted it. On March 13, 1918, Muck requested a pass from the Department of Justice to return to Germany, and Higginson supported his conductor, vouching for Muck's "absolute propriety, honesty, and honor." With Higginson's assurances, Muck was cleared for travel. All that was required to finalize his plans was a signature from Dewey.[19]

Muck's reportedly questionable relationship with Herter raised suspicion in Dewey's mind that perhaps there was more in Muck's background worth exploring before letting him leave the country. The ambitious and methodical Dewey saw an opportunity to advance his career by finding something condemning and potentially damaging in Muck's past. Arresting the famous German-born conductor during wartime would win Dewey praise and increase his reputation with Palmer and Hoover. Dewey refused to grant Muck the necessary travel passes.

Figure 6.2. The ambitious US attorney general A. Mitchell Palmer hated
"the Hun" and used his federal power against Muck and other immigrants.
Courtesy of the Library of Congress, Prints and Photographs Division, Digital
ID cph.3a37242. Harris and Ewing Collection.

Dewey began to search for scandalous information to use against the German conductor. He interviewed members of the Boston Symphony Orchestra as well as witnesses drawn from the broader musical community. So disturbed by the federal surveillance, Muck commented in a private letter, "Incredible as it seems, it is nevertheless not beyond the realm of possibility that there will be a search of the houses of all those people whom I personally know if once the 'hunt-down' part[y] gain the upper hand."[20] Pitting orchestra members against their beloved conductor, interrogations broke down good relationships within the orchestra, as players were urged to divulge whatever they knew about Karl Muck's personal life, for their own security depended upon it.[21] Thus, Mrs. Rudolph Nagel, the "patriotic" American wife of the "pro-German" Boston Symphony cellist, offered Dewey private details of Muck's romantic relationship with another young woman from Boston—a New England Conservatory mezzo-soprano named Rosamond Young.[22] As only a member of the Boston Symphony's inner circle would know, Rosamond and Karl often met at Symphony Hall, and they shared a brisk epistolary relationship as well. Proof of Muck's "wrongdoing," it was reported by Nagel, would be found in their secret correspondence.[23]

Federal Officials Raid the Home of Rosamond Young

During World War I, no one was safe from governmental intrusion, including the upper classes. Grateful for this new lead in the Muck case, Agent Dewey sent investigators to Rosamond Young's family home, and, "armed with the necessary authority, they persuaded Rosamond's mother to let them into her daughter's bedroom to hunt for evidence against Muck."[24] Initially, they found very little, but they got their opportunity when Mrs. Young heard the doorbell and went downstairs to answer it. While she was attending to the caller, investigators ransacked Rosamond's room and found a black metal box beneath a window seat.

Twenty-two-year-old Rosamond had been out horseback riding while her room was being searched. Completely unaware of the visitors in her home and bedroom, she arrived as investigators were rifling through her private possessions. Surprised to see them, she was frightened that her secret would be revealed. The investigators "forced the young woman to listen to [them] . . . about Dr. Muck." Appealing to her patriotism, they "showed her that it was her duty to the government to assist the nation in every way against a man who they felt was betraying America."[25]

Figure 6.3. Professional artist photo of Rosamond Young Chapin. Courtesy
of the Belknap Collection for the Performing Arts, Special and Area Studies
Collections, George A. Smathers Libraries, University of Florida, Gainesville,
Florida, as photographed by Joseph Abresch, 201 West 78th Street, New York
City.

Rosamond was given no options regarding the items taken from her bedroom. The Fourth Amendment of the Constitution should have protected her. It states, "The right of the people to be secure in their persons, houses, papers and effects, against unreasonable searches and seizures, shall not be violated."[26] Federal investigators took away Rosamond's right of security when they looted her individual space. Because of wartime powers, their actions were legal. Her personal life was suddenly thrust into public view. She was described as turning pale, feeling faint, and becoming angry. She lashed out at the investigators, exclaiming, "What a contemptible insult!"[27] Rosamond viewed the investigators' actions as an insensitive and demeaning invasion into her private world. Middle- and upper-middle-class Victorian society had received a degree of privacy behind heavy drapes, hedgerows, and secret gardens, unknown to the working-class majority of Americans. The theft of Rosamond's private correspondence and the act of making it public was a shocking and traumatic experience.

When federal investigators pressed Rosamond for the key to unlock her black metal box, her brother supported the investigators and urged Rosamond to produce it. Not given agency to manage her own possessions and feeling fraternal pressure from her own brother, Rosamond relented and produced the key. "It was a tense situation. She . . . inserted the key in the lock and lifted the cover of the box, (and) sank limply into a chair." The box was full of photographs of Muck as well as letters from him wrapped in ribbon, along with little trinkets and mementos of their time together.[28] The Boston Bureau of Investigation bullied and frightened Rosamond, arguing that the country's security was at stake and that it was Rosamond's national duty to hand over her personal letters. War powers gave the BOI the authority to disregard her constitutional rights. Weakened and traumatized by the whole episode, she relinquished her secret correspondence, giving the BOI insight into and evidence of the couple's private—sometimes emotional, sometimes erotic—relationship.[29]

The Arrest of Karl Muck

Late in the evening on March 25, 1918, Muck was rehearsing Bach's *Saint Matthew Passion* with the orchestra at Symphony Hall on the eve of its premier performance in Boston. Muck had spent a year preparing the piece, which had been recovered by Mendelssohn in 1829. Muck had worked diligently to analyze the original score and interpret Bach's markings, and he was eager to debut this work in Boston during Easter Holy Week.[30] His plans would be short lived, however.

To determine Muck's whereabouts, the BOI had sent a young messenger to the conductor's home with a note, essentially using Rosamond's forged name as a way to acquire information:

> Fearing that possibly Dr. Muck would be warned of the finding of the incriminating letters and would make his escape, a . . . message, signed with the initials of Miss [Rosamond Young] was sent, asking Dr. Muck to meet her at once at Symphony Hall. . . . The ruse worked to perfection and within a half an hour the boy returned with the information that Dr. Muck was conducting a rehearsal at the hall.[31]

Armed with this new information, BOI special agent Feri Weiss and members of the Boston Police Department stormed Symphony Hall during the private rehearsal and made a public display of Muck, demanding that he step down from the podium at once. Charles Ellis, the symphony manager, pleaded with the men to hold off until the rehearsal had concluded, which they agreed to do, strategically positioning themselves throughout the hall, sitting with their eyes fixed on Muck until he had finished his work. Following the rehearsal, the men accompanied Muck to his office, where he was informed that they would be taking him to the police station. "Dr. Muck made every effort to remain cool, but his shaking fingers belied his true inward agitation."[32]

Muck was forewarned that he would not be returning in time for the concert the next evening at Symphony Hall. He remarked several times that he regretted his inability to take part in the concert that he had worked so hard to prepare. His laments, however, were ignored by the authorities, and he was taken away on the eve of what the conductor considered to be the pinnacle of his efforts in America.

Meanwhile, the BOI raided Karl and Anita Muck's Fenway home, retrieving correspondence and other papers.[33] The BOI recklessly pored over personal items, pulled books off shelves, took pictures off the walls and out of their frames, and went through drawers, trunks, suitcases, and closets, looking for documents offering evidence of guilt. Investigators looked at Muck's collection of calling cards to see with whom he associated. They looked at his bank accounts to see where he spent his money, and they intercepted his mail.[34]

Local and federal officials did not have an organized plan when they took Karl Muck into custody. It would be years before the US government evolved into the bureaucratic and impersonal leviathan that we know today, but during World War I many governmental institutions were in their infancy. Muck was transferred from place to place, and decisions regarding his treatment were made at random. Initially,

Figure 6.4. The Arrest of Dr. Karl Muck. Surrounded by federal officials, Muck was physically taken from Symphony Hall in March of 1918. One official is holding Muck by his arm, while the conductor nervously grips a cigarette with his free hand. Boston Symphony Orchestra Manager Charles Ellis, on the right, looks visibly distraught as he accompanies the men. Courtesy of the National Archives, War Department. 1789-9/18/1947. File Unit: Enemy Activities, Series: World War I Photographs. Record Group 165.

he was taken to Boston's Back Bay Police Station. Muck's photograph was taken, and he was ordered to empty his pockets. BOI agents questioned him for six hours and told him he would remain there overnight.[35] In less than three hours, Muck had smoked several packs of cigarettes and remarked to the press that "this is the biggest predicament I have ever been in in my life." He was held, along with others arrested for various governmental infractions, and was interrogated at frequent intervals by District Attorney Dewey.[36] Muck was transferred the next morning to the US Marshal's office, where he was placed in an "iron prisoner's cage" with two other detainees. When Muck complained of his treatment, he was allowed for a time to sit outside the cage without handcuffs.[37] Still, Muck's privileged status offered him little protection from federal powers.

Conditions worsened for Muck when he was transferred to the East Cambridge Jail, a facility made infamous in 1841 by social reformer Dorothea Dix for its horrible conditions. There, Muck learned that he would not be allowed to smoke cigarettes, which he had come to rely on to calm his nerves. He complained of "inadequate treatment"—so bad, in fact, that one German American sent there during the same period committed suicide by jumping off a stairwell balcony during transport.[38] Prisoners like Muck expected preferential treatment based on their social class and their fame, but a transformation within the United States was taking place, for wartime authorities facing increasing responsibilities had little regard for class distinctions, consigning the privilege of gentility to a previous age. Muck had no choice but to endure the East Cambridge Jail for many days waiting for the final disposition of the case.[39] He was informed that he would remain in custody "indefinitely," and he was admonished to adjust to his harsher environment. During Muck's time in jail, he was allowed few visitors, although many adoring fans, including Isabella Stewart Gardner, waited for updates outside the facility. He sat there for days with no understanding as to why he was being detained.[40]

Removing a "Dangerous Enemy Alien" from Boston

On April 6, 1918, following a discussion of his options (that will be explained more thoroughly in chapter 7), the decision regarding Karl Muck's status was finalized. He was made aware of his formal arrest and his new classification as a "dangerous enemy alien" with an anticipated internment at Fort Oglethorpe, Georgia, for the duration of the war. On the morning of his scheduled journey to the southern camp, he received permission for a final visit to his home at 50 Fenway to gather personal items, to clean up his business affairs, and to say goodbye to his wife. "A taxi took the musician and a deputy marshal across the Harvard Bridge to his former residence. There, he was constantly under the eye of his guard. Mrs. Muck could not restrain the tears as she parted from him, but the prisoner himself bore up well."[41] Muck asked whether he could send a telegram to his orchestra in the care of concertmaster Anton Witek, to explain his circumstances and to say goodbye, but he was denied.[42] On the evening of April 6, accompanied by US deputy marshal Arthur J. Shinner and one other guard, Muck boarded the westbound Federal Express train to Washington, DC, where he transferred to a southbound train through the Appalachians and on to the internment camp.[43]

Muck had been removed from Boston and taken away from the social world that he was familiar with. He was placed in an institutional facility far from home without the benefit of a trial. Many prominent music patrons who knew their beloved conductor suggested a variety of alternative arrangements, offering to pay bail bond or provide escorts or guards to allow Muck's release from custody.[44] Boston patricians expressed their outrage against the Bureau of Investigation, claiming they had condemned an innocent man. They believed that Muck was a victim of a frame-up and that the whole story, when revealed, would show that he had been cruelly treated by the BOI. Rose Fay Thomas, the American-born widow of Chicago Symphony Orchestra conductor Theodore Thomas, winter resident of Cambridge, Massachusetts, and summer occupant of a New Hampshire mountain home, wrote to the *Boston Herald* on Muck's behalf, arguing that his arrest and internment was "shelling the one perfect and complete art creation of Boston . . . and will surely destroy this noble institution past all redemption."[45] Thomas and other influential and outspoken members of Boston's upper-class community seemed no match for an increasingly powerful federal government that disregarded their pleas for his release. The BOI, more concerned with national security in a threatening climate of anti-German hysteria, subordinated Boston's privileged citizens during World War I, never again granting them the level of deference they had been afforded in prior years.

The origins of Muck's treatment can be traced to the prior year. In 1917, the Wilson administration established the Committee of Internments of Alien Enemies, which drew up plans for the confinement of German enemy aliens, expanding federal powers even further.[46] The government pinpointed four distinct locations for internment: Fort Douglas in Salt Lake City, Utah, would receive all enemy aliens west of the Mississippi; and Fort Oglethorpe and Fort McPherson, Georgia, and Hot Springs, North Carolina, would receive prisoners east of the Mississippi.[47]

Conditions at Fort Oglethorpe Internment Camp

Fort Oglethorpe Internment Camp became a multipurpose facility to train US soldiers for war and to serve as a holding cell for German nationals and German American prisoners during World War I. In 1895, Congress established the Chickamauga National Military Park in Northern Georgia, near Lookout Mountain, to preserve the land and to honor those who fought in the Civil War at the Battle of Chickamauga, the bloodiest two-day encounter of the war. In 1902, the government expanded the site north of the park, creating a cavalry post, officers' quarters, barracks, stables, a parade ground, and a hospital. In the first decade of the new century, the National Guard and the army practiced maneuvers there, and, during World War I, it was home to five cavalry divisions. John J. Pershing and Dwight D. Eisenhower served for a short time at Oglethorpe in late 1917, overseeing military training exercises. In that same year, the War Department designated Fort Oglethorpe as an internment camp to house German prisoners of war and "enemy aliens," erecting 1,600 wooden cantonments adjacent to the existing base, serving sixty thousand troops and four thousand internees in total.[48] Construction was so vast that at the conclusion of the war, when the barracks were disassembled, the American House Wrecking Company of Chicago declared that the federal government had utilized three hundred miles of copper wire, thirty-two miles of pipe, eleven carloads of toilets, and enough wooden boards to stretch end-to-end from Chattanooga to Chicago, then on to New York.[49] This was a massive federal facility, hastily erected, to control the lives of the individuals housed within its walls.

Several correspondents during the war have described Muck's accommodations at Oglethorpe in glowing terms, as a "millionaire's club" and a "mountain resort" complete with a swimming pool, a polo field, a croquet lawn, and a ballroom.[50] Internees themselves called Muck and the men in his barracks "die Crème von Germany."[51] And yet, regardless of Muck's perceived privilege, his lodgings were not as grand as many imagined. Extravagant amenities may have been available to officers in the long-established military facility but not in the quickly constructed German prisoners' camp adjacent to the original site. It was in this new location in an empty field where row upon row of makeshift wooden barracks were assembled along the camp's only path, which internees humorously labeled the Chemin des Dames, after the French battlefields.[52] Each building housed upwards of forty men in an open and crowded room. The central structure contained two large mess halls and a kitchen.[53]

Two rows of barbed wire fence with spotlights surrounded the compound. American military soldiers guarded the inmates from tall machine-gun towers.[54] In addition, forty men and two officers stood guard beyond the perimeter of the fences, and two unarmed non-commissioned officers, an executive officer, and two assistants served inside the camp for added security. The corporals of the guard paced along the fencing, taking an hour to complete each round.[55] In total, some four hundred guards kept watch over the four thousand prisoners located there.[56]

Muck and the other inmates were told that if they came within eighty feet of the inner barbed wire fence, guards would shoot them on the spot. The *Chattanooga Times* reported, "There is one rule . . . at Oglethorpe, that means sudden death if violated—crossing the 'dead'

Figure 6.5. Fort Oglethorpe, Georgia. Panorama of the internment camp from the watchtower. Photograph by Sargent McGarrigle, May 3, 1919. Courtesy of the National Archives Records Administration. Records group 111, Records of the Office of the Chief Signal Officer, 1860–1985, Photographs of American Military Activities, ca. 1918–81.

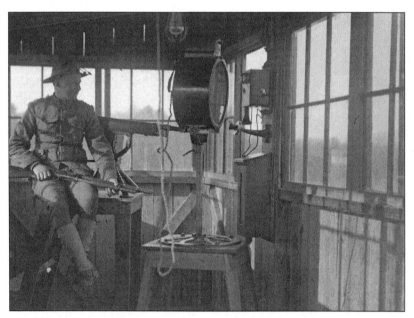

Figure 6.6. Fort Oglethorpe, Georgia, interior of one of the watchtowers, showing searchlight, guard, and gun. "The guard is always on alert to meet any outbreak of the prisoners." Photograph by Sargent McGarrigle, May 3, 1919. Courtesy of the National Archives Records Administration. Records group 111, Records of the Office of the Chief Signal Officer, 1860–1985, Photographs of American Military Activities, ca. 1918–81.

line."[57] Two men had been killed for crossing the line and attempting an escape: "They buried them, riddled with buckshot."[58] Searchlights were erected at all observation posts, which, it was said at the time, "spit their cruel, dazzling rays of light into the night and reach out for the shadows."[59] This was clearly a place of punishment, not a club resort.[60] The government sought to safeguard the country by creating conformity within its prison system, and yet, still somewhat disorganized, prisons did relent to social class pressures by the country's genteel classes. Accommodations were slightly better for wealthy men, whose barracks were more spacious, with thin dividers for privacy between metal beds, and they could purchase or prepare their food and eat separately from the other inmates. In general, however, detainees came from all economic backgrounds—laborers, merchantmen, diplomats, businessmen, musicians, and academics. The average working-class detainee did not enjoy special accommodations, sleeping in a barracks of one hundred men with a mattress on a wooden platform just inches from the next one, sharing a common shower and latrine, and eating collectively in the mess hall and lining up for every meal. Labor agitators and radical enemy aliens lived separately from the other men or were placed in solitary confinement, and they survived on bread and water rations. Every prisoner living at the camp experienced frustrations, regardless of status. In such tight quarters, they had to become accustomed to the smell of sweat or unwashed clothing, to tolerate fellow inmates who snored or groaned loudly while sleeping, who got up too early, who whistled or sang out of tune, or trudged their heavy, noisy boots through the barracks.[61] Train whistles from the Dixie Flyer express train that ran from Atlanta to Chattanooga and passed the camp regularly could be heard from morning through night. Muck had been wealthy and independent in Boston, living a very private life, but as a prisoner he was rarely alone. His persona as an upper-class man was much harder to maintain: known for his high-starched collars and expensive tailored suits, at Oglethorpe he wore a practical uniform of a "white duck shirt, without collar nor tie, white duck pants, that sadly needed an iron, and with feet encased only in tan socks and black overshoes," just as disheveled as every other inmate. Muck's individual identity was taken away and replaced with his prison identification—inmate number 1046.[62]

The climate at Oglethorpe was difficult to get accustomed to as well. Planners designed the property to give guards a complete panorama in case of escape, so the landscape was entirely barren and without shade trees. The wooden barracks did little to protect internees from the oppressive temperatures. Muck commented, "The heat, it is terrible. The first summer was bad enough, and I burned almost as black as a

Negro, but this second summer we all agree is the worst."[63] The men
had to contend with rattlesnakes and other creatures not present in
cooler climates. In the winter months, it rained, and the camp became
a muddy mess.[64] When Herbert Baldwin of the *Boston Post* visited Muck,
he recorded, "A figure hidden, almost beneath the folds of a raincoat,
his face obscured by a drooping black sou'wester, Muck came shuffling
along, a bit stoop-shouldered with a guard with a shotgun at his heels . . .
he plodded through the pelting rain. Prisoners referred to Oglethorpe
as 'Rio Grande de Orgelsdorf' or, a river that flows."[65]

Moreover, Oglethorpe was not a civilian prison where inmates
were confined for criminal activity. This was a military camp within
the federal system, where men are interned for political and security
threats to the country in general. Prisoners at Oglethorpe were divided
into two classes—prisoners of war and interned enemies. Within those
classifications, men were further categorized by their physical fitness,
such as those who could perform strenuous labor, those unable to perform it, and those labeled physically sick or disabled.[66] The men were
given a variety of pointless and mundane endeavors that were an inevitable part of war. A strict schedule was upheld. An internee's day at
Oglethorpe began at 6 a.m., with breakfast at 6:30 a.m., followed by
barracks cleaning and a 7:15 a.m. roll call and inspection. By 8 a.m.,
internees reported to their assigned work details, stopping at noon for
lunch and resuming work until 5:15 p.m.[67] Some prisoners fulfilled
their work duty by repairing the barracks, others performed back-
breaking work on the road crew, crushing rock at a nearby quarry to
make gravel for local roads. Others worked as groundskeepers, farmers, carpenters, mechanics, and electricians.[68] Karl Muck repaired
shoes, worked in the tinsmith shop, swept the barracks, made his bed,
and washed the windows each day.[69] Not performing anywhere near
the level of physical toil as working-class inmates, Muck still reported
to the press early in his confinement that he was ill, although the
prison doctor found him in perfect health. Muck complained that his
"iron constitution diminished: nerve pains and rheumatism began,
then a gall bladder disturbance, and then a rather severe heart condition. Now I am condemned to absolute rest!"[70] Muck saw himself as a
genteel soul attempting to alter his physical classification and get out
of manual labor assignments. He did not succeed.[71] Because this was a
military camp, discipline was strictly administered. For every one hundred men, a noncommissioned officer was placed in charge. As the
press reported at the time, the commander's "method for carrying out
these instructions rests more or less with the prisoners. They are well
aware of the fact that the more trouble they make the more severe the
control over them will become."[72]

In many regards, men interned at Oglethorpe were considered far more dangerous to the nation than those confined in local prisons for felonious behavior. Muck's arrest was an object of propaganda, a way to boost American morale and establish "legitimate" belligerents in the war. In a total war, he represented a human trophy, or a home-front prize of victory, a subduing of the enemy on home soil. US internment camps are illustrations of American might and power. They demonstrate the federal government's ability to rule with an iron fist and break the population. Fort Oglethorpe took respectable human beings and made them subhuman. It was a place where violations against internees went uncontested. The United States was not alone in this practice, as Europe interned four hundred thousand people during World War I. Sociologist Hans Speier speaks of internees as physical objects used for the expression of rage and hatred. These defeated individuals represent a national enemy by virtue of their incarceration and through the enforced control over their bodies.[73]

The emotional trauma that Muck endured in Oglethorpe cannot be understated. To adjust from the relative comfort of his Fenway home to a hostile prison camp in the southern heat was shocking to his system. Muck had to learn how to cope with his new circumstances. Thrust into a very public environment, he had to learn how to relate with fellow inmates and how to behave around the guards. Muck was a man who spoke his mind, and yet at Oglethorpe he had to practice self-restraint as a means of survival. No longer the leader of the country's most prominent symphony, Muck was absorbed into an indiscriminate institution, along with every other inmate, rich or poor, educated or not. His opinion was no more valuable than the next man's. The federal government imposed a subordinate status on all individuals, regardless of their social class.

Internees had difficulty arranging visits for their families. As the camp was too far away from Boston, Anita had moved to Chattanooga, Tennessee, where she remained throughout much of Muck's internment, traveling by train to see her husband.[74] Karl and Anita were allowed visits only once a week for two hours with an armed guard present.[75] They were required to speak in English, and if they unconsciously spoke in their home language, their visit would be over.[76] Alone and far away from not only Karl but also her friends in Boston and Germany, Anita's world was turned upside down. The couple could not maintain whatever level of intimacy they had shared before. Even hugs were difficult to come by. Poet and editor Erich Posselt, Muck's fellow inmate at Oglethorpe, who emigrated from Austria-Hungary in 1914 and attracted suspicion from nationalist Americans before he was interned, highlighted the difficulty he faced being separated from his partner:

You have never been so far to me,
Like now, you,
Who are far from me
Like never before.
Every hour of the long day
Only men—
Men in the early morning,
Men until late night—
But when everyone is moaning in deep sleep
And the floodlights
Are shining
With large skinny fingers
Through the camp and through the windows
Up to the sleeping ones;
And when the moon arduously flights his way
Through the waft of mist of the night
And when the stars come and go
And flare up
Like flashing light—
Then you, my faraway,
Are near me
Like never before.
So near.[77]

In a letter Posselt published in the camp newsletter, he describes his sadness and longing: "Here I am, sitting in the dry, while outside, cold autumn rain is changing our whole, big, sad, camp into a sea of loam and dirt. . . . I am like a homesick high school student, letting my thoughts wander, feeling lonely—thinking of the world outside the camp, sitting in front of my home-made most personally primitive table and writing—love letters."[78] Karl and Anita's separation was difficult, and Anita felt helpless to change the situation. In a letter to Charles Ellis, she expressed her anger over the entire ordeal: "It was a slap in the face . . . that Dr. Muck could be treated the way he was . . . that he was handled not much better than a horse thief might be by a half-bred sheriff's gang of ruffians in some Wild West place is an everlasting shame."[79]

Every attempt to make life bearable posed difficulty for Muck. Whether to get a pack of cigarettes, a little money, "luxury" foods such as sugar or coffee, a book, a musical instrument, a piece of sheet music, some comfortable clothes, or stamps to mail a letter—all took great effort. Every letter in or out of the camp was censored and often delayed. To handle the large flow of incoming mail, the government hired additional censors. Of Oglethorpe's mail service, the press recorded, "The censors are always on the lookout for coded messages,

messages in invisible ink, and other ways that are dark and tricks . . . to which the German spy is addicted. Relatives and especially wives are aware of this vigilance and realize that suspicion, once aroused, will mean that all the privileges of writing to the interned will be forfeited."[80] The camp newsletter alludes to this invasion of privacy and the surveillance of their most personal words: "Censorship—A soft object which floats above all, Which opens, reads, and then closes letters."[81] Fellow internee Richard Goldschmidt recorded that Oglethorpe's primary censor was "unanimously hated" because he inflicted "mental torture" on internees who worried about their families back home and waited far too long for news.[82] Perhaps even more disturbing, prisoners were limited to sending two letters a month and four postcards a week to relatives. Muck used his precious allotment to write to Anita. Only once did he write to Isabella Stewart Gardner, explaining his circumstance.[83] Punitive control measures caused great anguish for the inmates. Posselt recorded in the Oglethorpe newsletter, which, incidentally, was censored and eventually disbanded, "Someone is standing at the barbed wire and is staring across—to the outside. He is standing there for a long time, just staring. Then he sighs thoughtfully. And steals, as if being oppressed by a heavy weight, to his bed. The next night . . . he is standing there again . . . he just doesn't know why. He only knows that he wants to be free—free again."[84]

Federal power did not entirely crush individual spirit. Within the confines of the camp, inmates found ways to express themselves, demonstrating the limits of state power. Oglethorpe was a small town with a military base before Germans were interned there. Inmates outnumbered residents, and many of the local townspeople were frightened at the thought of living among dangerous enemies and spies. Intrigued by the new inhabitants, local people would bring their chairs and binoculars and sit outside the barbed wire fence to watch prisoner activity. In spite of the constant surveillance, the internees did what they could to make their situation more bearable. They found ways to acquire special meals through family members, or they created delicacies of their own in the camp. German American bakers prepared specialty breads using old family recipes.[85] Several inmates had been professors at leading universities, so they gave public lectures, and established the "Camp Oglethorpe University," teaching law, biology, zoology, physics, chemistry, engineering, European and American history, art and music history; languages such as Spanish, Italian, Arabic, Latin, French, English, Russian, Hebrew, Swahili, Sanskrit, Hindi, Chinese, and Japanese; and business courses such as bookkeeping, shorthand, and commercial letter writing.[86] Internees learned to survive their circumstances. They brought their own culture into the camp by forming clubs and

Figure 6.7. Fort Oglethorpe, Georgia. The outdoor movie theater allowed internees to pass the time. Photograph by Sargent McGarrigle May 3, 1919. Courtesy of the National Archives Records Administration. Records group 111, Records of the Office of the Chief Signal Officer, 1860–1985, Photographs of American Military Activities, ca. 1918–81.

musical organizations. They watched movies each week, outdoors if weather permitted.

People worked to keep busy. They set up gardens all around the camp and grew their own fresh vegetables. The press reported that they "remind one of the spick and span pictures in seed manuals," even though the soil was not adequate for "a bumper crop." Yet inmates managed to create "attractive designs for flower gardens, such as globes, crescents, crosses, and stars."[87] Inmates raised chickens and rabbits, which supplied them with ample eggs and meat. Scientifically inclined inmates had a still for making liquor. The men read magazines, newspapers, and books supplied by the YMCA. They played card games, chess, volleyball, football, and tennis and created a makeshift swimming pool. Prisoners recycled items available to them, turning the tin foil liners inside of cigarette cartons, floor linoleum, and cigar boxes into artwork.[88] They created toys, including tin soldiers, "representing every arm of the service of nearly all the nations." Using scrap lumber from the construction of the barracks and nails from the ground, they made furniture for their cabins and carved woodcuts in the German Expressionist style.[89] They made lamps, fruit dishes, and ashtrays from barbed wire. They made small boats that fit inside quart bottles, and their work was sold at Christmastime in Atlanta, New York, Philadelphia, and Chicago. The sale of these items indicates that anti-German sentiment did not win over the American people universally. After the May of 1918 passage of the Trading with the Enemy Act, however, inmates were prevented from selling their creations, signaling yet another expression of the federal government's coercive powers.

Internees festively decorated the camp for Christmas.[90] In other months, they put on vocal concerts, comedy shows, and theatrical events, such as Henrik Ibsen's *Ghost* and Hermann Sudermann's *Stein unter Steinen.*[91] Band concerts were held twice a week.[92] Internees listened to Cincinnati Symphony conductor Dr. Ernst Kunwald, who was interned at Oglethorpe in December of 1917 and later deported. Kunwald played the piano during their morning work breaks in front of the camp's car garage, "wearing blue working pants, old American army coats, and broad, mud covered shoes." The men stood "with their hands in their pockets, heads bowed and hardly moving," so affected were they by the sound of German music.[93] Karl Muck provided his musical services as a guest conductor with the eighty-piece Oglethorpe Tsing-Tau Orchestra, made up of medical men and amateur musicians from the Sanitary Corp of the German Third Sea Battalion who were captured by the Japanese army in China and interned in America.[94] Using handwritten scores, the ensemble performed Beethoven's *Eroica* and Brahms's *Akademische Festouvertüre* on December 12, 1918.[95] Posselt recalled that the concert was held in the mess hall and the audience included two thousand internees and government officials, and the music "rushed at us and carried us far away and above war and worry and barbed wire."[96] Goldschmidt writes that "when Muck raised his baton one could have heard a mouse running. The whole performance was unforgettable. . . . The American officers who attended said it was the greatest revelation they had experienced."[97] Townspeople from Chattanooga lined the streets outside the compound to hear the performance.[98]

Oglethorpe internee and novelist Hanns Heinz Ewers, Erich Posselt, and a group of young bohemian writers and artists created a newsletter, the *Orgelsdorfer Eulenspiegel,* as a way to survive their experience as well as to protest it.[99] The name *Eulenspiegel* consists of two words: *Eule* (owl) and *Spiegel* (mirror). The two words suggest surveillance. Also, the title refers to the tone poem by Richard Strauss of the German peasant folk hero, Till Eulenspiegel, known for his tricks and rebellion. For those outside Oglethorpe who had the privilege of receiving a copy, the newsletter offered insight into the life of German prisoners of war during World War I. Interestingly, printing was done on

Figure 6.8. The Tsing-Tao Orchestra was made up of medical men and amateur musicians from the German Third Sea Battalion who were captured by the Japanese army and interned at Fort Oglethorpe. The men often practiced outdoors with rudimentary instruments and scores. Although unconfirmed, Karl Muck appears to be seated on the far left front row with violin. Courtesy of the Deutsches Schiffahrtsmuseum in Bremerhaven, Germany.

poor-quality paper by a merchant marine wireless operator, using a small hand press that produced children's greeting cards and menus on steamer ships and, with much ingenuity, producing a full-sized camp broadsheet with thirty-page editions. The newspaper was sold for twenty-five cents a copy in the barracks canteen, and profits aided inmates without financial means. It consisted of original poems, jokes, stories, public protest letters, satirical artwork, comics, and scholarly articles.[100] Otto Schaefer, for example, offered an antidote for home-sickness, graphically describing images of German cathedrals and telling fellow inmates to "look east." Albrecht Montgelas shared connections between American art from the Hudson River School and Germany, providing a readily available source of comfort for weary prisoners. Ernst Fritz Kuhn offered biting sarcasm aimed at the Boston Symphony Orchestra in its quest to find Karl Muck's replacement. Each of these articles lifted internees' spirits until the newspaper was censored and shutdown.[101] Gerald H. Davis noted that the final edition included an illustration of the owl spreading its wings while perched on the *O* in "Orgelsdorf, soaring to freedom above a cluster of flames, just as the men were about to be released from the camp.[102] After the armistice, prisoners were not allowed to take copies of the *Orgelsdorfer Eulenspiegel* out of the camp, and, therefore, very few survive.

Men did whatever they could to remain sane in these strange and stressful surroundings. "Those who spend more than a short time behind the barbed wire are all more or less crazy. And the products of their imaginations are strange," the *Eulenspiegel* describes.

> We observe somebody named Dr. Phil, who hammers from early in the morning till late in the night, building sheds, clotheshorses, doorknobs, calendars, tables, picture frames, and other lovely things. He is only happy when he can hammer. Somebody else builds totem poles; by the sweat of his brow he collects stones and stones from the most remote corners of the camp. . . . [H]e leaves the monument unfinished and collects barbed wire. . . . [A] third somebody is contorting his arms and feet in an indescribable way.[103]

Erich Posselt published his recollections of Fort Oglethorpe in *American Mercury* magazine, describing an interned priest with a gambling addiction trying to offer his possessions to Muck and anyone else for five dollars so he could play his game.[104] In 1919, Adolf Lucas Vischer coined the clinical term "barbed-wire disease" to describe the psychological disorders found in people who had been imprisoned during World War I.[105] Mood changes, concentration problems, anxiety, boredom, confusion, and absentmindedness are symptoms of those incarcerated. Several internees committed suicide, and others were transferred to mental asylums.[106] Anita Muck records changes in her husband's personality in a letter to Isabella Stewart Gardner. She found him to be very nervous, depressed, and restless. "It is awfully hard for him."[107]

In August of 1918, the Spanish flu affected the men at Oglethorpe, spreading from Boston's military encampments to its civilian population and then to the rest of the country. Sixty-eight US sailors were taken off their ships at Boston's Commonwealth Pier and admitted to the Chelsea Naval Hospital, three miles north of the city, suffering from influenza.[108] In early September, the press reported that influenza victims filled all the hospital beds at the forts in Boston Harbor.[109] Thirty-five miles west of Boston, at Camp Devens army cantonment in Ayer, 1,543 soldiers became ill with the disease and, by September 22, nine thousand were on sick report, with six thousand filling every bed, corridor, and spare room at the base hospital. An extra-long barracks was evacuated where "bodies were piled up," and trains were arranged to carry away the dead.[110] Following a Win the War for Freedom parade that featured four thousand men, soldiers and residents alike became ill with the virus, filling Massachusetts hospitals. One thousand civilians died in September alone.[111] Boston novelist William Martin recalled that his forty-year-old grandmother Josephine Walsh Martin contracted the disease and died within a twenty-four-hour period, leaving ten children motherless, including his two-year-old father.[112] All Boston gathering places were closed, including all theaters, clubs, restaurants, and schools, but efforts to contain the illness were fruitless. Rose Howes Galbraith, a twenty-five-year-old Liggett-Rexall pharmaceutical saleswoman, who traveled by train each week from New York to Boston, witnessed a spike in sales during this period for an oral antiseptic product called Listerine.[113] Many hoped this germicide, and other sanitary measures, would prevent the spread of the disease. The Spanish flu traveled from Boston throughout the country—to the Philadelphia Navy Yard, to the Puget Sound Navy Base in Washington State, to the Great Lakes Naval Training Station in Chicago, to the Newport Rhode Island Naval Base, and on the steamer *Harold Walker* to New Orleans, among other places.[114] Army and navy installations were the incubators for disease. Today, reports indicate that, during World War I, 675,000 people died of influenza in the United States alone.[115] Worldwide, estimates suggest that as many as one hundred million people perished from the Spanish flu.[116]

At Camp Oglethorpe, in the fall of 1918, several thousand inmates became ill from the epidemic, and more than fifty died.[117] Emergency vehicles trekked in and out of Oglethorpe day and night bringing sick prisoners to the hospital. While almost half of the entire camp became afflicted, the remaining inmates were anxious as to whether their comrades would ever return to their quarters.[118] Rapidly developing symptoms included pneumonia that violently snapped rib cages or tore abdominal muscles, nose bleeds, hemoptysis (coughing up blood), bleeding from the ears, headaches, and vomiting. Within hours, victims developed cyanosis, a condition that turned the skin dark blue because of the lungs' inability to supply oxygen to the blood.[119] Internees complained of incompetent medical care.[120] Brave doctors and nurses were equally susceptible to the disease, which had no obvious cure, leaving hospital wards with minimal staffing. Camp quarantines were implemented to contain the outbreak. All recreational activities at Oglethorpe were cancelled, making life behind barbed wire a particularly unhappy affair.[121] Horse stables were converted to temporary morgues.[122] The camp newsletter reported:

> The big death came into the country. It also came here. . . . Someone died and someone else, the number five man and the number thirteen,

Figure 6.9. "Fort Oglethorpe, Georgia, Hospital in Prison Barracks."
Hospital tents were used during the Spanish flu epidemic. Photograph by
Sargent McGarrigle May 3, 1919. Courtesy of the National Archives Records
Administration. Records group 111, Records of the Office of the Chief Signal
Officer, 1860–1985, Photographs of American Military Activities, ca. 1918–81.

> the men's resistance to the disease had been paralyzed by long deten-
> tion or insidious illnesses which were in them and which had gnawed
> at their marrow of life like evil rats. Death laid on the prison camp
> like a shadow: it went round for a long time. . . . More than fifty peo-
> ple died. . . . [T]hey would not see home again; their home which
> had borne them. But one thought is a consolation to us, who have
> been brushed by but passed over by death with its icy breath: they
> died as Germans. They had lived here as Germans, like us.[123]

While this federally enforced internment was intended to crush dissent and enforce national conformity, the US treatment of these men
inspired many of them to become more German at heart and less
American.

Men developed solidarity with fellow inmates, for all suffered
unspeakable hardships. Dr. Hugo Letchtentritt of Harvard University, a
music critic of the Berlin *Vossische Zeitung* newspaper, remembered that
Muck spoke of his confinement during the last months of the war: "His
three companions in that camp were Ernst Kunwald, conductor of the
Cincinnati Orchestra, Dr. Bertling, Harvard professor and authority on
Ralph Waldo Emerson, and Director of the American Institute in Berlin, and Ferdinand von Scholley, manager of the Burkhardt Brewing

Company. All three spoke of their enforced residence in the camp without enthusiasm."[124] Disposed of behind steel wire and machine gun turrets, the men became each other's greatest supporters and life-long friends. Certainly, Muck's relationships with fellow musicians and academics greatly eased his hardship.

Muck's internment at Fort Oglethorpe lasted from April of 1918 to August of 1919, almost a year and a half. While Muck found friends to ease the burden of internment, the psychological impact of his experience cannot be understated. He was traumatized by his arrest and internment, and the distress and humiliation of that episode remained with him throughout his life. He had been cast out of Boston's cosmopolitan society. He had lost a year and a half of professional productivity that he would never get back. He had been ridiculed publicly in newspapers across the United States. He had lost his identity and his cultural moorings. Dehumanized, he never truly recovered from his incarceration.[125]

The Federal Seizure of Muck's Assets

Moreover, Muck had been made penniless. Less than one month after he had been sent to Fort Oglethorpe, President Wilson announced that interned aliens came under the term "enemy" in the Trading with the Enemy Act. The law gave the president the power to oversee or restrict any and all trade between the United States and its enemies in times of war, and by extension, as a result of this new classification, property of interned aliens was open to seizure by the Alien Property Custodian, requiring German Americans and German nationals to disclose their bank accounts and any other property to the US government. While Muck was serving his sentence at Fort Oglethorpe, A. Mitchell Palmer of the BOI seized his belongings, including his cash, stocks, bank accounts, house, and furniture at 50 Fenway in Boston. The value of Muck's property in 1918 was $82,181.82, roughly $1,500,000 in today's money.[126] Muck was entirely powerless to do anything about it.[127] He commented in a 1919 letter written at Fort Oglethorpe that he "learned the lesson myself, what it means to see everything destroyed that one has built by honest and hard work."[128]

Palmer was known for his vindictive and ruthless style. Per John Lord O'Brian, head of the War Emergency Division, Palmer "put the heat on us to intern individuals . . . if they could get the man interned then they could take his property without any ifs and ands."[129] As part of the spoils of war, Palmer's office in Washington seized an estimated $700 million in private property with dubious relevance to the war effort, amounting to almost the entire federal budget of prewar America. Most these assets came from German-owned businesses operating in the United States, and an additional $2.5 million from interned aliens like Karl Muck.[130] The mistreatment of civilians and the theft of enemy possessions were just parts of total war. Muck was destroyed financially by the seizure of his property. He had to begin his life anew with no assets. As he recorded later in life:

> Since they arrested me in Boston . . . and confiscated all our property, we left America, in September 1919, as paupers—I have not slept any more under a roof of my own, not even in a bed of my own. Hotels, furnished rooms, trains, trunks; today in Amsterdam, next week in Madrid; today in Copenhagen, next week in Rome—restless, homeless, alone. And I am in my 66th year. I beg your pardon for that side-trip in personal matters.[131]

Twenty years later, in 1940, the *Boston Post* gleefully reported that Mr. Charles Mills, a well-known stock broker, had purchased two prized German clocks once belonging to Karl Muck, seized from his home in 1918 and auctioned off. The photograph that accompanied the article expresses happiness for the "lucky bidder," while the couple who originally owned the clocks had suffered greatly, having lost all of their possessions.[132]

Long after Muck had given up hope of any recompense, Charles Ellis worked on Muck's behalf for many years to retrieve his property. In 1924, after much legal wrangling, he was still unable to make headway. In a letter to Ellis, Muck lashed out at Palmer, the man responsible for the seizure of his property and the dispersal of his letters to the press:

> I am utterly and thoroughly sick of the whole crooked business. May the poor U.S.A. get rich with the few dollars a simple musician has earned by hard work! It is against the dignity of man, for ever and ever to dance to a bunch of crooks and felon's pipes—The other day I met an American in Amsterdam. . . . That man, a full-blooded 100% American, said to me, "give it up, I am sure that not a single cent is left of your property; the Mitchell Palmer gang has stolen every bit of it!"[133]

Muck's property dispute did not end until 1928 with passage of the War Claims Act, which entitled Muck to 80 percent of his property. On May 15, 1928, he finally received $37,669.30 of his original $47,086.63 cash assets. The property and house and much of its contents, already auctioned by the government, were excluded from the claim. Legal battles over Muck's property carried on for many additional years. Because of governmental bureaucracy, progress was slow, stretching the case well beyond the war, leaving Muck utterly exhausted in his struggle to regain the wealth he had once enjoyed.

Not only was Muck's property seized but his professional reputation was damaged as well. He had to regain some semblance of his former identity and remind the world of the man it had come to forget.[134] Muck had to rebuild his life and cope with public assumptions placed on him, as criminal, spy, enemy, pervert, and abductor. Prior to his arrest, in early October of 1917, Muck and the full one hundred member Boston Symphony Orchestra had spent a week at the newly constructed Victor Talking Machine Company headquarters in its eighth-floor auditorium in Camden, New Jersey, making commercial acoustic recordings of works by Tchaikovsky, Wagner, Beethoven, Berlioz, and Wolf-Ferrari.[135] Victor had recorded smaller ensembles before, but as they pointed out in their 2001 commemorative album *RCA Red Seal Century*, the Karl Muck soundtracks were "the first known commercial recording sessions with a full symphony orchestra."[136] BSO management distanced itself from Muck after the war, however, and did not issue his work for seventy-five years. Many of his groundbreaking recordings were never marketed to the public, and are only now seeing the light of day.[137]

Climate of Fear and the Path to Deportation

Karl Muck had hoped that with the armistice he could put his internment behind him and resume his position as conductor in Boston. The country, however, had not lost its suspicion of foreign aliens. Just one month before the armistice, in October of 1918, President Wilson signed the Alien Anarchist Act, which, in summary, gave the government the power to deport any alien suspected of overthrowing the government or harboring malicious thoughts about America.[138] The law targeted immigrant aliens, allowing the federal government the power to deport members of social groups that professed any dissent from the war or expressed an anti-American viewpoint. The new expansion of powers extended its reach to all foreigners, no matter how long they had lived in America.[139] J. Edgar Hoover, who became the head of the BOI, took full advantage of these new laws to raid, arrest, and deport undesirable immigrants in the United States. Deportation, or the threat of it, according to John Higham, served an "instrumental function" as a way to purify American society, suppress potential radicalism, and maintain Americanism.[140]

Muck was disappointed that he was not given a simple, unconditional release from Fort Oglethorpe. When most other internees were paroled on the orders of US attorney general Palmer, Muck learned that he would be deported. Devastated by the news and eager to remain in the United States, he appealed to the government with the hope that he could overturn its decision. Muck willingly remained in custody at Fort Oglethorpe for nine months following the war, corresponding with influential people he believed could help him. He attempted to argue his way out of his sentence, and on the prisoner information form that he filled out before leaving Georgia, when asked whether he desired to return to Germany or Austria, Muck simply answered "no." He insisted repeatedly that his Swiss citizenship removed any "enemy alien" rank. Muck waited for a decision regarding his request to remain in the United States.

Between April and June of 1919, while Muck was still sequestered at Fort Oglethorpe awaiting his fate, a series of dramatic events occurred in the country that would have damning consequences for his future. In late April, bombs were mailed to thirty-six prominent politicians, judges, newspaper editors, and businessmen throughout the country. Notable targets included John D. Rockefeller and J. P. Morgan. Then, on June 2, 1919, a group of anarchists detonated large mail bombs simultaneously in eight different cities, including Boston, New York, Washington, DC, Philadelphia, Pittsburgh, and Paterson, New Jersey, intended for government officials who had endorsed anti-radical legislation that promoted deportation, like the Immigration Act of 1918. Anarchists targeted Georgia senator Thomas W. Hardwick, for example, whose African American housekeeper lost both of her hands in the attack, and Hardwick's wife Maude, who sustained injuries to her face, neck, lips, and teeth. Bureau of investigation head A. Mitchell Palmer's home was a target of one bomb, which upon detonation killed Carlo Valdinoci, an associate of perpetrator and Italian anarchist Luigi Galleani. Thus, the federal government "became centered upon activities of alien agitators, with the object of securing their deportation."[141]

Assistant Secretary of Labor Louis P. Post was assigned to the task of reviewing deportation cases. The liberal-minded Post reviewed each case carefully, rejecting 2,202 prospective deportees, much to Palmer's outrage, and endorsing 556 others.[142] Because of the nation's heightened fear regarding terrorism, Muck's request to remain in the United States was denied. The Justice Department concluded that "it would be dangerous for him to be permitted to remain at large."[143] Muck hoped until the day of his deportation that he could put his internment behind him and resume his position as the Boston Symphony conductor, but the federal government was not forgiving of its "enemy aliens." Animosity toward Germany, and toward foreigners in general, had only increased after the war, making Muck's request hopelessly impossible.[144]

On August 21, 1919, more than nine months after the armistice ending World War I was signed, Karl and Anita Muck were transported to New York where they boarded the SS *Frederik VIII*, a Swedish American line bound for Copenhagen. Muck wanted to stay in the United States so badly that federal agents remained onboard ship to guard him and ensure that he did not jump overboard and swim ashore. Rumor circulated that Muck was treated like a prisoner during the voyage, sequestered on a lower deck, while Anita was given a stateroom on an upper level. Anita, however, expressed it differently in a letter to her friend, Isabella Stewart Gardner:

> We are already in European waters and shall reach Norway tomorrow. Next we shall go to Sweden and stay until my husband feels completely recuperated and rested. The voyage already did him a lot of good; he sleeps well and eats with better appetite than I ever knew him to have. There is a nice sympathetic crowd on board; and the weather is favorable. The time slipped by; it seems unbelievable that it's already nine days since we left the States. Do you know we have our parrot with us? Dr. Muck daily spent hours in "taming him," as he hated men; now he adores my husband.[145]

Regardless of the pleasant voyage and Muck's newfound freedom, he was bitter. He was heard saying, "I am not a German, despite the fact they said I was. I consider myself an American, but see what America has done to me. I am going over to Denmark now, a man without a flag or a country."[146]

In the final analysis, the Bureau of Investigation successfully found Karl Muck's "one weak spot." Following up on Mrs. Jay's persistent attacks on his character and afraid of foreign nationals, they viewed him as a threat to the nation based on his nationality alone, and while they could not technically jail him as an "enemy alien" given his Swiss papers and they could not find any evidence that he was a spy, either, they pursued him until they found something—anything—that was illegal, so they could put him away. The middle-aged Karl Muck had moral shortcomings. They blackmailed him based on those weaknesses to accomplish their goals. Mrs. Jay had utilized anti-German hysteria in her campaign to dethrone Karl Muck. As a board director of the New York Philharmonic, her effort was a competitive maneuver intended to cause a shift in cultural leadership from Boston to New York. Karl Muck, the preeminent German conductor of the Boston Symphony Orchestra, was caught up in this changing time. He suffered incredible indignity; was stripped of his civil rights, his community, his position, his possessions, and his income; and was interned at Fort Oglethorpe, Georgia, and deported a year and a half later, even though specific charges were never publicly stated and the details of the case were shrouded in mystery.

On November 7, 1919, just two and a half months after Karl Muck's deportation, the Palmer Raids targeted Russian immigrants, many of whom were Jews, and suspected members of the Union of Russian Workers. A. Mitchell Palmer, who had "won national prominence" by "scourging the Hun" during the war, shifted his focus from the eradication of Germans to a "country wide drive against Bolshevism" by arresting, on December 21, 1919, 1,100 individuals and deporting 249 of them to Russia on the *Buford,* nicknamed the "Soviet Ark."[147] On January 2, 1920, an additional ten thousand innocent immigrants were arrested in a single day without warrants. Dragnet raids intruded into homes, schools, meeting halls, and other locations where foreigners were known to gather. Several hundred were arrested in Boston alone, and, using similar tactics that netted Karl Muck, individuals were intimidated, interrogated, and denied legal counsel while their property was seized.[148] Rather than arresting specific individuals for particular crimes, Palmer and Hoover suspiciously targeted entire ethnic populations in their effort to "secure" and "purify" the country.[149] Believing certain ethnic communities could not assimilate and prejudicially anticipating future criminal behavior from these groups, zealous government officials used their postwar authority to single out individuals with alleged communist, anarchist, socialist, or Bolshevik associations. Nativist in their thinking, fearing immigrants, and feeling deeply threatened by dissent, A. Mitchell Palmer and J. Edgar Hoover abused their power and overreacted, tragically destroying the lives of thousands. Dr. Karl Muck serves as a clear example of how such an abuse of power victimizes not just those on the margins of society but even those in the highest social echelons, like the renowned conductor of the Boston Symphony Orchestra.

Chapter Seven

"ONLY TOO PROUD TO SHOULDER IT ALL"

The Sexual Climate of Wartime Boston and Muck's Fall from Grace (1918–1919)

The letters seized illegally from Rosamond Young's home provided the only incriminating evidence federal officials could use to arrest Karl Muck. The BOI, at the instigation of Mrs. Jay, had been hunting for ways to catch Muck in some form of criminal activity, so it could then remove him from his important position in Boston. Its job would have been much easier if Muck had been a German spy or if he had sabotaged munitions plants. Unable to find any legitimate offense, investigators interrogated members of the Boston Symphony until they learned of Rosamond Young and the cache of letters in her home. The Muck-Young letters demonstrated a level of emotional and physical intimacy deemed inappropriate by certain BOI officials. Thomas Boynton, District Attorney Dewey's supervisor, wrote personally to John Lord O'Brian at the War Emergency Division of the Justice Department about the scandalous nature of the letters, saying "a very considerable number" were "entirely obscene in character."[1]

The Comstock Act of 1873 and the Mann White Slavery Act of 1910

The private correspondence between Karl Muck and Rosamond Young that was seized without her permission provided the BOI with proof that the BSO conductor was guilty of sex crimes.[2] While letters between two consenting adults having an affair may not seem criminal, there was a basis for the BOI to arrest and charge Muck through the provisions of two separate federal acts that he and Young had violated:

the Comstock Act of 1873 and the Mann White Slavery Act of 1910. The former law was named for anti-obscenity crusader and former dry goods salesman Anthony Comstock, who had received financial backing from capitalists J. P. Morgan and Samuel Colgate to push the bill through Congress. It prohibited the transportation of obscene items through the US Postal Service. The law reads:

> Be it enacted . . . that whoever shall sell . . . lend . . . give away, or in any manner exhibit or shall otherwise publish . . . have in his possession . . . an obscene book, pamphlet, paper, picture, advertisement, circular . . . or other articles of an immoral nature . . . shall be deemed guilty of a misdemeanor and or conviction thereof in any court of the United States . . . he shall be imprisoned at hard labor in the penitentiary for not less than six months nor more than five years for each offense.

The Comstock Act had been used to punish free love advocates such as Victoria Woodhull, Ezra Heywood, and Moses Harmon for their liberal publications dealing with sex, marriage, and radical politics.[3] Harmon was arrested in 1905 at seventy-five years of age and sentenced to a year of hard labor at Joliet State Prison in Illinois. The law was also applied to punish Margaret Sanger for distributing birth control literature and devices through the mail and for arresting 3,600 people for mailing "obscene" materials, such as condoms.[4] Muck's letters to Rosamond, transported through the US mail, were full of implied and explicit sexual content and were grounds for the maximum sentence according to this law.[5]

The Mann white slavery law was also utilized to find Muck guilty of a punishable crime. The Mann Act, named for Congressman James Mann of Illinois, was enacted to prevent the transportation of women across state lines for licentious purposes and illicit activities.[6] Because Muck's letters discuss traveling out of state with Rosamond when he conducted the orchestra on tour, the Mann Act was invoked.[7] In 1910, when the law was introduced, President William Howard Taft expressed enthusiastic approval and announced the allocation of $50,000 for the employment of special inspectors under the US Department of Justice and the BOI to track down violators. The law stated that persons found guilty of transporting any woman or girl across state lines for the "purpose of prostitution or debauchery or for any other immoral purpose" will be fined a maximum of $5,000 and up to five years in prison. There were no specific details regarding what constituted "an immoral purpose," however, leaving room for interpretation.[8] President Taft had told Congressman Mann when signing the law into effect, "Now let's hope they put some of the scoundrels in prison."[9] The BOI utilized the railroads to distribute circulars notifying ticket agents to be on guard for men traveling with young women and to be aware of women from "red light districts."[10]

The country became preoccupied with sexual trafficking during this period. The most famous World War I–era case of Mann Act persecution involved Jack Johnson, the famous black heavyweight boxing champion who had relationships with white women. Motivated by racial prejudice, federal officials arrested Johnson for Mann Act violations and sentenced him to a year in prison.[11] Cases of blackmail were rampant, and the Mann Act was often used as a threat to keep "violators" in line, notably in the divorce proceedings of architect Frank Lloyd Wright, whose estranged wife alerted FBI agents in 1926 that the architect and his girlfriend had crossed state borders to go into hiding together. Famous white Americans were not immune to prosecution, as exemplified by J. Edgar Hoover's pursuit in 1944 of Charlie Chaplin, whose radical politics and "un-American activities" inspired the FBI to monitor the actor's sexual life before arresting him and subsequently convicting him on Mann Act violations.[12] In 1918, the Department of Justice was just beginning to see that it could use the Mann Act to manipulate the law to force compliance. As the *Boston Post* duly noted, "The authorities rested their case against Dr. Muck on these letters, confident that no one can even read a small part of them without being convinced that the authorities were justified in placing Dr. Muck where he could do no further damage."[13]

Plea Bargain to Maintain Muck's Private Life

Muck was given two choices by the BOI: serve a military sentence as a "dangerous enemy alien" at Fort Oglethorpe, Georgia, or accept an indictment for the sexual charges under the Mann and Comstock Acts and serve a criminal sentence in a local penitentiary. Facing the possibility of a very public criminal trial as a sexual deviant, Muck communicated to Dewey his preference for internment over indictment.[14] In his judgment, in Boston it was better to be guilty of artificial and contrived offences against the government than to admit guilt for a sex crime. The BOI essentially blackmailed Muck with his own letters, making a bargain with him, on which they would later renege, to keep silent regarding his love affair with Rosamond Young, in exchange for accepting the charge of "dangerous enemy alien," even though he was entirely innocent of the latter charge. Technically, Muck was a Swiss citizen, so the BOI could not prosecute him as an enemy alien. The BOI could not link him to any "dangerous" activity.[15] Muck had to accept the charge of "dangerous enemy alien," however, or his sex life would have become a public affair.[16] He wrote to Rosamond that he was "only too proud to shoulder it all" and preferred to accept internment at Fort Oglethorpe to save Rosamond, his wife, and himself, the shame and embarrassment of a public spectacle. He hoped that, by keeping the sexual scandal a secret, he would be able to maintain his reputation and resume his position as the leader of the BSO after the war.

Complex factors lay beneath Muck's decision to accept the charge of "dangerous enemy alien" and internment at a military camp in Georgia over the charges of "sexual offender" with punishment in a local prison. To understand how and why he made his decision, this chapter will explore the sexual climate of Boston during the first two decades of the twentieth century to suggest why Muck would have gone to great lengths, such as submitting to prosecution for bogus enemy alien charges, to keep his extramarital relationship with Young concealed. Sex, particularly the knowledge of one's private sexual behavior, can be used as a powerful weapon to gain control of individuals and make them vulnerable and weak.[17] The federal government overstepped the limits of privacy to acquire sexual information and then used the nontraditional tactic of blackmail to arrest and intern him. Muck struggled to deal with the complexities of his intimate relationships amid an expanding US government investigative apparatus.

Commercialization of Sexuality in America and Boston's Conservative Backlash

During World War I, the pace of society changed rapidly, accelerating new ideas about sexuality and loosening up rules that had been rigidly adhered to before the war. Modern pragmatism replaced Gilded Age innocence. Sex became commercialized, and the mainstream marketplace became flooded with new print media and visual imagery.[18] The fledgling motion picture industry produced films that were increasingly erotic: Audrey Munson appeared entirely nude in *Inspiration* (1915). Annette Kellermann stood naked beneath a waterfall in *Daughter of the Gods* (1916). Theda Bara became an overnight sensation in *A Fool There Was* (1915), *Sin* (1915), and *Cleopatra* (1917). Every week, young couples held hands and snuggled close in darkly lit movie palaces like the Star Theater in Boston watching Rudolph Valentino and Clara Bow.[19] One of the earliest known pornographic films, *A Free Ride* (1915), directed by A. Wise Guy and photographed by Will B. Hard, graphically followed the sexual adventures of a man and two women having intercourse by the side of a country road. Technological

Figure 7.1. Australian actress Annette Kellemann appeared nude in the 1916 film *Daughter of the Gods*, a pre-censor-era production. Films like this one enflamed reformers who sought to clamp down on public immorality. Wikimedia Commons.

innovations like the movie projector brought sex into the public sphere. The hand-cranked Mutoscope machine appeared at penny arcades, train stations, and hotel lobbies and offered viewers short, erotic films, such as *The Birth of the Pearl* (1901) and Thomas Edison's *Trapeze Disrobing Act* (1901). One of the most popular short nickel films was *The Kiss* (1896), involving a middle-aged couple kissing, laughing, and talking, showing American audiences something they had "never seen before" in film—actual romance. Fascinated by it, people used their spare change to watch and then imitate the film. For many, movies were the earliest form of sexual education, in an era when none had existed.

Some people welcomed the changes, while others felt uneasy. Religious Americans worried about immorality during these years. They sought to influence sexual behavior, arguing that "two thousand years of Judeo-Christian sexual morality are not to be shrugged off in a couple of decades." God was utilized as a tool, pitting guilt against promiscuity.[20] Boston Methodist preacher Henry Morgan used his position at the pulpit in the 1880s and 1890s to write *Boston Inside Out! Sin of a Great City! A Story of Real Life*, a condemnation of immorality in the city. A nonfiction work that reads like a novel, Morgan's book told of sinister men preying upon innocent young women and made the claim that "Boston is New England's monster mill that grinds and crushes innocent beings, gathered from every New England State. The gigantic serpent that charms, envenoms and consumes. Thousands of guileless and unsuspecting ones are fascinated and enticed from their country homes, and become food for the serpent's maw."[21] In particular, Morgan visited the "haunts of iniquity" and the "most public and private spiritual mediums" in the city. He targeted "idle rich men" in Boston who considered themselves intellectually and morally superior and who debased themselves in prostitution and adultery: "Men, lecherous men . . . men of ease and luxury, leaders of fashion, magnates of society . . . The rich, idle spendthrifts are the city's curse. The law does not reach them. They go scot free."[22] A year before Muck's arrest, Billy Sunday, one of the most popular evangelical preachers of the day, appeared at Boston's specially erected tabernacle along Huntington Avenue, just down the street from Symphony Hall, to crusade against vice before a record crowd of more than one million people. Described as charismatic and handsome, the evangelist "denounced divorce, birth control, and the evils of ballroom dance." He devoted special condemnation for women who attempted to evade the "burden of motherhood." In a sermon just for men, Sunday attacked the perils of "masculine vice," arguing that sexual affairs outside of marriage are sinful.[23] Certainly, Muck would have been viewed as one of Morgan's "men of ease" who practiced the sort of masculine vice that Billy Sunday railed against.

As the conductor of the BSO, Muck was expected to uphold moral order in the city. Boston's upper classes believed themselves to be the custodians of musical and spiritual culture, and, by extension, they anointed Muck as leader of their cultural mecca who represented a conduit between the divine and the masses.[24] Muck was implicitly charged with disseminating moral values and spiritual uplift through music. He was expected to represent perfection in appearance and behavior as a model for others to follow. Like a preacher or a godlike figure, Muck was viewed as one of the most visible moral leaders of the city.[25] Audiences treated their experience at symphony as if they were in church, and Muck was their pastor. H. T. Parker, the Hard to Please columnist for the *Boston Transcript*, invoked evangelical rhetoric in his 1922 retrospective. Parker said, "Divining, penetrating, Dr. Muck enters into this emotion, transmits it, and sometimes releases and heightens it as though he were freeing that, which from sheer intensity of feeling, holds the composer almost tongue-tied. As widely as these composers' range, so ranges Dr. Muck's divination."[26] Joseph Horowitz insightfully compares Symphony Hall to a "spare church" or town meeting space with its hard upholstery and simple features. In part, Higginson's hall paid homage to Boston's Puritan past. Higginson admitted that he always liked "the severe in architecture, music, men and women."[27] Certainly, women came to Symphony Hall in droves to receive musical and spiritual inspiration, particularly as the home and the church encompassed the "female sphere of influence."[28] Symphony Hall became an extension of that sphere. The abstract nature of music and the emotions that it evokes make it a uniquely otherworldly art, one entirely opposite to the material existence of modern life.[29] Music served a missionary goal. Middle-class and elite female concertgoers were perhaps Muck's greatest supporters. Mrs. Henry Carmichael of Malden, Massachusetts, spared little emotion in her florid letter to Higginson that described music as the "religion of the masses, a vital force in wartime to bring about true peace. One and all nearer to the Divine God who gave music to the world to uplift mortals."[30] She continued, "I hope that nothing will overthrow the great monumental work you [Higginson and Muck] have done for humanity in bringing music into our lives."[31] To the women in Boston, Muck was on a pedestal, a figure of perfection. If news leaked out about Muck's transgressions, he would have disappointed his "congregants," and, worse, he would have destroyed the moral image that Higginson and the Boston Symphony had worked so hard to create. Knowledge of Muck's affair would have suggested a weakness in the argument that only Brahmins were arbiters of morality. The scandal would have called into question the private behavior of the city's most "morally elevated" elite.

In an era before television or radio, Muck and the symphony were a huge draw. He was expected to attract patrons to the symphony with his physical charisma. Conductors, like Muck, were considered "mythical heroes by their fans." Adoring audiences admired a strong, good-looking leader, and they worshipped Muck in cultlike fashion.[32] As a Stuttgart newspaper reported, for nearly two decades, Muck was "the idol of Boston's musical world."[33] Female students and older matrons flocked to the hall to see him conduct.[34] In the autumn of 1907, 1,500 people waited in line for hours in front of Symphony Hall to secure balcony seats for afternoon rehearsals. "Traffic on Huntington Avenue, including the trolley cars, had to stop, then inch their way through the crowd."[35] The *Boston Globe* reported that a thousand symphony girls, conservatory students, and adult women who had waited an entire day for tickets were turned away with tears in their eyes. Those who pushed their way through the crowds and into the hall, jumped across one another to obtain a seat, throwing bags and hats onto chairs in their eagerness.[36] When Muck was arrested and sent to an East Cambridge jail, women "walked to and fro in the corridors outside the office of the United States Marshal hoping to catch a glimpse of the distinguished prisoner."[37] Muck held great sexual appeal.

As Norman Lebrecht points out, conductors' image and magnetism were enhanced by their desirability.[38] Famous turn-of-the-century conductors were widely rumored to have transcended normative behavior, fondling colleagues' wives or taking female fans to bed following concerts. Mixed together, this combination of spiritual and sexual power produced a cultural hero figure that men could envy and emulate.[39] Like modern-day celebrities, conductors' sexual exploits were the stuff of fantasy. They were revered, and their behaviors were "accepted" with a wink and a nod.[40] But times were changing, and the public would not be so quick to accept lascivious behavior even from the most adulated figures.

On some levels, Muck had the requisite sex appeal for his occupation. He could exploit young women precisely because of his position in Boston, and it was through his relationships with women, with Rosamond, in particular, that he was able to summon the creative energy and passion that influenced his work. Muck was best known for his Wagner interpretations. As Laurence Dreyfus points out, Wagner created "an erotic high style" that utilized music as a "vehicle for simulating sexual impulse" and summoned the "torment of forbidden desire." Wagner's music was an acceptable way in Victorian society to express sexuality in a world that did not allow its expression otherwise.[41]

Parker, the music critic for the *Boston Transcript*, was very moved by the passionate nature of Muck's performance of Wagner's *Tristan und Isolde*, a tragic medieval romance about adulterous love between a knight and a queen. Parker mirrored the musical experience at Symphony Hall with erotic prose of his own. He describes Muck cueing the violins as Isolde "unbosomed (her) heart," and the "climax lift[ing] the tortures of longing, dying, desolate, from frenzy—measuring the mind, the spirit in the familiar union."[42] Muck's hands summoned a *forte*, while twice "rose the mighty surge of the climax to Isolde, yet the final f sharp upon which it dies into the sunset seemed not less to fill the theater." Describing the intercourse between the orchestra and the singing voices, "interweaving . . . leashing and unleashing," Dr. Muck "lays the flesh of heroic passion moving to the tragic fate: while through veins and arteries he sends beauty pulsing and manifold." Wrapped up in the nervous vitality and romance of the music, Parker describes the love duet as "in thrall with every other perspective faculty to the flaming incandescence of musical sound, ascending from the orchestra-pit. Upon the stage diffused, over the auditorium in flood descending . . . Tristan that blazed with the fires, of a firmament of passion into one pair and one fate concentrated."[43] Wagner's opera musically represents adultery and unfulfilled sexual tension, only resolved at the conclusion when Tristan and Isolde finally unite in death. Parker was clearly emotionally aroused by Muck's passionate performance, utilizing every possible titillating adjective to describe each note and dynamic marking.

As mentioned in chapter 4, provincial Bostonians were typically uncomfortable with opera and its voyeuristic display. Boston music journalist John Sullivan Dwight viewed opera as impure and hedonistic.[44] Muck, however, did not see it that way. He disliked "music of the stage in the stripped, actionless concert-hall," so he creatively found ways to meet Boston's criteria while infusing each performance with the sensuality and eroticism that one expected from a fully staged operatic performance. He called on his musicians, singers, and orchestra members alike to replace with sound and intensity all the drama that one could not see. As the press reported, "the imaginative listener saw the curtains part at the end of the overture" even though no curtain was actually present. Muck's power to draw on his own passion and demand it from his musicians charged his performances with a level of electricity that drew huge crowds to his concerts.[45]

During the first two decades of the twentieth century, the sexual climate in Boston changed as more people sought out erotic pleasure. The city's "red-light district," known as Scollay Square, was expanding.[46] City officials "allowed" provocative activities in this area, initially drawing patrons from immigrant and business communities but eventually becoming a more widespread attraction for all social classes.[47] The Old Howard burlesque house was the most popular, becoming a rite of passage for many Boston men. In the years prior to the war, Harvard College students and professors "rented" the balcony on Wednesdays to watch tableau artists covered in white powder pose nude like classical statuary. The audience fired slingshots and paperclips at the ladies onstage, attempting to break their pose. Crowds enjoyed watching "Little Egypt" perform her risqué hoochie-coochie dance. Isadora Duncan appeared in sheer fabric without shoes, dancing to classical music, oftentimes accompanied by Boston's German musicians. Duncan sought to cast off the rigidity of Victorian ballet, creating a more modern, natural art form. Prudish Bostonians viewed her act as vaudevillian.[48]

In 1916, Swiss composer Ernest Bloch conducted the Maud Allan Symphony Orchestra on a US tour with "Salome Dancer" Maud Allan in the starring role. Maud was known for taking Isadora Duncan's dance moves to an increasingly erotic level. The Allan-Bloch duo performed in Boston for a sellout crowd. Allan aroused audiences with her provocative striptease, revealing a see-through gown and beaded pasties, or breast patches. Described as "bare limbed and scantily draped in filmy gauzes, diaphanous in texture and unvivid in color, she floats from one pose to the next, emphasizing the plastic transitions with waving arms and raised legs and sundry poses of the head."[49] While the *New York Times* raved about the Allan-Bloch performance, finding it "artistic" and "graceful," Boston conservatives, including Mayor John F. Fitzgerald, were outraged, arguing that the city was home to many colleges and universities and parents had a right to expect performances that did not offend morality or public taste. Their act was "banned in Boston."[50] As Joseph Horowitz suggests, such performances "pushed and scraped" against the limits of New England taste. Muck went against the ban. In January of 1918, two years after the Allan-Bloch episode, Muck invited Bloch to Symphony Hall to conduct his new composition. He supported his colleague and countryman, who had been denounced in Boston for his association with Maud Allan.[51] The timing could not have been worse for Muck, for only two months after Bloch performed at the BSO, authorities began investigating Muck's sexual conduct.

Adding to the moral tension, Boston was a major port during the war, playing host to thousands of soldiers and sailors.[52] Estimates suggest that military men acquired some form of sexual service from upwards of twenty thousand women in the city.[53] People danced cheek-to-cheek at the Bowdoin Square or Independence Ballrooms. They did the bunny hug, the tango, the turkey trot, the grizzly bear, and the Chaplin wiggle. They listened to Sophie Tucker sing, "I'll let you have your way / Some one of these days." People drank more than they ever had before. In Boston, they enjoyed Medford rum punch and bourbon sours called Ward Eights as a tribute to Boston's Eighth Ward political district.[54] They watched burlesque at the Gaiety Theatre on Washington Street and B. F. Keith's Bijou Dream, the city's biggest vaudeville emporium.[55]

Figure 7.2. Isadora Duncan performed in sheer fabric accompanied by an orchestra of classical musicians, often German. Photographer Arnold Genthe, 1915–1923. Courtesy of the Library of Congress, Prints and Photographs Division, Arnold Genthe Collection. Negatives and Transparencies (Reproduction Number LC G432-0958-M-001) LC-DIG-agc-7a14273 (digital file from original).

Figure 7.3. "Maud Allan, Salome Dancer." Maud Allan toured with Swiss composer and conductor Ernest Bloch. Boston conservatives railed against the overt sensuality of these performances. Courtesy of the Dance Canada Danse Archive in Toronto, Canada.

Figure 7.4. Scollay Square. Sexuality became commercialized during the war years. Many Boston men frequented the Old Howard burlesque house in Scollay Square, the city's "red light district." Melissa D. Burrage Collection.

Figure 7.5. Washington Street, Keith's Burlesque and Gaiety Theater. Boston's entertainment district. Melissa D. Burrage Collection.

Some of Boston's upper classes had formed a vice society as early as 1882 based on the work of Anthony Comstock, and they called their organization the Watch and Ward Society. Charter officers included prominent iconic names, such as Hale, Brooks, Cabot, Lowell, Lawrence, Lodge, and Holmes. These privileged men enthusiastically supported the cause of "morality."[56] Watch and Ward's most energetic president, Godfrey Lowell Cabot, worked most diligently to prohibit all forms of sexual expression in the city.[57] The Watch and Ward succeeded in strengthening Massachusetts anti-obscenity laws. Members traveled to bookstores, movie houses, gambling parlors, brothels, and theaters to "clean up the city."[58] They read sexually provocative literature to label it "banned" and placed these "immoral" books in a locked room, called "the inferno," in the Boston Public Library.[59] They worked in conjunction with the Boston Art Commission to forbid "obscene" art, such as Frederick MacMonniess's sculpture *Bacchantes and Infant Faun* from being displayed in public spaces.[60] Harvard president Charles W. Eliot, Henry Lee Higginson's good friend, praised the Watch and Ward Society. In 1911, he described it as a "thoroughly scientific charity" because "it investigates the causes" of social ills and "undertakes to prevent these evils by drying up the sources of immorality and crime."[61] During the war, the Watch and Ward seized sexually explicit mail between soldiers and prostitutes in an effort to shut down local brothels.[62] The organization investigated the March 6, 1917, Mishawum Manor case, involving a sexual orgy hosted by Paramount Pictures executives at a Boston-area hotel.[63] For Muck's sexual relationship to come out into the open in this repressive climate would have been dangerous, as censoring in Boston was at its height during those years.[64] The city's moral authorities would certainly have labeled Karl Muck—the city's elite musical icon coming out of Boston's bastion of morality— "banned in Boston" if news of his infidelity became public.

Symphony Hall: A Virtuous Institution

Symphony Hall was Henry Lee Higginson's antidote to immorality in Boston, located far from the vice districts in the city. Elites like Higginson turned to art and culture to transmit civic values.[65] A heightened sexual tension brought urban leaders and local reformers together to restructure the social spaces in the city.[66] While some worked to "disinfect" the streets and alter the behavior and character within vice districts, many cultural capitalists, such as Higginson, worked to create a "geographical dividing line" or boundary between the sexual promiscuity of the waterfront vice district and the "moral" sector of Huntington Avenue and Boylston Street, building the Boston Public Library, the Museum of Fine Arts, Symphony Hall, the Boston Opera House, and New England Conservatory of Music's Jordan Hall on newly filled land.[67] Their goal was to create division between high art and popular entertainment. Such a partition intended to make clear a moral agenda of Brahmin leaders by reorganizing social space into good and bad districts. The "respectable" would dominate public space. Boston Symphony Hall would become a place where the public could go—far from brothels and burlesque houses. Symphony Hall was not simply an entertainment venue. It was a means of social control. Boston elites created institutions to uplift the masses, to socialize the poor, and to temper promiscuous behavior. Boston Symphony Hall, along with other arts institutions, lured people away from vice, offering affordable and more enriching alternatives.[68] If Muck's sexual liaison with Young became public, he would have tainted Higginson's vision of a respectable institution intended to uplift the lower classes. He would have blurred the geographical dividing line between Boston's "moral" musical and artistic region and its "immoral" red light district. A Muck scandal in the city would have been viewed as symptomatic of a very unhealthy society.

Double Standard of Morality among Boston's Upper-Class Men

While Boston Brahmins viewed themselves as the moral leaders of the city, they in fact were just as guilty of sexual permissiveness as working-class citizens. These privileged men had money to create private sexual spaces hidden from public view, behind the heavy mahogany doors of Boston's gentlemen's clubs. They drank port in Turkish robes, smoked cigars, and indulged in expensive "ladies of the evening." Fascinated by the sexual behaviors of people from foreign places, upper-class clubmen recited the sensual poetry of *The Rubáiyát of Omar Khayyám*. They studied paintings that depicted harems, nautch girls, and geishas and looked at graphic photographs of the tantric statuary of India's Khajuraho Temple with its orgy-like display. They dressed like sultans and studied foreign behaviors with a prurient interest that caused arousal yet publicly claimed that these cultures were debauched and lecherous.[69] They looked at "anthropological" depictions of nude African women in *National Geographic* magazine, and they studied carte-de-visite boudoir postcards from Paris.[70] They built conservatories to watch insects inseminate orchids, for orchids resembled the sexual organs of humans.[71]

Muck was a scholar of "orientalism," a term theorized by Edward Said to describe the Victorian obsession with the Eastern "other."[72] Like a lot of Victorian-era men titillated by the sexual behaviors and patterns of Eastern cultures, exposure of Muck's sexual behavior would have cast suspicions on other clubmen like himself. A sexual scandal involving Muck would have blown the lid off of Boston's upper-class sexual behavior—these men who were presumably the purveyors of morality and who viewed themselves to be above the law. The federal government's exposure of Muck's secret would have opened a Pandora's box regarding male privilege, laying bare the typical duplicity and hypocritical behavior going on in many of Boston's elite gentlemen's clubs, making them vulnerable too. Muck hoped to maintain his position as conductor of the BSO and continue his membership in Boston's upper-class gentlemen's clubs. The public exposure of his affair would show just how fragile and expendable he was in Boston, as "friends" in those clubs distanced themselves from him.

The Social Purity Movement against Prostitution, White Slavery, and Polygamy

During this period, many middle- and upper-middle-class matrons organized powerful moral reform and social purity movements, promoting a mission of abstinence before marriage for both sexes and complete fidelity in marriage.[73] For women reformers, sexuality outside of the family threatened their identities as wives and mothers, as well as the health of their families. They opposed any form of sexuality that was unrelated to reproduction or marital intimacy. Educated women, such as Elizabeth Blackwell and Caroline Winslow, argued that women should have responsibility for creating a single standard of sexual morality.[74] In the era of the suffragette, their purity campaign ran in parallel with their efforts for the vote, printing brochures to warn women of the dangers of illicit activity. They visited domestic servants who were often vulnerable to solicitations from the master of the house to let them know that they were supported. They followed men on the streets in the business districts and visited taverns and pubs to wage their "battle against sin."[75]

Complicating matters even further, close to three hundred thousand cases of venereal disease were reported in the United States. The epidemic shocked the promiscuous and caused many to reconsider and alter their behavior. Sexual diseases gave the purity movement great momentum, leading to a widespread decrease in risqué behavior.[76] This World War I–era public health crisis caused many people to take notice of the moral reform messages that they had otherwise ignored. Reformers were quick to take advantage of their position and market their propaganda to the public. The army launched its own anti-venereal-disease campaign to ensure the maximum number of healthy soldiers, extending its reach to local YMCAs, Knights of Columbus halls, and other national community organizations.[77] Throughout this period, the 1914 film *Damaged Goods* was shown, highlighting the dangers of prostitution. In it, the main character, George Dupont, visits a brothel and then transmits venereal disease to his innocent wife. Disease inflamed hostility toward men who sought sex outside marriage.[78]

The fear of venereal disease led many affluent men to take mistresses rather than prostitutes. They sought out young women who were "clean" virgins and not yet infected with disease.[79] Those who continued to frequent brothels demanded protective measures, which led to improvements in birth control technology, from sheep skin to rubber prophylactics, and a supposed rise in kidnappings of innocent young women for prostitution to satisfy the demand for hygienically pure sexual liaisons.[80]

"White slavery" was the term used to describe this global crime against vulnerable women, and reformers mobilized one of the largest campaigns in history to attack it, saturating the public arena with candid literature and movies. A popular journal quipped, "Our former reticence on matters of sex is giving way to a frankness that would even startle Paris."[81] Many Hollywood films popularized the topic of white slavery, dramatizing the dangers of sexual promiscuity. Theaters regularly showed films such as *The House of Bondage* (1914), *The Inside of the White Slave Traffic* (1913), *The Exposé of the White Slave Traffic* (1914), and *Little Lost Sister* (1917). By far the most popular film in this genre was Universal Studios' *The Traffic of Souls* (1913), which generated an incredible $450,000 in box office receipts.[82]

Using the momentum of the white slavery campaign, female reformers lashed out against polygamy, adultery, and the double standard. They fought against nontraditional, nonnuclear arrangements, seeing them as something that disenfranchised women, promoted male privilege, and disrupted the social order. They collectively organized into the National Women's Christian Temperance Union, launching a White Ribbon Campaign that encouraged faithful married men to wear small white banners. They called on states to increase the age of sexual consent for young women from age ten to eighteen. They pressured the federal government to prosecute men who had sex with young women with statutory rape.[83] The Woman's National Anti-polygamy Society called for legislation against "licentious men" who victimized women.[84] Anti-polygamists viewed plural marriage as

Figure 7.6. *Traffic in Souls* movie poster. Reformers mobilized against sexual promiscuity and "white slavery." Hollywood films, such as *Traffic in Souls* dramatized the dangers of licentious men who exploited young females. Wikimedia Commons.

a violation of women's rights, a threat to motherhood, the home, and the country.[85] Women sought to advance their political power and to protect the sanctuary of the home while maintaining their position as moral leaders within it.[86] Their efforts were not overlooked, and they did succeed at the state and federal levels in restricting male sexual privilege.

Muck's Behavior Reveals Hypocrisy, Privilege, and Deception

Muck's letters to Rosamond, if made public, would have cast a spotlight on upper-class male privilege, exposing the methods he used to maintain intimacy:

> My darling, since yesterday I find myself delirious with joy. . . . I have made arrangements to secure a small apartment, secret and secluded. . . . When tomorrow I meet you I will explain to you all the details. I will see to it that you have a duplicate key to the apartment, and after we have talked over every detail, we can meet at our new nest as often as it is mutually convenient and safe for you. And then my darling . . . drink the sweet cup to the last drop. Until tomorrow, with kisses, Your Karl.[87]

Muck's letters would have laid bare the duplicity of his actions—illustrating both Rosamond and Anita's victimized positions within their respective relationships with him. Rosamond was uncomfortable playing the role of mistress and had broken off the relationship. Her attachment to Muck, and his promise to obtain a divorce and "make you my own," brought her back to him, but the situation was difficult to maintain as this letter from Muck to Rosamond suggests:

> My Darling! I fail to find words to express my joy over your decision to renew our old friendship, which you so cruelly broke off in a moment of despondency. I feel happy to learn that you no longer feel worried. You say, and you are right in saying so, darling, that my marital entanglements make it very hard for you to continue our hitherto pleasant relationship. But can't you see, darling, how much harder it is for me to renounce the love that grew between us so sublimely? Must we, for the sake of foolish sentiments that are imposed on us by others, foreswear the love that is divine and inexpressible by common language? No, a thousand times no! You are mine and I am your slave and so I must remain. . . . It will perhaps surprise you to learn that to a certain extent Mrs. Muck knows our relationship. She has a noble

heart and her mind is broad beyond the comprehension of the swine-
like people among whom we must lie a little while longer.[88]

Muck's private letter to Rosamond would have been fodder for the
movement to abolish the double standard. The letters would have
exposed the ease with which upper-class men could "abduct" young
women in polite society. Muck, and the Brahmin clubmen with whom
he associated, would have been viewed as predators by white slavery reformers who were concerned about the vulnerability of young
women.[89]

In fact, moral reformers were so successful in their campaign that
in November of 1919, when Muck's affair eventually came to light, the
Tavern and St. Botolph Clubs, made up of Boston's most cultural elite,
publicly denounced him and voided his membership to avoid scandal within their own organizations.[90] The press reported that "Muck
was dropped like a hot coal and even his hitherto warm admirers had
nothing more to say."[91] Muck had been concerned about his relationship with these influential men. If his reputation was tarnished by a sex
scandal, this powerful clan would have decided his fate and influenced
whether he would retain his conducting position with the BSO.[92]
Muck's fears regarding the city's clubmen proved accurate.

Before the war, the country had turned a blind eye to the sexual indiscretions of privileged men, but the drama surrounding the
Muck case suggested that the BOI would target individuals regardless
of social class. In 1919, when news of his affair did come out, Holker
Abbot, secretary of the Tavern Club pointed out, "I think no questions had better be asked about the matter [Muck's internment]. We
all accept whatever the United States does without a single comment,
even in our own minds." Boston's (and the nation's) gentlemen's
clubs cut their ties with him.[93] They did not keep a code of silence
to protect him. These men severed their relationships with Muck to
protect their own reputations. Satirically, Henry Lee Higginson, president of the Tavern Club, commented that "if Dr. Muck should be
sent away, plenty of men should be sent away on the same ground";
however, he later altered his public response realizing that his BSO
audience was primarily female, and it was not wise to justify Muck's
immoral actions for fear of alienating his base of support. Thereafter, Higginson distanced himself from Muck and never spoke to
him again. Clearly, prosecuting an upper-class man for taking a lady
across state lines signaled something new—something that Boston
Brahmins were guilty of. Aware of this potential new threat, the city's
elite clubmen, including Henry Lee Higginson, publicly rebuked
Muck to protect their own interests.

Changing Gender Roles and
Muck's Support of Female Colleagues

Investigations into Muck's relationships with women also occurred as gender roles were being redefined, as women joined the suffrage movement and fought for their right to vote. The National American Woman Suffrage Association, led by Carrie Chapman Catt, supported the war, hoping it would lead to female equality.[94] Many young women abandoned old gender constructions that required them to maintain their home sphere and moved into the workforce, taking jobs that soldiers had left open. Escaping the drudgery of domesticity, they took jobs in local department stores, in munitions factories, as Red Cross workers, as nurses, mechanics, entertainers, and journalists. Women rented apartments and created new modern identities.[95]

Women filled 1.5 million job vacancies in the United States during the war. Women and men were in far greater contact than ever before, in gender integrated workplaces, college campuses, and public amusements.[96] World War I was the start of the flapper era, when women cut off their Gibson Girl hair styles and donated their metal corsets to the war effort. Women visited Boston's Old Corner Bookstore and picked up dime novels, such as *Madame Bovary* (1856) and *Fanny Hill* (1748). Mainstream popular literature began to have more sexual themes.[97] Novels of the period used a variety of vague and explicit language to describe body parts and sexual acts, portraying erotic behavior as a courageous act of liberation. The popular novel *Hermia Suydam* (1889) was the first in a series by Gertrude Atherton spanning several decades, featuring strong, independent women in pursuit of sexual pleasure.[98] Owen Johnson's 1913 novel, *Salamander*, unabashedly recounts the story of a young woman who enjoys her sexual freedom.[99] New character types became part of the literary lexicon, including the "new woman," "the mistress," and "the middle-aged woman."[100] As Dale Bauer points out, "Women writers began to treat sex, once considered an urge or impulse, as a conscious act and a choice."[101] With greater independence, "new women" defined a role for themselves that did not follow traditional patriarchal patterns. They set a fresh standard regarding their interactions with men. Not in any hurry to marry, they wanted meaningful relationships with men and women, based on intimacy, love, sexual gratification, and equality.[102] Not wanting to be objects that their fathers owned or the property of their husbands, they desired to possess themselves.[103]

Muck sought out independent-minded female musicians with whom he could collaborate and who would understand and support his work. Margaret Dows Herter is Muck's first such relationship that

Figure 7.7. Girl Stitchers. In 1917 and 1918, many men went to war, and women took the jobs soldiers left behind. As this advertisement shows, women were offered opportunities through the local newspapers to work outside of the home. *Boston Herald,* January 2, 1918.

Figure 7.8. Washington St. Shopping Hour. As this image shows, men and women were in greater contact than ever before. Melissa D. Burrage Collection.

we are aware of in the United States. As mentioned in the previous chapter, Herter was an accomplished violinist. We do know some details of Margaret's life and can piece together how the two would have come to know and appreciate one another. Margaret's father, Christian Archibald Herter, was an American physician and pathologist. Born in Glenville, Connecticut, Christian Herter was educated at Johns Hopkins University and became part of New York's scholarly community. In addition to his medical expertise, he was an accomplished cellist who had studied in Germany and who had performed professionally in New York City. His musical career certainly influenced his daughter, who became a gifted violinist in her own right. In 1910, Christian Herter died at the age of forty-five of a neurological disease, leaving his daughter in mourning. Six years later, in 1916, Margaret began her association with Muck, and at the same time her mother remarried. Muck may have been a substitute for Margaret's father, but their friendship was short lived, for Susan Dows Herter Dakin (Mrs. Henry Dakin), Margaret's mother, became uncomfortable with her daughter's association with the famous conductor and contacted the New York office of the BOI regarding Muck. With this investigation, the relationship ended.[104]

Margaret Herter went on to have an incredibly accomplished multifaceted career as a musician, composer, author, translator, and businesswomen. In 1925, Herter published *The Art of String Quartet Playing* with Carl Fischer. She married W. W. Norton, establishing the highly successful W. W. Norton Publishing firm. In 1927, she translated Paul Bekker's *The Story of Music: An Historical Sketch of the Changes in Musical Form.* She translated and published nine volumes of Rainer Maria Rilke's works, later set to music by George Perle and David Diamond. She collaborated with composer Roy Harris to arrange Bach's *Kunst der Fuge* for string quartet. She was an active member of the American Musicological Society, serving for ten years on its editorial board. She authored, edited, and translated articles for the *Musical Quarterly*, and she oversaw the operation of W. W. Norton Publishing after her husband's death in 1945, transferring ownership to company employees shortly thereafter. Since its founding, the Norton Company has published more than 250 musical books, a fitting legacy to Margaret's love of music.[105]

Rosamond Young, like Margaret, was an intellectual and musical companion for Karl Muck, having lived and trained in Germany. Challenging the old assumptions of separate spheres, Rosamond joined an exodus of women who traveled outside the United States to escape sexist social constraints and gain musical training denied to them at home. Rosamond "finished" her education and polished upper-class behavior with a European tour, visiting art museums, theaters, and concert halls and absorbing European history. Because of this experience, Rosamond could converse with authority about high culture.[106] Upon returning to the United States, she continued her studies at the New England Conservatory, bringing to her work a newfound knowledge from Europe.

A classic "new woman," Rosamond was part of a younger and educated generation that cast off established and repressive roles for women. A student of Percy F. Hunt at the New England Conservatory in Boston and Adrienne Remenyi-Von Ende at the Von Ende School of Music in New York City, Rosamond shunned the traditional role of marriage and housework in favor of a career.[107] On October 21, 1914, she made her professional debut in a vocal recital at Jordan Hall, and on June 6, 1916, she performed Berlioz, Beethoven, Schumann, and Strauss at the Astor Gallery of the Waldorf-Astoria Hotel in New York. Karl Muck attended both concerts and praised Rosamond's "unusually rich and full voice" in the local press. In July of 1917, promoter Antonia Sawyer of the Antonia Sawyer Agency, located in the Metropolitan Opera Company building on 1141 Broadway in New York, began managing Rosamond's concert career. On July 12, 1917, newspapers began reporting that Rosamond Young was "entering the concert field," enticing readers to future concerts with descriptions of her excellent vocal qualities and physical virtues.[108] Three months later, on October 18, she performed at the 3,500-seat Massey Hall in Toronto, returning to Boston for a full Jordan Hall recital on November 15 and a performance on January 15, 1918, as principal soloist with the Boston Symphony Orchestra under Karl Muck.[109] Rosamond's career was on the rise. Her relationship with Muck was one of musical collaboration and intimacy. Muck could share his culture and knowledge with her and expect a level of understanding that others perhaps could not give him. He saw a talent in her and he guided it.[110] While preparing for her BSO debut, he instructed Rosamond in the basic details of rehearsals—where she should practice, how she should stand to project her voice, and which critics commented favorably on her performances. He grew so close to her that he empathetically absorbed her performance anxiety as his own. In a letter to her he said, "Now you will perhaps understand why the last few days, and particularly yesterday, I was so nervous." Her success and happiness became equivalent to his own.[111] The pair became partners, discussing the interpretation of musical scores or what sort of feeling and musical phrasing the composer intended. They could channel their emotions for each other back into the music. Muck guided Rosamond's career as a companion and mentor. He wrote in a letter to her:

> I hope to see you tomorrow evening in the choir rehearsal. I am so absent minded that I really do not know for the moment whether the rehearsal begins at 7 or 7:30. I will telephone you as to this tomorrow forenoon. The whole choir and orchestra band must enter via the stage entrance; you must of course not do this. I shall take care that the main entrance shall remain open for you; respectively that somebody should wait there for you who will admit you. During the intermission and at the end of the rehearsal (perhaps also before the rehearsal begins) I may find an opportunity to hold your hands and glance into your eyes. And now God Bless you for today, my beloved darling! Be sweet to me!! Your karl.[112]

With Muck's arrest and subsequent deportation, the relationship ended. Years after their affair, Rosamond married Russell Chapin and with him, in 1946, became codirector of the New Boston Opera Company and the New Boston Music Festival in the Berkshires in western Massachusetts.[113]

We get a deeper glimpse into Karl Muck's professional relationships with women through a slightly more modern source. Antonia Brico, an American conductor and former student of Muck's, gained valuable experience under his tutelage.[114] In the 1920s in Germany, Muck gave Brico tickets to all Bayreuth performances, and he allowed her to sit in the pit to observe orchestra rehearsals. He coached Brico in opera conducting and helped her gain admission to the Master School in Conducting program at the Berlin Academy of Music. He wrote her a recommendation, saying she was "highly musically talented, gifted with a will of iron diligence concerning her studies; a person who has made enormous progress." He described her as "full of burning ambition to achieve the highest artistic goals."[115] In 1930, she debuted as guest conductor with the Berlin Philharmonic Orchestra. In 1931, Muck was in the audience when Brico conducted the Hamburg Philharmonic.[116] Throughout her career, Brico appeared as a guest conductor with many notable orchestras, including the Los Angeles Symphony, the San Francisco Symphony, the Detroit Symphony, and the New York Philharmonic, but, because of gender prejudice, she was never offered a permanent conductorship in a top-tier orchestra. Brico lived in Denver and conducted the Denver Community Symphony, which later became the Denver Philharmonic. She survived financially by teaching private piano lessons in her Denver home. She died in 1989.[117]

In 1939, Brico gave an interview to the press about her "great teacher" on Muck's eightieth birthday:

> Many people thought Muck austere and stern . . . but those of us who knew him well saw an entirely different side. His sometimes brusque exterior hid a most tender [and] sympathetic heart. The years I knew him he did not care to mingle in groups or go out socially, but he would sit for hours after a rehearsal or concert with one or two friends with whom he would exchange reminiscences. He had a keen sense of humor and loved to relate choice bits from his rich experiences all over the globe. When teaching me a score, he would make me sing the various instrumental parts.[118]

Karl Muck disregarded society's Victorian cues that suggested that women were delicate and not physically capable of careers.[119] Women had few opportunities to lead symphony orchestras during Muck's lifetime. Beth Abelson Macleod illustrates in her biographical exploration of female performers, composers, and conductors in the late nineteenth and early twentieth centuries, that women's musical activities were limited to their homes or they were not taken seriously in public professional settings.[120] Their appearance onstage in American concert halls challenged patriarchal control. Margaret Herter, Rosamond Young, and Antonia Brico managed to break out of their traditional consignments to become accomplished musicians, in great part because Karl Muck did not shun them as other male conductors or musicians had done.[121]

Figure 7.9. Antonia Brico, gifted pianist and conducting student of Karl
Muck's. Brico settled in Denver and conducted the Denver Community
Symphony, which later became the Denver Philharmonic. Courtesy of the
Denver Public Library, Western History Collection.

Muck rejected the notion that women should remain within their separate domestic sphere. In a field that overwhelmingly favored men and often systematically discredited women, Muck progressively guided talented musicians regardless of gender. Brico writes, "The world knew him as a conductor. Some few knew him as a brilliant teacher, philosopher, student of Oriental philosophy, and a profound and insatiable reader. As the sole recipient of five years' private training with Dr. Muck, and through the daily personal contacts of those years, I came to know him as few did in his later years."[122] Like Brico, Rosamond shared a mutually beneficial working relationship with Muck. Brico became one of the first eminent female conductors in America, in spite of gender obstacles, thanks in great part to Karl Muck.

Bureau of Investigation Backlash

Unwilling to see Rosamond Young (or Margaret Herter) as mature, adult women with minds of their own in professional, collaborative, and modern relationships, the BOI's perceptions of Rosamond and Margaret as passive victims colored its treatment of Muck and ultimately led investigators to do something about it. In part, their action against Muck was a conservative backlash against the "new women" and their rise in the workplace, as well as a response to progressive men like Muck for supporting them. In 1920, women did gain suffrage with the passage of the Nineteenth Amendment, and yet gender tensions continued. In 1921, Congress passed the Sheppard-Towner Act, financing instruction for infant care, hoping to entice women back into the home and thus allowing men to maintain their dominant positions over them.[123] Muck was untenably positioned between these competing forces.

In so many ways, Muck was on the precipice. His position in Boston was quite fragile during the war. Not as assimilated into the city as he thought he was, the social mores of the time played a large role in Muck's fall from grace. His relationship with Rosamond Young occurred as citizen organizations pressured the federal government, and as the state began to have greater control over the lives of individual citizens and more power and influence regarding the meaning of morality in America.[124]

Boston was clearly not the place to be involved in a sex scandal. The *Boston Post* reported "Muck feared scandal more than arrest."[125] Sex was the ultimate weapon used to punish and bring Karl Muck into compliance. It was a passionate topic among interest groups, and a high-profile figure like Muck would have inflamed the controversy.

Mrs. Jay could not have found a more perfect weakness to exploit than Muck's private sexual behavior. He knew that if his affair with Rosamond became public that his "enemies would rejoice."[126] He knew that Anita would have been humiliated. The relationship that had transpired between Karl Muck and Rosamond Young was private. It was not the business of the federal government, the newspapers, or matrons of city gossip. He wrote to Rosamond, "My Darling. In these days when the beast-like agents of the Department of Justice are following my every footstep we must make our plans with care lest these hunters will have a chance to drag our sweet friendship before public gaze. . . . We must not overlook any precaution that will save us both from a scandal. . . . dragging to vulgar public gaze our love that is sacred and which we alone understand."[127]

Finding no evidence of any subversive activities, federal officials doggedly built a case against Karl Muck as a sexual deviant. Vowing to protect Rosamond and Anita from public shame, he agreed to accept the conditions of his arrest and internment, including the bogus label of "dangerous enemy alien" in exchange for silence. Muck did not know when he made his decision that the federal government would ultimately expose his affair anyway. He did not know that he would face mandatory deportation. This was a cruel twist of fate. He had no idea that he would lose the opportunity to return to his post as the conductor of the Boston Symphony and that his personal property would be confiscated. The federal government had little regard for such matters. In his attempt to maintain his position and keep his indiscretion quiet, Muck lost his foothold in the United States altogether. Yet Karl Muck was willing to "walk through fire" to protect the privacy of his loved ones, as well as himself, for, as he wrote to Rosamond before his arrest, "Do not fear, darling, should our relationship result in disgrace (which God forbid), I would be only too proud to shoulder it all."[128] And shoulder it, he (and they) did.

Chapter Eight

MUCK'S FINAL YEARS

His Association with the Wagners and Adolf Hitler (1920–1940)

Muck's troubles were far from over when he and his wife Anita returned to Europe in September of 1919. The US federal government had expelled the couple with little regard for their well-being or their privacy. Utterly destroyed by America, a country they once called home, Karl and Anita attempted to reacclimate themselves to a world they had left behind many years before. Muck was initially unable to find stable employment as a musician in the post–World War I economy. He no longer had any savings to speak of, and he had no property. His close political connections to the kaiser did not help matters. In 1918, Wilhelm had abdicated the throne and was exiled to the Netherlands. As *New York Times* music critic Olin Downes pointed out, "Muck was no hero welcomed home."[1] The only work he could find was as an itinerant conductor, traveling from city to city, living in hotel after hotel. The transitory quality of their lives was difficult for the couple to bear.[2] Muck worked as a guest conductor at the Berlin State Opera and the Munich Opera Festival, among other places, but these assignments, while prestigious, offered no long-term financial security.[3] Economic instability was only part of the trouble Karl Muck would face, however.

BOI Fails to Maintain the Plea Bargain: The Sealed Muck-Young Letters Are Released to the Press

Just two and a half months after Muck's deportation, another series of events would prove that his troubles were far from over. On November 9, 1919, the *Boston Post* ran a twelve-part series exposing the real reason for Karl Muck's internment, publishing the very private (and supposedly sealed) letters of Karl and Rosamond. The sensational series was sent by the Associated Press across the United States and Europe, causing Karl, Anita, and Rosamond enormous suffering.

As mentioned in the previous chapter, Muck had accepted a plea bargain and agreed to internment as a "dangerous enemy alien" in exchange for secrecy regarding his affair with Rosamond. He had been assured that if he served his time at Fort Oglethorpe, the US government would not divulge the couple's love letters. Bureau of Investigation division superintendent George E. Kelleher and assistant superintendent Norman L. Gifford had ostensibly committed themselves to permanently sealing Muck's private correspondence in exchange for internment. They had promised Muck that they would not disclose the facts of his love affair in the "so-called spy case."[4] In the end, however, BOI officials reneged on their pledge of secrecy, because of a concern, ironically, for their own reputations, duplicitously agreeing to disseminate the letters to the press, highlighting the nature of federal power and the effect that it had on its victims.

Federal officials often worked together with journalists and newspaper companies to bring cases of suspicious activity to public attention. Many newspaper editors were eager to get their hands on sensational information that they could utilize to craft titillating reports in their daily tabloids to excite the public and sell papers.[5] Excitement is exactly what the *Boston Post* delivered to its readers by publishing the Muck-Young letters in a weekly series in 1919.

The BOI and the press exploited Muck and Young to suit their own agendas. The *Boston Post* weeks-long exposé used carefully chosen excerpts from Muck's letters, painting him as a depraved man of the worst sort. The series read like a romance novel and a crime thriller. The conductor came across as a conniving predator of young women with little regard for his wife.

District Attorney Thomas Jefferson Boynton at the BOI in Washington, DC, attempted to stop the newspaper series from continuing, to honor the original plea bargain. He notified C. B. Carberry, managing editor of the *Boston Post*, that a ban had been placed on the series. Carberry, refusing to let the insistent district attorney spoil his story, and having paid off the federal informant who leaked the letters in the first place, decided to appeal to powers above Boynton.[6] The next day, Carberry telegraphed Attorney General A. Mitchell Palmer, requesting that he lift the ban. Carberry communicated his paper's desire to print the articles and satisfy the public's insatiable curiosity, for "the Government should not protect Muck any longer." Acting swiftly, Palmer informed Boynton that the ban would be lifted. In the end, Palmer gave the press full access to the intimate letters between Karl Muck and Rosamond Young, ending a "conspiracy of silence" in favor of full public disclosure. Palmer believed that the evidence contained in the letters could justify the BOI's treatment of the maligned conductor. He explained to Robert Norton, the *Boston Post*'s chief correspondent on the story, "I know you understand the circumstances of the publication of this stuff. . . . I am glad, however, that the public now know the entire truth about Dr. Muck."[7] There had been sensational rumors concerning the sex charges against the former leader of the BSO, and Palmer saw no reason why he needed to keep the story hidden any longer. For Carberry and the *Boston Post*, the series reinforced the paper's tabloid reputation for bringing the most scandalous and lurid stories to the front page. The scandal, however, would not have seen the light of day without the intervention of Palmer, who disregarded Karl Muck's constitutional right to privacy and betrayed the agreement to keep the letters sealed. He was more concerned with his agency's reputation than any personal damage his decision might inflict.

When the first installment of the series was published, many of Muck's friends remained loyal to him, coming forward on his behalf to try to prevent the series from continuing. Boston socialite Isabella Stewart Gardner, known for her intimate friendship with the Mucks, was Karl's greatest defender. Her bold no-nonsense style and courage to confront this injustice was perhaps the greatest thorn in the BOI's side.[8] Mrs. Philip Hale, wife of the Boston music critic, wrote to Carberry in November of 1919. Her letter, along with Dr. Edmund von Mach's to Mr. Grozier, the publisher of the *Boston Post*, argued that "there was not a word of truth to the story" and that "the *Post* had printed an outrageous lie concerning Dr. Muck, and that the man who wrote it knew well it was a lie and every government official knew it was a lie also."[9] Von Mach distributed his attack to all the Boston newspapers, which fueled the *Post*'s desire to vindicate its treatment of Muck by acquiring the official transcript of the case. Following von Mach's appeal, Palmer "agreed that the public was entitled to know the facts, and he ordered delivered . . . the entire government file consisting of letters, reports and investigations . . . in fact, all the evidence the government had against Muck." The Boston intellectual community had put tremendous pressure on Palmer to change his decision and keep the remaining letters private. US Supreme Court associate justices Oliver Wendell Holmes Jr. and Louis D. Brandeis appealed to Palmer to change his instructions, but to no avail.[10] Because so many Bostonians complained about Muck's unfair treatment, from the earliest newspaper attacks against him by Mrs. Jay to his internment and eventual deportation, the BOI appeared corrupt. Palmer opted to utilize his position of power to expose the remainder of the letters and provide the full story of Muck's arrest and internment to defend the BOI's reputation.[11]

Muck Grief Stricken Over Anita's Death and Plagued by Rosamond and the Press

Even after the exposé was printed, Anita Muck remained silent about her husband's affair, expressing pride in her partner and complete devotion to him. Photos of Anita taken at the time demonstrate her strength and composure in the face of her husband's (and her own) difficulties.[12]

Anita supported her husband "for better or worse," enduring enormous heartache. The Mucks were in their sixties when they returned to Germany. The fatherland had been economically destroyed by World War I. Germans throughout the nation were suffering with the destruction of the old autocratic system of the kaiser, the fear of a communist revolution, and a humiliating peace treaty that required them to accept "guilt" for starting the war in the first place. To Germans, it felt as if the allies wanted to destroy them economically for generations.[13] The country was exhausted by war and hunger, suffering through a time of incredible inflation, when basic necessities were hard to come by and prices swelled beyond reasonable levels.[14] It was a time of political extremism, labor strikes, street violence, and hostile rhetoric. The country was saddled with heavy reparations, carved up and territorially smaller, and in financial ruin. In February of 1921, Anita became ill during a concert stop in Amsterdam and was taken by special car to a Berlin hospital for treatment. On April 14, 1921, sixteen months after the story of her husband's infidelity and desired divorce was released, Anita Muck passed away from cancer, broken in body and spirit, like Germany itself, too fragile to survive the trauma.[15]

Karl Muck was bereft over the loss of his companion, his wife of thirty-four years. Grief stricken, he lamented:

> During my whole life, I have been a tenacious energetic man, who could hardly be affected by anything. Now I know that it was all Anita's work. Anita for me meant strength, energy, pride, art—Light and air were not more indispensable to me than she. Now she has left me and has taken my life away with her. I have always been a rather peculiar man—a ponderer. Anita was the only person who really knew and thoroughly understood me and to whom I could fully reveal my whole being. I was always entangled in work, in my art, in science, in problems of many kinds. Anita shared everything with me, she was my

Figure 8.1. A picture of strength, Anita Muck is shown after registering as an alien enemy on June 1, 1918, two months after her husband's internment and after the couple's property was seized by the federal government. Boston Symphony Orchestra manager Charles Ellis, shown on the right, attempts to protect Anita from a crowd of reporters and photographers who surround the police station. Courtesy of the National Archives, War Department. 1789-9/18/1947. File Unit: Enemy Activities, Series: World War I Photographs. Record Group 165.

good genius, my inspiration, and at the same time the link between the world and myself. She guided my life in her quiet, simple, refined, self-confident way. Now she has left me alone, my "unworldliness" of which she so often smilingly reproached me, stares at me from every corner. I cannot anymore find my way in this world. With Anita, I have lost the best and most devoted wife, the noblest friend, the bravest companion. All that made life worth living died with her. Two beings that have existed only for each other during thirty-four years, inwardly entwined and dependent on each other cannot be separated without cutting off the life-thread of the remaining one. I am a restless, peace-less man, crushed by the wretched isolation and inconceivable solitude; day and night haunted by pictures of horror, reminding me the last four indescribably dreadful weeks of her fight with death.[16]

Of Anita's feelings for America, Muck wrote, "You know, *how much* Anita loved America, in spite of all our sad experience there. She really felt homesick for America. The *one* idea, to see Boston again, our nice, cozy house, our true loyal friends, the greatness and beauty of nature, the mountains and lakes, the fairy-land in the West—this one idea never left her. Until her death her thoughts were busy with it."[17] Of Anita's attachment to her Boston friend, Isabella Stewart Gardner, Muck wrote:

> Words cannot express the deep thanks my heart feels for you for your unchangeable, sincere friendship shown to my poor wife during those hard times in Boston. How often and with what love did Anita speak about you, of your true devotion and courage! She always carried the large photo of Fenway Court with her. A few days before she died, she asked me to give it to her. She looked at it for a long, long, while and silently returned it to me, big tears running down her cheeks; she had said good bye to the house and its magnanimous mistress.[18]

To Karl, Anita's death was another acute consequence of Palmer's actions, an abuse of power that caused unending hardship on the Muck family. He wrote, "Anita had suffered dreadfully being obliged to pack or unpack one's trunks nearly every week, without having a house or home of her own. . . . [W]eeks ago Anita has left me and the pain in my heart is still as terrible as on the day when I lost her."[19]

Muck kept busy, however, trying to ease the pain of his misfortune.[20] Bitter and bereaved, he wrote, "Cruel fate has taken my wife from me. I have worked year in year out without taking a single holiday." Following an exhaustive schedule of conducting throughout Europe, he asked, "And after that? Peaceless, restless, homeless. . . . As

Figure 8.2. Fenway Court and Fens, 1920. Anita Muck asked to see a photograph of Fenway Court just before she died. Courtesy of the Boston Public Library, Boston Pictorial Archives.

long as we were together, Anita's vital energy and cheerfulness helped us to overcome even this life of vagrancy. But now???"[21] Muck felt that his "constitution was wrecked," having been undermined by his wife's death and by his Boston experience. "I am now at the end of a life of conscientious, unceasing, sacrificing work; and must say to myself: 'It was in vain.' My life is finished."[22]

In 1922, Karl finally found some professional stability when he was appointed conductor of the Hamburg Philharmonic Orchestra.[23] Even while Germany was starving, music thrived, and the country's concert halls were packed with hungry audiences. The *New York Post* reprinted a Berlin report on March 27, 1922, that said "[Muck] has been slowly but surely working his way back into the enviable position he held in German musical circles prior to his departure to become head of the Boston orchestra."[24] His assignment with the Hamburg Philharmonic was described as an "ancient Pan-German seat" of the "greatest tradition" offering him "the highest recognition that has come to him since his return to Germany."[25] Muck also made guest appearances with the Concertgebouw Orchestra in Amsterdam and the Mozarteum Orchestra at the Salzburg Festival. He filled his calendar with musical assignments and social engagements to keep his mind occupied and free of sadness.

One month after Anita's death, twenty-seven-year-old Rosamond Young set out to contact Muck, traveling alone on board the *Caronia* to Hamburg to reestablish her relationship with him. The death of Anita Muck generated rumors across the United States regarding future wedding plans between Karl and Rosamond. Headlines in a San Francisco newspaper read, "Dr. Muck May Wed Society Girl Heiress," with the article going so far as to announce that an engagement "is daily expected from Germany as the result of recent society gossip overseas."[26] The *New York Times* reported:

> Miss Rosamond Young of Milton [Massachusetts] is to wed Dr. Karl Muck, former conductor of the Boston Symphony Orchestra who was interned during the war and later sent to Germany, is causing a stir in social circles in this section. Mrs. Frank L. Young, mother of the young woman, has made an emphatic denial that any such plan exists. The Young's [*sic*] are at their summer home at Duxbury [Massachusetts]. The girl's father is an invalid. The mother denied her daughter was at present in Munich, Germany. The news was received in this country in April of the death of Mrs. Muck in Germany. Miss Young, whose name was brought into the Dr. Muck investigation during the war when correspondence between the two was seized by Department of Justice agents, sailed for Europe the following month, and it was stated she would continue her musical education in Italy. Dr. Muck is 62 and Miss Young 24.[27]

Such newspaper reports were false. There were no plans between Karl Muck and Rosamond Young. Muck was grieving and feeling guilty for his earlier involvement with Rosamond. He expressed his devastation over the loss of Anita and refused to speak to Rosamond.[28] Victimized by the US and European presses that would not leave him alone, he seemed hopelessly unable to move on with his life. Rosamond was still in love with him, and she saw an opening with the death of Anita to resume their earlier romance. Muck wrote to Charles Ellis for his advice on how to handle his situation with Rosamond, hopeful that Ellis would intervene: "You know, that the young lady is in Europe. I cannot say how sorry I am for her. She too has had to suffer! But now she is doing inconsiderate things sometimes, placing herself and me in awkward positions. She evidently cannot see how fate has changed everything in the world. A personal interview between you and her may perhaps influence her to see things as they in reality are."[29] In the autumn of 1921, Muck remained anxious regarding Rosamond's repeated efforts to see him. Ellis, tied up with

Muck's legal battles in the United States, could not leave Boston for Europe to meet with her, and, given newspaper reporters' eagerness for any details about the couple, Muck believed he could not risk meeting with her himself. Distraught over the sensational gossip, he wrote to Ellis, "She is traveling over Europe like wildfire: from Paris to Munich and back; from Paris to Rome; from Rome to Munich and back. . . . What a topic for dirty newspapers again!"[30] Muck and Rosamond could not escape the relentless and torturous punishment that the press inflicted, which seemed to follow them wherever they traveled.[31]

On August 12, 1924, after spending three years in Europe, suffering unrequited love for Karl Muck, Rosamond boarded a Southampton, England, passenger ship for home. Certainly, feeling victimized by the government, the media, and now Karl, she had to let go of her dreams. At the same time, a new generation of law enforcement officials took charge of the Muck case and continued to withhold the original copies of Rosamond's letters as they were the only evidence that could be useful in preventing Muck from reentering the United States.[32] Charles Ellis, working on Muck's behalf, and Harrison Lyman, working for Rosamond Young, pressured the Justice Department to return the letters. In October of 1921, US Attorney Robert Harris ruled to keep the documents. "Even the comfort and reputation of a young woman who had so far forgotten herself as Miss Young ought not to prevent the U.S. from preserving at least some of the evidence in case this infernal scoundrel should attempt to re-enter the United States."[33] Harris made his personal feelings regarding Muck's behavior with Young apparent in his correspondence with his bosses in Washington, DC. Calling the letters "utterly indecent" and Muck the "sort of chap who would be dangerous anywhere," Harris explained what he believed to be the "proper punishment" for the conductor's indecent actions: "Muck deliberately seduced her and brought her down to a point of degradation which is almost beyond credibility in an American girl brought up as she has been. It was too bad that Muck could not have been shot when first arrested."[34]

Muck's troubles continued to multiply. The burden of his affair with Rosamond weighed heavily on him as the press reported that Rosamond had attempted suicide. Muck was blamed for the fragile state of her mental health. Headlines read, "Drove Girl to Attempted Suicide . . . Nothing Has Been Said about a Poor Deluded Young Woman, Caught Completely in the Toils of Dr. Muck, Who Attempted Suicide as the Best Way out of the Difficulty. She Did Not Succeed, but She Will Carry the Traces of Her Attempt to Her Grave."[35] German conductor Bruno Walter commented during this period that Muck had aged dramatically. Walter was "shocked at the difference between the man he knew twenty years before and the one who stood before him now." Almost unrecognizable, the high-energy perfectionist now appeared frail and weak, with little strength to guide his ensembles.[36]

Muck Occupies Himself with His Work, Develops Stronger Relationships with the Wagners and Adolf Hitler

Karl Muck carried on, however. He poured his sorrows into his work. The liberal German newspaper *Vossische Zeitung* claimed that "Muck is a magician the way he invokes the greatness of the *Prelude* from the mystical abyss, melding the divine and the human. Never have I heard the armor-plated theme of faith sound more despairing and the heartache and pained anguish of the love theme were struggling as if wrapped in fog."[37]

In 1924, three years after Anita's death, Muck returned to Richard Wagner's Bayreuth Opera House in southern Bavaria and carried on the prewar summer tradition of conducting *Parsifal*.[38] Interpreted variously, *Parsifal*, at the most obvious level, is a battle between good and evil, between the Christian and pagan worlds, and it deals with themes such as greed and longing. It is a story of giving in to sexual temptation, of resistance, and of religious redemption. *Parsifal* is an apology for getting sidetracked by lust. It is a religious homecoming. Muck performed this opera over and over throughout his later years. His interpretation of it was so dynamically slow and mournful that singers struggled with their breath control. English music critic Ernest Newman described it as so sluggish that "Good Friday had lasted until well into Easter Monday."[39] Transferring his own tragedy into the interpretation of the score, Muck drew on his personal experience to bring the opera to life.

As mentioned in chapter 1, Karl Muck spent a great deal of time in Bayreuth between 1900 and 1930. Particularly after Anita's death, he became intimately connected with many of the Wagner family members who lived there. The Germany that Muck returned to after the war was quite different from the one he had inhabited years before, however. In September of 1923, Cosima Wagner, Richard's widow, began entertaining a new and enthusiastic devotee of her husband's music at her dinner table. Adolf Hitler, a semi-educated would-be architect, had been an ordinary foot soldier during World War I. During the 1920s, his charismatic personality and political ambition won him favor with some members of the Wagner family, who backed his career. Like Karl Muck, Hitler was bitter and dispirited by a lost war.

He had become consumed with finding a way out of the national turmoil.[40] Hitler believed it was his "mission" to rebuild Germany "from the ruins of defeat."[41] He organized the National Socialist Party with the goal of seeking revenge against those who had crushed the fatherland. He used persuasive rhetorical skills and theatrical talents to voice his ideas and goals. Hitler appealed to Germans with his message of ending economic distress and political gridlock and making the country strong once again in the eyes of the world.[42] In an early speech before he became chancellor, Hitler declared that "Germans are the greatest people on earth." He went on to elaborate: "It is not your fault that you were defeated in the war and have suffered so much since. It is because you were betrayed in 1918 and have been exploited ever since by those who are envious of you and hate you. . . . Let Germany awake and renew her strength, let her remember her greatness and recover her old position in the world!"[43] Hitler attacked America for entering the Great War, believing Germany would have won without its involvement. He was resentful of the Treaty of Versailles's War Guilt Clause, which forced Germany to accept responsibility for the war and imposed extreme reparations.[44] Hitler offered hope to a German people who had suffered economic hardship during and after the war. Karl Muck's ultraconservative nineteenth-century view of the world was compatible with Hitler's thinking. Old German elites like Muck were keen to maintain stability and order, and he found enough common ground with Hitler to admire him. Muck's elitism, his sense of German superiority, his anti-Semitism, and his anti-communism, all were in alignment with Hitler's Nazi ideology. As Benjamin G. Martin records, Muck was "an outspoken anti-Semite" whose values matched the führer's agenda.[45]

Muck and Hitler shared a love of Wagner. Hitler's admiration for the composer went back to his childhood in Linz, Austria, saving whatever money he could to attend performances.[46] He saw *Lohengrin* at least ten times in Vienna, and in adulthood he kept a bust of Wagner in his office. Hitler wrote about the impact Wagner had on his thinking: "My youthful enthusiasm for the master of Bayreuth knew no bounds."[47] Hitler stated that "to understand Nazism one must first know Wagner."[48] Hitler saw in Wagner's music a way to remake the nation by removing people he thought undesirable from it. He was intoxicated by themes of German mythology and its depictions of fearless heroes that Wagner had employed in his operas and that Muck had brought to life with the stroke of his baton. Hitler was determined to utilize these stories to gain support for an ultranationalist, fascist movement.[49] Many Germans agreed with Hitler's thinking and believed that the country had come to a political dead-end and needed the sort of energy he seemed to provide.[50]

Hitler saw Wagner as part of Germany's musical heritage. He viewed German music as the backbone of the country and central to its national identity.[51] For centuries, central European composers had delivered music to the world, and, in Europe, every city precinct and small town had musical clubs and choirs that were important for middle- and working-class life. Germany had its great operas, including Wagner's, which were predominant features of German cultural identity. Both Hitler and Muck viewed the music of Germany in nationalistic terms, and Wagner was the country's greatest symbol of strength and power.

Perhaps Mrs. Jay and her New York associates had raised valid points regarding Karl Muck, arguing that he (and many of Boston's elites) were carriers not only of German culture but of extreme political ideology as well. Muck's very identity in the United States represented a contested battleground over the meaning of American culture. While he had remained publicly quiet during his time in Boston, Muck's views became more transparent when he returned to Germany.

In the post–World War I period, Bayreuth became an incubator for genocide in Germany.[52] Cosima Wagner's family and their numerous important guests, including Adolf Hitler, Karl Muck, and other German nationalist intellectuals, debated and discussed possible solutions to the country's crises by drawing on Richard Wagner's writings and music. Wagner had expressed anti-Semitic thinking as early as the 1850s, arguing in his infamous book *Judaism in Music* that the "Jewish spirit" was harmful to the nation. Feeling threatened by Jewish cultural success, his rhetoric was particularly dangerous and violent in tone. In 1881, for example, two years before his death, discussing a performance of Lessing's classic play *Nathan the Wise* and a scene involving a disastrous fire in the Vienna Ring Theater where more than four hundred people had died, many of them Jewish, Wagner said that "all Jews should burn in a performance of *Nathan*."[53]

In the early 1920s, the opinions of the Wagner family, their circle of friends, and of German society more generally, became increasingly extreme. Their deepening anti-Semitism was not unlike the movement of the Ku Klux Klan in America that victimized minorities during the same period. Cosima and her friends promoted their racist ideas through the periodical publication the *Bayreuth Papers*. She viewed her role as carrying on the wishes of her husband, whose "contact with Jews brought 'instinctive repulsion,' that Jewish speech sounded like a 'creaking, squeaking, buzzing, snuffle' and that the only music Jews could offer, that of the synagogue, was characterized by 'gurgle, yodel, and cackle.'"[54] As time went on, the Wagner clan not only talked about race but acted on their worst inclinations by removing Jewish musicians from Bayreuth productions and verbally attacking the remaining Jews on their payroll whose musical talents (and profits) they could not do without. Cosima routinely spoke in harsh language to the festival's only Jewish conductor, Hermann Levi, whom Karl Muck later succeeded.[55] In 1894, Levi complained about the degrading atmosphere for Jews at the festival: "I am a Jew and in and around Wahnfried it has become a dogma that a Jew appears a certain way, thinks and acts in a certain way, and above all that a Jew is incapable of selfless devotion to anything; as a result, everything I do and say is judged from this point of view and therefore everything I do and say is considered indecent or at least alien."[56] Famed opera singer Lilli Lehmann, who had sung the role of Brunhilde in 1869 at the world premiere of Wagner's *Ring* cycle, was described by the Wagner family after World War I as an "old Jewish grandmother without any talent."[57]

The Wagners were influenced by German art historian, philosopher, and author Julius Langbehn, who blamed Jews for Germany's problems and developed a language of hate against them. In 1897, he wrote, "Jews and idiots, Jews and scoundrels, Jews and whores, Jews and professors, Jews and Berliners." He wanted to "restore Germany to its former glory."[58] The Wagner circle also studied the works of French cultural theorist and member of the German Society of Race Hygiene, Ludwig Schemann, who in 1898 brought the term Aryan into vogue among German racists. He argued that cultural and political decline would occur if German Aryans intermingled with Jews.[59]

Cosima Wagner's son, Siegfried, and his English wife, Winifred, were staunch supporters of Hitler. They became "cultural royalty" to members of the Third Reich.[60] Cosima's daughter, Eva, married author and Englishman Houston Stewart Chamberlain (cousin of Neville Chamberlain), whose racial theories had a great impact on Hitler. In 1900, Chamberlain published *The Foundations of the Nineteenth Century*, which portrayed history as a struggle for supremacy between the Germanic and Jewish races. He argued that Jews were a supreme threat to human society. His most important (and dangerous) idea fused race with social Darwinism.[61]

The Wagners played a critical role in influencing Nazi ideology. Anti-Semitism and racial purity were integral to their thinking.[62] Throughout the 1920s, Muck's racial attitude became increasingly hostile toward Jews as he continued to associate himself with the rabidly anti-Semitic Wagner clan. Just as Muck had been friendly with Kaiser Wilhelm before World War I, he knew how to ingratiate himself into the top echelons of political and cultural society, and, as Hitler rose to power, Muck befriended him as well.

Figure 8.3. This 1930 Philipp Kester image shows Karl Muck with composer and conductor Siegfried Wagner and his family at Villa Wahnfried in Bayreuth. From left to right: Friedelind, Winifred, Verena, Siegfried, Wieland, and Wolfgang Wagner, Karl Muck, and Wagner stepsister Daniela Thode. Philipp Kester/ullstein bild via Getty Images. Used with permission.

Eva Rieger writes in *Friedelind Wagner: Richard Wagner's Rebellious Granddaughter* of the Wagner clan's September 1923 German Day Festival at Bayreuth, where Wagner family members (and possibly Muck) first met Hitler. Two months later, Hitler organized a coup, the Beer Hall Putsch, to take over the government in Munich. Siegfried Wagner viewed Hitler's failed attempt as "proof of his straightforwardness," regarding him thereafter "as the future savior of Germany."[63] In 1924, when Hitler was serving nine months of a five-year sentence at Landsberg Prison, Winifred Wagner sent "love parcels" to him that included "a woolen blanket, a jacket, socks, food, and books." Houston Chamberlain sent Hitler a note of solidarity praising his purity and suggesting that because he survived the experience that it was a "sign from God."[64] Muck empathized with Hitler during this time, as he recalled his own imprisonment at Oglethorpe.

In 1925, influenced by his anti-Semitic friends and authors at Bayreuth, Hitler published *Mein Kampf,* which railed against the Treaty of Versailles and the way Germany was punished after World War I. He detailed his plan for a Reich, and the National Socialist party, led by a strong central leader, the führer. Made paranoid by delusions that Jews were part of an international conspiracy to destroy Germany, he proposed their exclusion from society. *Mein Kampf* also revealed that he believed the country needed *Lebensraum,* or more territorial space, and suggested that Slavic people be reduced to slaves. When Hitler became chancellor in 1933, he required that all party members buy his book.[65]

Muck's Actions against Jewish Musicians at Bayreuth

In 1924, as principal conductor of Bayreuth, Karl Muck acted on racist and ethnocentric ideologies that he shared with Hitler when he black-listed two Jewish musicians, violinist Prins Hendrick and cellist Lucian Horwitz, from the reserve list of the festival. Horwitz, born in Vienna in 1879, played in the Berlin Philharmonic as well as in several Austrian orchestras. It was logical for Horwitz's name to appear as a substitute at the prestigious opera house, and yet Muck vetoed the selection by crossing his name off the list. A swastika indicated rejection. Horwitz continued to perform in Austria until 1927. When the Nazis annexed Austria in 1938, however, he was persecuted and deported in 1942 to the Theresienstadt concentration camp in Czechoslovakia and to Auschwitz two years later, where he perished.[66] Hendrick was born on September 12, 1881, and died in Auschwitz on June 29, 1943. More than a dozen Jewish orchestral musicians, chorus members, and solo-ists affiliated with the summer festival were murdered by the Nazis.[67] Given the company that Muck kept, it is not surprising that he became just as determined to "purify" Bayreuth of Jews as the rest of Wagner's inner circle. Muck had become a bitter old man who had clearly been mistreated in the United States. But one cannot attribute Muck's ugly behavior entirely to bitterness. As mentioned in chapter 1, he exhib-ited anti-Semitism in Boston. When he returned to Germany after the war, he found solace in Hitler's prejudicial statements, and he actively discriminated against and victimized Jewish musicians in his orchestras in the years before the Holocaust. There is continuity and complic-ity in Muck's behavior. Muck was part of an artistic and intellectual community in Boston and in Germany that shared varying degrees of intolerance.

Muck's actions against Jews at Bayreuth were not the only examples of his flawed personality. In 1924, Muck mentioned to Siegfried Wag-ner how much he disliked Fritz Busch, a Christian who was conducting at Bayreuth that summer. Muck had counseled Busch that to achieve success at the summer festival he needed to conform to the "Bayreuth way of thinking" and bring to the podium the "holy fanaticism of the Believer."[68] Busch was unable to accept this way of thinking.[69]

Historian Jonathan Carr claims that Muck was jealous and professionally threatened by Busch. Other sources claim that Busch opposed the
Nazi government.[70] Perhaps both stories contribute to Busch's short
stay at Bayreuth. Nine years later, on March 7, 1933, sixty Nazi soldiers
broke into a private rehearsal of Verdi's *Rigoletto* that Busch was conducting at the Dresden State Opera and heckled the conductor until
he was forced to stop.[71] They also terrorized him during a public performance by yelling, "Down with Busch." Busch quickly fled to Argen-
tina to save his own life.[72]

Conflict and Jealousy over Arturo
Toscanini and Changes at Bayreuth

In 1930, Muck resigned his position at Bayreuth after years of service.
Most sources claim that Muck had promised Cosima Wagner that he
would continue conducting there until Siegfried Wagner's death,
which occurred in 1930. A more intriguing drama also surrounds
Muck's retirement from Bayreuth. He did not simply withdraw because
his commitment was satisfied or because he disapproved of the festival's views on Jews. Rather, Muck also resigned because of petty jealousy.[73] In 1930, Siegfried Wagner booked Italian American Arturo
Toscanini, the conductor of the New York Philharmonic from 1926
to 1936, as the first non-German ever to conduct at Bayreuth. Muck
was jealous and perhaps resentful of Toscanini's connection with the
New York Philharmonic.[74] Muck viewed himself as the "keeper of the
grail" and the only conductor capable of authentically interpreting
Wagner's music. He did not want to share the podium or the acclaim
with anyone else. He was offended that Siegfried would hire Toscanini,
a man who would become a staunch anti-fascist supporter of Jewish
musicians throughout his life and who, in 1936, conducted the opening season of the Palestine Symphony Orchestra. Toscanini called
Muck "Beckmesser of conductors," an insult that referred to the Jewish
caricature in Wagner's *Die Meistersinger von Nürnberg*, who was humiliated and ejected from the community for following the rules. On one
level, Toscanini's comments referred to Muck's musical interpretations
as "terrible" and slow, but, on a deeper level, his remarks allude to a
darker anti-Semitic nature of both the composer and the conductor.[75]
Consequently, Muck "stormed and intrigued against Toscanini," but
Siegfried held firm.[76] Even Hitler, also unaware of Toscanini's political
views at that point, became involved in the conflict, remarking that he
was "beside himself because of Muck" and "horrified at Muck's with-
drawal," but even Hitler's attentions could not change Muck's opinion

on the matter.[77] Troubles really started when Toscanini arrived at Bayreuth, for both conductors had equally matched egos. Toscanini was assigned to conduct *Tannhäuser* and *Tristan und Isolde* and was given more rehearsal time, while Muck was assigned *Parsifal.* Toscanini had a temper, and he complained about the singers and instrumentalists. Siegfried, known for his easygoing nature, attempted to handle the two high-maintenance conductors with great diplomacy. He worked long hours, chain-smoked, and did not get enough rest. By mid-July, Siegfried collapsed of a heart attack, and, by the first week of August, he had died. On August 8, Muck and Toscanini conducted a memorial service, collaborating like they had never done while Siegfried was alive. Muck conducted the funeral march from *Götterdämmerung*, and Toscanini the *Siegfried Idyll.*[78] Mourners at the service described Muck's performance as "so old, like a piece of parchment, a piece of dusty old scenery," compared with Toscanini's conducting, which was described as "incredibly beautiful."[79] Muck created a tense environment at Bayreuth. Blinded by anger and petty jealousy, he could not see that Toscanini was an exciting celebrity conductor who brought new life (and an infusion of capital through ticket sales) to the organization.[80]

Not only was Muck unhappy with his changing status at Bayreuth, he was also upset that Winifred, Siegfried's widow, was making changes to the stage sets for *Parsifal* and entirely altering the appearance of the music hall. Muck wanted to keep the sets exactly as they were. He did not want to modernize, even though the sets needed to be refreshed. He grumbled about these changes to "aunts" Daniela and Eva Wagner, who were Winifred's fiercest foes. The old sets were the vestiges of his reign at Bayreuth. With new conductors taking his place, the sets had come to represent the only reminders of Muck's years of service.[81]

In addition to the newer generation of Wagners wanting to make innovative changes to the opera house, Hitler sought to change the famous theater as well. As the führer gained power after 1933, he co-opted the Bayreuth festival, attending all the Wagner productions for the ten-day period each year.[82] Hitler adopted Wagner as patron saint of the Nazi movement. He poured money into the opera house and began dictating his vision for how it should look. He commissioned monuments and memorials to Wagner and arranged full audiences for all productions. He even proposed tearing down the existing structure and building a new grandiose theater in its place. Hitler's ultramodern ideas horrified Muck, the conductor emeritus, and the Wagner family, who argued that the existing structure had perfect acoustics that a new building could never duplicate. Hitler complied with the Wagners' wishes to keep the existing theater, but this did not diminish Hitler's enthusiasm for Bayreuth or his penchant for taking control of the festival. Hitler greeted audiences from a balcony, his portrait appeared on the front of every program, patrons received Nazi propaganda in their hotel rooms, and swastika flags lined the streets and walkways surrounding the theater.[83]

While Hitler's interference at Bayreuth caused tension for Muck, his patronage brought a level of safety and protection that many other musicians in Germany's Third Reich failed to receive. Hitler seemed enamored of Muck's celebrity status. He liked to have home "listening parties" where he would play recordings of Muck conducting *Parsifal* and other works of Wagner.[84] Hitler was often heard whistling Wagner's music.

Growing Power of Adolf Hitler and Karl Muck's Declining Health

Adolf Hitler became German chancellor on January 30, 1933. In February, Hitler attended the concert marking the fiftieth anniversary of Wagner's death at the Leipzig Gewandhaus.[85] It was recorded that Muck was in ill health at this performance, "pitifully frail and shrunken." Muck smoked five packs of strong, specially made cigarettes a day throughout his life, and while his 1940 obituary states that he died of "nicotine poisoning," it was not until 1956 that the *British Medical Journal* published "Lung Cancer and Other Causes of Death in Relation to Smoking," equating "nicotine poisoning" to lung cancer.[86] And yet, on that day, Wagner's anniversary concert, Muck conducted excerpts from *Parsifal* and *Die Meistersinger* anyway, as he was "practically hoisted up on the podium by two stalwart attendants."[87] Muck's "magnificence, breadth, and vitality . . . stirred the overwrought gathering to a frenzy of enthusiasm."[88]

Over the next few months, the Nazis consolidated their power, destroying the Communist Party, eliminating trade unions, and suppressing civil liberties throughout the country.[89] Hitler's position on Jews became increasingly evident as he implemented his grand plan to dominate the world with a supposedly master race of Aryan people. On April 7, the Reichstag dismissed Jews from government jobs, from police and fire stations, from post offices, from libraries and museums, and from all cultural institutions supported by state or local governments. SA Storm Troopers, or Nazi police, terrorized Jewish civilians on the streets.[90] In early 1933, Muck's hometown of Darmstadt was the first city in Germany that Nazis targeted, forcing Jewish store owners to close.[91] Fear became commonplace. There was less public spontaneity, and people began to distrust everyone around them.[92]

Figure 8.4. Muck with Adolf Hitler, February 1933. Courtesy of the Library of Congress, Prints and Photographs Division, Lot Number 11378.

Figure 8.5. Richard Wagner Gedächtnisfeier im Großen Saal des Gewandhauses (Memorial Service for Richard Wagner in the Great Hall of the Gewandhaus), February 1933. Muck conducting before Hitler (seated in the front row). Courtesy of the Library of Congress, Prints and Photographs Division, Lot Number 11378.

Public music performances in Germany came under the control of the Reich Music Censorship Office, formed by Hitler in 1933, to scrutinize "acceptable" music. Musical associations of all kinds, including orchestras, bands, choirs, and music appreciation societies, were taken over by the Nazis and purged of Jewish members. These measures were accompanied by a barrage of propaganda in the musical press.[93] The regime demanded absolute ideological conformity.[94] It clamped down on state-supported theaters, orchestras, and opera companies. Virtually overnight, thousands of Jewish actors and musicians were unemployed and Brownshirts (another name for the SA), forced a mass exodus of Jewish performers.[95] Surveillance and control took over every aspect of German society.[96]

Well-known Jewish musicians were popular targets. A statue in Leipzig of Jewish composer Felix Mendelssohn was pulled down by the Nazis. Much of Richard Wagner's initial anti-Semitism stemmed from his jealousy toward Mendelssohn, who had been the most famous conductor of the Leipzig Gewandhaus Orchestra in the 1830s and 1840s. Hitler adopted Wagner's earlier view of Mendelssohn, arguing that his music was not genuine German music but a Jewish imitation. His name was removed from public programs and music catalogs, and the wreath that appeared annually at his memorial after his death in 1847 was anonymously destroyed.[97]

In 1933, Otto Klemperer, one of Germany's leading conductors, was in the process of rehearsing a new production of *Tannhäuser* with the Berlin State Opera when his appointment was cancelled because he was Jewish. Hitler's minister of propaganda, Dr. Joseph Goebbels, declared that Klemperer did not understand Wagner's music. Klemperer had held important posts in Hamburg, Bremen, Cologne, and Wiesbaden and had received the Goethe Medal from President Hindenburg years earlier for his contributions to the advancement of German culture. The Nazi regime confiscated his property and a warrant was issued for his arrest. Klemperer escaped to Switzerland.[98]

Bruno Walter, distinguished conductor of the Leipzig Gewandhaus Orchestra and a Jew, arrived for rehearsal on March 16, 1933, to find that the concert hall had been padlocked. Walter demanded an explanation and was informed by the *Reichskommissar* that patrons of the orchestra were unhappy that a Jew was in charge. The regime ordered the upcoming concert cancelled.[99] A week later, Bruno Walter was scheduled to conduct the Berlin Philharmonic, and again he found the doors of the concert hall locked. This time, he was informed that the hall would be set on fire if he dared to fulfill his commitment to the orchestra.[100] Bruno Walter packed his bags and left Germany, first for Vienna, and then for New York.

Arnold Schoenberg, a Jewish composer and professor of composition at the Berlin Music Academy, was dismissed from his post for composing atonal music, which Hitler believed "disrupted the idea of a harmonious German racial community with its dissonance." Schoenberg emigrated to California.[101] Before the war, Muck had conducted the American premiere of Schoenberg's *Five Pieces for Orchestra* with the Boston Symphony. He admitted when he conducted it that he did not like the piece, but he performed it anyway. Modern works such as this were disagreeable to Hitler and to the Nazi regime that wanted to maintain the German Romantic musical tradition. Certainly, Muck would not have objected to a world with fewer Schoenberg compositions.

Christian conductor and composer Richard Strauss agreed to substitute for Bruno Walter at the Berlin Philharmonic. The Nazi press praised the new replacement, but he received much criticism from those who felt he harmed the Jewish conductor.[102] Martin Goldsmith writes, "It seems fair to conclude that he sincerely believed that he could exert a positive influence on German musical life from this new position."[103] Strauss ran into difficulties with the Nazi regime in 1943 when he refused to turn over part of his villa to SS soldiers. He is reported to have said, "I did not want this war, it is nothing to do with me." He appealed to Hitler directly for assistance, reminding him of their mutual interest in music and their meeting at Bayreuth during *Parsifal* a few years before. Hitler refused to assist Strauss and insisted that the conductor accommodate Nazi officers in his home.[104] When it came time to celebrate the composer's eightieth birthday in June of 1944, Hitler sent only a curt telegram. "His music, in particular his songs, is certainly wonderful," Hitler apparently remarked, "but his character is simply miserable." In an angrier mood, Hitler once announced that Strauss was "completely second rate."[105]

Like Strauss, Muck knew that it was nearly impossible to be politically correct. He witnessed both Jewish and "Aryan" conductors treated poorly by the Nazis. One had to remain on Hitler's good side, for he was an incredibly vindictive and murderous man. No one was exempt from difficulty. Hitler either loved his celebrity musicians or he despised them. Muck had to be very careful not to cross the führer.[106]

The Nazis were clearly manhandling musicians. Wilhelm Furtwängler bravely wrote an open letter to the press protesting the persecution of Jewish musicians.[107] After reading Furtwängler's plea, American institutions and musicians got involved to protest Hitler's actions. On April 1, 1933, a group of musicians including conductors Serge Koussevitzky of the Boston Symphony Orchestra, Fritz Reiner of the Curtis Institute in Philadelphia, and Arturo Toscanini of the New York Philharmonic cabled Hitler to complain. Consequently, the Nazi regime promptly banned from state radio all concerts and recordings of Koussevitzky, Reiner, and Toscanini.[108]

Certainly, Karl Muck knew of the US attempt to assist Jewish musicians, and if he had any reservations about their treatment, he said nothing publicly. In fact, Muck himself was actively involved in the persecution of Jews in the Third Reich. In early April of 1933, the Hamburg Philharmonic Society published an announcement of its concert festival to be performed on May 7, to celebrate the one hundredth anniversary of the birth of Hamburg composer Johannes Brahms.[109] Hitler planned to attend the opening concert, make a few remarks, and lay a wreath at Hamburg's Brahms memorial. There was just "one small problem." Hitler had noted the participation of several Jewish musicians on the printed brochure. When questioned about the racial membership of the orchestra, conductor Karl Muck acted swiftly to make sure all Jewish artists were removed from the orchestra and program.[110] He reported that the orchestra was "free of Jews," and, sounding very much like Cosima Wagner at Bayreuth, he remarked that only in the direst of circumstances would he bite "the Jewish sour apple."[111] On April 6, 1933, the Hamburg Philharmonic Society published an addendum to its original announcement: "The choice of soloists, which had to be made in December last year, will of course be amended so that no Jewish artists are participating. Frau Sabine Kalter and Herr Rudolf Serkin will be replaced by artistes who are racially German."[112] Both Muck's racism and his loyalty to Hitler seem genuine. Hitler had the power to destroy successful people, to take away their livelihood or their lives with a single command. Muck was selfishly willing to sell out Jews in his orchestra to maintain his own security, and, based on his statements, he truly wanted to cleanse the orchestra of its "sour apples."

Muck resigned his position immediately after the concert, putting his baton down permanently from the Hamburg Philharmonic, but not because of anything to do with Jewish musicians. David Josephson writes that Muck was feeling political pressure from Nazi authorities over the city's cultural affairs:

> The Veteran Karl Muck, in his seventy-fifth year, was resigned from the conductorship of the Hamburg Philharmonic Orchestra, finding himself unable to acquiesce in the ideas of the new Nazi holders of power concerning the musical consolidation of the Hamburg Philharmonic with the Hamburg Opera and the political "coordination" of both. The Senate of Hamburg begged Dr. Muck at least to conduct the first five orchestra concerts on the program for the Autumn, but he emphatically declined and requested to be relieved of all his official duties forthwith.[113]

Muck was unhappy about the consolidation of the orchestras. Once again, jealousy became a factor, because the two orchestras had two conductors. Muck wanted complete control. He never voiced any public opposition regarding the Nazis' Jewish policies. He seemed perfectly willing to comply with Hitler's request to remove Jews from his ensemble. When Muck resigned over the consolidation of the orchestras, he publicly commented that he was not a Jew. Muck wanted to be clear that his motives for retiring were based on consolidation alone and Nazi control over musical institutions, and not because he sympathized with Jews.[114]

Other evidence suggests that Muck supported and remained loyal to Hitler throughout his life. In 1934, at Muck's retirement celebration from the Hamburg Philharmonic, Hitler named the square in front of the Hamburg Music Hall the Karl Muck Platz. Muck had conducted there for eleven years. Frank Pieter Hesse writes that the plaza was so named, "among other things, because of [Muck's] admiration of Hitler."[115] Goebbels marched Nazi troops on this plaza in the ensuing decade to demonstrate German strength to the world. In 1997, the name of the square was changed to Johannes Brahms Platz to commemorate one hundred years since Brahms's death, which offered a "much larger reference" and more identifiable presence in Hamburg than Karl Muck.[116]

In 1935, Heinrich Hoffman published a book of photographs of Hitler in the Alpine Mountains of southern Bavaria. The photographs attempt to humanize Hitler, and he is shown in various poses with his black Alsatian dog, named Muck. Moreover, Hitler ordered Nazi commanders to present new soldiers with SS rings with the accompanying instruction to use the secret code word "Muck" for loyalty.[117] Clearly, Muck was well thought of by the führer as a trustworthy friend.

In 1938, Muck went into semipermanent seclusion, a move certainly related to his ill health but also coinciding with Kristallnacht, Hitler's violent pogrom against German and Austrian Jews that resulted in the killing of almost one hundred people and the burning of synagogues and businesses, which preceded the internment of more than thirty thousand Jews.[118] In that same year the German army began forcibly deporting Jews from Berlin to ghettos in the East.[119] Thousands of Jewish musicians were impressed into labor brigades or sent to death camps where they perished.[120]

On September 1, 1939, Hitler invaded Poland, effectively beginning World War II. Just seven weeks later, on October 22, 1939, Karl Muck gratefully accepted the Eagle Shield from the German Empire on his eightieth birthday. The Eagle Shield was first awarded in 1922 by President Hindenburg to artists "whose intellectual creations have

Figure 8.6. Karl Muck-Platz, Hochhaus Deutscher Ring, Hamburg, engraving. The Karl Muck Platz in Hamburg, named in honor of the famous conductor by Adolf Hitler. Melissa D. Burrage Collection.

benefited the German people." Hitler personally awarded the medal to Muck.[121] The shield was a bronze medallion with a large national emblem with Muck's name embossed on the back. The medal was mounted on a pedestal and engraved with the inscription, "Dem Grossen Dirigenten" (to the Great Conductor).[122]

Muck's Final Years

Without children of his own, as his only child had died young, Muck spent the final years of his life in Stuttgart, Germany, at the home of Baroness Ruth von Scholley, the daughter of fellow Fort Oglethorpe internee and former Prussian military leader Baron Ferdinand von Scholley, who, before World War I, had been the German consul general in New York and son-in-law in the Burkhardt Brewing family in Boston. The Mucks had been close friends with the von Scholleys and had often visited them at their Massachusetts homes.[123] Anita was particularly close to their daughter, Ruth. Anita's letters suggest a motherly attachment to her that went beyond mere friendship. When the Mucks were deported, Anita struggled being so far away from Ruth. Anita wrote, "I haven't had a letter from the dear child since long

Figure 8.7. Adolf Hitler is pictured playing with his Alsatian dog Muck at Wachenfels, his mountain retreat in the Bavarian Alps near Berchtesgaden. Courtesy of the Library of Congress, Prints and Photographs Division, dated March 2, 1935, Class J, XXC no. 16299, 48025.

[ago]. We are traveling. . . . There is little chance for foreign correspondence to reach us."[124] In Anita's last letter before she died, she
told Isabella Stewart Gardner, "Yesterday, I had a letter from my Baby.
. . . [S]he is very lonely." In her absence, Anita implored Isabella to
develop a deeper relationship with Ruth, saying, "She worships you.
. . . [Y]ou are the only link connecting her with a world of wide hori-
zons and artistic temperament in which she belongs, and for which she
is longing."[125] Anita praised Isabella for attending Ruth's art exhibit
at the Museum of Fine Arts, telling her that it made Ruth proud to
have her there.[126] After Anita died, Karl sent a letter to Isabella telling
her that Anita's spirit was present when the von Scholleys were in her
company: "In her true love she shares the pleasure of the friends who
came together through Ruth, Anita's 'Baby.'" Muck's letter provides
a glimpse of their parental fondness for Ruth in the development of
her career: "How many plans had Anita made with regard to Ruth's
coming; how much did she look forward to their traveling and studying together! Now Ruth has at last come—and Anita is sleeping the
eternal sleep. I am perfectly sure that Ruth with her extraordinary gifts
will attain the highest aims. Anita expected the utmost from Ruth, and
Anita's overflowing blessings will be with her."[127]

Ruth von Scholley remained close to Karl after Anita's death. In
1927, Ruth's father passed away, followed by her mother four years
later. Both Ruth and Karl had lost their closest family members, and
they needed one another more than ever for support. Ruth continued
her work as an artist in Stuttgart.[128] She used her considerable talents
to paint Muck's portrait and provide him with a comfortable home in
his final days.[129] During his retirement years, Muck devoured books
on oriental philosophy and looked back on his years with the BSO as
"the greatest artistic pleasure I ever had in my life, in my heart as well
as in performance. Even in the most harrowing times the people of
Boston were very nice to me."[130] Still, Muck could never overcome the
torment of his treatment in the United States. He dwelled in bitterness
and guilt wrought by what he had done to Anita and Rosamond.[131]

Karl Muck passed away on March 3, 1940, at eighty years of age.
He was buried next to Anita at the Steinfeld Friedhof Cemetery in
Graz, Austria. When news reached Symphony Hall in Boston, all
110 members of the orchestra under the baton of Jewish conductor
Serge Koussevitzky rose from their chairs and bowed their heads for
a two-minute silent tribute to their former leader.[132] The *Boston Globe*
reported in Muck's obituary that he "was not the man to have gloried
in the achievements of the present Nazi regime. Muck was an ardent
and uncompromising patriot, but his intellectual and ethical standards
were both too high for any cordial relationship to have existed between

Figure 8.8. Ruth von Scholley (1893–1969) painted *Japanese Women around a Kettle*, 1919 (Accession Number P33w16). It hangs in the Vatichino (little Vatican), in the Isabella Stewart Gardner Museum in Boston. Courtesy of the Isabella Stewart Gardner Museum.

himself and National Socialism."[133] The Boston press polished Karl Muck's image, not wanting to admit that perhaps his (and their) racial temperament was less than ideal.[134]

Muck's final years in Germany could look like a shocking departure from his earlier life in America until we look at them in context. His journey, as a man of aristocratic bearing who epitomized the nineteenth-century bourgeois value system, connects that world with the catastrophic crimes of the Nazi era. Muck's actions were typical of the varieties of intolerances in both European and American culture in the first half of the twentieth century. The evidence suggests that Karl Muck was loyal to Hitler from their first meeting in 1923 to Muck's death in 1940. He fired Jewish musicians at Bayreuth and in Hamburg. He made public statements in support of Hitler's Jewish policies, and yet he rejected Nazi cultural practices with regard to orchestra mergers. Muck seems clearly anti-Semitic based on his public statements, and while it is possible he feared Hitler's severe draconian punishment for having a dissenting viewpoint, he continued to show his admiration for the führer. Hitler awarded Muck the Karl Muck Platz in part because of Muck's devotion to the chancellor, and Hitler named his beloved Alsatian dog after him. SS officers used the code word "Muck" for loyalty, which certainly suggests that Hitler held him in high regard. Lastly, Hitler personally presented Muck with the Eagle Shield five months before the celebrated conductor's death, demonstrating a consistent and warm affection between the men. Upon Muck's passing, *New York Times* music critic Olin Downes described Muck as "one of the greatest musicians and conductors of his epoch."[135] Certainly he was an enormous talent. We can only know a person by his actions, however, and in Muck's case, his actions became increasingly negative after his deportation from the United States. Befriended by the Wagners, Muck was an ardent anti-Semite who played a contributing role in the terrifying persecution of Jews prior to the Holocaust. The link between Muck's racial conditioning before he came to America, Boston Brahmins' anti-Semitism, America's injustice against German immigrants during World War I, and Karl Muck's later actions in Germany cannot be overlooked. Muck was part of an artistic and intellectual culture that was venerated around the world but that nevertheless grew in tandem with an elite society that was ultraconservative and anti-Semitic. No matter how the American press tried to spin the story, Muck will forever be identified with Hitler and his tyrannical Nazi regime.

Figure 8.9. Portrait of Karl Muck. Courtesy of the Stadtgeschichtliches Museum Leipzig, F/2690/2005.

CODA (1919 TO PRESENT)

Regardless of Karl Muck's complex personality and his anti-Semitic actions in Europe following World War I, he was, from our present-day point of view, severely mistreated in the United States during the Great War, and his professional reputation, which he had earned and worked so hard to achieve, was repeatedly and often dishonestly assaulted. His personal life became front-page news. Victimized by Lucie Jay and the New York capitalist class, by the American news media, and by the federal government, there was very little that he could do to fight this injustice. "Here in America there is no place for a German," Muck told a reporter before his deportation. "I never had any idea that such discrimination could take place."[1] But he was not entirely defeated.

Before Muck was released from the Fort Oglethorpe Internment Camp, he committed an act of rebellion against the federal authorities there. Muck gave an interview to radical journalist and social critic H. L. Mencken, the most renowned political commentator of the era. Mencken was a German sympathizer who mocked the Americanization movement and viewed the world in racial and elitist terms.[2] He recounted his postwar interview with Muck:

> I had met Muck in America, and we sat down for a friendly chat. He had been interned after his dismissal and he told me that in the camp he was sent to, somewhere in Tennessee, he found more than a hundred other German musicians. Most of them had their instruments with them, and they soon formed an orchestra, with Muck as its leader. He said that they gave some of the best concerts he had ever conducted. . . . Once, on a very hot day, they played Beethoven's *Eroica* Symphony stark naked. "It was," said Muck, "a really magnificent performance though the heat was hard on the violin strings. Beethoven would have been proud of it."[3]

While this nude performance appears to be an innocent act of climate control, it also represents a significant act of defiance. One can imagine the musicians seated with their instruments before them, somewhat concealing their genitalia from view. Muck, as the conductor, however, would have stood directly before the entire ensemble, arms outstretched and in full visual display. He would have been the first to peel away layers of clothing and stand entirely exposed before them. His players would have understood his implicit directive, removing their garments as well in a demonstration of unity. The meaning of this rebellious act cannot be overlooked. For that hour, Muck and his orchestra took over their prison space, performing in complete view of the machine gun turrets and guards. Within their barbed-wire cage, the men symbolically cast off the shackles of their imprisonment. By removing their clothing, they gave themselves a level of autonomy not offered or allowed during their internment. They performed *Eroica*, music that refers to a fallen hero, perhaps as a metaphor for German American musicians who were loved and admired in America before the war, and who now sought their freedom from captivity at the height of the conflict. Their performance was a "Fick Dich!" to a federal system that guarded and controlled them at the point of a gun.[4] It was a way of saying, go ahead and shoot me, for you've already taken everything I have. In those few moments of defiance, the guards were left helpless in their response. By sharing this story with Mencken, Muck knew that he would get "the last word" in the American press. This single act was his way of standing up, quite literally, to his oppressors.

Karl Muck was not the only one to speak his mind about the actions taken by federal officials. Performer and patron of the arts Rosamond Young (Chapin) left clues concerning her feelings about her mistreatment during the war and about her relationship with Muck. Years after the affair, Rosamond named her eldest daughter Isolde, after *Tristan und Isolde*—perhaps Wagner's most sexually provocative opera—which Rosamond had performed with Muck and the BSO years before. By naming her daughter Isolde, Rosamond signaled that she had not forgotten Karl Muck.[5] In 1946, Isolde graduated from Vassar College in Poughkeepsie, New York, and several years later received a master's degree from George Washington University in Washington, DC. She lived most of her life in the DC area, working as the executive director of Washington Independent Writers and as a freelance columnist with the *Washington Post*, fighting for the sexual rights of women, as well as protecting sexual, musical, and literary expression from federal interference. The scandal that her mother had experienced affected Isolde's worldview quite deeply, for Rosamond passed this influence on to her children.[6] In 2002, for example, Rosamond's grandson, lawyer Eric MacLeish, heroically represented three hundred victims in the well-publicized Catholic Church sexual-abuse scandal in Boston. Isolde's work on behalf of sexual and artistic expression and Eric's efforts in support of sexual abuse victims speaks to Rosamond's earlier hardships and her courageous desire to prevent others from suffering as well.[7]

The postwar years appear to have been uneventful for Lucie Jay. She continued to winter in New York City and divide her summers between Newport, Rhode Island, and New York State, cared for by a large entourage of "chauffeurs, cooks, kitchen and chamber maids, carpenters, gardeners and farmers, laundresses, governesses, and a butler."[8] She died on January 30, 1931, at her home in the Hotel Madison in New York City at the age of seventy-five and was buried in the St. Matthew's Episcopal Church Cemetery in Bedford, New York. Her obituary fashions her legacy as that of an American patriot. It does not mention the Oelrichs family, her father's successful steamship enterprise, or her connection to capitalists in New York. Several of the North German Lloyd ships were seized by the US Navy during World War I, and, by 1921, immigration restriction had severely reduced the flow of passengers traveling to the United States, presumably affecting her fortunes. North German Lloyd Steamship Line eventually merged with its longtime competitor, the Hamburg-America Lines, becoming the Hapag-Lloyd container freight company.[9] Her obituary speaks of her marriage to William Jay and her connection to John Jay, the first chief justice of the United States. It also refers to the John Jay Homestead in Katonah, New York, where her daughter Eleanor lived with her family until 1952.[10] Lucie Jay's obituary boasts of her valiant effort to remove German music and musicians from American orchestras. No mention is made of her membership on the board of the New York Philharmonic.[11]

Beyond the principal figures in this manuscript, World War I transformed America into a global power and left its mark more broadly on US citizens who were no longer as naïve or innocent as they had been before the conflict. Many soldiers returned home from Europe and became politically active. In 1932, seventeen thousand World War I veterans marched on Washington in the "Bonus Army," demanding payment promised to them by the World War Adjusted Compensation Act of 1924. In 1944, Great War veterans helped to push the GI Bill through Congress, insisting that World War II soldiers receive better treatment than they had. Their collective activism inspired, in part, the welfare state, and the civil rights movements of the 1950s, 1960s, and beyond.

American internment camps in World War I set a precedent for more far-reaching confinement policies practiced against Japanese Americans, German Americans, and Italian Americans during World War II.[12] The expansion of bureaucratic structures and logistical know-how used against internees in World War I provided a template for later incarcerations, as state power remains ever-present in the lives of citizens and noncitizens alike, and as the country continues to this day to debate issues of criminal justice, immigration, and belonging set against a backdrop of national security.

Enough time has passed for the United States to recognize and memorialize German victims of World War I on American soil and to acknowledge the contributions of German civilians in American society more generally. In honor of German prisoners of war who died in American internment camps, the German consul general lays a wreath every November on Volkstrauertag, Germany's National Day of Mourning, at a 1935 monument erected at the Chattanooga National Cemetery, eight miles from Fort Oglethorpe.[13] Seventy-eight German World War I POWs are buried at the site, many having died of influenza at Fort Oglethorpe in 1918. Each year US Army musicians play "Ich hatt' einen Kameraden" (I Had a Good Comrade), in honor of the dead. A local German ladies' organization called the Klub Heimatland tend the graves. In October of 2015, President Barack Obama proclaimed October 6 German American Day, encouraging all Americans to learn more about the history of this ethnic group and reflect on their many contributions to the nation. Today, some forty-eight million Americans claim German heritage, though most have a weak sense of ethnic identification.[14]

German influence in Boston has slowly revived since World War II, continuing quietly and reappearing more vigorously in the latter decades of the twentieth century, in its schools, cultural and social service organizations, churches, and restaurants. Its strength is evident in the Goethe Society, Goethe Institut Boston, German International School Boston, German Language School, German Saturday School, Boston German Language Meetup, German American Business Council, Boylston Schul-Verein, Musikgarten, Kinderchor, Sängerchor, Sängerfest, Sommerfests, Oktoberfests, Christmas concerts, holiday markets, lectures, hunting excursions, films, and theater. Compassion is clear in its German Ladies Aid Society, and in its Deutsches Altenheim Nursing Home and Assisted Living facility. German influence extends throughout Massachusetts to German American Clubs of Bristol, Berkshire, and Worcester Counties, Cape Cod and the Lowell area, to the New England states of Connecticut, Rhode Island, New Hampshire, and Maine, and throughout the entire country. In addition, Boston–area restaurants such as Jacob Wirth, Bronwyn, Hofbrauhaus, Munich Haus, Student Prince, and Karl's Sausage Kitchen, among others, continue to feed the community.

The immediate postwar years brought significant changes to the Boston Symphony Orchestra as well. The transition to a post-Higginson directorship was difficult. In 1920, one year after Higginson's death, BSO musicians collectively attempted to improve wage and working conditions by asking for a 50 percent pay increase. Management refused to negotiate. The conflict came to a head when seventy-three musicians joined the American Federation of Musicians union. During the March 5 BSO concert, American-born concertmaster Frederic Fradkin refused to rise when conductor Pierre Monteux gestured the orchestra to stand at the conclusion of Berlioz's *Symphonie Fantastique.* The rebellious leader of the violin section was fired. Thirty-six musicians supported Fradkin, and they, too, were dismissed, forcing Monteux to replace one-third of the orchestra.[15] To solve the labor shortage, the strikers were invited to return if they relinquished their union membership. Fradkin and many others did not return, and they "practically disappeared from the concert world."[16] The strike demonstrated a level of instability within the BSO, as the board attempted to maintain nonunion control over the musicians. By the end of the 1924 season, management sought a new conductor and after an extensive search hired Russian-born Serge Koussevitzky as Monteux's successor.[17]

According to Mark Volpe, the current managing director of the Boston Symphony, Koussevitzky was viewed "as a god" in pre-Communist Russia. "He's still talked about there all the time," becoming a conductor that future maestros seek to emulate.[18] Koussevitzky expanded BSO offerings, introducing important international masterpieces such as Bartók's *Concerto for Orchestra*, Hindemith's *Konzertmusik*, Mahler's Ninth Symphony, Messiaen's *Turangaîla Symphony*, Mussorgsky's *Pictures at an Exhibition* (in the Ravel orchestration), Prokofiev's Violin Concerto nos. 1 and 2, and Stravinsky's *Symphony of Psalms*.[19] Koussevitzky also championed American music.[20] In 1926, Aaron Copland, a leading figure in the League of Composers, helped the new conductor to commission American symphonic works that were presented on BSO programs with equal importance as standard European pieces.[21] By the end of his twenty-five years with the Boston Symphony, Koussevitzky had given first performances of eighty-five American scores and performed almost two hundred new American compositions.[22] Second New England School composers such as Amy Beach and George Chadwick, who emulated German style, were absent from Koussevitzky's programs, however. Koussevitzky had "little use for Chadwick and other turn of the century Bostonians," forging a new cultural direction for the BSO.[23]

In 1942, Koussevitzky unionized the Boston Symphony after years of management resistance. The change occurred upon the death of Brahmin banker Ernest B. Dane, chairman of the board of directors, who had donated his own fortune to the BSO and had maintained control over the decision making of the organization for more than twenty years. According to Harry Ellis Dickson, associate conductor of the Boston Pops Orchestra, Dane was "fiercely opposed to anything smacking of organized labor." He would rather "have seen the orchestra collapse than join a union."[24] In 1942, however, the AFM forced RCA Victor Records to cease its exclusive recording arrangement with the BSO, threatening the orchestra's reputation. The publicity from this action affected the stagehands union, which refused to allow the BSO to appear in unionized halls on tours.[25] Koussevitzky was forced to act before the situation spiraled out of control. He invited James Caesar Petrillo, Chicago-born son of Italian immigrants and AFM president, to his Berkshires estate. "Little Caesar" Petrillo arrived in a bulletproof limousine accompanied by bodyguards. He was known to fight for better working conditions for union members by using strong-arm tactics, such as placing a gun on the table before him, screaming, or pounding his fist.[26] Koussevitzky was apparently "amazed by Petrillo's knowledge of the orchestra's finances and impressed by his candor and tact."[27] Petrillo pledged not to interfere with Koussevitzky's ability to hire qualified musicians, and thus the BSO signed an agreement with the AFM in December of 1942, bringing the orchestra members and its conductors into the musicians' union.[28]

The AFM was a step in the right direction for symphony musicians, giving them a measure of self-respect, a more equitable pay structure, and reforms that cultivated goodwill.[29] With the passing of the Immigration Restriction Act of 1921, employers had to rely more heavily on an American labor pool. It made good economic sense for business owners to practice kindness and to "tolerate" the union.[30] Both the Great Depression and World War II gave additional momentum to that effort, providing a sense that "all Americans needed to share a common burden."[31]

The union was credited with improving the relationship between players, conductors, and management, but it was and is by no means perfect. As Julie Ayer points out, for generations, "deeply engrained paternalism and autocracy characterized the top-heavy relationship between the conductor and 'his' musicians." New, formal audition procedures for hiring the most qualified candidates, including blind auditions, eliminated some of the prejudice concerning gender, race, age, and physical appearance.[32] Conductors could no longer fire musicians without a valid reason or hire musicians on the basis of cronyism.[33] While the relationship between conductor and musician has improved from one hundred years ago, the professional landscape has flaws, as several well-known conductors today have made front-page news with allegations of sexual misconduct and misuse of power, as top-tier orchestras uphold gender discrimination by failing to appoint female or minority conductors, and as female musicians file suit over unfair wages.[34]

Regardless of the imperfections in the workplace, the BSO and the NYP have continually sought to modernize their orchestras following World War I. Within two years of Mrs. Jay's resignation from the NYP board, Josef Stransky was eased out of his position as conductor.[35] From 1922 to 1956, Arthur Judson managed the New York Philharmonic, and, in 1926, he contracted Italian maestro Arturo Toscanini as the philharmonic's full-time conductor, achieving worldwide acclaim under his guidance.[36] The philharmonic continued to perform German music as it had before and during the war, indifferent to anything but the established classics.[37] The notion of Americanization had faded rapidly at the NYP.[38] New York audiences were tired of "threats and pressures" of anti-German hysteria.[39] Germans, and their music, were "once more restored to favor through another swift reversal of judgment."[40] Even the *New York Transcript* noted on Mrs. Jay's death in 1931 that she must have been upset to see the "regained ascendency" of German music after the war.[41] The New York Philharmonic maintained its 1884 creed to exclusively perform "standard works" and "old masters, and to be thus conservative and not given to experimenting with the new musical sensation of the hour."[42] It would be decades before the orchestra ventured from its creed.[43] The philharmonic, under Toscanini, conducted only six American works in ten years, becoming what Joseph Horowitz has described as a "showcase for German antiquities."[44]

Today, the Boston Symphony Orchestra and the New York Philharmonic work to reimagine their cultural positions, to remain competitive, and to adjust to changing times. To compete in an ever-expanding commercial entertainment industry, they have partnered with management agencies, recording engineers, advertisers, cellular providers, music producers, television, radio, and internet professionals to bring music to consumers who may not attend live events. In 2003, for example, the NYP was the first orchestra to perform on the televised Grammy Awards. In 2004, it became the first major American orchestra to offer downloadable live concerts, and, in 2009, it began offering an iTunes subscription series. The BSO has invested heavily in its internet presence by launching BSO.org in 1996, the largest and most visited orchestral website in the United States. This site offers video podcasts and free audio concerts, receiving approximately seven million visitors annually in its full site and mobile device formats.[45]

NYP executive director Matthew Van Besien has acknowledged the challenges facing symphony orchestras around the country today:

"We understand that we have to operate smarter, and as responsibly as we can, while still being the New York Philharmonic, with everything that's great about the Philharmonic. . . . No one is looking to diminish what the Philharmonic does, and what it means for New York."[46] The Boston Symphony Orchestra also works to remain significant in the Boston community. Mark Volpe writes, "We want to do things the Boston way, to figure out what's right for Boston in terms of programming and what's appropriate in the dynamic with our players."[47] Blessed with the largest endowment of any American orchestra (well over $400 million) and with three splendid revenue streams (the Boston Symphony itself, the Pops, and the summertime Tanglewood season), Volpe boasts, "our orchestra faces little chance of closure."[48] And yet management works hard to sell tickets and to entice the community to attend performances in its spectacular hall.

Just as in Karl Muck's time, symphony orchestras today struggle to remain relevant within a complex and politically changing world. They are business enterprises that compete, innovate, and adapt to fluctuating cultural conditions in order to survive. During World War I, the demand for European music declined as America grappled to define its own national identity. The Boston Symphony, the New York Philharmonic, and American musical institutions more broadly had to implement reforms and respond to that new agenda as they struggled to develop and modernize. Karl Muck, caught on America's changing cultural battleground, became an expendable victim in that process.

ACKNOWLEDGMENTS

This project is more than a decade in the making. I have been assisted by so many wonderful people along the way. I'm grateful for the late Michael Hager, chairman of the Board of Directors of the Goethe Society of New England, who kindly guided me toward people in the German community of Boston who could assist my work. I interviewed the late Martha Engler, first-generation German American, who grew up in Boston during World War I. She recalled that her formerly warm and friendly multicultural city became a scary place during those years. I am thankful to the staff at the Deutsches Altenheim Nursing Home for allowing me to visit. I am indebted to the Holy Trinity German Catholic Church and to the parishioners there who shared their family stories and showed me their magnificent church before its doors closed in 2008.

I interviewed the late Anthony Pierro, a Boston World War I veteran and Italian immigrant, who provided me with a sense of what mobilization felt like in Boston, and how he, specifically, felt about the conflict. Warren Cutler, owner of Muck's Boston home, graciously offered an intimate perspective into the conductor's private world. I imagined Muck sitting on his balcony looking out over the Fens or walking down the brick sidewalk on Westland Avenue to the back door of Symphony Hall.

I am grateful for archivist Maryalice Perrin-Mohr, at the New England Conservatory Spaulding Library, who directed me to Muck's correspondence with composer and NEC director George Chadwick, giving me a deeper understanding of Muck's personal relationships and emotional well-being in the city. The Boston Public Library staff introduced me to their scrapbook on Karl Muck, which offered a sense of his professional reception in Boston before the war, as well as the day-to-day crises he experienced after the war began. I am indebted to Bob Cullum for allowing me to use his grandfather Leslie Jones' photographs, taken in Boston during the height of the conflict. I appreciate Bridget Carr and Barbara Perkel at the Boston Symphony Orchestra Archives for providing several images and cheerfully helping me to learn about Muck's experience in Boston, as well as Henry

Lee Higginson's evolving opinions of Germans as the war progressed. Thank-you to BSO violinist Bo Youp Hwang and Boston Pops principal cellist Ron Lowry, my children's teachers, for their twenty-first-century insights regarding the BSO. In 2007, I spent cold winter months at a Brandeis University microfiche machine studying the *Boston Herald* from 1915 to 1919, which provided a daily chronology of Boston's vibrant European-based musical culture and home-front landscape. I am grateful to Therese Mosorjak of the Thomas Crane Public Library for the Fore River Shipyard image; to Stephanie Krauss of Historic New England Library; Alexandra Bush, Shana McKenna, Elizabeth Reluga, and Molly Phelps of the Isabella Stewart Gardner Museum Archives; Sabina Beauchard of the Massachusetts Historical Society, for providing wonderful images and interesting correspondence; Katie Baxter and Isa Schaff of the Putnam Library at Noble and Greenough for material on Arthur Volkmann; Susanna Coit of the Perkins School for the Blind for the illustrative World War I propaganda poster, and to Robert Seyffert for sharing stories about Seal Harbor and for contributing his grandfather's portrait of Muck to this book; and Kirk Mohney of the Maine Historic Preservation Commission for the photograph of Lichen House.

I am indebted to archivists Barbara Haws, Matthew McDonald, Sarah Palermo, and Gabryel Smith at the New York Philharmonic for graciously providing several images and for allowing me to pore over board of directors' minutes and war-era correspondence, to better understand the history of the philharmonic and Mrs. Jay's role there as that institution sought to develop and grow. I am grateful to Allan Weinreb and Carolyn DePalma of the John Jay Homestead State Historic Site for information about the Jay family. I am thankful for Matthew Laudicina from the New York State Library for their World War I poster collection.

I am grateful to the Richmond Hill History Museum for directing me to the Henry Ford Research Center, and to Jim Orr for providing photographs of Henry Lee Higginson's Cottenham Plantation; to Coi Drummond-Gehrig at the Denver Public Library for her help in tracking down an image of Antonia Brico; and to William D. Keel at the University of Kansas for providing me with the Yearbook of German-American Studies. I appreciate the Post Community Association, and the Fort Oglethorpe Sixth Cavalry Museum, and most especially Paula Muina and Christine McKeever, for their assistance in understanding the internment camp experience. I shared several enlightening emails with Mary Prevo, whose great grandfather, Federico Stallforth, was incarcerated at Fort Oglethorpe until 1920. Thank-you to James Liversidge of George A. Smathers Library at the University of Florida, and

Jonathan Eaker and Alexis Valentine at the Library of Congress for helping me to acquire several pertinent photographs for this book. I owe a debt of gratitude to the US National Archives War Department for its photograph collection on Fort Oglethorpe. The First World War Galleries of the Imperial War Museum in London gave me a much deeper understanding of total war. In October 2017, I presented a paper on Karl Muck for the Remembering Muted Voices World War I Centennial at the National World War I Museum in Kansas City that proved particularly helpful in refining this book.

I am grateful for Amy Bowring from Dance Collection Danse in Toronto for the photograph of Maud Allan; David Mawhinney at Mount Allison University Archives in New Brunswick, Canada, for sharing photos and information on the Halifax Explosion. To Fuest Klaus of the Bremerhaven Museum, I am most grateful for the image of the Tsing Tao Orchestra at Fort Oglethorpe. Nadja Staab from the Stadtgeschichtliches Museum Leipzig was particularly kind in obtaining a lovely portrait of Karl Muck in his senior years. I value my conversation with John Froning and Herr von Scholley, Baroness Ruth von Scholley's nephew in Stuttgart, for providing me with family stories about Ruth and her care of Karl Muck during his retirement. I am grateful to the Bergen Public Library in Norway for their image of Leonora Speyer.

I want to thank professors and colleagues over the past decade for their valuable insights, guidance, and editorial assistance: Bob Allison, Sven Beckert, Hugh Brogan, Chris Capozzola, Richard Crockett, Kathleen Dalton, Jackie Fear-Segal, Rebecca Fraser, Matt Guilford, Kunio Hara, Steve Holmes, Eric Homberger, Chris Huggard, Tomas Jaehn, Chris Ketchersides, Malcolm McLaughlin, Tom O'Connor, Don Ostrowski, Rebecca Tillett, Sue Weaver Schopf, and Liping Zhu. I am enormously indebted to Sonia Kane and Ralph Locke, for seeing something important in my manuscript and kindly shepherding it to publication, along with their team—Julia Cook, Jacqueline Heinzelmann, Tracey Engel, Rosemary Shojaie, Carrie Watterson, Marilyn Bliss and others. Thank you to my anonymous reviewers who offered excellent suggestions for improvement and who boosted my morale with their encouragement.

Going further back in time, I want to highlight the unsung heroes in my own humble musical development, who inspired my love for the arts, which ultimately led to this project: my first teacher, my mom, Marilyn Procknik Burrage, is a talented pianist and vocalist who, in the 1950s, studied voice with Wilma Thompson at Boston University and Frederick Jagel at New England Conservatory, who gave up an amazing operatic career to take care of her family, cultivating a love for music in our home. In my childhood, her nightly practice sessions after bedtime were intended to lull my brother and me to sleep but had just the opposite effect. Her powerfully rich mezzo-soprano voice frankly blew the roof off the house when she sang.

I also want to acknowledge my early private voice and piano teachers, school music teachers, community choral directors, and civic club leaders in my hometown of Middleboro, Massachusetts, who influenced my musical life in countless ways: Brenda Hartford, Sylvia and Fred Thornton, Jan Bichsel, Dick Brooks, Dennis Smith, Rose and Tom Weston, and Genie Mullen. It was through their efforts that I learned to love music making and was guided by them in group and solo performances in church basements, prisons, hospitals, nursing homes, clubhouses, religious sanctuaries, school auditoriums, and concert hall stages. These childhood experiences gave meaning to my life and enriched not only myself but our small community.

I also wish to express my gratitude to the quiet, often invisible patrons in my life who worked behind the scenes to ensure that I had meaningful experiences. My dad, Philip Burrage, financially and emotionally supported (and continues to encourage) whatever projects I take on with love, patience, humor, and pride. His infectious passion for American history, Boston most especially, and his abiding support for his family's (musical) endeavors has deeply shaped my identity and life's work. Also, civic-minded women, like Cynthia Carver (and my mom), among others, came together cooperatively in organizations like the Junior Cabot Club and the Middleboro Music Guild and hosted fairs and bake sales to raise money for music scholarships. I was a very lucky recipient of their generosity. Thank you to public school administrators, like Superintendent Lincoln D. Lynch, who, in the 1970s-era of Massachusetts Proposition 2 1/2, supported the arts despite budget cuts and made possible yearly school-funded bus trips to Symphony Hall, which had a lasting impact on my love for music and my later interest in the BSO.

I am also grateful for the excellent instruction I received from the music faculty at Keene State College during my undergraduate years there, notably Carlesta Henderson Spearman, Carroll Lehman, Chonghyo Shin, Meriam Goder, and Raymond Rosenstock, who developed my musical interests and skills and made performance opportunities a routine part of my New Hampshire experience. I, in turn, passed this knowledge on to my children and to friends and students that I've had the opportunity to work with.

I am thankful for my supportive and jovial brother Scott Burrage; my dear friends Linda Kennedy, Joanne Mullen, Sheila Belletete, and Chris Huggard; to my in-laws Elizabeth, Cathy, Michael, and Nancy

Goodwin, and Stacie Macricostas; and Karen Rodriguez, Ryan Fuss, Mimi Harding, Jonathan Lovett, and Sam Sanders.

My most precious moments have been spent with my children, Lydia, Miranda, and Zachary Burrage-Goodwin. I cannot possibly describe in words what an impact they have had on my life. In terms of this book, they have performed in countless ensembles from Weston High School orchestras, Rivers Conservatory orchestras, New England Conservatory, Handel and Haydn Society, Wellesley Symphony, Boston Civic Symphony, Massachusetts All State Orchestras and Choruses, All Eastern Chorus, Florida State University Summer Orchestras, Soundfest with the Colorado String Quartet, University of South Carolina Symphony and Concert Choir, Long Bay Symphony, Brevard Philharmonic, and the South Carolina Philharmonic, among others. They have taught string education at MusiConnects in Mattapan, Massachusetts; USC String Project; and the school districts of Columbia, South Carolina; Fairfax, Virginia; and Wayland, Weston, Hopkinton, and Lexington, Massachusetts. My children have been my greatest teachers, and their feelings about music, the ensembles they have performed in, and the conductors they have worked under, have informed this book.

Finally, I also could not have done any of this without the love, patronage, and emotional support of my husband, Tom Goodwin, who has sacrificed the most to ensure that my dream for this book became a reality. This has been an extremely long journey and I have appreciated every act of kindness, encouragement, and patience along the way.

NOTES

Introduction

1. Irving Lowens, "L'affaire Karl Muck: A Study in War Hysteria (1917–1918)," *Musicology* 1 (1947): 272; Celia Applegate, *Bach in Berlin: Nation and Culture in Mendelssohn's Revival of the St. Matthew Passion* (Ithaca, NY: Cornell University Press, 2005), 255–56.

2. Richard B. Goldschmidt, *In and Out of the Ivory Tower: The Autobiography of Richard B. Goldschmidt* (Seattle: University of Washington Press, 1960), 165.

3. John Higham, *Strangers in the Land: Patterns of American Nativism, 1860–1925* (New Brunswick, NJ: Rutgers University Press, 2002), 196.

4. Joseph Horowitz, *Moral Fire: Musical Portraits from America's Fin De Siècle* (Oakland: University of California Press, 2012), 14.

5. "18 Germans Dropped by Boston Symphony: Among Them Is Ernest Schmidt, Successor to Dr. Karl Muck," *North American,* June 22, 1918.

6. Robin Moore, *The Colorful Mr. Pops: The Man and His Music* (Boston: Little, Brown, 1968), 59. Also discussed in Carol Green Wilson, *Arthur Fiedler: Music for the Millions. The Story of the Conductor of the Boston Pops Orchestra* (London: Evans, 1968), 24.

7. Jessica C. E. Gienow-Hecht, *Sound Diplomacy: Music and Emotions in Transatlantic Relations, 1850–1920* (Chicago: University of Chicago Press, 2009), 205.

8. Gienow-Hecht, *Sound Diplomacy,* 186–87. Joseph Horowitz, *Wagner Nights: an American History* (Oakland: University of California Press, 1994), 296.

9. New England Conservatory Archives, Fritz Kreisler to George Chadwick, n.d.

10. Barbara L. Tischler, *An American Music: The Search for an American Musical Identity* (New York: Oxford University Press, 1986), 88.

11. Gienow-Hecht, *Sound Diplomacy,* 186–87.

12. The Great Depression inspired Copland's sympathy for working-class people. He reviewed the *Workers' Song Book* for the *New Masses* magazine in June 5, 1934. He composed *Into the Streets May First* in 1934; *El Salón México,* first performed in 1937 by the Mexico Symphony Orchestra under Carlos Chávez; and *Fanfare for the Common Man* in 1942.

13. Julie Ayer, *More Than Meets the Ear: How Symphony Musicians Made Labor History* (Minneapolis: Syren Book, 2005), 69–70.

14. "Muck Feared Massacre of Germans in Boston," *Boston Post*, November 12, 1919.

Chapter One

Epigraph: Poem by Kuno Francke read at the dedication of the Germanic Museum at Harvard University in 1903.

1. Ellis Island Research Center, Microfilm Series T715, Roll T715_774, http://www.ellisisland.org/search/shipManifest.asp?MID=1689904709 0177072224&FNM=KARL&LNM=MUCK&PLNM=MUCK&first_kind= 1&last_kind=0&RF=5&pID=101000100017&.

2. John Spitzer, *American Orchestras in the Nineteenth Century* (Chicago: University of Chicago Press, 2012), 3, 314; Michael Broyles, *"Music of the Highest Class": Elitism and Populism in Antebellum Boston* (New Haven, CT: Yale University Press, 1992).

3. Spitzer, *American Orchestras*, 314.

4. Karen Kupperman, "International at the Creation: Early Modern American History," in *Rethinking American History in a Global Age*, ed. Thomas Bender (Oakland: University of California Press, 2002), 15; William Webber, "Orchestral Programs in Boston, 1841–55, in European Perspective," in Spitzer, *American Orchestras*, 373.

5. Peter Muck, *Dr. Karl Muck: Ein Dirigentenleben in Briefen und Dokumenten* (Tutzing: Verlegt Bei Hans Schneider, 2003), 1–20. According to Peter Muck, Jacob Muck composed his own opera and conducted it in the local opera house.

6. Richard J. Evans, *Coming of the Third Reich* (London: Allen Lane, 2003), 20.

7. Jonathan Carr, *Wagner Clan: The Saga of Germany's Most Illustrious and Infamous Family* (New York: Atlantic Monthly Press, 2007), 67–69.

8. "Boston's New Conductor," *Independent*, 61 (July–December 1906), 1219.

9. Thomas Weber, *Our Friend "The Enemy": Elite Education in Britain and Germany before World War I* (Stanford, CA: Stanford University Press, 2008), 112.

10. "Where Students Fight: Scarred Faces are Common Sights at Heidelberg," *Daily Bulletin Supplement* (San Francisco), July 12, 1890. "Dueling in Germany: The Bane of the Universities—Burial of a Student Victim to the Brutal Practice," *New York Times*, March 18, 1877. "Dueling in Berlin," *Galveston Daily News*, November 9, 1886.

11. Steven P. Remy, *The Heidelberg Myth: The Nazification and Denazification of a German University* (Cambridge, MA: Harvard University Press, 2002), 117–20.

12. Muck, *Dr. Karl Muck*, 1–20.

13. Patrick Carnegy, *Wagner and the Art of the Theatre* (New Haven, CT: Yale University Press, 2013), 208.

14. "Karl Muck, Former Head of Boston Symphony: Noted Wagnerian Interpreter Was Friend of Hitler. Stuttgart, Germany," *New York Times*, March 4, 1941. "Musical Matters Abroad," *New York Times*, May 14, 1899.

15. Harold C. Schonberg, *The Great Conductors* (New York: Simon and Schuster, 1967), 216–17, 222.

16. Ferdinand Portugall (1837–1901) was the son of a baker, and he studied law at the University of Graz, receiving the rank of juris doctor. As mayor, Portugall was influential in the development of Graz, expanding the University of Graz, and developing the Mountain Railway, the road system, and electric lighting for the city. Anita Muck to Mrs. Gardner, June 4, 1920. Isabella Stewart Gardner Museum Archives. In 1920, the Portugall address in Graz was Karl Ludwig Ring 2.

17. Egon Pelikan and Heidemarie Uhl, "Culture, Identity and Politics: Aspects of National Politics in Graz and Ljubljana at the Close of the Nineteenth Century," in *The Postmodern Challenge: Perspectives East and West*, ed. Bo Strath and Nina Witoszek (Amsterdam: Rodopi, 1998), 219.

18. Eric J. Hobsbawm, *The Age of Empire, 1875–1914* (New York: Pantheon Books, 1987), 152.

19. "Wore the Kaiserin's Gifts," *Boston Post*, November 12, 1919.

20. Klara Moricz, *Jewish Identities: Nationalism, Racism and Utopianism in Twentieth Century Music* (Oakland: University of California, 2008), 160.

21. Frederic Spotts, *Bayreuth: A History of the Wagner Festival* (New Haven, CT: Yale University Press, 1994), 20, 115–16. Muck conducted all fourteen Bayreuth festivals from 1901 to 1930.

22. Colleen Walsh, "When the Genius Is also a Symbol of Hate, Where Does That Leave Us?" *Harvard Gazette*, April 23, 2018.

23. Evans, *Coming*, 32.

24. Mark Twain's *Travel Diary*, as quoted by the *Chicago Daily Tribune*, December 6, 1891. http://www.twainquotes.com/Travel1891/Dec1891. html.

25. Mark Twain, *Travel Diary*.

26. Isadora Duncan, *My Life* (New York: Boni and Liveright, 1927), 105.

27. Evans, *Coming*, 32.

28. Evans, *Coming*, 32.

29. Mark DeVoto, "Taking a Knee in 1918," *Boston Musical Intelligencer*, November 2017. DeVoto describes a rumor shared with him by American composer Roger Sessions that Muck was the illegitimate son of Richard Wagner and socialite Isabella Stewart Gardner. DeVoto exclaimed that he was fascinated by Muck and had been gossiping about him for more than half a century.

30. Schonberg, *Great Conductors*, 218.

31. "Karl Muck, Former Head of Boston Symphony"; "Musical Matters Abroad," *New York Times*, May 14, 1899.

32. Henry Lee Higginson Files, Boston Symphony Orchestra Archives, Series 1096, Reel 2, 534–35, xii-9-2.

33. Henry Lee Higginson Files, Boston Symphony Orchestra Archives, Series 1065 Reel 2, 427, xii-8-73.

34. Henry Lee Higginson Files, Boston Symphony Orchestra Archives, Series 123, Reel 4, 328–31 (263–66), xv-1.

35. Henry Lee Higginson Files, Boston Symphony Orchestra Archives, Series 125, Reel 4, 335–39 (270–74), xv-1.

36. Joseph Horowitz, *Classical Music in America: A History of Its Rise and Fall* (New York: W. W. Norton, 2005), 77.

37. Horowitz, *Classical Music in America*, 77.

38. Paul DiMaggio, "Cultural Entrepreneurship in Nineteenth Century Boston: The Creation of an Organizational Base for High Culture in America," *Media, Culture and Society* 4 (1982): 47; Melissa Burrage, "Albert Cameron Burrage: An Allegiance to Boston's Elite through a Lifetime of Political, Business and Social Reform" (MA thesis, Harvard University, 2004), 40. Roosevelt was connected to the Boston upper classes through Harvard and his first wife, Alice Lee.

39. Henry Lee Higginson Files, Boston Symphony Orchestra Archives, Series 188, Reel 4, 444–45 (396–97), xv-1.

40. Henry Lee Higginson Files, Boston Symphony Orchestra Archives, Series 198, Reel 4, 457–59 (409–12), xv-1.

41. Bliss Perry, *Life and Letters of Henry Lee Higginson* (Boston: Atlantic Monthly Press, 1921), 319. Henry Lee Higginson Files, Boston Symphony Orchestra Archives, Series 957, Reel 2, 251, xii-7-59.

42. M. A. DeWolfe Howe, *The Boston Symphony Orchestra: An Historical Sketch* (Boston: Houghton Mifflin, 1914), 210.

43. Alexandra Haueisen, *Das Bostoner Intelligenz-Blatt: Kulturgeschichte der deutschen Immigration in Boston im 19. Jahrhundert. Zur Biographie einer deutschen Kolonie* (Hamburg: Verlag Dr. Kovač, 2009); personal conversation with Haueisen, March 22, 2009. In the early to mid-nineteenth century, working-class German immigrants who arrived in Boston received a cold reception from the city's inhabitants. They were greeted with signs in store windows that read, "No Need Apply." Between 1815 and 1900, more than five million Germans came to the United States, and fewer than two thousand Germans remained in Boston, moving on to other communities, such as the Midwest; Wolfeboro, Maine; Braintree, Massachusetts; Manchester, New Hampshire; and the mill regions of Lawrence or Holyoke, Massachusetts. By the time Muck lived there, most German immigrants had assimilated years before and had gained acceptance, and 85 percent of all Germans in Boston had obtained citizenship. By the turn of the century, many first-generation Germans had passed away, and successive generations identified as American with strong German affinities, even though new generations may never have been to Germany. Cultural

traditions were passed down and kept alive in Boston in the pre–World War I years.

44. Edwin Monroe Bacon, *Bacon's Dictionary of Boston* (Cambridge, MA: Riverside Press, 1886), 170.

45. Alexander von Hoffman, *Local Attachments: The Making of an American Urban Neighborhood, 1850–1920* (Baltimore: John Hopkins University Press, 1994), 3–14; Liz Sonneborn, *German Americans: Immigrants in America* (Philadelphia: Chelsea House, 2003), 57.

46. Massachusetts Historical Commission and the Boston Landmarks Commission, Jamaica Plain Preservation Study, July 31, 1983. Fifteen hundred German immigrants were living in the Stony Brook Valley area of Jamaica Plain by the late 1860s.

47. Sonneborn, *German Americans*, 58. German American Conrad Mohr and his staff of German American workers manufactured cigars, which he sold at the Boston Cigar Store. He lived in Jamaica Plain.

48. Goethe Society of New England, *Germans in Boston* (Boston: Goethe Society of New England, 1981), 77. In 1750, Germans began settling in Quincy, Massachusetts, in the village of Germantown, thirteen miles south of Boston. Many Germans manufactured glass there before the American Revolution, providing a domestic solution to the Non-importation Agreement signed by Boston merchants that embargoed glass from England. Christopher Seider, a German boy whose parents lived and worked in Germantown, was the first casualty of that conflict.

49. Panikos Panayi, *German Immigrants in Britain during the Nineteenth Century, 1815–1914* (Providence, RI: Berg, 1995) 78–89.

50. Goethe Society of New England, *Germans in Boston*, 84–88; Von Hoffman, *Local Attachments*, 145. The original Boylston Schul-Verein building at 45 Danforth Street, built in 1874, is currently a community cultural-arts center called Spontaneous Celebrations.

51. Edwin Monroe Bacon, *Bacon's Dictionary of Boston*, 170.

52. The German Music Club at 276 Amory Street was designed in 1896 by carpenter and Jamaica Plain resident John Albrecht, who was also president of the club. The name of the structure was later changed to The German Club before it was sold in 1919 to the Jamaica Plain Neighborhood House Association, a community education center. The building became a condominium complex in the 1990s.

53. Goethe Society of New England, *Germans in Boston*, 70–72; Oscar Handlin, *Boston's Immigrants: 1790–1880* (Cambridge, MA: Harvard University Press, 1991), 172; Jamaica Plain Historical Society, *Boylston Schul-Verein and the German Saturday School*, accessed November 25, 2012, https://www.jphs.org/victorian-era/boylston-schul-verein-and-the-german-saturday-school.html. Many members of the BSO maintained their culture by teaching the German language or performing impromptu concerts for the enjoyment of members.

54. Carl Wittke, *The German Language Press in America* (Lexington: University of Kentucky, 1957), 1–3.

55. Panayi, *German Immigrants*, 253.

56. Russell A. Kazal, *Becoming Old Stock: The Paradox of German-American Identity* (Princeton, NJ: Princeton University Press, 2004). Germans found common ground in America by speaking the same language, often realigning along professional and class lines.

57. Higham, *Strangers*, 68; Jonathan D. Sarna and Ellen Smith, *Jews of Boston* (New Haven, CT: Yale University Press, 2005), 5–7.

58. The German Methodist Church at 169 Amory Street is a granite rock-faced gothic-style church built in 1899 by Jamaica Plain architect Jacob Luippold.

59. Goethe Society of New England, *Germans in Boston*, 84.

60. Dennis P. Ryan, *A Journey through Boston Irish History* (Charleston, SC: Arcadia, 1999), 76. Irish-born architect Patrick C. Keely designed the structure in cooperation with German church members, creating "as perfect a specimen of the early German gothic as it was possible to reproduce."

61. Robert J. Sauer, *Holy Trinity German Catholic Church of Boston: A Way of Life* (Dallas, TX: Taylor, 1994), 18.

62. Anita Muck to Mrs. Gardner, November 23, 1918, Isabella Stewart Gardner Museum Archives. Gardner had visited the pope on a trip to Italy and shared her experience with Anita, who found it fascinating. Anita writes, "I gave my husband a brief report of it, which he enjoyed very much."

63. Frederick C. Luebke, *Bonds of Loyalty: German Americans and World War I* (DeKalb: Northern Illinois University Press, 1974), 30.

64. Edwin Monroe Bacon, *Bacon's Dictionary of Boston*, 170. Bacon mentions a German restaurant on Hawley Street, which was a popular destination, another "of cheaper grade" opposite the Court House, located in a basement, and Sherman's German Restaurant on La Grange Street.

65. "Don't Go Hungry for Want of Variety," *Boston Globe*, January 3, 1916.

66. Nancy Gailor Cortner, *Great German-American Feasts* (Dallas, TX: Taylor, 1987), 6–7; Susan Williams, *Food in the United States, 1820–1890* (Westport, CT: Greenwood Press, 2006), 31, 105.

67. Williams, *Food in the United States*, 24.

68. Marcia Morton and Frederic Morton, *Chocolate: An Illustrated History* (New York: Crown, 1986), 34, 71, 77.

69. Morton and Morton, *Chocolate*, 34, 71, 77.

70. Maureen Ogle, *Ambitious Brew: The Story of American Beer* (New York: Harvest-Harcourt, 2006). Haffenreffer Brewery complex occupied several brick industrial buildings on Germania and Bismarck Street, where the current Sam Adams Brewery is located today.

71. Hoffman, *Local Attachments*, 55–60; *Boston Daily Globe*, January 12, 1879. German workers in the area who were members of the German

Arbeiter Club socialized in Arbeiter Hall and drank beer at the Apollo Garden and Hotel, located at 107 Amory Street behind the Rockland Brewery.

72. Walter Muir Whitehill, *A Seidel for Jake Wirth* (Lunenburg, VT: Stinehour Press, 1964), 16.

73. *United States Investor* 15 (New Jersey: Princeton University, 1904), 29–101; *Commercial and Financial New England Illustrated* (Boston: Boston Herald, 1906). Selg's Palm Garden at 116–20 Sudbury Road, was owned by Eugene Selg.

74. Williams, *Food,* 156, 172.

75. Joseph Horowitz, *Classical Music in America,* 38.

76. Anita Muck to Mrs. George Chadwick, New England Conservatory Archives, n.d.

77. Williams, *Food,* 184.

78. Stephen Nissenbaum, *The Battle for Christmas* (New York: Knopf), 176–218. Goethe Society of New England, *Germans in Boston,* 78. Paul Revere reflected on his childhood having admired a beautifully decorated Christmas tree displayed by German Puritans at Christ Church.

79. T. Nast and T. N. St. Hill, *Thomas Nast: Cartoons and Illustrations* (New York: Dover, 1974), 2.

80. "German Toy Shipment at Boston," New *York Times,* August 27, 1919. Five hundred cases of German-made toys were purchased and brought to Boston by the Holland-American Shipping Line.

81. Higham, *Strangers,* 25.

82. James F. Harris, *German-American Interrelations, Heritage, and Challenge: Joint Conference Held at the University of Maryland, April 2–April 5, 1984* (Tübingen: Attempto Verlag, Tübingen University Press, 1985), 148.

83. Michael Broyles, "'Music of the Highest Class': Elitism and Populism in Antebellum Boston," in Spitzer, *American Orchestras,* 314.

84. Hajo Holborn, *A History of Modern Germany* (New York: Knopf, 1969), 45.

85. Holborn, *Germany,* 40.

86. Martin B. Green, *The Problem of Boston: Some Readings in Cultural History* (New York: W. W. Norton, 1966), 61.

87. Ticknor received his undergraduate training at Dartmouth College, went on to study law in Boston, passing the bar and then abandoning that enterprise, traveling to Germany to study classical philology. In 1819 he began teaching at Harvard.

88. Green, *Problem of Boston,* 44.

89. Green, *Problem of Boston,* 90.

90. Thomas Adam and Gisela Mettele, *Two Boston Brahmins in Goethe's Germany: The Travel Journals of Anna and George Ticknor* (Plymouth, UK: Rowman and Littlefield, 2009), 8.

91. Green, *Problem of Boston,* 50.

92. Horowitz, *Classical Music,* 96.

93. Green, *Problem of Boston,* 75.

94. Green, *Problem of Boston*, 114.

95. Harris, *German-American Interrelations*, 148.

96. Harris, *German-American Interrelations*, 148.

97. Alan Wallach, "The Battle of the Casts' Revisited" (paper delivered at the Association of Historians of American Art Symposium, Boston Athenaeum, October 12, 2012).

98. Goethe Society of New England, *Germans in Boston*, 56; Peter Nesbit and Emilie Norris, *The Busch-Reisinger Museum: History and Holdings* (Cambridge, MA: Harvard University Press, 1991), 5–39.

99. Green, *Problem of Boston*, 12, 35; Horowitz, *Classical Music*, 94.

100. DiMaggio, "Cultural Entrepreneurship," 34.

101. Nancy Glaze and Thomas Wolf, *And the Band Stopped Playing: The Rise and Fall of the San Jose Symphony Orchestra* (Cambridge, MA: Wolf, Keene, 2005), 16.

102. Goethe Society of New England, *Germans in Boston*, 23; Christine Merrick Ayars, *Contributions to the Art of Music in America by the Music Industries of Boston 1640–1936* (New York: H. W. Wilson, 1937), 9.

103. Ayars, *Contributions*, 3.

104. Publishers included Elias Howe Co., W. H. Oakes Co., Charles Edward Horn Co., Eben H. Wade Co., George P. Reed Co., Joseph M. Russell Co., Nathan Richardson Co., Jean White Co., John F. Perry Co., George W. Stratton Co., E. A. Samuels Co., Thompson and Odell Co., Damm & Gay Co., Ginn and Co., C. C. Birchard Co., E. C. Schirmer Co., Oliver Ditson Co., Carl Fischer Co., Louis H. Ross Co., H. B. Stevens and Co., L. F. Whipple Co., E. C. Ramsdell Co., Cundy-Bettoney Co., J. B. Millet Co., C. W. Thompson and Co., William H. Gerrish Co., Boston Music Co., Schmidt & Co., Herbert F. Odell Co., Ernest S. Williams Co., the Wa Wan Press, G. Shirmer Co., the Musicians Library Co., Charles A. White Co., Charles W. Homeyer and Co., Inc., Parish Choir Co., McLaughlin and Reilly Co., Walter Jacobs Co., and Vega Co.

105. Ayars, *Contributions*, 38.

106. Ayars, *Contributions*, 43.

107. Richard Crawford, *American Musical Life: A History* (New York: W. W. Norton, 2001), 149. Spitzer, *American Orchestras*, 378; Broyles, *"Music of the Highest Class,"* 203.

108. "Patronage—and Women—in America's Musical Life," in *Cultivating Music in America: Women Patrons and Activists since 1860*, ed. Ralph P. Locke and Cyrilla Barr (Oakland: University of California Press, 1997), https://publishing.cdlib.org/ucpressebooks/view?docId=ft838nb58v;query=;brand=ucpress, 35. By 1900, music education was a rapidly expanding field dominated by women. That trend changed after 1910 as more men became attracted to the profession.

109. Ayars, *Contributions*, 54.

110. Ayars, *Contributions*, 65.

111. Ayars, *Contributions*, 87.

112. Ayars, *Contributions*, 61.

113. Ayars, *Contributions*, 19, 78; Horowitz, *Classical Music*, 20.

114. Ayars, *Contributions*, 99.

115. Ayars, *Contributions*, 111.

116. Liszt Ferenc Memorial Museum and Research Center, *Exhibitions*, accessed April 25, 2018, Lisztmuseum.hu.

117. Ayars, *Contributions*, 110–28. Several other piano manufacturers thrived in the "Piano Row" region of Boston in addition to Chickering and Sons: Henry F. Miller Piano Company sold fifty-five thousand pianos during its years in the city. Ivers and Pond Piano Company sold eighty thousand instruments. Poole Piano Company, founded in 1893 by William H. Poole, sold twenty-five thousand pianos. Mason & Hamlin, M. Steinert and Sons, and Vose and Sons are a few of the most prominent piano manufacturers in Boston at the time. Those who did not have the time or discipline to learn an instrument could purchase a player piano with accompanying rolls from M. Welte and Son, Ludwig Hupfeld, and Charles Fuller Stoddard, pioneers in modern player piano technology. With the huge number of pianos in the region, it follows that Boston needed many piano tuners to keep their sound. Perkins Institute for the Blind trained its students to repair and tune pianos in Boston city schools and in local homes.

118. Ayars, *Contributions*, 197, 201–11. Edmund F. Bryant, Oliver H. Bryant, J. H. Elder, George Gemunder, Albert Lind, Walter Solon Goss, F. Lincoln Johnson, and Jerome Bonaparte Squier duplicated Cremona, Stradivarius, Guarnerius, and Amati violins. Goss experimented with glass violins that he filled with sand. Many of these men experimented with varnishes and oils and created their own formula for rosin. Hugo Schindler made violin strings using aluminum, gold, and other metals to alter their tone quality.

119. Ayars, *Contributions*, 216. William S. Haynes also manufactured flutes using silver. He also improved the mechanism of the clarinet, selling eight thousand in the first eight years of production.

120. Eric Hobsbawm and Terence Ranger, *The Invention of Tradition* (Cambridge: Cambridge University Press, 1983), 220; Benedict R. Anderson, *Imagined Communities: Reflections on the Origin and Spread of Nationalism* (New York: Verso, 2006), 75.

121. Eric Hobsbawm, *Invention of Tradition*, 7.

122. Ayars, *Contribution*, 7.

123. William Weber, "*Orchestral Programs in Boston*, 1841–55," in Spitzer, *American Orchestras*, 371.

124. Spitzer, *American Orchestras*, 13.

125. Spitzer, *American Orchestras*, 15–19.

126. Spitzer, *American Orchestras*, 104.

127. Mary Wallace Davidson, "John Sullivan Dwight and the Harvard Musical Association Orchestra: A Help or a Hindrance," in Spitzer, *American Orchestras*, 246–68.

128. Horowitz, *Classical Music*, 30; Spitzer, *American Orchestras*, 367.

129. Weber, "Orchestral Programs in Boston," in Spitzer, *American Orchestras*, 381.

130. Spitzer, *American Orchestras*, 8.

131. Nancy Newman, "Gender and the Germanians: 'Art Loving Ladies' in Nineteenth Century Concert Life," in Spitzer, *American Orchestras*, 289.

132. Gienow-Hecht, *Sound Diplomacy*, 70.

133. Horowitz, *Classical Music*, 30.

134. Weber, "Orchestral Programs in Boston," in Spitzer, *American Orchestras*, 388; Spitzer, *American Orchestras*, 20.

135. Davidson, "John Sullivan Dwight . . . ," in Spitzer, *American Orchestras*, 247, 256.

136. Davidson, "John Sullivan Dwight . . . ," in Spitzer, *American Orchestras*, 247, 256.

137. Davidson, "John Sullivan Dwight . . . ," in Spitzer, *American Orchestras*, 262.

138. Davidson, "John Sullivan Dwight . . . ," in Spitzer, *American Orchestras*, 247.

139. Anna-Lise P. Santella, "Modeling Music: Early Organizational Structures of American Women's Orchestras," in *The American Bourgeoisie: Distinction and Identity in the Nineteenth Century*, ed. Julia Rosenbaum and Sven Beckert (London: Palgrave Macmillan, 2010), 53.

140. Frank Trommler and Joseph McVeigh, *America and the Germans: An Assessment of a Three Hundred Year History*, vol. 2, *The Relationship in the Twentieth Century* (Philadelphia: University of Pennsylvania Press, 1985), 193; Howe, *Boston Symphony Orchestra*; Perry, *Life and Letters*, 297; Goethe Society of New England, *Germans in Boston*, 23–26.

141. Horowitz, *Classical Music*, 82.

142. Horowitz, *Classical Music*, 10.

143. Spitzer, *American Orchestras*, 9.

144. Brenda Nelson Strauss, "Theodore Thomas and the Cultivation of American Music," in Spitzer, *American Orchestras*, 395; Howard Shanet, *Philharmonic: A History of New York's Orchestra* (New York: Doubleday, 1975), 167.

145. Spitzer, *American Orchestras*, 8.

146. Davidson, "John Sullivan Dwight . . . ," in Spitzer, *American Orchestras*, 261.

147. Broyles, *"Music of the Highest Class,"* 237.

148. Spitzer, *American Orchestras*, 3.

149. Karen Ahlquist, "Performance to 'Permanence': Orchestra Building in Late 19th Century Cincinnati," in Spitzer, *American Orchestras*, 59.

150. Horowitz, *Classical Music*, 45; Hobsbawm and Ranger, *Invention of Tradition*, 220; DiMaggio, "Cultural Entrepreneurship," 375.

151. Hobsbawm, *Invention of Tradition*, 306.

152. Spitzer, *American Orchestras*, 109.

153. Davidson, "John Sullivan Dwight . . . ," in Spitzer, *American Orchestras*, 258.

154. Higham, *Strangers*, 22; Barbara Miller Solomon, *Ancestors and Immigrants: A Changing New England Tradition* (New York: John Wiley, 1956), 130–36 and 158. Henry Cabot Lodge praised Germans on the senate floor in 1896 as welcome representatives of the Teutonic race, admiring them for fitting seamlessly into Anglo-Saxon society. Handlin, *Boston's Immigrants*, 246–56 and 135. "The Germans could be as optimistic, rational and romantic as the natives, for their emigration rested on hope rather than on bare necessity. . . . And in America their economic and physical adjustment was relatively simple, so that within a short time they shared the ideas of the natives."

155. Perry, *Life and Letters*, 14. Higginson's family network in Boston included the Cabots, Lowells, Lees, Perkins, Morses, Jacksons, Channings, and Paines.

156. Robert F. Dalzell Jr., *Enterprising Elite: The Boston Associates and the World They Made* (Cambridge, MA: Harvard University Press, 1987), 5; Burrage, "Albert Cameron Burrage," 113; DiMaggio, "Cultural Entrepreneurship," 34, 46.

157. Spitzer, *American Orchestras*, 50; DiMaggio, "Cultural Entrepreneurship," 35.

158. DiMaggio, "Cultural Entrepreneurship," 45.

159. Green, *Problem of Boston*, 23.

160. DiMaggio, "Cultural Entrepreneurship," 375.

161. DiMaggio, "Cultural Entrepreneurship," 40.

162. Richard Hofstadter, *The Age of Reform* (New York: Random House, 1955), 8; Higham, *Strangers*, 26.

163. Higham, *Strangers*, 39.

164. Jonathan D. Sarna and Ellen Smith, *Jews of Boston* (New Haven, CT: Yale University Press, 2005), 343.

165. Sarna and Smith, *Jews of Boston*, 271.

166. Sarna and Smith, *Jews of Boston*, 8.

167. Alton Gal, *Brandeis of Boston* (Cambridge, MA: Harvard University Press, 1980), 31.

168. Sarna and Smith, *Jews of Boston*, 8.

169. Sarna and Smith, *Jews of Boston*, 8.

170. Sarna and Smith, *Jews of Boston*, 9.

171. Gal, *Brandeis of Boston*, 64.

172. Gal, *Brandeis of Boston*, 110.

173. Gal, *Brandeis of Boston*, 109.

174. Gal, *Brandeis of Boston*, 174.

175. Gal, *Brandeis of Boston*, 9.

176. Gal, *Brandeis of Boston*, 195. In spite of bitter opposition from Boston's upper-class circles, Brandeis's nomination was confirmed in June of 1916.

177. Gal, *Brandeis of Boston*, 192.

178. Solomon, *Ancestors and Immigrants*, 123; Gal, *Brandeis of Boston*, 193.

179. Higham, *Strangers*, 101.

180. Higham, *Strangers*, 103.

181. Higham, *Strangers*, 134.

182. Higham, *Strangers*, 276.

183. Higham, *Strangers*, 9.

184. Higham, *Strangers*, 275.

185. Higham, *Strangers*, 157.

186. Edward Lurie, "Louis Agassiz and the Races of Man," *Isis* 45, no. 3 (1954): 227–42.

187. Higham, *Strangers*, 143.

188. Higham, *Strangers*, 137.

189. Higham, *Strangers*, 98.

190. Higham, *Strangers*, 96. 162.

191. Higham, *Strangers*, 311. While the 1924 law excluded Eastern Europeans, it did not restrict Latin American immigration. Employers encouraged this population to come to the United States, where their labor supported the American economy. Today, immigrants from Latin America (and Muslim communities) face increasing animosity from isolationists, in a repeating pattern of exclusion.

192. DiMaggio, "Cultural Entrepreneurship,"40.

193. Burrage, "Albert Cameron Burrage," 275.

194. Burrage, "Albert Cameron Burrage," 275.

195. Burrage, "Albert Cameron Burrage," 274; Frederic Cople Jaher, *The Urban Establishment: Upper Strata in Boston, New York, Charleston, Chicago, and Los Angeles* (Urbana: University of Illinois Press, 1982), 59.

196. Horowitz, *Classical Music*, 89.

197. Cleveland Amory, *The Proper Bostonians* (Orleans, MA: Parnassus, 1947), 173.

198. Perry, *Life and Letters*, 312.

199. Henry Lee Higginson File, Boston Symphony Orchestra Archive, Series 525, Reel 1, 526, xii-3-91.

200. DiMaggio, "Cultural Entrepreneurship," 35.

201. Henry Lee Higginson File, Boston Symphony Orchestra Archives, Series 562, Reel 1, 601–2, xii-4-11; Series 555, Reel 1, 586–88, xii-4-11.

202. DiMaggio, "Cultural Entrepreneurship," 47.

203. Perry, *Life and Letters*, 312.

204. DiMaggio, "Cultural Entrepreneurship," 42.

205. Henry Lee Higginson File, Boston Symphony Orchestra Archives, Series 899, Reel 2, 131–32. Higginson used the Agassiz Calumet and Hecla Iron Works to build the railings and stairways at Symphony Hall.

206. Henry Lee Higginson File, Boston Symphony Orchestra Archives, Series 827, Reel 2, 16, xii-6-57; Adrienne Fried Block, "Thinking about Serious Music in New York, 1842–82," in Spitzer, *American Orchestras*, 436;

Mark Evan Bonds, "Idealism and the Aesthetics of Instrumental Music at the Turn of the Nineteenth Century," *Journal of the American Musicological Society* 50, no. 2 (Summer/Autumn, 1997): 392. Musical idealism emerged in the late eighteenth and early nineteenth centuries based on the notion that "the aesthetic effect of an artwork resides in its ability to reflect a higher ideal." Instrumental music, Beethoven symphonies in particular, was believed to be able to communicate what could not be seen or named, carrying the listener upward into a "spirit realm," a transcendent consciousness.

207. Cecile died in 1875 at the age of five. Alexander was born a year later, in 1876.

208. Ida Agassiz and her siblings left Germany after their mother died in 1849. They lived in Cambridge, Massachusetts, with their father, Louis Agassiz, and their step-mother, Elizabeth Cabot Cary. Cary became the president of Radcliffe College and a staunch supporter of Higginson's BSO endeavor.

209. Perry, *Life and Letters*, 297; Henry Lee Higginson File, Boston Symphony Orchestra Archives, Series 946, Reel 2, 229–30. x11-7-59.

210. Perry, *Life and Letters*, 297; Henry Lee Higginson File, Boston Symphony Orchestra Archives, Series 946, Reel 2, 229–30. x11-7-59.

211. Ahlquist, "'Performance to 'Permanence,'" in Spitzer, *American Orchestras*, 157.

212. Joseph Horowitz, "Reclaiming the Past: Musical Boston Reconsidered," *American Music* 19, no. 1 (Spring 2001): 22.

213. DiMaggio, "Cultural Entrepreneurship," 38–42.

214. Spitzer, *American Orchestras*, 29.

215. Ronald G. Walters, "Afterword: Coming of Age," in Spitzer, *American Orchestras*, 452.

216. Perry, *Life and Letters*, 295.

217. DiMaggio, "Cultural Entrepreneurship," 34; Burrage, "Albert Cameron Burrage," 155; Margo Miller, *Chateau Higginson: Social Life in Boston's Back Bay, 1870–1920* (Charleston, SC: Arcadia, 2017). Higginson also invested in real estate, building the Hotel Agassiz, a luxury brick apartment building on the corner of Commonwealth Avenue and Exeter Street. His own residence at 191 Commonwealth Avenue was attached to it.

218. Perry, *Life and Letters*, 303.

219. Perry, *Life and Letters*, 293.

220. DiMaggio, "Cultural Entrepreneurship," 44.

221. DiMaggio, "Cultural Entrepreneurship," 44.

222. Horowitz, *Classical Music*, 2–3.

223. DiMaggio, "Cultural Entrepreneurship," 45; Paul DiMaggio, "The Problem of Chicago," in Rosenbaum and Beckert, *American Bourgeoisie*, 209.

224. Ronald G. Walters, "Afterword," in Spitzer, *American Orchestras*, 451; Ahlquist, "Performance to 'Permanence,'" in Spitzer, *American Orchestras*,

170. As Ahlquist has noted, the BSO was a model for a permanent orchestra in Cincinnati. The "Boston Symphony Orchestra model seemed to offer Cincinnati the possibility of an orchestra that was both permanent and local—if only a local Higginson could be discovered."

225. Horowitz, "Reclaiming the Past," 18–38.

226. Green, *Problem of Boston*, 110. Higginson paid his musicians a yearly salary of $1,500.

227. "Muck Talks of America: Observations in Musical Matters Here by the German Conductor," *New York Times*, May 31, 1908.

228. Henry Lee Higginson File, Boston Symphony Orchestra Archives, Series 1440, Reel 3, 109–10, xii-15-Ellis, 1914–15. On October 5, 1915, Higginson wrote to Ellis in Minneapolis with suggestions for Muck's investments as related to the copper market.

229. Gienow-Hecht, *Sound Diplomacy*.

230. Perry, *Life and Letters*, 292.

231. Perry, *Life and Letters*, 302.

232. Spitzer, *American Orchestras*, 20.

233. Horowitz, *Classical Music*, 52–53.

234. Schonberg, *Great Conductors*, 221.

235. Schonberg, *Great Conductors*, 220.

236. Olin Downes, "Dr. Karl Muck: His Death Recalls Problems of the Artist in Time of War," *New York Times*, March 10, 1940.

237. James J. Badal, "The Strange Case of Dr. Karl Muck Who Was Torpedoed by the Star-Spangled Banner During World War I," *High Fidelity* 20, no. 10 (October 1970): 55–60; "Considering Two Great Leaders: Dr. Koussevitzky and Dr. Muck are Comparable," and "Muck of the Wasting Years, Yet Power of Prime," *Boston Transcript*, August 1926.

238. David Ewen, *Dictators of the Baton* (New York: Ziff-Davis, 1943), 97.

239. Moricz, *Jewish Identities*, 160.

240. Moricz, *Jewish Identities*, 160.

241. Moricz, *Jewish Identities*, 160.

242. Bill Faucett, *George Whitefield Chadwick: The Life and Music of the Pride of New England* (New Hampshire: University of New England Press, 2012), 312–14. Muck's good friend, composer George Chadwick, shared a similar anti-Semitism, describing the "little New York Hebrew Ornstein" as "feebleminded" and a "lunatic."

243. "Famed Violinist Kreisler Dies," *Traverse City (Michigan) Eagle Record*, January 30, 1962.

244. "Famed Violinist Kreisler Dies."

245. Horowitz, *Classical Music*, 78.

246. Hobsbawm, *Invention of Tradition*, 4.

247. Kathleen Dalton, *Theodore Roosevelt: A Strenuous Life* (New York: Alfred A. Knopf, 2002), 52.

248. Graeme Turner, *Understanding Celebrity* (London: Sage, 2004), 5.

249. Turner, *Understanding Celebrity*, 6. 25. The function of celebrity often parallels functions ascribed to religion, with audiences looking to a special individual as a congregation looks upon a religious figure.

250. Turner, *Understanding Celebrity*, 10.

251. *Constitution* (Atlanta, GA), December 8, 1912. Muck's face appeared in advertisements such as this one: "Music critics all agree that the highest standard of piano tone and piano construction was not attained until the advent of the Mason and Hamlin Piano. Read what Dr. Karl Muck says of the Mason and Hamlin Piano. 'Their beautiful tone which no adjectives can adequately describe and their inspiring perfection of mechanism render them noble instruments worthy of the highest place in my esteem.' Dr. Karl Muck, Director of Music and Conductor of the Boston Symphony Orchestra, Conductor of the Royal Opera, Berlin, Conductor of Bayreuth Wagner Festival, one of the most distinguished musicians now living."

252. Turner, *Understanding Celebrity*, 37.

253. Hobsbawm, *Invention of Tradition*, 23–24.

254. Gienow-Hecht, *Sound Diplomacy*, 127. Two music critics from Boston's leading newspapers were musicians themselves, having trained in Germany. Philip Hale, editor of the *Boston Herald*, and Louis C. Elson, editor of the *Musical Herald, Musical Courier*, and the *Boston Advertiser*.

255. Allen A. Brown Music Collection, Boston Public Library, Muck File. Perry, *Life and Letters*, 320.

256. Allen A. Brown Music Collection, Boston Public Library, Muck File. Perry, *Life and Letters*, 320.

257. Horowitz, *Classical Music*, 79; Perry, *Life and Letters*, 320.

258. "The World of Music," *Constitution* (Atlanta, GA), October 21, 1906.

259. Henry Lee Higginson Files, Boston Symphony Orchestra Archives, Series 206, Reel 4, 463, 437, xv-1.

260. Henry Lee Higginson Files, Boston Symphony Orchestra Archives, Series 216, Reel 4, 482, 454, xv-1.

261. Perry, *Life and Letters*, 321.

262. Henry Lee Higginson Files. Boston Symphony Orchestra Archives, Series 223, Reel 4, 494–96.

263. Henry Lee Higginson Files, Boston Symphony Orchestra Archives, Series 223, Reel 4, 497, 473, xv-1.

264. George Chadwick Files, New England Conservatory Archives.

265. Perry, *Life and Letters*, 316; Henry Lee Higginson Collection, Baker Business Library, Harvard University. The collection contains correspondence between Higginson and his musicians demonstrating his paternalism.

266. Gienow-Hecht, *Sound Diplomacy*, 331. Passenger liners were filled with middle-class Americans attending music schools and concerts in Germany and Austria. In 1893, there were 112 music schools in Berlin,

60 in Vienna, collectively teaching 1,500 students each year, and producing 1,800 professional musicians from 1890 to 1897. Elam Douglas Bomberger, "The German Musician Training of American Students, 1850–1900" (PhD diss., University of Maryland, 1991), 1–2, 60–61.

267. Horowitz, *Classical Music*, 98.

268. Horowitz, "Reclaiming the Past," 18–38.

269. Adrienne Fried Block, *Amy Beach: Passionate Victorian; The Life and Work of an American Composer, 1867–1944* (New York: Oxford University Press, 1998), 21, 294, 38; Fletcher Dubois, "Celebrating Margaret Ruthven Lang's 150th Birthday," accessed April 12, 2018, https://hampsongfoundation. org/. Margaret Ruthven Lang was the first American woman to have a composition performed by a top-tier US symphony. *Dramatic Overture* was performed by the Boston Symphony Orchestra in 1893. Lang was a prolific composer of hundreds of choral, chamber, and orchestral works. Margaret's father, B. J. Lang, was a prominent Boston organist and conductor and founder of the Apollo Club and the Cecilia Society, and her mother, Frances Morse Burrage, was a vocalist who traveled abroad with young Margaret for music lessons. The family hosted Dvořák and Paderewski at their Back Bay home and dined with Franz Liszt and his daughter Cosima Wagner on trips to Europe. B. J. Lang served as a pall bearer at Liszt's funeral. Ralph P. Locke, "Living with Music: Isabella Stewart Gardner," in Locke and Barr, *Cultivating Music in America*, 106. Isabella Stewart Gardner and B. J. Lang were also friends. Upon his death, Gardner gave Margaret Ruthven Lang her harpsichord in memory of him.

270. Block, *Amy Beach*, 41.

271. "If You Don't Behave I'll Call Dr. Muck," *Boston Globe*, March 12, 1940.

272. Anita Muck to Mrs. George Chadwick, New England Conservatory Archives, n.d.

273. *Sandusky Star-Journal*, January 2, 1908.

274. Jaher, *Urban Establishment*, 109; E. Digby Baltzell, *The Protestant Establishment: Aristocracy and Caste in America* (New Haven, CT: Yale University Press, 1987), 2.

275. St. Botolph Club History, https://www.stbotolphclub.org/ Club_History.

276. Tavern Club of Boston, *A Partial Semi-centennial History of the Tavern Club, 1884–1934* (Boston: 1934), 261. Muck became a full member in 1912.

277. "The Meistersingers of Nuremberg," *Boston Daily Globe*, January 27, 1907.

278. *Music News* 11, no. 24 (June 13, 1919): 2.

279. Thorstein Veblen, *The Theory of the Leisure Class* (New York: Dover, 1994), 24.

280. New England Conservatory Archives. Dr. and Mrs. Muck hosted a dinner with a formal invitation at their home at the Tuileries on

Commonwealth Avenue on Tuesday, May 7, 1912, from 4 p.m. to 6:30 p.m. The *Boston City Directory of 1914* lists Muck's address as 382 Commonwealth Avenue.

281. The author met with Warren Cutler, owner of 50 Fenway, on April 6, 2007, and received a tour of the property. The home has a basement kitchen, formal dining room on the first floor, bedrooms on the second and third floors, and servants' quarters on the fourth floor.

282. Cynthia Zaitzevsky, *Frederick Law Olmsted and the Boston Park System* (Cambridge, MA: Harvard University Press, 1982); personal walking tour of the area, strolling as Muck did on the pathways of the Back Bay Fens.

283. Hoffman, *Local Attachments*, 151.

284. Horowitz, *Classical Music*, 81.

285. The Mucks, the Gardners, and the Higginsons had each lost a child early in their marriages. Perhaps they bonded with one another and became closer in part because of their collective family tragedies. Anita Muck to Isabella Stewart Gardner June 14, 1916 and December 25, 1917, Isabella Stewart Gardner Museum Archives, Papers of Isabella Stewart Gardner. In 1917, the Mucks and Mrs. Gardner spent Christmas together. They often met for lunch and maintained an epistolary relationship from 1916 to 1921.

286. Ralph P. Locke, "Living with Music: Isabella Stewart Gardner," in Locke and Barr, *Cultivating Music in America*, 90–109. In 1908–10, Gardner hosted two full seasons of Kneisel Quartet concerts. Ahead of her time, she sponsored an early performance of Schoenberg's String Quartet no. 1 in D Minor, op. 7. Isabella and her husband Jack were longtime friends of Henry Lee Higginson and devoted supporters of the BSO. So devoted, in fact, that when Isabella broke her ankle, unwilling to miss a single BSO concert, she had her servant carry her by hammock to her seat.

287. Goethe Society of New England, *Germans in Boston*, 48.

288. New England Conservatory Archives, Anita Muck to Mrs. George Chadwick, January 31, no year listed.

289. New England Conservatory Archives, the Mucks to the Chadwicks, May 1915.

290. *Constitution* (Atlanta, GA), September 10, 1906.

291. Muck, *Dr. Karl Muck*, 104–5.

292. "Dr. Muck and the First War," *New York Times*, March 10, 1940.

293. "Dr. Karl Muck, Retired Wagner Conductor, Dies," *New York Times*, March 4, 1940.

294. *Washington Post*, September 8, 1907. "Dr. Karl Muck the conductor of the Boston Symphony Orchestra has spent the summer at Tobelbad in Austria. He returns to Berlin for a few days on September 10 and will sail to this country at the end of the month. It was he who engaged all the new members of the orchestra that are coming from abroad. This work, together with the making of programmes and the studying of new scores has kept him busy this summer."

295. "Boston Symphony Orchestra Will Give the Last of Its New York Concerts This Week—What Is Promised at the Opera Houses," *New York Times*, May 15, 1908. Higginson had donated the money to build a dining hall called the Harvard Union.

296. Henry Lee Higginson Files, Boston Symphony Orchestra Archives, Series 252, Reel 4, 542–43 (201–2), xv-2.

297. Perry, *Life and Letters*, 319. "Berlin's Farewell to Muck: Conductor Is Overcome by the Demonstration in His Honor," *New York Times*, June 15, 1912. In 1912, during his final Berlin performance before returning to America, the audience "engaged in a rival series of cheers every time the conductor made his appearance before the curtain. One section shouted 'Come back! Come back!' Another group yelled, Stay here! Don't go! Dr. Muck was entirely overcome by emotion and unable to respond to the frantic appeals for a speech."

298. "Example from Cambridge for Boston to Outdo," *Boston Transcript*, April 30, 1917.

299. Irwin Altman and Setha M. Low, *Place Attachment* (New York: Plenum Press, 1992), 1–10. Altman and Low describe the type of transformation the Mucks experienced as a "place attachment," whereby interacting within one's neighborhood, environmental spaces, and social networks can increase self-esteem, happiness, and provide a sense of emotional belonging.

300. Richard D. Alba, *Ethnic Identity: The Transformation of White America* (New Haven, CT: Yale University Press, 1990). Alba speaks about ethnic communities creating cultural attachments through food, friendships, family, community, and organizational affiliations.

301. Zaitzevsky, *Frederick Law Olmsted*, 2.

302. Michael Broyles, "Bourgeois Appropriation of Music: Challenging Ethnicity, Class, and Gender" in Rosenbaum and Beckert, *American Bourgeoisie*, 236, 238.

Chapter Two

1. Christopher Clark, *The Sleepwalkers: How Europe Went to War in 1914* (New York: Penguin, 2013), xxxvii, 562. Clark refers to the policy makers as "sleepwalkers, watchful but unseeing, haunted by dreams, yet blind to the reality of the horror they were about to bring into the world."

2. Clark, *The Sleepwalkers*, xiv–xxvii.

3. Clark, *The Sleepwalkers*, xiv–xxvii.

4. Wilhelm I's son Friedrick III died shortly after taking power, leading to the reign of Wilhelm II, Friedrick's son, from 1888 to 1918. Frank B. Tipton, *A History of Modern Germany since 1815* (Oakland: University of California Press, 2003), 249.

5. Margaret MacMillan, *The War That Ended Peace: The Road to 1914* (New York: Random House, 2013), 88.

6. Imanuel Geiss, *German Foreign Policy, 1871–1914* (Boston: Routledge and Kegan Paul, 1976); Niall Ferguson, *The Pity of War: Explaining World War I* (New York: Penguin Press, 1998).

7. Tipton, *History of Modern Germany*, 255. Because Germany felt hemmed in by France on one side and by Russia on the other, German militarist General Count Alfred von Schlieffen developed a strategy based on the assumption that Germany would have to conduct a two-front campaign against France and Russia if either side waged war. The Schlieffen Plan assumed that Russia would be slow to mobilize in wartime and that Germany could quickly defeat France before repositioning troops on the eastern front against Russia. Because this plan involved attacking neutral Belgium, which Britain had agreed to protect, Germany risked a British declaration of war.

8. Tipton, *History of Modern Germany*, 252; Robert K. Massie, *Castles of Steel: Britain, Germany, and the Winning of the Great War at Sea* (New York: Ballantine Books, 2004).

9. David E. Barclay and Elisabeth Glaser-Schmidt, eds., *Transatlantic Images and Perceptions: Germany and America since 1776* (New York: Cambridge University Press, 1997).

10. Warren Zimmermann, *First Great Triumph: How Five Americans Made Their Country a World Power* (New York: Farrar, Strauss and Giroux, 2002), 301–2.

11. Philip A. Crowl, *Alfred Thayer Mahan: The Naval Historian in Makers of Modern Strategy from Machiavelli to the Nuclear Age* (Oxford: Clarendon Press, 1986); MacMillan, *The War That Ended Peace*, 97–98. Wilhelm ordered a copy of Mahan's book placed on every German warship.

12. Zimmermann, *First Great Triumph*, 318. The US purchased Guam as part of the treaty negotiations after the Spanish American War.

13. William N. Tilchin, *Artists in Power: Theodore Roosevelt, Woodrow Wilson And Their Enduring Impact on U.S. Foreign Policy* (Westport, CT: Praeger Security International, 2006), 31–35.

14. Tilchin, *Artists in Power*, 31–35.

15. Anthony F. Sarcone and Lawrence S. Rines, *A History of Shipbuilding at Fore River* (Quincy, MA: Thomas Crane Public Library, 1975).

16. Sarcone and Rines, *A History of Shipbuilding*.

17. "Children Provide Shoes for Destitute Lads of Belgium," *Boston Herald*, April 13, 1915.

18. "Tin Boxes in Boston to Aid Belgian Babies: For the Child in Belgium, Put in Three Cents; It Will Give a Child One Meal," *Boston Herald*, February 4, 1917.

19. Frank Trommler and Joseph McVeigh, *America and the Germans: An Assessment of a Three Hundred Year History*, vol. 2, *The Relationship in the Twentieth Century* (Philadelphia: University of Pennsylvania Press, 1985), 8.

20. Trommler and McVeigh, *America and the Germans*, 8.

21. *Boston Herald*, February 1, 1917; Jake Klim, *Attack on Orleans: The World War I Submarine Raid on Cape Cod* (Gloucestershire, UK: History Press, 2014). On July 21, 1918, long after American entry into the war, the German U-boat U-156 attacked and sank five unarmed vessels, including four barges and the tugboat *Perth Amboy*, in the waters off Nauset Beach, in Orleans, Cape Cod. Two planes from the Chatham Naval Air Station fought off the U-boat by dive-bombing it until it submerged. Forty-one people were rescued, and one crew member was wounded by a shell fragment. Summer tourists along the beach watched in horror, for they too were targets of machine-gun fire.

22. Harris, *German-American Interrelations*, 150.

23. "Germany asks Mexico and Japan to Join Her in War on United States," *Boston Herald*, March 1917.

24. "3000 Bostonians Urge State of War Declared," *Boston Herald*, April 1, 1917.

25. "3000 Bostonians Urge State of War Declared."

26. "President Wilson Proclaims War: Sends Out Notice to the World; Calls for Nation to Rally to Flag," *Boston Herald*, April 7, 1917.

27. "S.S. Canadian Torpedoed," *Boston Herald*, April 6, 1917.

28. "Supposed German Vessel Is Sighted 50 Miles South of Island," *Boston Herald*, April 7, 1917.

29. Burrage, "Albert Cameron Burrage," 113.

30. Joseph Garland, *The Gold Coast: The North Shore, 1890–1929* (Manchester, MA: Commonwealth Editions, 1998), 238, 298–99, 301; Burrage, "Albert Cameron Burrage," 360; personal conversation with Garland, 1998.

31. "Francis Bellamy, the Pledge of Allegiance, the Bellamy Salute, & Edward Bellamy," http://rexcurry.net; Margarette S. Miller, *Twenty-Three Words: A Biography of Francis Bellamy: Author of the Pledge of Allegiance* (Printcraft Press, 1976), 103, 257.

32. John W. Baer, *The Allegiance, a Centennial History, 1892–1992* (Annapolis, MD: Free State Press, 1992).

33. Hobsbawm and Ranger, *Invention of Tradition*, 11, 30.

34. David M. Kennedy, *Over Here: The First World War and American Society* (New York: Oxford University Press, 2004), 150.

35. Kennedy, *Over Here*, 49.

36. Kennedy, *Over Here*, 136.

37. "To Camouflage State House Dome as Protection against Air Raids. A Grim Reminder That the Terrors of War Are Nearing Boston Will Be Apparent to Bostonians within a Few Days . . . the Gilded Dome of the State House Is the Most Conspicuous Object in Boston, as the City Is Seen from the City or from the Air," *Boston Herald*, June 6, 1918; Brett Howard, *Boston—a Social History* (New York: Hawthorn, 1976), 244–48.

38. "Will Provide $8,000,000 for Port of Boston: Army Construction Program Includes Work in this City; Make Boston Great Shipping Point for Army; Plan of $8,000,000 Terminal Hailed with Delight by Business Men," *Boston Herald*, February 13, 1918.

39. "Commonwealth Pier Joins The U.S. Navy: Officially Known as the 'U.S. Receiving Ship Annex' Great Pier Now 'Home' for Nearly 1000 Men of New England Naval Militia—Will Stay a Ship Until War Ends," *Boston Herald*, April 15, 1917.

40. Howard, *Boston*, 247–48.

41. Brian Fitzgerald, "General Pershing's Legacy Stands Tall in Memorabilia Collection," *BU Bridge* 5, no. 14 (November 23, 2001), https://www.bu.edu/bridge/archive/2001/11-23/pershing.htm.

42. Burrage, "Albert Cameron Burrage," 344. Albert Burrage offered his hospital on Bumpkin Island to the war effort, and he gave his yacht to the navy, which was outfitted with weapons as a harbor defense. "Burrage Offers Hospital and Yacht to the Navy," *Boston Herald*, March 28, 1917.

43. Jennifer Keene, *Doughboys, the Great War, and the Remaking of America* (Baltimore: Johns Hopkins University Press, 2001). Initially, selective service included men aged twenty-one to thirty, but, by 1918, that number expanded to include eighteen to forty-five-year-olds. Conscription, in theory, attempted to create a fair system that spread the burden of service equally among the states. One in five soldiers was an immigrant, however, and African Americans were overrepresented as well, calling into question the fairness of the draft system. Kennedy, *Over Here*, 94.

44. "Governors Deplore Roosevelt Speech: 'Rash and Unwise' Says Haines of Maine; Others Support President; See 7,000 Militia PARADE Massachusetts Gives Demonstration of Preparedness," *New York Times*, August 27, 1915; "Plattsburg List Is Full: New England Alone Has More Than 4000 Recommended to Attend: More Than 4000 New England Men Have Been Recommended to Attend Officer's Training Camp at Plattsburg."

45. Anatole Sykley, "Boston at War," *Over the Top Magazine of the World War I Centennial* (May 2009): 10. Sykley records that 125 MIT alumni were killed in action.

46. Clyde W. Barrow, *Universities and the Capitalist State: Corporate Liberalism and the Reconstruction of American Higher Education, 1894–1928* (Madison: University of Wisconsin Press, 1990), 135, 142, 283; *Boston Herald*, April 28, 1917.

47. *New York Times*, March 9, 1917.

48. Sykley, "Boston at War," 9.

49. Brian Fitzgerald, "General Pershing's Legacy Stands Tall in Memorabilia Collection," *B.U. Bridge*, http://www.bu.edu/bridge/archive/2001/11-23/pershing.htm. The Pershing Collection is displayed at the Military Science Department at Pershing House at Boston University.

General Pershing's grandson, Colonel John W. Pershing, is a Boston University Alumni.

50. Boston Public Library Print Department, Leslie Jones Collection, 1917.

51. "Mrs. Cynthia E. Hollis of 1780 Beacon Street, Brookline Has Promised to Give the Mayor $100 to Be Spent in Hiring Buglers to Tour Greater Boston in Automobiles to Encourage Recruiting," *Boston Herald*, April 1917.

52. Alan Seeger's brother, pacifist and musicologist Charles Seeger and his wife, composer Ruth Crawford Seeger, are the parents of American folk singer Pete Seeger.

53. *Boston Herald*, May 27, 1917.
Rendezvous—I have a rendezvous with Death
At some disputed barricade
When Spring comes back with rustling shade
And apple-blossoms fill the air—
When Spring brings back blue days and fair
It may be he shall take my hand
And lead me into his dark land
And close my eyes and quench my breath—
It may be I shall pass him still
I have a rendezvous with Death
On some scarred slope of battered hill
When Spring comes round again this year
And the first meadow-flowers appear
God knows 'twere better to be deep
Pillowed in silk and scented down
Where love throbs out in blissful sleep
Pulse nigh to pulse, and breath to breath
Where hushed awakenings are dear
But I've a rendezvous with Death
At midnight in some flaming town
When Spring trips north again this year
And I to my pledged word am true
I shall not fail that rendezvous.

54. "City Registration for Military Draft Swamps Officials: 75,767 Willing Men Crowd Booths and Enrollment Continues Through the Night," *Boston Herald*, June 5, 1917.

55. Merrill Katz, *The Great Boston Trivia and Fact Book* (New York: Turner, 1999), 51. More than 198,000 men from Massachusetts served in World War I, some 5,700 died.

56. Voluntary Committee of the Regiment, *History of the 101st United States Engineers American Expeditionary Forces, 1917—1918—1919* (Cambridge, MA: University Press, 1926), 40–51.

57. "12,000 Army Engineers to Go to France," *Boston Herald*, May 1917. Twelve thousand army engineers left for France in May 1917.

58. "Dynamite Blasts 'Shell' Hole on Training Field at Camp Devens in Ayer: Then 200 Soldiers Are Set to Work Enlarging Crater—Bombs and Grenade on the Instruction Program," *Boston Herald,* November 13, 1917; Voluntary Committee of the Regiment, *History of the 101st,* 22–39.

59. Sykley, "Boston at War," 12. The Twenty-Sixth Division recorded twelve thousand casualties, including both killed and wounded soldiers. Of the 3,800 men in the 101st Infantry, 560 were killed in action.

60. Sykley, "Boston at War," 8.

61. *Hope, Valor, and Inspiration: 1896–1918; The World of George Dilboy—Greek Immigrant and American Hero,* Somerville Museum, Somerville, Massachusetts, 2006–7. George Dilboy died during the war and became an icon of patriotism and national pride for Boston's Greek community, which traces its ancestry to Dilboy and has celebrations in honor of him still.

62. Interview with Anthony Pierro and his nephew, Nick Pierro, January 2007. Tony came to America at sixteen and enlisted five years later with the US Army to fight in France. He was a private in Battery E, 320 Field Artillery, sailing overseas on May 18, 1918, and serving in the Aisne, St. Mihiel, and Meuse Argonne offenses. Tony died one month after my interview, on February 12, 2007. He was Massachusetts' oldest surviving soldier, living to the age of 110. He recalled that New England Italians were happy to fight the Germans in World War I. He put the ugliness of war out of his mind when he returned to Boston and got a good job at General Electric with excellent benefits. He "never looked back," recalling that he "never wanted to return to Italy. Things were really better in America," and he was "proud to be an American."

63. "Local Doctors Going to Front: Dr. Cushing Ordered to Prepare His Hospital Unit for Active Service," *Boston Herald,* May 1, 1917.

64. "Boston Woman Makes New Faces for Poilus," *Boston Herald,* May 19, 1917.

65. Sargent's most famous war-era painting, a room-sized mural called *Gassed* (1918), portrays a standing row of wounded soldiers after a mustard gas attack. It hangs in the Imperial War Museum in London.

66. The inscription above the sculpture reads:

While a bright future beckoned
they freely gave their lives and fondest hopes
for us and our allies
that we might learn from them courage
in peace to spend
our lives making a better world for others.

The sanctuary also recognizes four German students who gave their lives for their country. In 2001, Harvard College unveiled a plaque in this same sanctuary to honor three Radcliffe College nurses who were not recognized just after the war.

67. The Civil War Commission erected cemeteries to their war dead. The United States honored those who participated in World War I with public sculptures, murals, and parks.

68. "23 Towns Exceed Quotas on Loans," *Boston Herald*, April 7, 1918.

69. *Boston Herald,* June 16, 1917.

70. Howard, *Boston*, 244–48.

71. *Boston Herald*, April 6, 1918.

72. "Thousands Sing and Cheer on Boston Common. Patriotic Mass Meeting under Auspices of City Draws Many to Hear Major and Military Men Speak upon Needs of Nation," *Boston Herald*, April 4, 1917.

73. "20,000 Sing National Anthem when Flag Is Unfurled at Chelsea," *Boston Herald*, April 23, 1917.

74. Albert E. George, *Pictorial History of the Twenty-Sixth Division United States Army* (Boston: Ball, 1920), 301–2.

75. "6000 State Troops to Parade in Honor of the Visiting French," *Boston Herald*, May 11, 1917.

76. "Preparedness—Excitement—Innocence—Boston's Big Store Employees Are Hard at Work Learning Military How's and Why's: Scores of Stores Are At It," *Boston Herald*, May 13, 1917.

77. "5000 Boy Scouts Drill in the Stadium Today: Girl Scouts of the Bay State . . . Rally in Boston Arena Come Next Saturday," *Boston Herald*, June 9, 1917.

78. "Fighting Tank Parades Today," *Boston Herald*, April 5, 1918.

79. *Boston Herald*, May 7, 1917.

80. "How Women Can Aid U.S.: Raise Own Vegetables, Can Own Fruit and Prevent Waste at Home," *Boston Herald*, April 12, 1917.

81. "14,000,000 Pounds of Frozen Fish for Allied Armies: Plant Turns Out 75,000 Pounds of Coffee Daily," *Boston Herald* May 5, 1917.

Chapter Three

1. John U. Bacon, *The Great Halifax Explosion: A World War I Story of Treachery, Tragedy, and Extraordinary Heroism* (New York: Harper Collins, 2017), 8, 168. *Mont Blanc* carried one of the largest cargoes of explosives ever loaded onto a ship: sixty-two tons of gun cotton, almost 250 tons of combustible benzol airline fuel, 250 tons of TNT, 2,366 tons of picric acid, packed barrel to barrel, crate to crate, with slabs of flammable plywood between them.

2. "Halifax is Swept by Blizzard. Many Die by Cold and Hunger. Raging Snowstorm Blows through Unprotected Buildings. Rescuers Forced to Suspend Efforts—Injured Buried in Ruins. Perish with Lookers on Helpless—Outlook Is Appalling—Population Threatened with Epidemic of Pneumonia—Trains Bring Relief from All Quarters Held Up in

Drifts—Stricken City Now Faces Famine—Many Victims Will be Buried as Nameless Dead. All Blankets Requisitioned for Hospitals," *Boston Herald,* December 8, 1917.

3. "Halifax Almost Wiped Out: Crews Killed on Vessels in Port; Telegraphers Struck Dead at Desk Four Miles Off," *Boston Herald,* December 7, 1917; "Boston Leads in Relief," *Boston Herald,* December 9, 1917.

4. Higham, *Strangers,* 196.

5. *Boston Herald,* January 18, 1918.

6. "Maple Sugar Replaces White," *Boston Herald,* June 2, 1917.

7. "Finds Tons of Sugar in Back Bay. Inspector Uncovers 40,000 Pounds in Furniture Warehouse. Held for Candy Makers. . . . 40, 000 Pounds under Lock and Key Had Been Located at the Boston Storage Warehouse," *Boston Herald,* November 13, 1917.

8. "Many Women Hurt in Sugar Riot at Brockton: Mob of 15,000 Storms City Hall," *Boston Herald,* November 19, 1917.

9. Kennedy, *Over Here,* 117. Newspapers started mentioning food shortages in the fall of 1917 into the winter of 1918.

10. "Mrs. Godfrey L. Cabot is Pushing Campaign to Raise Chickens. Any Woman with Ground 10 Feet Square Ought to Have 20 Chickens. Care Takes Only 15 Minutes a Day. Is Profitable If One Does All the Work," *Boston Herald,* April 22, 1918.

11. Kennedy, *Over Here,* 123. "Ignoring Nation-Wide Protest, Garfield Puts Fuel Order into Effect," *Boston Herald,* January 18, 1918; *Boston Herald,* January 6, 1918.

12. "President Upholds Garfield Order as Necessity of War. Hundreds of Plants in East Shut Down. All Industries Except Those Making "Essentials" Obey Decree—Thousands of Workers Made Idle. Mills Full of War Orders. Nearly Half Machinery Making Woolen Goods for Government," *Boston Herald,* January 19, 1918.

13. "Fuel Committee Forbids Sale of Coal to Boston Business Houses and Office Buildings: New England Swells Chorus of Protest at Garfield Order," *Boston Herald,* January 1918.

14. *Boston Herald,* January 6, 1918.

15. James R. Green and Hugh Carter Donahue, *Boston's Workers: A Labor History* (Boston: Trustees of the Public Library, 1979), 97.

16. Green and Donahue, *Boston's Workers,* 97. Telephone operators went on strike for a week in 1919. They won their strike, getting back pay, better wages, and a cafeteria.

17. Boston police went on strike after the war in 1919. They lost their strike, and the entire police force was replaced.

18. "Elevated Employees May Strike: Shipyard Strike Is Called Off," *Boston Herald,* February 20, 1918; "Telephone Girls to Vote on Strike: Boston Police Officers Were Talking during the Spring about Unionizing," *Boston Herald,* February 25, 1918; "Western Union Men Ordered to Strike Week from Today," *Boston Herald,* July 1, 1918; "Government Ready to Seize

Telegraph and Telephone Lines: U.S. May Settle Lowell Strike; Federal Intervention is Expected by Both Sides Now," *Boston Herald*, July 2, 1918; "Carmen Win Wage Advance Strike Is Off," *Boston Herald*, February 28, 1918; "Wool Men Will Make Protest: Boston Committee to Go to Washington," *Boston Herald*, March 2, 1918; "All Strikes Off Until War Ends: Adoption of a Plan to Prevent Strikes Had Been Achieved," *Boston Herald*, March 29, 1918.

19. *Boston Herald*, January 20, 1918. Residents became depressed without entertainment or educational outlets to attend. Somerville Hospital employees came up with a clever way to bring lightheartedness to the problem. During their annual minstrel show fundraiser, guests were asked to bring ten-pound bags of coal to keep the hall open.

20. "Harvard Teacher Opposes Daylight Saving Bill: Measure Rejected Last Year Finds New Advocates in Congress; Million Tons of Coal to be Saved," *Boston Herald*, January 1918.

21. "War Workers' Week on Today: Opens with Display of Photographs of Actual Trench Fighting. Pictures Which Have Revealed to Wives and Parents the Circumstances under Which Their Husbands and Sons Gave Their Lives, Pictures That Show in Detail the Character of the Country over Which the German Army Is Now Dashing to Wholesale Immolation," *Boston Herald*, March 29, 1918.

22. "Artist to the Front: Yankees Strike on Aisne Front," *Boston Herald*, February 22, 1918.

23. Higham, *Strangers*, 214.

24. "Bay State Boys on Pershing's Latest List," *Boston Herald*, April 13, 1918.

25. Ferguson, *Pity of War*, 24.

26. Clark, *Sleepwalkers*, xxi.

27. Tipton, *History of Modern Germany*, 270.

28. Post-traumatic stress disorder is a condition and definition officially added to the *Diagnostic and Statistical Manual* of mental disorders in 1980.

29. "198,000 Men from MA Served, and Some 5, 700 Died," *Boston Herald*, May 26, 1918.

30. "Cape Cod Hit by the War," *Boston Herald*, April 16, 1918.

31. At 4 p.m. on December 10, Americans throughout the country sang the "Star-Spangled Banner" in workplaces, office buildings, schools, and homes in honor of the Halifax Explosion victims.

32. Harold Lasswell, *Propaganda Technique in the World War* (Cambridge: Massachusetts Institute of Technology Press, 1971). Lippman invented the phrase in 1921.

33. George Creel, *How We Advertised America, the First Telling of the Amazing Story of the Committee on Public Information that Carried the Gospel of Americanism to Every Corner of the Globe* (New York: Harper and Brothers, 1920), 3.

34. "Find Ground Glass in Peanut Butter," *Boston Herald*, February 4, 1918; "Report Is Absurd, Says Chocolate Co. Official," *Boston Herald*,

February 10, 1918. "Officials of the Massachusetts Chocolate Company, regarding with the utmost incredulity, the report from Camp Dix, N.J. that ground glass was found in candy made at their factory, yesterday sent on to the camp a special representative to demand an investigation which they declare will exonerate the company from stigma of unfound assertions." "Warns of Glass from Bakeries," *Boston Herald*, March 21, 1918.

35. "Dynamite Bomb Is Found Near Cordage Plant: Boys Playing near Factory of Plymouth Concern Discovered Missile Which Would Have Caused Heavy Damage," *Boston Herald*, March 20, 1917.

36. "Catch Two Suspects Near Holbrook Factory," *Boston Herald*, April 8, 1917.

37. "Plot to Wreck State's Pier: Telephone Girl Reports Hearing Men Talk in German of Using a Bomb," *Boston Herald*, April 13, 1917.

38. "Tried to Kill Dr. Cabot with Bomb at Door: Persons Assumed to Resent Strong Anti-German Attitude of Doctor Leave Explosive in Vestibule of His Home—Fuse Goes Out—Three Previous Attacks Recorded," *Boston Herald*, March 21, 1917. Cabot found the bomb and hurled it into the Charles River, where the fuse went out.

39. "Bomb Exploded under Trolley in Cambridge," *Boston Herald*, March 28, 1917. "Cambridge took its turn in the bomb scare series last night. Eight trolley car passengers, a motorman and a conductor had the fright of their lives. The front trains ran over something on the rails, blowing the roof and windows out. A thick black smoke filled the car. No one was injured."

40. Creel, *How We Advertised America*.

41. Walton H. Rawls, *Wake up, America! World War I and the American Poster* (New York: Abbeville Press, 1988).

42. Byron Farwell, *Over There: The United States in the Great War, 1917–1918* (New York: W. W. Norton, 1999), 124.

43. Farwell, *Over There*, 24.

44. Scott Eyman, *Lion of Hollywood: The Life and Legend of Louis B. Mayer* (New York: Simon and Schuster, 2005), 98.

45. "Boston Yachtsmen Work in War Service," *Boston Herald*, November 4, 1917. Theodore Roosevelt and Kaiser Wilhelm took part in a series of yacht races between the German and American teams prior to the war. Germany entertained TR and many American elites at Kiel and Hanover, and Boston men entertained German high officials at the Eastern Yacht Club on the North Shore of Boston in 1901 and 1907. To American elites, Germans turned from friend to foe with the onset of war.

46. Luebke, *Bonds*, 144, 68. This was an interesting response, given Theodore Roosevelt's Dutch German ancestry, and his competitive yachting escapades with the kaiser.

47. Luebke, *Bonds*, 145–50; Albert Shaw, *The Messages and Papers of Woodrow Wilson* (New York: George H. Doran, 1924), 150–52.

48. Luebke, *Bonds*, 209.

49. David Cole, *Enemy Aliens: Double Standards and Constitutional Freedoms in the War on Terrorism* (New York: New Press, 2003), 92.

50. John C. Miller, *Crisis in Freedom: The Alien and Sedition Acts* (Boston: Little Brown, 1951), 52–53.

51. Cole, *Enemy Aliens*, 86.

52. "More than 3000 Apply for Right to Enter Barred Areas," *Boston Herald*, June 7, 1917.

53. Debs's sentence was commuted in 1921.

54. Higham, *Strangers*, 196.

55. Don H. Tolzmann, *German-Americans in the World Wars*, vol. 1, *The Anti-German Hysteria of World War One* (New Providence: KG Saur, 1995), 195.

56. Cole, *Enemy Aliens*, 106.

57. Jorg Nagler, "Nationale Minoritaten im Krieg: 'Feindliche Auslander' und die amerikanische Heimatfront wahrend des Ersten Weltkriegs" [National minorities in war: "Enemy foreigners" and the American home front during World War I], *Journal of American History* 89, no. 2 (2002): 672–90.

58. US Department of Justice, "History: The U. S. Marshals during World War I; Protection of the Homefront," August 9, 2007, accessed November 25, 2012, https://www.usmarshals.gov/history/ww1/ww1.htm; Higham, *Strangers*, 210; Cole, *Enemy Aliens*, 106; Chad Millman, *The Detonators: The Secret Plot to Destroy America and an Epic Hunt for Justice* (Boston: Little, Brown, 2006). The most well-known act of sabotage is the 1916 Black Tom munitions factory explosion in Jersey City, New Jersey. Frank Holt, alias Eric Muenter, a German American spy, posed as a German-language professor at Cornell and Harvard and planted a bomb in the US Capitol, shot J. P. Morgan for funding the allies, and committed suicide while in police custody.

59. Christopher Capozzola, *Uncle Sam Wants You: World War I and the Making of the Modern American Citizen* (New York: Oxford University Press, 2008), 210.

60. Luebke, *Bonds*, 157.

61. Luebke, *Bonds*, 237.

62. Thomas Fleming, "The Flames of Hatred, Then—and Now: The Illusion of Victory; America in World War I," *Once upon a Time . . .* (blog), May 13, 2004, http://powerofnarrative.blogspot.com/2004/05/flames-of-hatred-then-and-now.html.

63. "Urges America to Shoot Spies: Marcosson Declares Man Who Even Thinks Peace Now is a Traitor. Tells of Travels in War Countries. Isaac F. Marcosson of the Saturday Evening Post, Speaking at the Boston City Club Last Night on 'The Business of the War,'" *Boston Herald*, March 1918.

64. "Urges America to Shoot Spies."

65. "Charges Plot to Stir Negroes Here to Revolt: German Spies at Work, Says Pastor of Zion A. M. E. Church—He Would Have Them Shot for Treason," *Boston Herald*, April 8, 1917.

66. Farwell, *Over There*, 149.

67. "Kaiser Chained at Gilchrist's: Patriotic Americans to Overthrow Prussian Rule," *Boston Herald*, May 5, 1918.

68. Jack Tager, *Boston Riots: Three Centuries of Social Violence* (Boston: Northeastern University Press), 149.

69. Tager, *Boston Riots*, 148.

70. Luebke, *Bonds*, 9; Sonneborn, *German-Americans*, 84; Robert Siegel and Art Silverman, "During World War I, U.S. Government Propaganda Erased German Culture," *All Things Considered*, April 7, 2017, http://www.npr.org/2017/04/17/523044253/during-world-war-1-u-s-government-propaganda-erased-german-culture.

71. "Illinoisan Lynched for Disloyalty," *Chicago Daily Tribune*, April 5, 1918; Donald R. Hickey, "The Prager Affair: A Study in Wartime Hysteria," *Journal of the Illinois State Historical Society* (Summer 1969): 126–27.

72. Luebke, *Bonds*, 22.

73. Duane C. S. Stoltzfus, *Pacifists in Chains: The Persecution of Hutterites in the Great War* (Baltimore: John Hopkins University Press, 2013), 150.

74. John Hofer, *The History of the Hutterites* (Altona: D. W. Friesen and Sons,1988), 62; Stoltzfus, *Pacifists in Chains*, 115.

75. Frederick C. Luebke, *Germans in the New World: Essays in the History of Immigration* (Champaign: University of Illinois Press, 1999), 40; personal conversation with Dora Maendal of the Fairholme Hutterite Colony of Manitoba, Canada, October 20, 2017.

76. National Archives Records Administration, US District Court for the Second (Mankato) Division of the District of Minnesota. John Meintz sued thirty-two of the men who attacked him. The judge acquitted the men and argued that evidence proved that Meintz was disloyal. In 1922, four years after the attack, anti-German hysteria had abated, and Meintz won an appeal in the case.

77. "German Flees, Escaping Rope—Portland Man Has Close Call Following Alleged Disloyal Talk—Knocked Down by a Patriot," *Boston Herald*, June 4, 1918.

78. "Italians Attack Idle German Ships: Riotous Outbreak in Boston Attends the Sailing of 1400 Reservists for War," *New York Times*, August 16, 1915.

79. "Patriotic Climate in Boston: Made Him Kneel and Kiss Flag," *Boston Herald*, March 3, 1918.

80. Olge, *Ambitious Brew*, 174.

81. Olge, *Ambitious Brew*, 175.

82. Nisbet and Norris, *Busch-Reisinger Museum*, 10–11, 27–28. Kuno Francke, professor of German culture at Harvard, was curator of the museum during World War I and instrumental to its survival.

83. La Verne J. Rippley, The *German-Americans: Immigrants in America* (Boston: Twayne, 1976), 84.

84. Richard T. Flood, *The Story of Noble and Greenough School, 1866–1966* (Dedham, MA: Noble and Greenough, 1966), 53–55; Noble and Greenough Archives.

85. "Volkmann School Lockers Burned," *Boston Herald*, May 26, 1918.

86. Flood, *The Story of Noble and Greenough*, 53–55.

87. *New York Times*, November 23, 1917.

88. Whitehill, *Seidel*, 6.

89. Sykley, "Boston at War," 5. In addition to the support that some German Americans received from the Boston Police Department, a Roxbury organization called the Friends of Irish Freedom offered its sympathetic support during World War I, passing a resolution that reminded city residents of German Americans' patriotic service during the Civil War.

90. "Drop German in Boston Schools," *Boston Herald*, June 3, 1918.

91. Interview with Martha Engler, November 12, 2007, and December 16, 2007, at Deutsches Altenheim Nursing Home, West Roxbury, Massachusetts.

92. Kurt Vonnegut, *Palm Sunday* (New York: Delacorte Press, 1981), 21.

93. Personal conversation with Reverend William T. Schmidt, at the Holy Trinity German Catholic Church, December 9, 2007.

94. Luebke, *Bonds*, 245.

95. Luebke, *Bonds*, 245.

96. Hoffman, *Local Attachments*.

97. The concept of total war is defined by a lack of restriction regarding weapons, territory, combatants, or laws.

98. Higham, *Strangers*, 183–242.

99. Luebke, *Bonds*, 268.

100. Kazal, *Becoming Old Stock*. As Russell Kazal tells us, under wartime pressure, many German Americans "became old stock" and erased their ethnic identities.

101. Kathleen N. Conzen, "Germans," in *Harvard Encyclopedia of American Ethnic Groups*, ed. Stephan Thernstrom (Cambridge, MA: Harvard University Press, 1980), 409–22; John A. Hawgood, *The Tragedy of German-America: The Germans in the United States of America during the Nineteenth Century—and After* (New York: Putnam, 1940).

Chapter Four

1. Perry, *Life and Letters*, 321.

2. Muck, *Dr. Karl Muck*, 104. "Arrest Karl Muck as an Enemy Alien," *New York Times*, March 26, 1918.

3. John Koegel, *Music in German Immigrant Theater: New York City 1840–1940* (Rochester, NY: University of Rochester Press, 2009), 1.

4. DiMaggio, "Cultural Entrepreneurship," 33–50.

5. DiMaggio, "The Problem of Chicago," in Rosenbaum and Beckert, *American Bourgeoisie*, 219.

6. Horowitz, *Moral Fire*, 47.

7. Horowitz, "Reclaiming the Past," 33.

8. "Dr. Karl Muck—the New Conductor of the Boston Symphony Orchestra and His Career," *New York Times*, June 10, 1906.

9. Shanet, *Philharmonic*, 200.

10. "The World of Music," *Constitution*, October 21, 1906.

11. Angela M. Blake, *How New York Became American: 1890–1924* (Baltimore: John Hopkins, 2006), 6.

12. Blake, *How New York*, 6.

13. Blake, *How New York*, 51.

14. Blake, *How New York*, 59, 69.

15. Blake, *How New York*, 81–83

16. Blake, *How New York*, 8.

17. Blake, *How New York*, 49, 53.

18. Blake, *How New York*, 94.

19. Edward White, *The Tastemaker Carl Van Vechten and the Birth of Modern America* (New York: Farrar, Straus and Giroux, 2014), 57.

20. White, *The Tastemaker*, 135, 78.

21. John Koegel, *Music in German Immigrant Theater*, 97, 35. Another German neighborhood included broadly in Klein Deutschland is Yorkville on the Upper East Side, which attracted audiences to its Deutsches Theater on East Street, the Yorkville Casino, numerous cabarets, churches, restaurants, and shops.

22. Koegel, *Music in German Immigrant Theater*, 2.

23. Koegel, *Music in German Immigrant Theater*, 32–35, 44.

24. Koegel, *Music in German Immigrant Theater*, 37, 53. Oscar Hammerstein I (1847–1919), got his start as manager at the Stadt Theater, and went on to open several opera houses in New York, throughout the United States, and in London. His grandson, Oscar Hammerstein II became Broadway's most influential lyricists.

25. Adolf Neuendorff, former violinist with the New York Philharmonic, opened the Germania Theater and championed the works of German composers, playing an important role in bringing opera to New York audiences.

26. Koegel, *Music in German Immigrant Theater*, 85. By the turn of the century, the Atlantic Garden offered vaudeville acts, boxing matches, and motion pictures. John Koegel and Jonas Westover, "Beethoven and Beer: Orchestral Music in German Beer Gardens in Nineteenth Century New York City," in Spitzer, *American Orchestras*, 150.

27. Koegel, *Music in German Immigrant Theater*, 93, 97.

28. Koegel, "Beethoven and Beer," 152; Koegel, *Music in German Immigrant Theater*, 95.

29. Koegel "Beethoven and Beer,"130.

30. Spitzer, *American Orchestras*, 104.

31. "German Opera at the Stadt," *New York Times*, March 1, 1871.

32. DiMaggio, "The Problem of Chicago," in Rosenbaum and Beckert, *American Bourgeoisie*, 107; Walters, "Afterword," in Spitzer, *American Orchestras*, 456.

33. DiMaggio, "The Problem of Chicago," in Rosenbaum and Beckert, *American Bourgeoisie*, 209.

34. Spitzer, *American Orchestras*, 370.

35. Adrienne Fried Block, "Thinking about Serious Music in New York, 1842–1882," in Spitzer, *American Orchestras*, 450.

36. Ora Frishberg Saloman, "The Leopold Damrosch Orchestra, 1877–78," in Spitzer, *American Orchestras*, 283.

37. Michael Broyles, "Bourgeois Appropriation of Music," in Rosenbaum and Beckert, *American Bourgeoisie*, 233.

38. Broyles, "Bourgeois Appropriation of Music," in Rosenbaum and Beckert, *American Bourgeoisie*, 108–9.

39. Jaher, *Urban Establishment*, 275.

40. Jaher, *Urban Establishment*, 275.

41. Russell B. Adams, *The Boston Money Tree* (Boston: Thomas Y. Crowell, 1977), 219.

42. Adams, *Boston Money Tree*, 140, 220, 261–74. Higginson's money rested in railroad and copper investments and inherited money. Higginson was considered Boston's leading financier. By 1925, Lee, Higginson and Company had moved out of its State Street office to a smaller space after an investment in the Swedish Match Company had failed. Lee, Higginson and Company closed its doors in the late 1920s.

43. Adams, *Boston Money Tree*, 267; Hofstadter, *Age of Reform*, 137.

44. Barbara Haws, "Ureli Corelli Hill: An American Musician's European Travels and the Creation of the New York Philharmonic," in Spitzer, *American Orchestras*, 348–63.

45. Haws, "Ureli Corelli Hill," in Spitzer, *American Orchestras*, 348–63.

46. Broyles, "Bourgeois Appropriation," in Rosenbaum and Beckert, *American Bourgeoisie*, 238.

47. Shanet, *Philharmonic*, 110; Horowitz, *Understanding Toscanini*, 70.

48. Haws, "Ureli Corelli Hill," in Spitzer, *American Orchestras*, 363.

49. Mark Clague, "Building the American Symphony Orchestra: The Nineteenth Century Roots of a Twenty-First Century Musical Institution," in Spitzer, *American Orchestras*, 27; John Graziano, "Invisible Instruments: Theater Orchestras in NY, 1850–1900," in Spitzer, *American Orchestras*, 110. Because there were so many theaters in New York, musicians could fill their weekly schedule with performance opportunities and provide a yearly income.

50. DiMaggio, "Cultural Entrepreneurship," 37.

51. DiMaggio, "Cultural Entrepreneurship," 34.

52. *The Longest Run,* New York Philharmonic Brochure, New York Philharmonic Archives. Ahlquist, "Performance to 'Permanence,'" in Spitzer, *American Orchestras,* 156.

53. Shanet, *Philharmonic,* 206.

54. Broyles, "Bourgeois Appropriation," in Rosenbaum and Beckert, *American Bourgeoisie,* 241–43; Ahlquist, "Performance to "Permanence," in Spitzer, *American Orchestras,* 156.

55. Shanet, *Philharmonic,* 294.

56. Karen J. Blair, *The Torchbearers: Women and Their Amateur Arts Associations in America, 1890–1930* (Bloomington: Indiana University Press, 1994), 4; Linda Whitesitt, "Women as 'Keepers of Culture': Music Clubs, Community Concert Series, and Symphony Orchestras," in Locke and Barr, *Cultivating Music,* 65–86.

57. Shanet, *Philharmonic,* 110.

58. Shanet, *Philharmonic,* 209.

59. Shanet, *Philharmonic,* 206.

60. Martin Goldsmith, *The Inextinguishable Symphony—a True Story of Music and Love in Nazi Germany* (New Jersey: John Wiley and Sons, 2000), 201.

61. Shanet, *Philharmonic,* 210.

62. Shanet, *Philharmonic,* 229.

63. Boston Symphony used only half of its musicians on tours.

64. Horowitz, *Understanding Toscanini,* 71.

65. Horowitz, *Understanding Toscanini,* 70.

66. Shanet, *Philharmonic,* 218.

67. Shanet, *Philharmonic,* 222.

68. Shanet, *Philharmonic,* 221.

69. Shanet, *Philharmonic,* 226.

70. Shanet, *Philharmonic,* 213.

71. Shanet, *Philharmonic,* 230

72. Shanet, *Philharmonic,* 226.

73. New York Philharmonic Archives, July 22, 1913, director's minutes.

74. New York Philharmonic Archives, administrative listing notebook, Papers of Felix Leifels, 1903–1921 Managing Director February 21, 1910, Mahler and New York Philharmonic letter. Mrs. Katie Wilson Greene to Richard Arnold, April 11, 1910.

75. Spitzer, *American Orchestras,* 22.

76. Glaze and Wolf, *And the Band,* 57.

77. Mark Clague, "Building the American Symphony Orchestra: The Nineteenth Century Roots of a Twenty-First Century Musical Institution," in Spitzer, *American Orchestras,* 49; DiMaggio, "The Problem of Chicago," in Rosenbaum and Beckert, *American Bourgeoisie,* 215.

78. Glaze and Wolf, *And the Band,* 54.

79. Glaze and Wolf, *And the Band,* 54.

80. New York Philharmonic Archives, April 9, 1914, director's minutes.

81. New York Philharmonic Archives, April 9, 1914, director's minutes.

82. New York Philharmonic Archives, April 9, 1914, director's minutes.

83. Faucett, *George Whitefield Chadwick*, 287.

84. New York Philharmonic Archives, February 1915, director's minutes.

85. New York Philharmonic Archives, March 4, 1915, director's minutes.

86. New York Philharmonic Archives, March 4, 1915, director's minutes.

87. New York Philharmonic Archives, April 1916, director's minutes.

88. *New York Herald*, March 16, 1918.

89. "Would Abolish German Music," *Boston Herald*, March 29, 1915.

90. "Would Abolish German Music."

91. "Would Abolish German Music." "Suspect's Mail Is Read," *Boston Post*, November 12, 1919.

92. "Would Abolish German Music."

93. "Kaiser Wilhelm's Birthday," *Boston Herald*, January 28, 1915. Between August of 1914 and April of 1917, several German ships took refuge in American harbors, for attempting to cross the Atlantic would have been suicidal during wartime. Once the United States declared war on Germany, these ships were interned and their crews were taken to temporarily holding stations such as Gallops Island in Boston Harbor before being interned as prisoners of war in interior camps.

94. FBI Records, 1909–1921, Old German Files, Baron Ferdinand von Scholley.

95. On December 29, 1912, the *New York Times* reported that Muck had tonsillitis while in Boston, and, on January 17, 1916, the *Boston Transcript* reported that Muck had required a tonsillitis operation years before, and he feared a reoccurring problem.

96. Henry Taylor Parker, "Music and Musicians: The Wrong of Current Gossip about Dr. Muck. Malicious and Wholly Unfounded Tales that He Declined to Conduct for Mme. Melba," *Boston Transcript*, January 17, 1916.

97. Parker, "Music and Musicians."

98. "Boston Rushes Relief," *Boston Post*, December 7, 1917; Anita Muck to Mrs. Gardner, June 29, 1920, Isabella Stewart Gardner Museum Archives. "Yesterday we were so pleased to receive a very dear letter from Nellie from London." Melba had been in London helping Guglielmo Marconi transmit Britain's first official radio broadcast.

99. "New York was entertained last week with the report that for ten days Dr. Muck had been feigning illness because he and Mr. Higginson were at odds," *Boston Transcript*, May 6, 1916.

100. Horowitz, *Classical Music in America*, 79. Parker was an eccentric man who wore a German cavalry coat and a fedora and carried a bamboo walking stick.

101. Henry Taylor Parker, "The Final Programme of the Season, with a Glance Backward and Forward upon Dr. Muck and Other Matters," *Boston Transcript*, May 6, 1916.

102. Parker, "Final Programme."

103. Shanet, *Philharmonic*, 221.

104. Shanet, *Philharmonic*, 230.

105. Shanet, *Philharmonic*, 230.

106. "Josef Stransky Avows American Sympathies, Symphony Conductor Says Attack on Him Unfair," *American*, April 2, 1918.

107. "Stransky Attack Will Be Ignored," *American*, April 3, 1918.

108. "Stransky Attack Will Be Ignored."

109. "Hermann Oelrichs Dies on a Liner at Sea," *New York Times*, September 6, 1906.

110. George Bessell, *Norddeutscher Lloyd, 1857–1957* (Bremen: Schunemann, 1957), 130–35.

111. "The Allen Collection," *Anchor Line History*, accessed November 21, 2013, www.benjidog.co.uk/allen/Anchor%20Line.html.

112. Jennifer P. McLean, *The Jays of Bedford* (New York: Friends of John Jay Homestead, 1984), 41.

113. Bessell, *Norddeutscher Lloyd*, 130–35; Kenneth T. Jackson, *The Encyclopedia of New York City* (New Haven, CT: Yale University Press, 2010), 854.

114. Sven Beckert, *The Monied Metropolis: New York City and the Consolidation of the American Bourgeoisie, 1859–1896* (New York: Cambridge University Press, 2001), 323.

115. "Ward McAllister Gives out the Official List," *New York Times*, February 16, 1892.

116. *New York Times*, September 4, 1906.

117. Shanet, *Philharmonic*, 228.

118. New York Philharmonic Archives, 1917 director's minutes.

119. New York Philharmonic Archive, March 2, 1916, director's minutes.

120. New York Philharmonic Archives, March 22, 1916, director's minutes.

121. New York Philharmonic Archives, May 7, 1917, director's minutes.

122. New York Philharmonic Archive, Letter File.

123. New York Philharmonic Archives October 15, 1917, director's minutes.

124. New York Philharmonic Archives. October 27, 191,7 director's minutes.

125. New York Philharmonic Archives. January 1918, director's minutes.

126. New York Philharmonic Archives April 18, 1918, director's minutes.

127. "Keen Speculation as to Wealth Left by Hermann Oelrichs," *Dawson Daily News*, October 4, 1906.

128. Blake, *How New York*, 112; Higham, *Strangers*,159.

129. Higham, *Strangers*, 15.

130. Higham, *Strangers*, 17.

131. Panayi, *German Immigrants*, 61.

132. Higham, *Strangers*, 17.

133. Alvaro Vargas Llosa, *Global Crossings: Immigration, Civilization, and America* (Oakland, CA: Independent Institute, 2013), 8, 5, 3.

134. Higham, *Strangers*, 144.

135. Higham, *Strangers*, 4, 8.

136. Blake, *How New York*, 112; Higham, *Strangers*, 159.

137. Higham, *Strangers*, 143.

138. Higham, *Strangers*, 308. Prostitutes, political radicals, criminals, alcoholics, and mentally or physically handicapped people were included in this classification.

139. Perry, *Life and Letters*, 474.

140. "Teuton Ships are Seized," *New York Times*, February 4, 1917.

141. Higham, *Strangers*, 198. Also, see Lucie Jay, "Intern All German Music!," *Musical Leader* 36 (July 1918): 213, for her views on citizenship.

142. Higham, *Strangers*, 115.

143. Higham, *Strangers*, 187, 52.

144. Higham, *Strangers*, 187, 52.

145. Higham, *Strangers*, 130.

146. Beckert, *Monied Metropolis*, 267.

147. Beckert, *Monied Metropolis*, 4, 323; Eric Homberger, *Mrs. Astor's New York: Money and Social Power in a Gilded Age* (New Haven, CT: Yale University Press, 2009), 226.

148. Homberger, *Mrs. Astor's New York*, 226.

149. Mrs. Astor, nee Caroline Webster Schermerhorn, was a New York socialite who determined who was accepted into New York's fashionable aristocratic society.

150. Homberger, *Mrs. Astor's New York*, 226.

151. Beckert, *Monied Metropolis*, 4.

152. The name Knickerbocker refers to New York upper classes whose families descend from the earliest Dutch colony.

153. Homberger, *Mrs. Astor's New York*, 275.

154. Alan Wallach, "The Birth of the American Art Museum," in Rosenbaum and Beckert, *American Bourgeoisie*, 248.

155. McLean, *The Jays of Bedford*, 36–37. William Jay was a member of the City, Century, and Metropolitan Clubs; the New York Historical, Huguenot, St. Nicholas, and American Geographic Society; and the Metropolitan Museum of Art. He was also a director of the Valley Farm Company, Commercial Cable Company, the Manhattan Storage and Warehouse Company, and the New York Cab Company.

156. Homberger, *Mrs. Astor's New York*, 10.

157. Beckert, *Monied Metropolis*, 49; McLean, *The Jays of Bedford*, 38–39. As a new wife of the only male descendent in the Jay family, Lucie "felt it was her prerogative to have what she considered the best guest room and most desirable nursery for her children" at the Jay homestead, taking ownership of bedrooms that rightfully belonged to her in-laws. She often

traveled abroad with her daughters, buying them the most current London fashions, much to their disgust.

158. Lucie Jay was born in 1854 and died in 1931. She was in her mid-sixties during her attacks on Muck.

159. Hobsbawm and Ranger, *Invention of Tradition*, 9.

160. McLean, *The Jays of Bedford*, 39.

161. "Society and Its Horses," *New York Times*, November 11, 1896.

162. McLean, *The Jays of Bedford*, 40.

163. Irving Lowens, "L'affaire Muck: A Study in War Hysteria (1917–1918)," *Musicology* 1 (1947): 265–74, as told by Barbara Tischler, "One Hundred Percent Americanism and Music in Boston during World War I," *American Music* 4, no. 2 (Summer 1986): 164–76; "Major Higginson Defends Muck," *Boston Herald*, November 6, 1917. "The request of the ladies was not mentioned to Dr. Muck and the orchestra, and the concert was, as usual, quiet and well received." *Providence Journal*, October 30, 1917.

164. William E. Walter, "Dr. Muck and the First War," *New York Times*, March 10, 1940. In November 1917, Muck conducted the anthem in New York City, where critics complained that the Victor Herbert arrangement of the piece was "undignified." In December 1917, those same critics approved of an arrangement by BSO concertmaster, Bohemian-born Anton Witek.

165. Perry, *Life and Letters*, 480–85; Schonberg, *Great Conductors*, 217.

166. "Karl Muck," *New York Times*, March 5, 1940.

167. Badal, "The Strange Case of Dr. Karl Muck," 55–60.

168. Garrett D. Byrnes and Charles H. Spilman, *The Providence Journal 150 Years* (Providence, RI: Providence Journal, 1980), 289–90.

169. *Providence Journal*, October 29, 1917; October 31, 1917; November 1, 1917; "Dr. Muck Is Hurt by Request to Play the National Anthem," *Philadelphia Evening Telegraph*, November 1, 1917; "Boston Orchestra Will Not Play U.S. Anthem," *Philadelphia Inquirer*, November 2, 1917.

170. "1918: Fiction Writer," *Providence Journal*, July 21, 2004.

171. "Spies in Boston Says Rathom: He Tells Pilgrim Publicity Body of Greetings to 'Imperial Master,'" *New York Times*, November 22, 1917.

172. "Sees Radicals Active Here, John R. Rathom Warns against Bolshevist Propaganda," *New York Times*, February 1, 1919.

173. "Dr. Karl Muck had Prussian View Always," *Boston Post*, November 12, 1919.

174. William E. Walter, "Dr. Muck and the First War," *New York Times*, March 10, 1940.

175. Badal, "The Strange Case of Dr. Karl Muck," 55–60; Matthew Mugmon, "Patriotism, Art, and 'The Star-Spangled Banner': A New Look at the Karl Muck Episode," *Journal of Musicological Research* 33 (2014): 4–26.

176. Perry, *Life and Letters*, 485.

177. Perry, *Life and Letters*, 462–27.

178. "Rathom Speaks about German Spies in Boston," *New York Times*, November 21, 1917.

179. The New York Philharmonic had performed at Infantry Hall establishing a connection to the people there.

180. "On Doktor Muck: One Solid Phalanx to Oppose Prussian Orchestra Leader and His Enemy Alien Musicians," *New York Herald*, March 13, 1918.

181. *New York Times*, September 1, 1919.

182. *American*, April 29, 1918.

183. Tischler, "One Hundred Percent Americanism," 173; "Dr. Muck Resigns, Then Plays Anthem," *New York Times*, November 3, 1917.

184. Benedict R. Anderson, *Imagined Communities: Reflections on the Origin and Spread of Nationalism* (New York: Verso, 2006), 23.

185. Homberger, *Mrs. Astor's New York*, 13.

186. Homberger, *Mrs. Astor's New York*, 11.

187. Homberger, *Mrs. Astor's New York*, 13, 24.

188. Wayne Craven, *Gilded Mansions: Grande Architecture and High Society* (New York: W. W. Norton, 2009), 169.

189. Homberger, *Mrs. Astor's New York*, 75.

190. "Ex-Gov. Warfield Would Mob Muck: Volunteers to Lead Baltimore Citizens to Prevent Concert Conducted by German," *New York Times*, November 5, 1917.

191. Faucett, *George Whitefield Chadwick*, 302.

192. Tischler, "One Hundred Percent Americanism," 168–69.

193. Muck, *Dr. Karl Muck*, 8.

194. "Arrest Karl Muck as an Enemy Alien," *New York Times*, March 26, 1918.

195. Badal, "The Strange Case of Dr. Karl Muck," 55–60.

196. "Muck's Claim to Be a Swiss Boldly Made," *Boston Post*, November 12, 1919. "Honored Doctor. . . . Your father acquired Swiss citizenship for himself and his family in 1866, and that since then this citizenship has continued to exist unchanged. In connection herewith I desire to remark that, notwithstanding this verification, unfortunately you will be denied entrance into Washington by virtue of the regulations of the Department of Justice."

197. "Find No Direct Overt Act," *Boston Post*, April 7, 1918.

198. Tischler, *An American Music*, 170; Gienow-Hecht, *Sound Diplomacy*, 484.

199. Perry, *Life and Letters*, 493.

200. Perry, *Life and Letters*, 490.

201. Higginson to Mrs. Jay, January 30, 1918, Perry, *Life and Letters*, 490.

202. Perry, *Life and Letters*, 496.

203. Perry, *Life and Letters*, 490–91. "I have thought and still think that I know about that man very well, for I have seen considerable of him for the last eight years, and I think he is a typical artist who holds strong opinions

about art. . . . Of course he is a German, and of course he sympathizes with that side, but he has done us great services which it is fair to recognize. When they talk about his having done this or that which is disloyal to us, when they say that he is pushing schemes here, they are saying what they do not know. . . . He is very shrewd and he would not give himself away on any account, no matter what he thinks or what he wants. But I do feel very badly that the public should throw so many stones at him."

204. Perry, *Life and Letters*, 497.

205. Perry, *Life and Letters*, 496.

206. McLean, *The Jays of Bedford*, 36.

207. James L. Crouthemel, *Bennett's "New York Herald" and the Rise of the Popular Press* (New York: Syracuse University Press, 1989), 2.

208. Horowitz, *Understanding Toscanini*, 9.

209. *New York Herald*, February 27, 1918. Rathom cabled his German plot stories to the editor of the *World*.

210. Horowitz, *Wagner Nights*, 15.

211. Richard Wetzel, *The Globalization of Music in History* (New York: Routledge, 2012), 109.

212. *New York Herald*, March 12, 1918.

213. Lucie Jay, "Intern All German Music!," *Musical Leader* 36 (July 1918): 213. Jay linked Muck to a Bernstorff conspiracy, suggesting that the ambassador "had given his instructions and had outlined his campaign along what he perhaps thought was very clever" before leaving the United States.

214. "Links Muck to the Kaiser," *New York Herald*, March 12, 1918.

215. *New York Herald*, March 12, 1918.

216. *New York Herald*, March 12, 1918.

217. *New York Herald*, March 12, 1918.

218. *New York Herald*, March 15, 1918.

219. "On Doktor Muck," *New York Herald*, March 12, 1918.

220. *New York Herald*, March 12, 1918.

221. *New York Herald*, March 12, 1918.

222. *New York Herald*, March 12, 1918.

223. *New York Herald*, March 12, 1918.

224. *New York Herald*, March 12, 1918.

225. "Dr. Muck Resigns, Then Plays Anthem," *New York Times*, November 3, 1917; Stacy Horn, *Imperfect Harmony: Finding Happiness Singing with Others* (Chapel Hill, NC: Algonquin Books, 2013), 96. Interestingly, in 1918, Walter Damrosch's brother Frank, conductor and founder of the New York Institute of Musical Art, now known as the Julliard School, received a letter from Richard Fletcher, editor of the *Chronicle*, on behalf of Mrs. Jay, asking for his support. Frank replied, "Why deprive ourselves of the things that are good and beautiful at a time when the world cannot have too much of just such things? German militarism will not be defeated by the exclusion of the masterworks of German music. . . . Nor will it be

defeated by the persecution of harmless German artists, nor by the efforts to incite a mob-spirit against the works of art which have nothing to do with German autocracy or militarism. Let us preserve our dignity and fairness and appreciation of what is true, beautiful, and noble." Clearly, even close family members like the Damrosches disagreed on political matters in wartime.

226. Damrosch Collection, New York Public Library, Box 1, Folder 2.

227. *New York Herald*, March 12, 1918.

228. *New York Herald*, March 12, 1918.

229. "Doktor Muck Must Go," *Chronicle*, March 1918.

230. "Opposition," *New York Herald*, March 12, 1918.

231. "Opposition."

232. *New York Herald*, March 12, 1918.

233. "Dr. Manning Joins Attack on Dr. Muck," *New York Times*, March 13, 1918.

234. Badal, "The Strange Case of Dr. Karl Muck," 55–60.

235. "D.A.R. Joins in Protest," *New York Tribune*, March 14, 1918.

236. *New York Tribune*, March 14, 1918.

237. "Miss Scoville's School, Miss Spance's School and Miss Ely's School made this offer," *New York Herald*, March 12, 1918.

238. "Mrs. Jay Moves to Stop Muck's Concerts," *American*, March 13, 1918.

239. "BSO Must Answer Questions Concerning His Patriotism or She Will Take Other Measures, She Declares," *New York Tribune*, March 14, 1918.

240. "BSO Must Answer."

241. *New York Tribune*, March 17, 1918.

242. *New York Herald*, March 14, 1918.

243. "War Growing Warmer," *New York Herald*, March 14, 1918.

244. "War Growing Warmer."

245. *New York Herald*, March 14, 1918.

246. "Threat to Tear Down Carnegie Hall: A White Livered Lot," *New York Tribune*, March 1918.

247. "Threat to Tear Down Carnegie Hall."

248. "Threat to Tear Down Carnegie Hall."

249. "Threat to Tear Down Carnegie Hall."

250. "Muck Plays Here Guarded by Police," *New York Times*, March 15, 1918.

251. *New York Herald*, March 14, 1918.

252. *New York Herald*, March 16, 1918.

253. Cole, *Enemy Aliens*, 23–24.

254. "Conference at His House," *Boston Post*, November 12, 1919.

255. "Dr. Muck Had Fear of Being Assassinated: Dreaded Being Shot by American Fanatic," *Boston Post*, November 12, 1919.

256. "Muck Feared Massacre of Germans in Boston," *Boston Post,* November 1919. Muck commented in another exchange that he enjoyed outdoor recreation, including hunting.

257. "Muck Plays Here, Guarded by Police: Only Subscribers Admitted to Concert, Which Was Not Interrupted; Opens with Our Anthem," *New York Tribune,* March 15, 1918. "Dr. Muck Plays Again without Causing a Riot: 23 Grand Army Posts Protest against Performance as a 'Disgrace'; Many Secret Service Men There," *New York Herald,* March 16, 1918.

258. "Muck Plays Here, Guarded by Police: Only Subscribers Admitted to Concert, Which Was Not Interrupted; Opens with Our Anthem," *New York Tribune,* March 15, 1918; "Dr. Muck Plays Again without Causing a Riot: 23 Grand Army Posts Protest against Performance as a 'Disgrace'; Many Secret Service Men There," *New York Herald,* March 16, 1918.

259. "Brooklyn Acts to Bar Its Doors to Doktor Muck," *World,* March 16, 1918.

260. "Brooklyn Audience Cordial to Muck," *World,* March 16, 1918.

261. "Brooklyn Audience Cordial to Muck."

262. "Muck Victory at Carnegie and Brooklyn Academy," *World,* March 16, 1918.

263. "Brooklyn Acts to Bar Its Doors to Doktor Muck," *World,* March 16, 1918.

264. *World,* March 17, 1918.

265. "Brooklyn Wants No More of Muck: Contract with Boston Symphony Will Not Be Renewed If Leader Is Retained," *New York Herald,* March 17, 1918; "Second Concert Is Given in Brooklyn with U. S. Flags as Drapery: Opposition Not Ended," *New York Herald,* March 16, 1918.

266. "Brooklyn Wants No More of Muck: Contract with Boston Symphony Will Not Be Renewed If Leader Is Retained," *New York Herald,* March 17, 1918; "Second Concert Is Given in Brooklyn with U. S. Flags as Drapery: Opposition Not Ended," *New York Herald,* March 16, 1918.

267. "Brooklyn Audience Cordial to Muck: Crowded House Gives Conductor Ovation but His Sacrifice Is Hinted," *New York Sun,* March 16, 1918.

268. "Brooklyn Audience Cordial."

269. *New York Herald,* March 16, 1918.

270. Higham, *Strangers in the Land,* 211.

271. Capozzola, *Uncle Sam Wants You,* 213.

272. Higham, *Strangers,* 211.

273. Capozzola, *Uncle Sam Wants You,* 211–13.

274. Capozzola, *Uncle Sam Wants You,* 211–13; Jorg Nagler, "Victims on the Home Front: Enemy Aliens in the United States during the First World War," in *Minorities in Wartime: National and Racial Groupings in Europe, North America and Australia during the Two World Wars* (Oxford: Berg, 1993), 205.

275. Kelly J. Baker, *Gospel according to the Klan: the KKK's Appeal to Protestant America, 1915–1930* (Lawrence: University of Kansas Press, 2017).

276. "Defense Society against Muck," *New York Herald*, March 16, 1918.

277. "Retired Wagner Conductor, Dies," *New York Times* via Stuttgart, Germany, March 4, 1941.

278. "Calls for Strict Ban on German Language," *New York Times*, February 24, 1918. C. Wright Mills, *The Power Elite* (Oxford: Oxford University Press, 2000), 11.

279. Muck to Rosamond Young, *Boston Post*, November 12, 1919, published in the Boston newspaper after Muck's deportation.

280. Muck to Rosamond Young.

281. "The Real Facts," *Boston Post*, April 7, 1918.

282. *Boston Transcript*, March 31, 1918; *Boston International News Bureau*, March 28, 1918.

283. New York Philharmonic Archives, March 28, 1918, director's minutes.

284. Capozzola, *Uncle Sam Wants You*, 2.

285. Mills, *The Power Elite*, 9.

Chapter Five

Epigraph: "Lady Speyer's Poem to Muck," *Boston Post*, November 12, 1919. When the Department of Justice agents raided Muck's cottage in Seal Harbor, Maine, they found among his papers this poem dedicated to him by Leonora Speyer.

1. Gienow-Hecht, *Sound Diplomacy*, 125; Horowitz, *Wagner Nights*, 41–43, 346.

2. Perry, *Life and Letters*, 481.

3. Green and Donahue, *Boston Workers*, 94.

4. Henry Lee Higginson Files, Boston Symphony Orchestra Archives, 1312, Reel 2, 851–55, xii-14 Music 1913.

5. "Symphony Orchestras Much Disturbed," *Boston Globe*, November 3, 1917.

6. Michael Broyles, "'Music of the Highest Class': Elitism and Populism in Antebellum Boston," in Spitzer, *American Orchestras*, 237.

7. DiMaggio, "Cultural Entrepreneurship," 42–44.

8. Perry, *Life and Letters*, 470.

9. Green, *Problem of Boston*, 59.

10. FBI Records, 1909–1921, Old German Files, Gustav F. Heim #56999, 44.

11. *Boston Post*, November 12, 1919.

12. Spitzer, *American Orchestras*, 84.

13. Horowitz, "Reclaiming the Past," 32.

14. Perry, *Life and Letters*, 492.

15. Spitzer, *American Orchestras*, 107.

16. DiMaggio, "Cultural Entrepreneurship," 44–45; Howe, *Boston Symphony Orchestra,* 67–69, 121–23.

17. Henry Lee Higginson Files, Boston Symphony Orchestra Archives, 1626, 3, 385–87, xii-17-1915, Music and 1627, reel 3, 388–90.

18. Gienow-Hecht, *Sound Diplomacy,* 156, 96.

19. Henry Lee Higginson Files, Boston Symphony Orchestra Archives, 1410, Reel 3, 61–65, xii-15, Ellis 1914–15.

20. Henry Lee Higginson Files, Boston Symphony Orchestra Archives, 1417, Reel 3, 85–86, xii-15, Ellis 1914–15.

21. Henry Lee Higginson Files, Boston Symphony Orchestra Archives, 1472, Reel 3, 164–65, xii-15, Ellis 1914–15.

22. Henry Lee Higginson Files, Boston Symphony Orchestra Archives, 1494, Reel 3, 201–3, xii-15, Ellis 1914–15.

23. Henry Lee Higginson Files, Boston Symphony Orchestra Archives, 1522, Reel 3, 242, xii-15, Ellis 1914–15.

24. John Spitzer, "American Orchestras and their Unions," in Spitzer, *American Orchestras,* 80–84.

25. Boston Musicians Association, "Oral History," http://www.bostonmusicians.org/history/, April 12, 2011.

26. Gienow-Hecht, *Sound Diplomacy,* 17.

27. Gienow-Hecht, *Sound Diplomacy,* 162.

28. Gienow-Hecht, *Sound Diplomacy,* 171.

29. Ayer, *More Than Meets the Ear,* 11.

30. Henry Lee Higginson to Miss Francis Snell, November 14, 1917, Henry Lee Higginson Papers, Baker Business Library, Harvard University,.

31. Howe, *Boston Symphony Orchestra,* 90.

32. Gienow-Hecht, *Sound Diplomacy,* 275.

33. Green and Donahue, *Boston Workers,* 94.

34. Tager, *Boston Riots.*

35. Horowitz, "Reclaiming the Past," 18–38.

36. Boston Musicians Association, "The Emergence of Classical Players in Local 9-535," accessed December 3, 2017, http://www.bostonmusicians. org/history/the-emergence-of-classical-players-in-local-9-535.

37. Horowitz, "Reclaiming the Past," 19.

38. Lawrence W. Levine, *Highbrow / Lowbrow: The Emergence of Cultural Hierarchy in America* (Cambridge, MA: Harvard University Press, 1988), 124. Lawrence Levine recorded, "The Boston Symphony Orchestra is Mr. Henry L. Higginson's yacht, his racing stable, his library, and his art gallery, or it takes the place of what these things are to other men of wealth with other tastes."

39. Henry Lee Higginson Files, Boston Symphony Orchestra Archives, Higginson to Muck, March 20 and 25, 1912.

40. Buddy Sullivan and the Richmond Historical Society, *Richmond Hill* (Charleston, SC: Arcadia, 2006), 20, 53. The property was later purchased by Henry Ford. Met with Vince Askew, Director of the Waterways Township

on May 9, 2015, and toured Richmond Hill and the site of Cottenham Plantation.

41. Perry, *Life and Letters*, 247, 252.

42. Mary Lawton, *Schumann-Heink: The Last of the Titans* (New York: Macmillan, 1928), 264. The audience learned after the first act that war was declared. Orchestra members who were in the German and Austrian armies left immediately to report to duty. Muck conducted a skeletal orchestra for the final act. Egon Voss, *Die Dirigenten der Bayreuther Festspiele* (Regensburg: Gustav Boss Verlag, 1976), 135.

43. Henry Lee Higginson Files, Boston Symphony Orchestra Archives, 1409, Reel 3, 59–60, xii-15, Ellis 1914–15.

44. Henry Lee Higginson Files, Boston Symphony Orchestra Archives, 1411, Reel 3, 66–68 and 76–80, xii-15, Ellis 1914–15.

45. Henry Lee Higginson Files, Boston Symphony Orchestra Archives, 1395, Reel 3, 41–43, xii-15, Ellis 1914–15.

46. Henry Lee Higginson Files, Boston Symphony Orchestra Archives, 1417, Reel 3, 85–86, xii-15, Ellis 1914–15.

47. Perry, *Life and Letters*, 472.

48. Henry Lee Higginson Files, Boston Symphony Orchestra Archives, 1607, Reel 3, 362–63, xii-17, Ellis 1914–15.

49. Perry, *Life and Letters*, 480.

50. Perry, *Life and Letters*, 489.

51. *Boston Post*, November 12, 1919.

52. White, *The Tastemaker*.

53. White, *The Tastemaker*, 124.

54. White, *The Tastemaker*, 114.

55. White, *The Tastemaker*, 127.

56. Carol J. Oja, "Women Patrons and Crusaders for Modernist Music," in Locke and Barr, *Cultivating Music*, 240–44. New York became the central location for activism against European classical music. Spearheaded in many cases by wealthy patrons like Gertrude Vanderbilt Whitney (benefactor of the 1913 Armory Show), Alma Morgenthau Wertheim, Blanche Wetherill Walton, and Claire Raphael Reis. These women were instrumental in forming the League of Composers and championing new works by Edgard Varèse, Aaron Copland, Henry Cowell, Ruth Crawford, and Charles Seeger. Blair, *Torchbearers*, 44. Blair argues that the National Federation of Music Clubs also promoted American composers with their "Hear America First" campaign. Jay may have been influenced by these efforts, although her sincerity is questionable, as her target was the BSO and not the NYP, of which she was a part.

57. Personal conversation with Bridget Carr at Boston Symphony Orchestra Archive, March 2009; "Mrs. Jay Starts League to Combat German Music," *New York Herald*, March 22, 1917.

58. *New York Herald*, March 22, 1917.

59. Alex Ross, *The Rest Is Noise* (New York: Macmillan, 2007), 26.

60. Jay, "Intern All German Music!," 213. Jay equated America's addiction to German music and the need to sever dependence on it, as "almost like curing a person of an unfortunate love affair, and how well do we know that deep suggestion of a fragment of melody and how it awakens thoughts and yearnings." Joseph Horowitz, *Wagner Nights*, 297. Jay attacked the Metropolitan Opera for its reliance on German music, but her opinion was contested by influential German Americans in that city. In 1918, the Met reluctantly banned Wagner and other German composers and eliminated six Met singers.

61. Jay, "Intern All German Music!," 213.

62. MacDonald Smith Moore, *Yankee Blues: Musical Culture and American Identity* (Bloomington: Indiana University, 1985), 6; Joseph Horowitz, "*Reclaiming the Past*," 18–38.

63. Liane Curtis, "Why Amy Beach Matters" (lecture given at Forest Hills Cemetery, Jamaica Plain, Massachusetts, March 25, 2018). Curtis is the president of the Women's Philharmonic Advocacy and resident scholar at the Women's Studies Research Center of Brandeis University.

64. Block, *Amy Beach*, 214.

65. Block, *Amy Beach*, 194.

66. Horowitz, "Reclaiming the Past," 28–29.

67. Horowitz, *Classical Music in America*, 68. Beach retreated to her Hillsboro, New Hampshire, home for the duration of the conflict. Curtis, "Why Amy Beach Matters." Following the war, Beach cofounded the Society of American Women Composers to assist other marginalized female composers. Through perseverance, she published more than three hundred works in her lifetime. Margaret Ruthven Lang stopped composing altogether after the war. Tragically, she destroyed all of her symphonies; 130 art songs, however, survive.

68. Gail Bederman, *Manliness and Civilization: A Cultural History of Gender and Race in the United States, 1880–1917* (Chicago: University of Chicago Press, 1995), 170.

69. Moore, *Yankee Blues*, 9; personal conversation with trombonist Matt Guilford following a March 2009 BSO performance of Charles Ives Symphony no. 4.

70. Gienow-Hecht, *Sound Diplomacy*, 17.

71. Moore, *Yankee Blues*, 40.

72. Horowitz, "Reclaiming the Past," 18–38.

73. Schonberg, *Great Conductors*, 221.

74. Erik Kirschbaum, *The Eradication of German Culture in the United States, 1917–1918* (Stuttgart: Hans-Dieter Heinz,), 35; Tipton, *History of Modern Germany*, 223.

75. Applegate, *Bach in Berlin*, 45–79.

76. Gienow-Hecht, *Sound Diplomacy*, 79. "Karl Muck's goal in Boston, recorded the *Berliner borsen-Courier*, was to create traditions in the New

World, and to defend German music against encroachment of the French school."

77. Schonberg, *Great Conductors*, 21.

78. Faucett, *George Whitefield Chadwick*, 312–14.

79. Faucett, *George Whitefield Chadwick*, 222.

80. Faucett, *George Whitefield Chadwick*, 353.

81. Jessica C. E. Gienow-Hecht, "Trumpeting Down the Walls of Jericho: The Politics of Art, Music and Emotion in German-American relations, 1870–1920," *Journal of Social History 36, no. 3 (2003): 585–13*.

82. Gienow-Hecht, *Sound Diplomacy*, 102. The Venezuela Crisis is mentioned in more detail in chapter 2. Sebastian Conrad, *German Colonialism* (Cambridge: Cambridge University Press, 2011), 27, 137. German colonialism lasted for thirty years prior to World War I in an effort to find settlements for Germans who wished to emigrate, to find natural resources, and to provide locations for the exportation of surplus German goods. The United States was not on Germany's radar as a colony because immigrants there assimilated too rapidly. Wilhelm looked for colonial opportunities in Africa, Australia, and Latin America as alternatives to the United States.

83. "Intended to Be Citizen," *Boston Post*, November 12, 1919.

84. Panayi, *German Immigrants*, xix.

85. Llosa, *Global Crossings*, 259–60.

86. Llosa, *Global Crossings*, 259–60.

87. Higham, *Strangers*, 202.

88. Gienow-Hecht, *Sound Diplomacy*, 102.

89. Gienow-Hecht, *Sound Diplomacy*, 181; Reinhard R. Doerries, *Imperial Challenge: Ambassador Count Bernstorff and German-American Relations, 1908–1917* (Chapel Hill: University of North Carolina Press, 1989), 41, 260.

90. Margareta Anna Adelheid Münsterberg, *Hugo Münsterberg: His Life and Work* (New York: D. Appleton, 1922), 276.

91. Münsterberg, *Hugo Münsterberg*, 276.

92. Münsterberg, *Hugo Münsterberg*, 276.

93. Allen A. Brown Music Collection, Boston Public Library, Karl Muck File.

94. On April 1, 1917, Muck was called into the US District Attorney's office in Boston and asked what corps he belonged to at Heidelberg with Bernstorff. He answered, "Schwaben Corps. Chum and Crony of Bernstorff," *Boston Post*, November 12, 1919.

95. "Conference with Bernstorff," *Boston Post*, November 12, 1919.

96. *Boston Post*, November 12, 1919.

97. *Boston Post*, November 12, 1919.

98. *Boston Post*, November 12, 1919.

99. *Boston Post*, November 12, 1919.

100. "My Report Has to Go to Berlin," *Boston Post*, November 12, 1919.

101. "His Relations with Bernstorff Revealed," *Boston Post*, November 12, 1919.

102. FBI Records, 1909–1921, Old German Files, Museum of Fine Arts. Boston School, *Thirty-Sixth Annual Report of the School of Drawing and Painting* (Boston: 1913), 20. Ruth von Scholley was a student from 1912 to 1913.

103. The properties were located on Bellevue Avenue in Squantum and 19 Alton Place, Brookline, Massachusetts.

104. FBI Records, 1909–1921, Old German Files.

105. FBI Records, 1909–1921, Old German Files.

106. FBI Records, 1909–1921, Old German Files.

107. FBI Records, 1909–1921, Old German Files.

108. The Hotel Buckminster was on Beacon Street on Grosvenor Square in Boston.

109. FBI Records, 1909–1921, Old German Files.

110. FBI Records, 1909–1921, Old German Files. Von Scholley had several estates in Germany to return to, including Hamburg, Sieferling, Bavaria, Oberensingen, Wurtenberg, and Stuttgart.

111. Antony Lentin, *Banker, Traitor, Scapegoat, Spy? The Troublesome Case of Sir Edgar Speyer; An Episode of the Great War* (London: Haus, 2013), xx.

112. "Leonora Speyer Pulitzer Poet, 83: Prizewinner for 1927 Dies Here," *New York Times*, February 11, 1956.

113. Lentin, *Banker, Traitor, Scapegoat, Spy?*, 18.

114. Lentin, *Banker, Traitor, Scapegoat, Spy?*, 33.

115. Lentin, *Banker. Traitor. Scapegoat, Spy?*, 33.

116. Lentin, *Banker, Traitor, Scapegoat, Spy?*, 27.

117. Lentin, *Banker, Traitor, Scapegoat, Spy?*, 49.

118. Lentin, *Banker, Traitor, Scapegoat, Spy?*, 49.

119. Lentin, *Banker, Traitor, Scapegoat, Spy?*, 49.

120. Lentin, *Banker, Traitor, Scapegoat, Spy?*, 44.

121. Lentin, *Banker, Traitor, Scapegoat, Spy?*, 50.

122. Lentin, *Banker, Traitor, Scapegoat, Spy?*, 60. Fifty-eight thousand German residents in Britain became enemy aliens in 1914 with the declaration of war. They were rounded up at a rate of one thousand per week and sent to the Isle of Man, while some thirty thousand others, mostly elderly, women, and children, were forcibly taken from their homes and deported to Germany.

123. Lentin, *Banker, Traitor, Scapegoat, Spy?*, 86.

124. Lentin, *Banker, Traitor, Scapegoat, Spy?*, 123.

125. Email correspondence with artist Robert Seyffert, September 21, 2018. The author visited these Maine properties in December 2014. The Speyer "cottage" was built in 1892 by Boston architect Rotch Tilden. It was located on Highbrook Road in Bar Harbor. More of a mansion than a cottage, it was torn down in 1945. Only the Tea House and surrounding stone walls still exist today. Equally large, Muck's 1900 shingle-style Lichen House at 14 Ox Hill Way in Seal Harbor was designed by Duncan Candler for Edsel Ford. Located high on a ledge, and surrounded by pines and a spectacular view of the ocean, Ford rented the cottage to Dr. A. E.

Lawrence of New York, who sublet the property to the Mucks. The cottage was torn down, replaced by formal gardens. In recent years, Martha Stewart has acquired the gardens and the adjoining Tower Cottage that was also a part of the Ford property.

126. Robert Seyffert shared that, in 1916, his grandfather, artist Leopold Seyffert, a native of Seal Harbor, created charcoal drawings of several of these musicians, including Karl Muck, as they sat by gaslight for evening concerts. His portraits are exhibited at the Artemis Gallery in Northeast Harbor, Maine.

127. Lentin, *Banker, Traitor, Scapegoat, Spy?*, 127.

128. Muck to Rosamond, August 4, 1916, Allen A. Brown Music Collection, Boston Public Library.

129. "Discover Wireless Plant Parts in Apartment," *Boston Post*, November 12, 1919.

130. "Discover Wireless Plant Parts in Apartment."

131. FBI Records, 1909–1921, Old German Files.

132. "Conference at His House," *Boston Post*, November 12, 1919.

133. "Boston People Gave Cash to Dr. Muck to Help Germany in War," *Boston Post*, November 12, 1919.

134. "Telephoned to Münsterberg," *Boston Post*, November 12, 1919.

135. *Boston Post*, November 12, 1919.

136. Allen A. Brown Music Collection, Boston Public Library, Karl Muck File, May 31, 1915.

137. "Griesheimer Goes to Cell: Chicagoan of National Notoriety Swindled Mr. Muck," *Iowa City Citizen*, January 11, 1916.

138. "Rathom Strikes Again Saying He Gives Money to Germany," *Providence Journal*, November 7, 1917.

139. Lentin, *Banker, Traitor, Scapegoat, Spy?*, 26.

140. Lentin, *Banker, Traitor, Scapegoat, Spy?*, 90.

141. Lentin, *Banker, Traitor, Scapegoat, Spy?*, 92.

142. Lentin, *Banker, Traitor, Scapegoat, Spy?*, 85.

143. Lentin, *Banker, Traitor, Scapegoat, Spy?*, 130.

144. Lentin, *Banker, Traitor, Scapegoat, Spy?*, 138.

145. Lentin, *Banker, Traitor, Scapegoat, Spy?*, 101.

146. "German Officer 'Muck; Not Orchestra Leader," *New York Times*, May 15, 1918; "Muck on Stand in Rifle Probe," *New York Times*, May 22, 1918. Muck had been accused of storing large quantities of arms and ammunition in the United States for a suspected uprising. Sometime later, officials determined that they were searching for Henry Muck; Henry having no relationship to the conductor.

147. "Undertook Work for Country," *Boston Post*, November 12, 1919.

148. "Dare Not Speak to Own Brother," *Boston Post*, November 12, 1919.

149. Allen A. Brown Music Collection, Boston Public Library, Karl Muck File.

150. Allen A. Brown Music Collection, Boston Public Library, Karl Muck File.

151. *Boston Post*, November 12, 1919.

152. Allen A. Brown Music Collection, Boston Public Library, Karl Muck File, April 1, 1916.

153. "Raid Made by Collector Billings when the German Ships Were Seized in Boston," *Boston Herald*, January 28, 1916.

154. Perry, *Life and Letters*, 486.

155. Perry, *Life and Letters*, 486.

156. Henry Lee Higginson Files, Boston Symphony Orchestra Archives, Series 1743, reel 3, 561 xii-20-Music 1917.

157. Henry Lee Higginson Files, Boston Symphony Orchestra Archives, Series 1743, reel 3, 561 xii-20-Music 1917.

158. "U.S. Flag Drapes Symphony Hall: Hangs over Main Entrance and Manager Says It Will Remain," *Boston Herald*, November 2, 1917.

159. Perry, *Life and Letters*, 495.

160. Perry, *Life and Letters*, 495.

161. Perry, *Life and Letters*, 469.

162. Perry, *Life and Letters*, 469.

163. Perry, *Life and Letters*, 469.

164. Perry, *Life and Letters*, 504.

165. On June 5, 1890, Higginson presented Harvard College thirty-one acres of land to be called the Soldier's Field, in honor of Robert Gould Shaw and five other Civil War friends who lost their lives in battle.

166. Perry, *Life and Letters*, 477.

167. Burrage, "Albert Cameron Burrage." Boston mining capitalists were investing heavily in South America during World War I when Germany was forced to abandon its exploration and investment there.

168. Perry, *Life and Letters*, 480.

169. Perry, *Life and Letters*, 480.

170. Perry, *Life and Letters*, 480; Adam Tooze, *The Deluge: The Great War and the Remaking of Global Order 1916–1931* (London: Allen Lane, 2014).

171. Perry, *Life and Letters*, 479.

172. Perry, *Life and Letters*, 466.

173. Perry, *Life and Letters*, 466.

174. Perry, *Life and Letters*, 481.

175. Perry, *Life and Letters*, 495.

176. Perry, *Life and Letters*, 495.

177. Perry, *Life and Letters*, 513.

178. Perry, *Life and Letters*, 513.

179. Faucett, *George Whitefield Chadwick*, 302.

180. *Boston Herald*, July 5, 1917.

181. Perry, *Life and Letters*, 483.

182. "In Position of Guilty One," *Boston Post*, November 12, 1919.

183. Horowitz, *Classical Music in America*, 83.

184. FBI Records, 1909–1921, Old German Files, Gustav Heim, September 4, 1918, to November 26, 1918.

185. FBI Records, 1909–1921, Old German Files. Karl Rissland, November 26, 1918.

186. "Dr. Karl Muck Had Prussian View Always: Entirely and Blindly Biased with Attitude of Bitter Hostility to U.S. on All War Questions," *Boston Post*, November 12, 1919.

187. Perry, *Life and Letters*, 500.

188. Perry, *Life and Letters*, 500.

189. Perry, *Life and Letters*, 500.

190. "18 Germans Dropped by Boston Symphony: Among Them Is Ernest Schmidt, Successor to Dr. Karl Muck," *North American*, June 22, 1918; "Symphony Proves Patriotism Discharges Germans; Hires French," *Boston Post*, June 30, 1918; "Germans Dropped from Orchestra," *Christian Science Monitor*, June 1, 1918; "Boston Orchestra Cleans Out Its German Element," *New York Review*, June 28, 1918.

191. *Boston Post*, March 31, 1918.

192. *World*, April 29, 1918.

Chapter Six

Epigraph: "Dr. Muck of the Wasting Years, yet Power of Prime," *Boston Transcript*, August 1926. Howard Zinn, "The Problem Is Civil Obedience," in *The Zinn Reader* (Seven Stories Press, 1970), 1.

1. Herter published "The Art of String Playing" under her married name, M. D. Herter Norton.

2. "Dr. Muck Real Opinion of Americans," *Boston Post*, November 12, 1919. Muck complained about the press and the government in private letters that were printed later in the *Boston Post* in 1919.

3. "Muck Involved in Plans for German Revolt: Visited Spot Where Guns Were Stored," *Traveler*, May 15, 1918.

4. Goldschmidt, *In and Out of the Ivory Tower*, 165–66; Horowitz, *Understanding Toscanini*, 222; Gienow-Hecht, *Sound Diplomacy*, 281.

5. "Dr. Muck Real Opinion of Americans," *Boston Post*, November 12, 1919.

6. "Says Sympathies Entirely with Germany," *Boston Post*, November 12, 1919; "Discover Wireless Plant Parts in Apartment" and "Complete Wireless Outfit in Muck's House," *Boston Post*, November 12, 1919; "The House Was Located Not Far from That of a German Propagandist from Whose Windows Many Colored Signal Lights Had Been Observed" and "Muck's Arrest Leads to Talk of Wireless," *American*, March 29, 1918.

7. "Says Sympathies Entirely with Germany," *Boston Post,* November 12, 1919; "Discover Wireless Plant Parts in Apartment" and "Complete Wireless Outfit in Muck's House," *Boston Post,* November 12, 1919; "The House Was Located Not Far from That of a German Propagandist from Whose Windows Many Colored Signal Lights Had Been Observed" and "Muck's Arrest Leads to Talk of Wireless," *American,* March 29, 1918; email correspondence with Robert Seyffert, September 21, 2018.

8. *Boston Post,* November 12, 1919.

9. *Boston Post,* November 12, 1919.

10. In 1921, the Immigration Act made it illegal to pass nationalistic literature or currency to a home country. Muck's actions on behalf of Germany would have been illegal in 1921 but not in 1918. The law was not in place during World War I.

11. Capozzola, *Uncle Sam Wants You,* 190.

12. Michel Foucault, *Discipline and Punish: The Birth of the Prison* (New York: Pantheon, 1977), 26.

13. *New York Sun,* April 6, 1918.

14. Capozzola, *Uncle Sam Wants You,* 2.

15. Capozzola, *Uncle Sam Wants You,* 190.

16. Higham, *Strangers,* 229.

17. Capozzola, *Uncle Sam Wants You,* 201.

18. Cole, *Enemy Aliens,* 116. The Bureau of Investigation was the name of the organization until 1935, when it became the Federal Bureau of Investigation.

19. Henry Lee Higginson, Boston Symphony Orchestra Archives, Series 288, 4, 623–24, xv-3.

20. *Boston Post,* November 12, 1919.

21. Gienow-Hecht, *Sound Diplomacy,* 484

22. FBI Records, 1909–1921, Old German Files, Interview with Gustav Heim, BSO member, September 4, 1918. "Nagel is understood to have been divorced from his wife recently on account of domestic troubles caused by her patriotic sentiments toward this country which were distasteful to her husband."

23. *New York Sun,* April 6, 1918.

24. "The Story of Retrieving the Letters from Rosamond Young—Girl Enters during Hunt for Letters," Allen A. Brown Music Collection, Boston Public Library, Karl Muck File, 21.

25. "Story of Retrieving the Letters"; Daniel P. Toomey, *Massachusetts of Today: A Memorial of the State, Historical and Biographical, Issued for the World's Exposition at Chicago* (Boston: Columbia, 1892), 94. Rosamond lived in a beautiful colonial revival home at 294 Ashmont Street, Dorchester (formerly Milton). The house no longer exists, but one can get a sense of the neighborhood Rosamond lived in by visiting there. Her home was located

between Adanac Terrace and Cavalry Baptist Church. Her father was Frank L. Young, the head of the Frank L. Young Oil Company of South Boston.

26. David Cole, *Enemy Aliens*, 116.

27. "Story of Retrieving the Letters."

28. "Story of Retrieving the Letters."

29. Foucault, *Discipline and Punish*, 6, 8, 16, and 26.

30. Lowens, "L'affaire Karl Muck," 272; Applegate, *Bach in Berlin*, 255–56.

31. Allen A. Brown Music Collection, Boston Public Library, Karl Muck File. Foucault, *Discipline and Punish*, 40. Foucault speaks of authority figures deceptively acquiring knowledge at all costs.

32. Allen A. Brown Music Collection, Boston Public Library, Karl Muck File. Foucault, *Discipline and Punish*, 40.

33. Allen A. Brown Music Collection, Boston Public Library, Karl Muck File, 85–86; "Dr. Muck Sent to Jail; All Pleas Are Vain . . . Home is Ransacked, Documents Seized: Papers Found May Incriminate Others, Including Prominent Person, Boston, March 26, 1918—Dr. Karl Muck, Personal Friend of Count von Bernstorff and Conductor of the Boston Symphony Orchestra, Was Committed to the East Cambridge Jail Late This Afternoon, While Ernest Schmidt Led the Orchestra in a Concert at Symphony Hall. Before Muck Departed from the Federal Building He Learned That Agents of the Department of Justice Had Visited His Home and Other Places Frequented by Him and That a Seizure of Correspondence and Papers Was Made. The Other Warrants Were Served in Other Localities and When the Raiding Officers Returned to the Federal Building They Had a Mass of Papers Which They Had Taken from the Three Places Searched, but Most of the Matter Was Taken from Dr. Muck's Studio," and "Raid on Muck's Home Reveals Papers," *New York Evening Journal*, March 27, 1918.

34. FBI Records, Old German Files, 1909–1921, Gustav F. Heim (Boston Symphony Orchestra musician).

35. "Dr. Karl Muck Arrested as Alien Enemy: Symphony Conductor Is Taken as He Leaves Motor Car at His Home; Locked Up at Back Bay Station," *Boston Herald*, March 26, 1918; Foucault, *Discipline and Punish*, 38–40. Foucault speaks of the variety of ways that the accused is coerced into providing information and interrogated with graduated severity, moving the accused from place to place in an effort to extract a confession.

36. "Dr. Muck Quizzed, Then Sent to Jail," *New York Sun*, March 27, 1918; "Dr. Muck Faces Fresh Quizzing: Federal Attorneys Planning Reexamination of Prisoner," *Boston Herald*, March 27, 1918.

37. "Dr. Muck Quizzed, Then Sent to Jail," *New York Sun*, March 27, 1918; Foucault, *Discipline and Punish*, 25. Foucault speaks about the use of the body in the punishment process, first sentencing the accused to jail, followed by the public display of the individual, the ride to jail, followed by the removal of personal liberty, and the physical misery of incarceration.

38. "Enemy Alien Dies from Fall in Jail," *Boston Herald,* June 24, 1918; Goldschmidt, *In and Out of the Ivory Tower,* 166–68. German biologist Richard Goldschmidt describes his arrest and jail experience prior to his internment at Oglethorpe during World War I: "The feelings of a cultured man suddenly locked in a cage can hardly be described . . . for years this cage was to appear in dreams that filled me with horrors." He tells of his jail cell with its waste pail "emptied once a day" sitting next to his evening meal. He describes the haunting sound of steel bars slamming shut, the lines of inmates, including murderers, filing past the guards to wash and grab coffee, and the indignity of the entire episode.

39. "No Decision in His Case Is Reached, Despite Long Examination: Charges Kept Secret," *New York Sun,* April 6, 1918.

40. *New York Sun,* April 6, 1918. The government detectives seized a large quantity of letters and other papers. They were closely examined while Muck sat in jail.

41. "Tearful Farewell," *Boston Herald,* April 7, 1918; "Muck Taken South for Internment," *American,* April 7, 1918; "Muck Off for Camp Oglethorpe: Bids Farewell to Wife at Fenway Home," *Boston Transcript,* April 6, 1918.

42. Anita Muck to Mrs. Gardner, May 18, 1918, Isabella Stewart Gardner Museum Archives. Anita reported that federal refusal to allow Muck to communicate with his orchestra "hurt him terribly."

43. Charles Ellis accompanied Muck on the first leg of the journey to Washington, DC. Muck was allowed to bring one suitcase including personal items and several orchestral scores.

44. Allen A. Brown Music Collection, Boston Public Library, Karl Muck File. An undated article from the *Boston Post* records, "Patrons Intercede in Vain—One group of ten patrons of the Symphony concerts interceded with the officials but made it clear that their interest was entirely musical, and that they were not seeking Dr. Muck's release except under suitable restraint, long enough to conduct the orchestra at the concerts which were arranged far in advance of any suggestion that the leader was to be arrested."

45. Horowitz, *Moral Fire,* 65.

46. Capozzola, *Uncle Sam Wants You,* 186.

47. Capozzola, *Uncle Sam Wants You,* 186. Hot Springs was a former mountain resort that received primarily interned seamen. Most of the inmates from Hot Springs were transferred to Fort Oglethorpe in late autumn of 1918 following a typhoid epidemic, caused by polluted drinking water from the French Broad River that killed twenty-nine men.

48. "Just How Interned Germans are Treated," *Chattanooga Times,* July 21, 1918.

49. "Looking Backwards," *Chattanooga Times,* February 6, 1945; "Largest War Prison Barracks in U.S. May Soon Be Abolished," *Chattanooga News,* May 20, 1919.

50. Gienow-Hecht, *Sound Diplomacy*, 281. Hot Springs, North Carolina, internment camp was, in fact, a former mountain resort, but Fort Oglethorpe was a standard army facility.

51. *Orgelsdorfer Eulenspiegel* [2], n.d.

52. Chemin des Dames means "the ladies' path," named for King Louis XV's mistress and daughters, who traveled this route between Paris and Chateau de Boves. Three World War I battles were fought along this road.

53. "Just How Interned Germans are Treated," *Chattanooga Times*, July 21, 1918.

54. Foucault, *Discipline and Punish*, 202–3. Foucault speaks of a panoptic aerial view within the prison architecture, where "anonymous power" reins within the central tower and where guards "can gain a clear idea of the way of surveillance."

55. "War Prison Is Enlarged," *Chattanooga Times*, June 30, 1918. In the summer of 2009, the author and her children hiked in this area. Fort Oglethorpe, the German cantonment, was located behind the current Post Office, encompassing the former K-Mart Plaza at 526 Battlefield Parkway to the Gilbert-Stephenson City Park, including Lafayette, Forrest, Stephenson, Gilbert, and Van Cleave Streets. Very little evidence exists to mark the World War I camp. There is a small dirt road, a stone entrance, several concrete pilings, and platforms where buildings had been. Overgrown vegetation indicates the location of garden plots. There is a small housing settlement in the camp now, and urban growth continues to erase structures from the World War I camp.

56. "War Prison Now Empty: Last of Alien Enemies Gone and Stockade Deserted," *Chattanooga Times*, April 28, 1920.

57. "War Prison Now Empty."

58. "War Prison Now Empty."

59. *Orgelsdorfer Eulenspiegel* [5], December 5, 1918, 2–4.

60. Heather Jones, *Violence against Prisoners of War in the First World War: Britain, France and Germany, 1914–1920* (Cambridge University Press, 2011). Comparatively, conditions in United States internment camps were better than in Europe.

61. *Orgelsdorfer Eulenspiegel* [5], December 5, 1918, 10–11.

62. "United States War Prison Barracks, No. 2," *Boston Post*, June 24, 1919; Dr. Karl Muck to Mrs. Gardner, August 9, 1919, Isabella Stewart Gardner Museum Archives. Muck signed his letter from the War Prison Barracks, Fort Oglethorpe, Georgia, "Prison No. 1046."

63. "United States War Prison Barracks, No. 2," *Boston Post*, June 24, 1919; Dr. Karl Muck to Mrs. Gardner, August 9, 1919, Isabella Stewart Gardner Museum Archives; *New York Times*, March 24, 1940. The *New York Times* described Muck as "gaunt and bronzed like an Indian brave."

64. "United States War Prison Barracks, No. 2," *Boston Post*, June 24, 1919; Dr. Karl Muck to Mrs. Gardner, August 9, 1919, Isabella Stewart Gardner Museum Archives; *New York Times*, March 24, 1940.

65. *Orgelsdorfer Eulenspiegel* [7], January 7, 1919.

66. "Just How Interned Germans Are Treated," *Chattanooga Times*, July 21, 1918.

67. "Just How Interned Germans Are Treated."

68. "Just How Interned Germans Are Treated."

69. Muck, *Dr. Karl Muck*, 113.

70. Muck, *Dr. Karl Muck*, 113; Anita Muck to Mrs. Gardner, May 18, 1918, November 23, 1918, and January 12, 1919, Isabella Stewart Gardner Museum Archives. Anita describes Muck's appearance during her visits as "physically quite well" and in good health.

71. "United States War Prison Barracks, No. 2." When Muck complained to Herbert Baldwin, a *Boston Post* reporter, about his shattered health, Colonel Penrose sarcastically remarked, "Well, they all have something the matter with them."

72. "Just How Interned Germans Are Treated."

73. Hans Speier, "The Social Types of War," *American Journal of Sociology* 46, no. 1 (1941): 445–54; Elizabeth Head Vaughan, *Community under Stress: An Internment Camp Culture* (Princeton, NJ: Princeton University Press, 1949).

74. New England Conservatory Archives, George Chadwick Letters. Anita wrote to "Chaddie," or Mrs. Chadwick, that the hardest part about leaving Boston was not being able to see her best friend anymore. Chaddie attempted to make her feel better by having Anita's favorite flower, an Arbutus, shipped to her. Anita stayed at the Signal Mountain Inn in Chattanooga, Tennessee, which is currently the Alexian Village Retirement Community. The author visited there in 2009. Anita Muck to Mrs. Gardner, May 18, 1918, November 23, 1918, and January 12, 1919, Isabella Stewart Gardner Museum Archives. Anita also stayed at the Georgian Terrace Hotel on Peachtree Street in Atlanta, Georgia, and the city's first skyscraper, the Hotel Patten on Market and East Street in Chattanooga. The Hotel Patten is currently called the Patten Towers, an affordable housing community. Anita occupied her time by attending concerts, "reading a lot," including Willa Cather's *My Antonia*, and cooking, since she "abhorred the Southern Style." Anita wrote that she had no definite plan regarding her lodging, "just drifting along and letting providence shape my life."

75. "United States War Prison Barracks, No. 2." When a *Boston Post* correspondent visited Muck in June 1919, the reporter commented on "a keen-eyed square jawed doughboy" who sat nearby "with buckshot loaded." Anita Muck to Mrs. Gardner, January 12, 1919, Isabella Stewart Gardner Museum Archives. "It is a wonderful comfort to be so near my dear husband, even if I can see him only once a week; and I am loathe to tear myself away."

76. "Just How Interned Germans Are Treated."

77. *Orgelsdorfer Eulenspiegel* [1], October 15, 1918.

78. *Orgelsdorfer Eulenspiegel* [2], n.d., 9–10.

79. Anita Muck to Charles Ellis, June 3, 1919, Boston Symphony Orchestra Archives.

80. "Just How Interned Germans Are Treated."

81. *Orgelsdorfer Eulenspiegel*, n.d., 11.

82. Goldschmidt, *In and Out of the Ivory Tower*, 177.

83. Karl Muck to Mrs. Gardner, August 9, 1919, Isabella Stewart Gardner Museum Archives. "The first letter I can spare certainly belongs to you."

84. *Orgelsdorfer Eulenspiegel* [5], December 5, 1918.

85. Paula Muina, *Remembering Fort Oglethorpe Post* (Fort Oglethorpe, GA: Post Community Association, 2008).

86. Goldschmidt, *In and Out of the Ivory Tower*, 176. *Orgelsdorfer Eulenspiegel* [5], December 5, 1918; personal conversation with Mary Prevo in February of 2012, whose great-grandfather, Federico Stallforth, was interned at Fort Oglethorpe until 1920.

87. "Just How Interned Germans Are Treated."

88. *Orgelsdorfer Eulenspiegel* [1], October 15, 1918, 18.

89. Hans Stengel and others created a series of woodcuts for the *Orgelsdorfer Eulenspiegel* newsletter illustrating various aspects and people within the Oglethorpe prison camp. Karl Muck, P.O.W. 1046, was one of the first woodcarvings for the first issue of the magazine on October 15, 1918.

90. Anita Muck to Mrs. Gardner, January 12, 1919, Isabella Stewart Gardner Museum Archives. Anita called it very "stimmungsvoll."

91. *Orgelsdorfer Eulenspiegel* [5], December 5, 1918. Gerald H. Davis, "Orgelsdorf: A World War I Internment Camp in America," *Yearbook of German-American Studies* 26 (1991): 259.

92. "Just How Interned Germans Are Treated."

93. *Orgelsdorfer Eulenspiegel* [5], December 5, 1918.

94. "Celebrated Tsing-Tau Orchestra Is Engaged," *Meriden Morning Record*, January 27, 1917.

95. "Largest War Prison Barracks in U.S. May Soon Be Abolished." "An eighty-piece orchestra has been organized among the prisoners under the leadership of O.K. Wills [Witte]. He was brought to this country with two (German) bands from the German protectorate on mainland China at the beginning of the war and was first sent to Hot Springs, Arkansas, being later transferred with some of the band members to Oglethorpe. The orchestra gives concerts once a week."

96. "Muck's Last Concert in America," *New York Times*, March 24, 1940. "Never Return to Boston," *Boston Post*, June 1919. Muck conducted "many of their weekly concerts." The reporter commented that Muck said that "it helped the spirit of the men but compared with my Boston orchestra, 'no,' and the 'no' was an emphatic one."

97. Goldschmidt, *In and Out of the Ivory Tower*, 176.

98. Goldschmidt, *In and Out of the Ivory Tower*, 33.

99. Hanns Heinz Ewers was a novelist, poet, and literary critic who praised Edgar Allen Poe for his experiments with altered states of consciousness. In 1915, he published a book of German war songs called *Deutsche Krigslieder* that included translations of American, Yiddish, and Irish poems directed against England and Russia.

100. *Orgelsdorfer Eulenspiegel* [5], December 15, 1918. Davis, "Orgelsdorf," 259–60. Ten editions of the camp magazine appeared between October 1918 and May 1919.

101. *Orgelsdorfer Eulenspiegel* [5], December 15, 1918. Davis, "Orgelsdorf," 259–60.

102. *Orgelsdorfer Eulenspiegel* [5], December 15, 1918. Davis, "Orgelsdorf," 259–60.

103. *Orgelsdorfer Eulenspiegel* [5], December 5, 1918, 2–4.

104. Erich Posselt, "Prisoner of War Number 3598," *American Mercury Magazine*, May–August 1927.

105. Adolf Lucas Vischer, *Barbed Wire Disease: A Psychological Study of the Prisoner of War* (London: Bale and Danielsson, 1919).

106. Posselt, "Prisoner of War Number 3598."

107. Anita Muck to Mrs. Gardner, May 18, 1918, and November 23, 1918, Isabella Stewart Gardner Museum Archives. On February 7, 1920, she records that Muck still suffers with problems relating to nerves.

108. John M. Barry, *The Great Influenza: The Epic Story of the Deadliest Plague in History* (New York: Viking, 2004), 183–88.

109. Barry, *The Great Influenza*, 310.

110. Barry, *The Great Influenza*, 188.

111. American Experience, "Influenza, 1918. City Snapshots: Boston," http://www.pbs.org/wgbh/americanexperience/features/influenza-boston/; Barry, *The Great Influenza*, 203.

112. Personal conversation with historical novelist William Martin, Harvard University, April 19, 2018. Josephine and her family lived at 9 Gloucester Place in Boston's South End.

113. Personal conversation with historian Robert J. Allison, Harvard University, April 18, 2018, about his grandmother Rose.

114. Barry, *The Great Influenza*, 2, 4, 192, 271, 372. Baltimore, Pittsburgh, Louisville, New York, and many smaller cities were affected as well.

115. Barry, *The Great Influenza*, 238.

116. Thomas H. O'Connor, *Boston A to Z* (Cambridge, MA: Harvard University Press, 2000), 177. Barry, *The Great Influenza*, 5.

117. Posselt, "Prisoner of War Number 3598."

118. Goldschmidt, *In and Out of the Ivory Tower*, 178.

119. Barry, *Great Influenza*, 2, 250.

120. Davis, "Orgelsdorf," 256.

121. *Orgelsdorfer Eulenspiegel*, n.d., 16.

122. Sixth Cavalry Museum, 2 Barnhardt Circle, Fort Oglethorpe, Georgia.

123. *Orgelsdorfer Eulenspiegel* [3].

124. Von Scholley was arrested in Boston seven months after Muck, on October 29, 1918, arriving at Fort Oglethorpe on November 8, 1918.

125. *Orgelsdorfer Eulenspiegel* [3]. Fellow internee B. Nientiedt describes the destruction of the human spirit in his poem "Riddle of the Waves": "What are you, little man, in the dance of the waves? A puny craft soon to be shattered."

126. US Alien Property Custodian, *Annual Report, Office of the Alien Property Custodian* (Washington, DC: US Printing Office, 1919), 601.

127. "See Move to Seize Muck's Properties," *Record* March 29, 1918; "May Seize Muck's Properties Here: $50,000 Home May be Taken," *Boston Herald* March 30, 1918.

128. Dr. Karl Muck to Mrs. Gardner, August 9, 1919, Isabella Stewart Gardner Museum Archives.

129. John Lord O'Brian, *Reminiscences* (Glen Rock, NJ: Microfilming Corp of America, 1972), 313; Gayle K. Turk, "The Case of Dr. Karl Muck: Anti-German Hysteria and Enemy Alien Internment during World War I" (BA thesis, Harvard University, 1994). Christopher Capozzola, *Uncle Sam Wants You*, 189. Capozzola relays the story of Georg Roenitz, a former German consul to Hawaii and vice president of H. Hackfield and Company, a sugar enterprise. Roenitz was arrested and his property was seized by Palmer, parceled out to Roenitz's competitors, and reorganized under the new name, American Factors, Ltd.

130. Joan M. Jenson, *The Price of Vigilance* (Chicago: Rand McNally, 1969), 165; Daniel A. Gross, "World War One: 100 Years Later; The U.S. Confiscated Half a Billion Dollars in Private Property during WWI," *Smithsonian Magazine*, July 28, 2014.

131. Karl Muck to Charles A. Ellis, August 11, 1921, Boston Symphony Orchestra Archives.

132. *Boston Post*, March 6, 1940.

133. Karl Muck to Charles A. Ellis, June 1, 1924, Boston Symphony Orchestra Archives.

134. Alexander H. Leighton, *The Governing of Men: General Principals and Recommendations Based on Experience at a Japanese Relocation Camp* (New York: Octagon Books, 1964).

135. In 1917, Muck recorded Wagner's *Lohengrin*, prelude act 3 with the BSO. LP: RCA Victor LM 2651; CD: *The First Recording of the Boston Symphony Orchestra, BSO Classics*, 171002 (1995); *Wagner—Overtures and Preludes Muck*, Naxos (2002). See Jim Cartright and Christopher Dyment, "Karl Muck: A Discography," *Journal of the Association for Recorded Sound Collections* 1 (1977): 69–77, for a full discography of Karl Muck's original recordings.

136. "RCA Red Seal Century" (RCA 63861). Ernst Kunwald and Frederick Stock had made orchestral recordings before Muck's BSO recordings, with significantly fewer musicians. In late October 1917, Leopold Stokowski and the full Philadelphia Orchestra followed the BSO at Victor.

137. Gienow-Hecht, *Sound Diplomacy*, 281; *Gramophone* magazine, November 1999, 122; Jonathan Brown, *Great Wagner Conductors: A Listener's Companion* (Canberra, Australia: Parrot Press, 2012), 191. Christopher Dyment's notes in the Appian CD APR5521. After Muck's deportation, he made several other important recordings in Europe: In 1927, he conducted excerpts from *Parsifal* acts 1 and 2 at the Bayreuth Festival for the English Columbia Gramophone Company. The Transformation and Grail scenes are praised for their control of phrasing. In that same year, he conducted *Parsifal*'s prelude with the Berlin State Opera for the Gramophone Company (HMV), in Berlin. In December 1928, he made a nearly complete recording of act 3 of *Parsifal* using singers from that year's Bayreuth performances. Music critic Alan Blyth described it as "the most uplifting, superbly executed reading . . . in the history of recording." In 1929, Herman Klein wrote, "Nothing [is] more grandiose or imposing, more gorgeous in tone or color, has been heard from the gramophone." Roughly 40 percent of the opera score was recorded over a three-year period, and all the *Parsifal* recordings have been released on CD. They are described as a cutting-edge achievement in the history of the gramophone, an amazing accomplishment given the primitive recording conditions. The church bells that toll in the recording were later destroyed in World War II. HMV also recorded Muck in eight other Wagner orchestral pieces between 1927 and 1929. Several radio broadcasts supposedly conducted by Muck include *Faust Overture* and Siegfrieds Trauermarsch, *Gotterdammerung* with the Berlin Radio Orchestra, and an excerpt from the Adagio from Bruckner's Symphony no. 7 with the Hamburg Philharmonic.

138. Capozzola, *Uncle Sam Wants You*, 202; Burdett A. Rich and M. Blair Wailes, *American Law Reports Annotated*, vol. 12 (Rochester, NY: Lawyers Cooperative, 1921), 197. The federal statute relating to the Deportation of Seditious Aliens Act October 16, 1918, provides for the deportation of the following classes of aliens:

Aliens who are anarchists, aliens who believe in or advocate the overthrow by force or violence of the government of the United States or of all forms of law; aliens who believe in or are opposed to all organized government; aliens who advocate or teach the assassination of public officials; aliens who advocate or teach the unlawful destruction of property; aliens who are members of or affiliated with any organization that entertains a belief in, teaches, or advocates the overthrow by force or violence of the government of the United States or of all forms of law, or that entertains or teaches disbelief in or opposition to all organized government, or that advocates the duty, necessity, or propriety of the unlawful assaulting or killing of any officer or officers, either of specific individuals or of officers generally, of the government of the United States or of any other organized government, because of his or their official character, or that advocates or teaches the unlawful destruction of property.

139. Cole, *Enemy Aliens*, 114–22.

140. Higham, *Strangers*, 221, 228.

141. Louis F. Post, *The Deportation Delirium of Nineteenth Century: A Personal Narrative of an Historic Official Experience* (New York: Da Capo Press, 1923), 53–54.

142. Higham, *Strangers*, 231. "Palmer fumed at Post for coddling and encouraging Bolsheviks, and a group of 100 per cent American Congressmen tried to impeach him for disloyalty."

143. Barbara L. Tischler, *An American Music*, 170.

144. Anita Muck to Mrs. Gardner, August 30, 1919, Isabella Stewart Gardner Museum Archives. The Department of Justice had "made out Dr. Muck's papers for Boston" before the May Day Riots. Also, BSO manager Charles Ellis thought that "new trouble might come from a visit to Boston by my husband . . . the mere possibility was enough to scare him into a fit of panics!"

145. Anita Muck to Mrs. Gardner, August 30, 1919, Isabella Stewart Gardner Museum Archives.

146. "Interned Germans Sail for Denmark: Dr. Muck Says He's a Man without a Flag or Country," *Fort Wayne Journal Gazette*, August 22, 1919.

147. Cole, *Enemy Aliens*, 120; Higham, *Strangers*, 229, 255.

148. Cole, *Enemy Aliens*, 120; Higham, *Strangers*, 229, 255.

149. Higham, *Strangers*, 220.

Chapter Seven

1. Turk, "Case of Dr. Karl Muck." Boynton to Gregory, April 1, 1918, General Records of the Department of Justice.

2. "Given His Choice," *Boston Post*, November 12, 1919.

3. Victoria C. Woodhull, *Steinway Speech* (New York: Woodhull and Claflin, 1871). "I am a Free Lover. I have an inalienable, constitutional and natural right to love whom I may, to love as long or as short a period as I can; to change that love every day if I please, and with that right neither you nor any law you can frame have any right to interfere."

4. Maura Shaw Tantillo, *American Sexual Politics: Sex, Gender and Race Since the Civil War* (Chicago: University of Chicago Press, 1993), 162, 155.

5. Tantillo, *American Sexual Politics*, 119.

6. Jessica R. Pliley, *Policing Sexuality: The Mann Act and the Making of the FBI* (Cambridge, MA: Harvard University Press, 2014), 66.

7. "Woman's Name Brought In," *Boston Post*, November 1919. "Authorities were assisted by patriotic members of the Symphony Orchestra, it developed that the name of a young woman in the Back Bay was closely connected with that of Dr. Muck. She had made frequent trips out of the State in Dr. Muck's company and it was felt that he should be arrested and charged with a violation of the Mann White Slavery Act."

8. Karen Abbott, *Sin in the Second City* (NY: Random House, 2007), 208.

9. Abbott, *Sin*, 223.

10. Abbott, *Sin*, 260.

11. Abbott, *Sin*, 290.

12. Abbott, *Sin*, 291.

13. "Could Have Prosecuted under Mann Act," *Boston Post*, November 12, 1919. In the judgment of the authorities it was better to punish him for his offenses against the government, and this was done. "Letters to Hub Woman Damning Factor," *Boston Post*, November 1919.

14. "Muck on Way to Internment: Starts for Fort Oglethorpe Under Guard; How Muck Landed in Detention—Preferred Internment to Trial Involving a Woman—Faced with Proof of Mann Law Violation Chose Prison," *Boston Post*, April 7, 1918; "Muck Chose Internment to Jail Term: Preferred to Be Taken as Enemy Alien Rather Than Face More Serious Charge: Many Damaging Admissions in Letters," *Boston Post*, November 9, 1919.

15. "Letters to Hub Woman Damning Factor," Allen A. Brown Music Collection, Boston Public Library, Karl Muck File, 17; "Could Have Prosecuted under Mann Act."

> Dr. Muck could have been prosecuted under the Mann Act and likewise for sending unlawful matter through the mails. This would have involved a great scandal, resulted in deep injury to innocent people and in the judgment of the authorities it was better to punish him for his offenses against the government, and this was done. Had Dr. Muck chosen to deny the charges of unlawful activity on behalf of Germany and attempted to escape by way of his alleged Swiss citizenship he would have been promptly prosecuted for the other offenses. Dr. Muck wisely decided to go to an internment camp and later face deportation.

16. Excerpt from the Comstock Law, 2012, accessed November 25, 2012, http://law.jrank.org/pages/12349/Comstock-Law-Excerpt-from-Comstock-Law.html; "Dr. Karl Muck, conductor of the Boston Symphony Orchestra, was taken into custody last night as an Enemy Alien," *Boston Post*, March 26, 1918.

17. Michel Foucault, *History of Sexuality* (New York: Vintage Books, 1988).

18. T. J. Jackson Lears, *Fables of Abundance: A Cultural History of Advertising in America* (New York: Basic Books, 1994), 144; Peter N. Stearns, *Sexuality in World History* (New York: Routledge, 2009), 82.

19. David Kruh, *Always Something Doing: A History of Boston's Infamous Scollay Square* (Boston: Northeastern University Press, 1999), 115.

20. Tantillo, *American Sexual Politics*, 436.

21. *Boston Herald*, December 2, 1878; Ivan D. Steen, "Cleansing the Puritan City: The Reverend Henry Morgan's Anti-vice Crusade in Boston," *New England Quarterly* 54, no. 3 (1981): 400.

22. *Boston Herald,* December 2, 1878; Ivan D. Steen, "Cleansing the Puritan City: The Reverend Henry Morgan's Anti-vice Crusade in Boston," *New England Quarterly* 54, no. 3 (1981): 400.

23. Margaret Bendroth, "Why Women Loved Billy Sunday: Urban Revivalism and Popular Entertainment in Early Twentieth Century American Culture," *Religion and American Culture: A Journal of Interpretation* 14, no. 2 (Summer 2004): 254.

24. Moore, *Yankee Blues,* 1.

25. Moore, *Yankee Blues,* 44, 63.

26. Horowitz, *Classical Music in America,* 79.

27. Horowitz, *Classical Music in America,* 73.

28. Moore, *Yankee Blues,* 44, 63.

29. Moore, *Yankee Blues,* 10; Robert H. Wiebe, *The Search for Order, 1877–1920* (New York: Hill and Wang, 1967).

30. Turk, "Case of Dr. Karl Muck," 20.

31. Henry Lee Higginson Papers, Baker Business School, Harvard University.

32. Norman Lebrecht, *The Maestro Myth* (NY: Birch Lane Press, 1991), 2–3.

33. "Dr. Karl Muck Dies in Reich: Long Conductor of Symphony Was 80," *New York Times* via Stuttgart, Germany, March 4, 1941.

34. Turk, "Case of Dr. Karl Muck," 20.

35. "Thousand Women Unable to Hear Symphony Rehearsal, *"Boston Globe,* October 14, 1907.

36. Gienow-Hecht, *Sound Diplomacy,* 130.

37. Gienow-Hecht, *Sound Diplomacy,* 130.

38. Norman Lebrecht, *The Maestro Myth* (New York: Birch Lane Press, 1991), 4.

39. Norman Lebrecht, *Great Conductors in Pursuit of Power* (New York: Birch Lane Press, 1991), 8.

40. Lebrecht, *Maestro Myth,* 1.

41. Laurence Dreyfus, *Wagner and the Erotic Impulse* (Cambridge, MA: Harvard University Press, 2010), 76, 88.

42. "Dr. Muck of the Wasting Years, yet Power of Prime."

43. "Dr. Muck of the Wasting Years, yet Power of Prime"; Brown, *Great Wagner Conductors,* 32, 178–80.

44. Horowitz, *Classical Music in America,* 129.

45. "Dr. Muck of the Wasting Years, yet Power of Prime."

46. Kruh, *Always Something Doing,* 115–20, 25. A shooting gallery replaced Woolworths in Scollay Square. A bowling alley opened during the war. Bars were plentiful—Marty's, the Tasty, the Half Dollar Bar, and the Old Brattle Tavern. The area had character, and people enjoyed visiting there to eat at the Crescent Grill, the Hub Barbeque, or Albiani's Luncheonette. Sailors visited Tanya's Tattoo Parlor or Sal's Barbershop. Residents were drawn to Epstein's Drug Store for the best fountain drink in

the city, or they bought clothing at Bond's, Leopold and Morse, or Houghton Dunton. One could rent a room at the William Tell Hotel for five dollars a week including meals or eat a full-course meal for a quarter.

47. Stearns, *Sexuality in World History*, 99.

48. White, *The Tastemaker*, 79, 131. During the war, in New York City, Duncan danced nude with an American flag draped around her body. Audiences there were thrilled. Gertrude Stein commented, "She drives 'em mad; the recruiting stations are full of her converts."

49. White, *The Tastemaker*, 83, 58.

50. Horowitz, *Classical Music in America*, 82.

51. "Maud Allan Dances Anew," *New York Times*, October 17, 1916.

52. Kruh, *Always Something Doing*, 25.

53. Michael Lowenthal, *Charity Girls* (Boston: Houghton Mifflin, 2007), 2.

54. Jerry Thomas, *How to Mix Drinks, or The Bon Vivant's Companion* (New York: Dick and Fitzgerald, 1876).

55. Bendroth, "Why Women Loved Billy Sunday," 262.

56. Paul Boyer, "Boston Book Censorship in the Twenties," *American Quarterly* 15, no. 1 (Spring 1963): 8.

57. John D'Emilio and Estelle B. Freedman, *Intimate Matters: A History of Sexuality in America* (New York: Harper and Row, 1988), 160. Lowell attacked vice in the city and simultaneously (and hypocritically) wrote provocative letters to his wife, graphically detailing their own erotic sexual behavior.

58. Neil Miller, *Banned in Boston: The Watch and Ward Society's Crusade against Books, Burlesque, and the Social Evil* (Boston: Beacon Press, 2010), 27; Kruh, *Always Something Doing*, 67. *Harvard Magazine*, November 1973. The Watch and Ward Society reported in 1916 that the Old Howard Burlesque House was "the Shame of Boston." The report told of the "flimsy attire of the women" and of the "innovation of standing all the women upon the stage in a semicircle and having each one in turn make her debut to the audience by making a smutty remark."

59. Neil Miller, *Banned in Boston*, 17.

60. Stearns, *Sexuality in World History*, 91; D'Emilio and Freedman, *Intimate Matters*, xi.

61. Boyer, "Boston Book Censorship," 5–7.

62. Neil Miller, *Banned in Boston*, 68. Because of increased restrictions during the war, traditional brothels in Boston were replaced by "cafes," where a variety of sexual activities occurred.

63. Neil Miller, *Banned in Boston*, 64, 77.

64. Boyer, "Boston Book Censorship," 10.

65. Peter Dobkin Hall, "Rediscovering the Bourgeoisie: Higher Education and Governing Class Formation in the United States, 1870–1914," in Rosenbaum and Beckert, *American Bourgeoisie*, 199–200.

66. Boyer, "Boston Book Censorship," 10. Mayor Malcolm A. Nichols of Boston said, "We have an epidemic of indecency . . . which constitutes a

most perplexing problem." Following the Civil War, the city actively filled its mud flats and swamps, creating more space for development.

67. DiMaggio, "Cultural Entrepreneurship," 35; Boyer, "Boston Book Censorship," 8. Reverend William McVickar told the Watch and Ward at their annual meeting in 1901, "There are other streets in Boston besides Beacon Street and Commonwealth Avenue . . . and these spots, these localities, these purlieus—may I say, "slums" of Boston?—are the danger spots . . . which threaten your better neighborhoods; and this Society is the agency to which the people of this city must largely look for their disinfection, if not obliteration."

68. Boyer, "Boston Book Censorship,"10.

69. Stearns, *Sexuality in World History*, 95.

70. Kruh, *Always Something Doing*, 114.

71. Eric Hansen, *A Horticultural Tale of Love, Lust and Lunacy* (New York: Random House, 2000).

72. Edward W. Said, *Orientalism* (New York: Vintage, 1993); Reina Lewis, *Rethinking Orientalism: Women, Travel and the Ottoman Harem* (New Brunswick, NJ: Rutgers University Press, 2004); Richard Bernstein, *The East, the West, and Sex: A History of Erotic Encounters* (New York: Knopf, 2009); Joan Del Plato, *Multiple Wives, Multiple Pleasures: Representing the Harem, 1800–1875* (Madison, NJ: Fairleigh Dickinson University Press, 2002); Ursula Wokoeck, *German Orientalism: The Study of the Middle East and Islam from 1800 to 1945* (New York: Routledge, 2009).

73. Pamela Haag, *Consent: Sexual Rights and the Transformation of American Liberalism* (Ithaca, NY: Cornell University Press, 1999), xvii, 161.

74. Haag, *Consent*, 149.

75. Haag, *Consent*, 149.

76. Reay Tannahill, *Sex in History* (Cardinal, UK: Sphere Books, 1990), 367.

77. Kennedy, *Over Here*, 186.

78. Stearns, *Sex in World History*, 126.

79. Tannahill, *Sex in History*, 367.

80. Stearns, *Sex in World History*, 126.

81. Abbott, *Sin*, 289.

82. Abbott, *Sin*, 289.

83. Abbott, *Sin*, 152

84. Tantillo, *American Sexual Politics*, 7, 123; Joan Smyth Iversen, *The Antipolygamy Controversy in U.S. Women's Movements, 1880–1925* (London: Taylor and Francis, 1997), 7–8.

85. Tantillo, *American Sexual Politics*, 123, 129.

86. Tantillo, *American Sexual Politics*, 131.

87. "Plan for Secret Apartment," Allen A. Brown Music Collection, Boston Public Library, Karl Muck File, 22.

88. "Wife Knew of Love for Girl," *Boston Post*, November 9, 1919.

89. Dale M. Bauer, *Sex Expression and American Women Writers, 1860 to 1940* (Chapel Hill: University of North Carolina Press, 2009), 74.

90. "Musical Temperament Blamed For Letters," *Boston Transcript*, November 9, 1919; Allen A. Brown Music Collection, Boston Public Library, Muck File, 6.

91. "Muck Dropped Like Hot Coal," *Boston Transcript*, November 9, 1919; "Read Out of Tavern Club," *Boston Transcript*, November 9, 1919; Allen A. Brown Music Collection, Boston Public Library, Karl Muck File, 9, 32.

92. "Muck Feared Scandal More Than Arrest," *Boston Post*, November 12, 1919.

93. *Music News* 11, no. 24 (June 13, 1919), 2. The supreme secretary-treasurer of Phi Mu Alpha Sinfonia reported to *Music News* that Karl Muck's name was stricken from the list of that fraternity and that "the action was supported by the unanimous vote of the Supreme Governing Council."

94. Kennedy, *Over Here*, 284.

95. Janet Staiger, *Bad Women: Regulating Sexuality in Early American Cinema* (Minneapolis: University of Minnesota Press, 1995), 4.

96. Stearns, *Sexuality in World History*, 119.

97. Bauer, *Sex Expression*, 2.

98. Bauer, *Sex Expression*, 35.

99. Bauer, *Sex Expression*, 184–85.

100. Bauer, *Sex Expression*, 12

101. Bauer, *Sex Expression*, 19.

102. Kristin Celello, *Making Marriage Work: A History of Marriage and Divorce in the Twentieth Century United States* (Chapel Hill: University of North Carolina Press, 2009), 22.

103. Tantillo, *American Sexual Politics*, 162.

104. "Mary Crena De Longh Is Dead; Co-founder of W. W. Norton," *New York Times*, April 20, 1985. Margaret Herter married William Warder Norton and cofounded in 1924 the Norton and Company Publishing House.

105. Michael Ochs, "Who Was M. D. Herter Norton?," *Musicology Now*, accessed January 22, 2014, http://musicologynow.ams-net.org/2014/01/who-was-m-d-herter-norton.html.

106. James Buzard, *The Beaten Track: European Tourism, Literature, and the Ways to "Culture" 1800–1918* (New York: Oxford University Press, 1993), 6–7; James Duncan and Derek Gregory, eds., *Writes of Passage: Reading Travel Writing* (London: Routledge, 1999), 5; Dean MacCannell, *The Tourist: A New Theory of the Leisure Class* (Oakland: University of California Press, 1999.

107. *Music News* 6, no. 2 (October 23, 1914); *The Music Magazine–Musical Courier* 72 (June 15, 1916).

108. Rosamond was described as having excellent diction, style, and timbre, with "reliable musicianship," a "likeable personality," a "wholesome

viewpoint," and "an easy stage presence and fascinating abandon in her presentation." Various reports described her as having a "fine physique" due to her athleticism as a swimmer and equestrian.

109. "Schedule of the Ellis Courses," *Music Magazine–Musical Courier* 75 (September 20, 1917). The January 15, 1918, BSO concert occurred in Providence, Rhode Island.

110. Advertisement, *Musical America* 22 (October 25, 1915): 64. Muck was on the board of directors of the Montclair New Jersey Conservatory of Music that Sawyer had helped to establish. She was also involved with Muck in the promotion of Mason and Hamlin Piano's. It is perhaps not coincidental that Sawyer became Rosamond's agent.

111. "Knew German Note Was Coming," *Boston Post*, November 1919. Letter dated February 1, 1917.

112. Allen A. Brown Music Collection, Boston Public Library, Karl Muck File, 12.

113. "Rosamond Y. Chapin," *New York Times*, August 15, 1984. Rosamond and Russell Chapin lived at 52 Maple Street, Springfield, Massachusetts. The Chapin family controlled the Chapin and Gould Paper Company, later known as Texon Mill in the Russell region of Springfield.

114. *Gramophone* magazine, December 1972. Austrian Conductor Karl Böhm recalled in a 1972 interview that Muck had invited Böhm to study all of Wagner's scores with him, helping him with dynamics and Bayreuth acoustics. According to Böhm, Muck was a fine teacher.

115. Beth Abelson MacLeod, *Women Performing Music: The Emergence of American Women as Classical Instrumentalists and Conductors* (Jefferson, NC: McFarland, 2000), 128.

116. MacLeod, *Women Performing Music*, 128.

117. MacLeod, *Women Performing Music*, 128.

118. "Karl Muck Is Remembered by Edward Downes: A Pupil Speaks," *Boston Transcript*, March 9, 1940; Schonberg, *Great Conductors*, 218–20.

119. Geraldine Farrar, *Such Sweet Compulsion: The Autobiography of Geraldine Farrar* (New York: Greystone Press, 1938), 40, 142. Soprano Geraldine Farrar describes performing "Elsa's Dream" from Wagner's *Lohengrin* in 1901 under Karl Muck at the Berlin State Opera, and from that performance receiving a three-year contract. Farrar defended Muck in her book, arguing that "many musicians envied him his high position" and that "the emotions of the time—and matters of a private nature, foolishly made public—provided the weapons for an all too successful effort to discredit him."

120. MacLeod, *Women Performing Music*, 124–39.

121. According to MacLeod, Brico remained frustrated throughout her life, for gender prejudice prevented her from receiving the level of acclaim that her equally talented male colleagues enjoyed.

122. "Karl Muck Is Remembered." Schonberg, *Great Conductors*, 218–20.

123. Kennedy, *Over Here*, 287.

124. Foucault, *History of Sexuality*, xvii

125. "Muck Feared Scandal More Than Arrest."

126. "Muck Feared Scandal More Than Arrest."

127. "Muck Feared Scandal More Than Arrest."

128. *Boston Post*, November 1919.

Chapter Eight

1. Olin Downes, "Dr. Karl Muck: His Death Recalls Problems of the Artist in Times of War" *New York Times*, March 10, 1940.

2. Anita Muck to Mrs. Gardner, August 30, 1919 and October 27, 1921, Isabella Stewart Gardner Museum Archives. Without a permanent address, Anita sent word to her friend that mail could be sent to Deutsche Bank, Potsdamerstrasse, Berlin. Two years later, Karl records their mailing address at the Hotel Adlon in Berlin, writing that "whenever I travel, I leave my new address at this hotel, and all my mail is forwarded to me."

3. Gienow-Hecht, *Sound Diplomacy*, 281.

4. "Palmer Refuses to Conceal Case," *Boston Post*, November 1919.

5. Homberger, *Mrs. Astor's New York*, 11.

6. Charles H. McCormick, *Hopeless Cases: The Hunt for the Red Scare Terrorist Bombers* (Lanham, MD: University Press of America, 2005), 19–21.

7. Turk, "Case of Dr. Karl Muck." A. Mitchell Palmer to Robert L. Norton, December 8, 1919, General Records of the Department of Justice.

8. Douglass Shand-Tucci, *The Art of Scandal: The Life and Times of Isabella Stewart Gardner* (New York: Harper Collins, 1998), 92, 291–92. Dr. Karl Muck to Mrs. Gardner, August 9, 1919, Isabella Stewart Gardner Museum Archives. "Courage and independence always seemed to me to be an integrate part of you. . . . It was your wonderful loyalty which helped Anita over the bitterness of many a hard hour."

9. Letter to Mrs. Philip Hale from C. B. Carberry, Managing Editor, the *Boston Post*, November 26, 1919, Allen A. Brown Music Collection, Boston Public Library, Karl Muck File.

10. "Muck Treated Badly, So Say the Elites—Trying Hard to Clear His Reputation" *Boston Post*, November 1919.

11. "Muck Treated Badly."

12. "Karl Muck Is Remembered."

13. Laurence Riis, *Hitler's Charisma: Leading Millions into the Abyss* (New York: Pantheon, 2012), 21–22.

14. Anita Muck to Mrs. Gardner, February 7, 1920, Isabella Stewart Gardner Museum Archives. Anita spoke of living in cold, uncomfortable rooms in Europe because of a coal shortage. She remained positive, however, pointing out that the sun had reduced their suffering.

15. Advertisement, *Musical America* 33–34 (April 17, 1921), 43.

16. Dr. Karl Muck to Mrs. Gardner, October 27, 1921, Isabella Stewart Gardner Museum Archives.

17. Dr. Karl Muck to Mrs. Gardner, October 27, 1921, Isabella Stewart Gardner Museum Archives.

18. Dr. Karl Muck to Mrs. Gardner, October 27, 1921; Anita Muck to Mrs. Gardner, June 29, 1920, Isabella Stewart Gardner Museum Archives. In Anita's last letter to Isabella Stewart Gardner, she reflected fondly on Fenway Court: "For every mood you can find instantly the company that would be most welcome just then: you go and stand before one picture if you are gay, or even frivolous (which, I hope, happens frequently!); and you go to another one for strength; and again, to another one if you are sad (which, I trust, scarcely ever occurs!).

19. Karl Muck to Charles A. Ellis, August 11, 1921, Boston Symphony Orchestra Archives.

20. Dr. Karl Muck to Mrs. Gardner, October 27, 1921, Isabella Stewart Gardner Museum Archives. Muck wrote that his physician forced him to work.

21. Dr. Karl Muck to Mrs. Gardner, October 27, 1921, Isabella Stewart Gardner Museum Archives. Quite unable to recover from the tragedy, he commented that "the war and the revolution have destroyed the big B— Berlin, Bayreuth, Boston, to which I devoted my whole life's work."

22. Dr. Karl Muck to Mrs. Gardner, October 27, 1921, Isabella Stewart Gardner Museum Archives.

23. William Lines Hubbard, *History of American Music* (New York: AMS Press, 1976), 277. Hamburg Philharmonic hosted important musicians and conductors, including Clara Schumann, Franz Liszt, Gustav Mahler, Sergei Prokofiev, Igor Stravinsky, and Karl Muck.

24. "Dr. Muck Goes to Hamburg," *New York Post*, March 27, 1922.

25. "Dr. Muck Goes to Hamburg."

26. Press Clippings, September 26, 1921, Boston Symphony Orchestra Archives. "Report Karl Muck to Wed, Mother of Rosamond Young, Singer, Denies Troth with Daughter: Special to the New York Times," *New York Times*, September 27, 1921.

27. "Report Karl Muck to Wed." Rosamond was three years older than the newspaper claimed, emphasizing a stark difference in age between the pair.

28. Karl Muck to Charles A. Ellis, August 26, 1921, Boston Symphony Orchestra Archives.

29. Karl Muck to Charles A. Ellis, August 26, 1921, Boston Symphony Orchestra Archives.

30. Karl Muck to Charles A. Ellis, September 5, 1921, Boston Symphony Orchestra Archives.

31. "Love and Intrigue Mingle in the Story of Karl Muck Departed Orchestra Leader," *Washington Times*, December 17, 1919. Rosamond's reputation was greatly harmed by the Muck scandal. She moved to

Washington, DC, to escape the public spotlight, and for a few years after the war she changed her name to Adele Marvin.

32. Allen A. Brown Music Collection, Boston Public Library, Karl Muck File, 87. "The Letters—To prevent Muck from Reentering the Country, the BOI Kept the Letters."

33. Robert Harris to Harry Daugherty, October 24, 1921, FBI Records, 1909–1921, Old German Files. They "left the indictment in a secret file . . . but informed O'Brian of its existence, who in turn notified Muck."

34. Robert Harris to Harry Daugherty, October 24, 1921, FBI Records, 1909–1921, Old German Files.

35. Allen A. Brown Music Collection, Boston Public Library, Karl Muck File, 32.

36. Badal, "The Strange Case of Dr. Karl Muck," 55–60. "Considering Two Great Leaders: Dr. Koussevitzky and Dr. Muck Are Comparable," "Muck of the Wasting Years, Yet Power of Prime." "His hair is thin and grizzled, his face wrinkled and shrunken. . . . As he chooses to believe, the future holds nothing for him."

37. Brown, *Great Wagner Conductors*, 188.

38. Spotts, *Bayreuth*, 20.

39. "Bayreuth Revisited," *Sunday Times*, August 10, 1930. Voss, *Die Dirigenten*, 153.

40. Riis, *Hitler's Charisma*, 18–19.

41. Riis, *Hitler's Charisma*, 21.

42. Riis, *Hitler's Charisma*, 24.

43. Goldsmith, *Inextinguishable Symphony*, 27.

44. Goldsmith, *Inextinguishable Symphony*, 206.

45. Benjamin G. Martin, *The Nazi-Fascist New Order for European Culture* (Cambridge, MA: Harvard University Press, 2016), 38.

46. Evans, *Coming*, 163.

47. Adolf Hitler, *Mein Kampf* (Boston: Riverside Press, 1943), 17.

48. William Shirer, *The Rise and Fall of the Third Reich* (New York: Simon and Schuster, 1960), 102.

49. Riis, *Hitler's Charisma*, 35; Richard J. Evans, *The Third Reich in Power: 1933–1939* (New York, Penguin, 2005), 167.

50. Evans, *Coming*, 38.

51. Evans, *Coming*, 122.

52. Evans, *Third Reich in Power*, 199.

53. Evans, *Coming*, 32.

54. Carr, *Wagner Clan*, 79.

55. Carr, *Wagner Clan*, 63.

56. Voss, *Die Dirigenten*, 22.

57. Carr, *Wagner Clan*, 62.

58. Evans, *Coming*, 32.

59. Evans, *Coming*, 32.

60. Evans, *Third Reich in Power*, 99.

61. Evans, *Coming*, 33.

62. Riis, *Hitler's Charisma*, 24; Evans, *Coming*, 38.

63. Eva Rieger, *Friedelind Wagner: Richard Wagner's Rebellious Granddaughter* (Woodbridge, UK: Boydell Press, 2013), 17.

64. Rieger, *Friedelind Wagner*, 17.

65. Adolf Hitler, *Mein Kampf*, 532.

66. *Silenced Voices*, exhibit, Wagner Festspiele. "Exhibit Examines Anti-Semitism in Bayreuth Using Bayreuth Archives," July 27, 2012, http://www.rappler.com/entertainment/9323-exhibit-examines-anti-semitism-in-bayreuth.

67. *Silenced Voices*.

68. Voss, *Die Dirigenten*, 43.

69. Voss, *Die Dirigenten*, 147.

70. Carr, *Wagner Clan*, 157; *Silenced Voices*.

71. Evans, *Coming*, 293.

72. Carr, *Wagner Clan*, 157; *Silenced Voices*.

73. Rieger, *Friedelind Wagner*, 32; Spotts, *Bayreuth*, 158.

74. Anita Muck to Mrs. Gardner, June 4, 1920, Isabella Stewart Gardner Museum Archives. Of Toscanini, Anita writes from Turin, Italy, "He is just trying to get it together here; but meets unexpected difficulties, as the musicians dislike him thoroughly, and call him a terrible ruffian."

75. Christopher Dyment, *Toscanini in Britain* (Woodbridge, UK: Boydell Press, 2012), 238; Christopher Dyment, *Conducting the Brahms Symphonies: From Brahms to Boult* (Woodbridge, UK: Boydell Press, 2016), 98; Tom Service, "Die Meistersinger: It's Wagner's Most Heartwarming Opera," *Guardian*, May 19, 2011. Conductor David McVicar said Wagner "dropped big fucking clanging clues" for how he wanted the opera interpreted. "The hapless Beckmesser who embodies stereotypical qualities of Jews so vilified by Wagner in racist diatribes."

76. Dyment, *Toscanini in Britain*; Dyment, *Conducting the Brahms Symphonies*, 98; Service, "Die Meistersinger"; Egon Voss, *Die Dirigenten*, 158.

77. Rieger, *Friedelind Wagner*, 32.

78. Carr, *Wagner Clan*, 158. After this episode at Bayreuth, Toscanini became vehemently anti-fascist. In 1936, he conducted the opening season of the Palestine Symphony Orchestra, now known as the Israel Philharmonic Orchestra.

79. B. H. Haggin, *The Toscanini Musicians Knew* (New York: Horizon Press, 1967), 62.

80. Carr, *Wagner Clan*, 159.

81. Lucy Beckett, *Richard Wagner: Parsifal* (Cambridge: Cambridge University Press, 1981), 97.

82. Evans, *Third Reich in Power*, 200.

83. Horowitz, *Wagner Nights*, 327.

84. Ross, *The Rest Is Noise*, 334.

85. Schonberg, *The Great Conductors*, 222.

86. R. Doll and A. B. Hill, "Lung Cancer and Other Causes of Death in Relation to Smoking," *British Medical Journal* 2, no. 5001 (November 1956): 1071–81.

87. *American Music* 25, no. 3 (2007), 440.

88. Herbert Peyser, "Wagner in Germany," *New York Times*, March 5, 1933.

89. Goldsmith, *Inextinguishable Symphony*, 40.

90. Evans, *Coming*, 412.

91. www.darmstadt.de. The city's official website.

92. Goldsmith, *Inextinguishable Symphony*, 49.

93. Evans, *Coming* 394.

94. Evans, *Third Reich in Power*, 202.

95. Evans, *Coming*, 493; Goldsmith, *Inextinguishable Symphony*, 40, 51.

96. Evans, *Coming*, 295.

97. Evans, *Third Reich in Power*, 191.

98. "Otto Klemperer Conductor Dead at 88," *New York Times*, July 8, 1973; Evans, *Coming*, 392.

99. Goldsmith, *Inextinguishable Symphony*, 41.

100. Goldsmith, *Inextinguishable Symphony*, 41.

101. Evans, *Third Reich in Power*, 191; Goldsmith, *Inextinguishable Symphony*, 43.

102. Evans, *Coming*, 392, 293.

103. Goldsmith, *Inextinguishable Symphony*, 70.

104. Ross, *The Rest Is Noise*, 336.

105. Ross, *The Rest Is Noise*, 336.

106. Goldsmith, *Inextinguishable Symphony*, 41.

107. Horowitz, *Understanding Toscanini*, 147.

108. Erik Levi, *Music in the Third Reich* (London: Macmillan, 1994), 246n5.

109. Goldsmith, *Inextinguishable Symphony*, 43.

110. Goldsmith, *Inextinguishable Symphony*, 43.

111. Frank Pieter Hesse, *The Little Music Hall: A Contribution to the 100th Anniversary of the Laeiszhalle* (Hamburg: Conservation Hamburg, Ministry of Culture, Sports and Media, Heritage Institute, 2008), 9–10.

112. Evans, *Coming*, 394.

113. David Josephson, "The Exile of European Music: Documentation of Upheaval and Immigration in the *New York Times*," in *The Musical Migration from Nazi Germany to the United States: Driven into Paradise*, Reinhard Brinkmann and Christoph Wolff (Oakland: University of California Press, 1999), 128. "Muck was sympathetic to the Nazis."

114. Josephson, "The Exile of European Music," in Brinkmann and Wolff, *Musical Migration*, 128.

115. Hesse, *Little Music Hall*, 10.

116. Hesse, *Little Music Hall*, 10.

117. Henry Makow, "Did Hitler Betray Rudolf Hess (and Germany)?," January 27, 2017, http://henrymakow.com/hess_was_on_peace_mission_from.html#sthash.y4qoDlKw.dpuf; "Hitler's Dogs," *Axis History Forum*, September 22, 2005, http://forum.axishistory.com/viewtopic.php?f=45&t=86325; Heinrich Hoffman, *Hitler in Seinen Bergen* (Berlin: SS Totenkopf Library, 1935).

118. Goldsmith, *Inextinguishable Symphony*, 137.

119. Goldsmith, *Inextinguishable Symphony*, 290.

120. Goldsmith, *Inextinguishable Symphony*, 291, 137.

121. *New York Times*, March 5, 1940.

122. Henry Doehl, *The Awards of the Greater German Reich: Orders, Decorations, Badges* (Berlin: Berlin Book and Magazine, 1943), 68–69.

123. Dr. Karl Muck to Mrs. Gardner, October 27, 1921, Isabella Stewart Gardner Museum Archives. Muck later wrote of his attachment to the von Scholley's as "noble, faithful, straight-forward people."

124. Anita Muck to Mrs. Gardner, June 12, 1919, June 4, 1920, and June 29, 1920, Isabella Stewart Gardner Museum Archives.

125. Anita Muck to Mrs. Gardner, June 12, 1919, June 4, 1920, and June 29, 1920, Isabella Stewart Gardner Museum Archives. In honor of this relationship, Isabella Stewart Gardner acquired one of Ruth von Scholley's paintings, called *Four Japanese Women around a Kettle*, that she hung in Fenway Court in the Vatichino, or "little Vatican Room."

126. Anita Muck to Mrs. Gardner, June 12, 1919, June 4, 1920, and June 29, 1920, Isabella Stewart Gardner Museum Archives.

127. Dr. Karl Muck to Mrs. Gardner, October 27, 1921, Isabella Stewart Gardner Museum Archives.

128. American Federation of Arts, *American Magazine of Art* 11 (November 1919–December 1920), 241. Ruth's painting called *Roses* appears in this issue. Archaeological Society of Washington, *Art and Archaeology: An Illustrated Magazine* 12 (1921): 171. Her portrait of Isabel and Marion Neilson and Ruth Morris are mentioned in this magazine as part of the Mrs. Francis Neilson Gallery. Her portrait of Carl Johannes Fuchs was acquired in 2012 by the Nuremberg City Museum at Fembohaus. Her work called *Still Life with Asian Vase and Wackelpagode* was exhibited at the Wurttembergischer Kunstverein in Stuttgart. Her portrait of Ludwig von Kohler hangs in the Professor Gallery of the University of Tubingen.

129. Email correspondence with Herr von Scholley, the Baroness's nephew, and John Froning, Stuttgart, Germany, May 16, 2013, July 16, 2013, July 17, 2013, July 30, 2013, and August 26, 2013. Muck had lost three very significant friends, Ferdinand von Scholley died in 1927, his wife died in 1931, and Edgar Speyer died in Berlin in 1932 while undergoing nose surgery.

130. "Artistic Zenith in Boston," *Boston Post*, June 1918.

131. *High Fidelity* 20 (October 1970).

132. "Boston Symphony Rises in Tribute to Dr. Karl Muck: Former Conductor Here Dies in Germany at 80; Left U.S. under Fire," *Boston Globe*, March 5, 1940.

133. "Boston Symphony Rises."

134. "Karl Muck, Former Head of Boston Symphony," *Boston Globe*, March 4, 1940; Sarna and Smith, *Jews of Boston*, 271. Only six years before Muck's death, in 1934, the Brahmins of Harvard University hosted fellow alumnus, Nazi officer, and Hitler confidante, Ernst Hanfstaengl, to marshal its commencement parade.

135. Olin Downes, "Dr. Karl Muck: His Death Recalls Problems of the Artist in Times of War," *New York Times*, March 10, 1940.

Coda

1. "Army to Determine Attitude," *Boston Post*, June 1919.

2. Higham, *Strangers*, 276. Koegel, *Music in German Immigrant Theater*, 10. H. L. Mencken, a descendent of German immigrants, wrote in 1928, "The melting pot has swallowed up the German Americans as no other group."

3. Henry Louis Mencken, *Thirty-Five Years of Newspaper Work: A Memoir* (Baltimore: Johns Hopkins University Press, 1994), 113. The camp was on the border of Georgia and Tennessee.

4. German phrase "Fick Dich!" meaning "Fuck you!"

5. As mentioned in chapter 7, *Tristan und Isolde* is a tragic opera based on the adulterous love between a knight and a princess, musically representing unfulfilled love and sexual tension, only resolving at the conclusion when Tristan and Isolde finally unite in death.

6. Rosamond's daughter, Diana Chapin, married political commentator and journalist Roderick MacLeish, nephew of poet Archibald MacLeish. Eric MacLeish is their son.

7. Rosamond Chapin died in 1984 at the Mediplex Nursing Home in Beverly, Massachusetts, and is buried in Jamaica Plain at Forest Hills Cemetery in the Young family lot on Milton Hill.

8. McLean, *Jays of Bedford*, 46.

9. Jackson, *Encyclopedia of New York City*, 854.

10. Eleanor Jay (1882–1953), Lucie Jay's daughter, inherited the ancestral home of John Jay and lived there with her husband, Arthur Iselin, a textile merchant, until their deaths in 1952 and 1953, respectively. Westchester County, New York, subsequently purchased the property, and in 1958 it became a New York State Historic Site.

11. "Mrs. Jay, 75, Dies; Ex Social Leader," *New York Evening Post*, January 30, 1931.

12. Richard B. Speed III, *Prisoners, Diplomats, and the Great War: A Study in the Diplomacy of Captivity* (New York: Praeger, 1990), 141.

13. Gerry Depken and Julie Powell, *Fort Oglethorpe* (Charleston, SC: Arcadia, 2009), 44; John Shearer, "The German Connection at Chattanooga's National Cemetery," *Chattanoogan*, August 29, 2008. The monument reads, "During the war years died here far from the homeland. Germany will always remember you."

14. Koegel, *Music in German Immigrant Theater*, 10.

15. Horowitz, *Classical Music in America*, 297.

16. Ayer, *More Than Meets the Ear*, 23–25.

17. Horowitz, *Classical Music in America*, 297.

18. "BSO Poised for Great New Beginning," *MetroWest Daily News*, January 7, 2014.

19. Horowitz, *Classical Music in America*, 301–2.

20. Tischler, *An American Music*, 86.

21. Tischler, *An American Music*, 109. The estimated one million listeners tuned in to Koussevitzky and the BSO's live NBC radio broadcast in 1926.

22. Ross, *The Rest Is Noise*, 264.

23. Horowitz, *Classical Music in America*, 268.

24. Ayer, *More Than Meets the Ear*, 26.

25. Ayer, *More Than Meets the Ear*, 23–25.

26. Ayer, *More Than Meets the Ear*, 14.

27. Horowitz, *Classical Music in America*, 300.

28. Ayer, *More Than Meets the Ear*, 23–25.

29. Higham, *Strangers*, 257.

30. Higham, *Strangers*, 301.

31. Higham, *Strangers*, 340.

32. Ayer, *More Than Meets the Ear*, 118. Oja, "Women Patrons and Crusaders for Modernist Music," in Locke and Barr, *Cultivating Music*, 43.

33. Ayer, *More Than Meets the Ear*, 141.

34. Ralph Locke and Cyrilla Barr, *Cultivating Music in America*, 10; Jocelyn Gecker, "Famed Conductor Accused of Sexual Misconduct," *Associated Press*, December 22, 2017; Anastasia Tsioulcas, "Sexual Assault Claim against Conductor Dutoit Is Credible, Boston Symphony Says," *National Public Radio*, March 2, 2018; Michael Cooper, "James Levine's Final Act at the Met Ends in Disgrace," *New York Times*, March 12, 2018; Michael Cooper, "Met Opera Accuses James Levine of Decades of Sexual Misconduct," *New York Times*, May 18, 2018; Douglas Shadle, "Systemic Discrimination: the Burden of Sameness in American Orchestras," https://www.icareifyoulisten.com/2018/02/systemic-discrimination-burden-sameness-american-orchestras/; "Top Flute Player Sues Boston Symphony Orchestra under Mass. Equal Pay Law," *Associated Press*, July 6, 2018.

35. Horowitz, *Understanding Toscanini*, 93.

36. Horowitz, *Understanding Toscanini*, 114. Judson also managed the Philadelphia Orchestra from 1915–1935, bringing conductor Leopold Stokowski to the city from 1912 to 1937, where he conducted more than two thousand premiere performances by American composers.

37. Shanet, *Philharmonic*, 291.

38. Higham, *Strangers*, 260.

39. Higham, *Strangers*, 254.

40. Higham, *Strangers*, 304.

41. "Dr. Muck's Adversary," *New York Transcript*, February 3, 1931.

42. Horowitz, *Understanding Toscanini*, 136.

43. Horowitz, *Wagner Nights*, 305. New York simply had a love affair with Wagner and could not give that up. By 1922, the Metropolitan Opera Company had offered twenty-three performances of *Tannhauser, Lohengrin, Die Walkure, Tristan und Isolde,* and *Parsifal.*

44. Ross, *The Rest Is Noise*, 264; Horowitz, *Understanding Toscanini*, 136; Shanet, *Philharmonic*, 271.

45. Both orchestras are visible on Facebook, Twitter, and YouTube.

46. *New York Times*, December 17, 2013.

47. BSO, *A Brief History of Symphony Hall* (Boston: Boston Symphony, 2016).

48. "BSO Poised for Great New Beginning," *MetroWest Daily News*, January 7, 2014.

BIBLIOGRAPHY

Archives, Exhibits and Manuscript Collections

Allen A. Brown Music Collection, Boston Public Library, Boston, Massachusetts. Karl Muck File.

Baker Business Library, Harvard University, Cambridge, Massachusetts. Henry Lee Higginson Collection.

Boston Symphony Orchestra, Boston, Massachusetts. Henry Lee Higginson Files.

Brandeis University Library, Waltham, Massachusetts. Newspaper Collection.

Eda Kuhn Loeb Music Library, Harvard University, Cambridge, Massachusetts.

Ellis Island Research Center, Jersey City, New Jersey. Microfilm Series.

Isabella Stewart Gardner Museum Archives, Boston, Massachusetts. Papers of Isabella Stewart Gardner.

John Jay Homestead State Historic Site. Katonah, New York.

Library of Congress, Washington, District of Columbia. Prints and Photographs Division.

Massachusetts Historical Commission, Boston, Massachusetts. Jamaica Plain Preservation Study.

National Archives and Records Administration, Washington, District of Columbia. Records of the Office of the Chief Signal Officer, 1860–1985. Photographs of American Military Activities, 1918–81. FBI Records, 1909–21, Old German Files.

New York Philharmonic Archives, New York, New York. Director's Minutes.

New York Public Library, New York, New York. Damrosch Collection.

New York Times Archives, New York, New York. Online Collection, 1851–1980.

Putnam Library, Noble and Greenough School, Dedham, Massachusetts. Volkmann School Papers.

Richmond Hill History Museum, Richmond Hill, Georgia.

Sixth Cavalry Museum and the Post Community Association, Fort Oglethorpe, Georgia. Fort Oglethorpe Internment Camp Memorabilia.

Smithsonian American Art Museum, Washington, District of Columbia. National Portrait Gallery, Ruth von Scholley File.

Somerville Museum, Somerville, Massachusetts. Exhibit entitled "Hope, Valor, and Inspiration: 1896–1918: The World of George Dilboy— Greek Immigrant and American Hero."

Spaulding Library, New England Conservatory, Boston, Massachusetts. George Chadwick Papers.

Widener Library, Harvard University, Cambridge, Massachusetts. Walter Damrosch Correspondence, 1936–37.

Interviews

Allison, Robert J. April 18, 2018. Informal conversation. Harvard University, Cambridge, Massachusetts.

Askew, Vince. May 9, 2015. Informal discussion and driving tour. Waterways Township. Cottenham Plantation. Richmond Hill, Georgia.

Cutler, Warren. April 6, 2007. Informal interview and property tour. 50 Fenway, Boston, Massachusetts.

Engler, Martha. November 12, 2007, and December 16, 2007. Formal interview. Deutsches Altenheim Nursing Home, West Roxbury, Massachusetts.

Froning, John, and Herr von Scholley [Baroness Ruth von Scholley's nephew]. May 16, 2013, July 16, 2013, July 17, 2013, July 30, 2013, and August 26, 2013. Email correspondence. Stuttgart, Germany.

Garland, Joseph. 1998. Informal conversation. Spirit of '76 Bookstore. Marblehead, Massachusetts.

Haueisen, Alexandra. Informal conversation. March 22, 2009. Goethe Institute, Boston.

Maendal, Dora. October 20, 2017. Personal conversation. Fairholme Hutterite Colony, Manitoba, Canada. National World War I Museum, Kansas City, Missouri.

Martin, William. April 19, 2018. Informal conversation. Harvard University, Cambridge, Massachusetts.

Pierro, Anthony, and Nick Pierro [his nephew]. January 7, 2007. Formal interview. Swampscott, Massachusetts.

Prevo, Mary. February 2012. Internet correspondence.

Schmidt, Reverend William. December 9, 2007. Informal conversation. Holy Trinity German Catholic Church, Boston, Massachusetts.

Journals

American Federation of Arts. *American Magazine of Art* 11 (November 1919–December 1920) 241.

Angoff, Charles. "Boston Twilight." *American Mercury Magazine* (December 1925) 439–44.

Archaeological Society of Washington. *Art and Archaeology: An Illustrated Magazine* 12 (1921): 171.

Badal, James J. "The Strange Case of Dr. Karl Muck Who Was Torpedoed by the Star-Spangled Banner during World War I." *High Fidelity* 20, no.10 (October 1970): 55–60.

Bendroth, Margaret. "Why Women Loved Billy Sunday: Urban Revivalism and Popular Entertainment in Early Twentieth Century American Culture." *Religion and American Culture: A Journal of Interpretation* 14, no. 2 (Summer 2004): 251–71.

Bonds, Mark Evan. "Idealism and the Aesthetics of Instrumental Music at the Turn of the Nineteenth Century." *Journal of the American Musicological Society* 50, no. 2 (Summer/Autumn 1997): 392.

Boyer, Paul. "Boston Book Censorship in the Twenties." *American Quarterly* 15, no. 1 (Spring 1963): 3–24.

Cartright, Jim, and Christopher Dyment. "Karl Muck: A Discography." *Journal of the Association for Recorded Sound Collections* 9, no. 1 (1977): 69–77.

Chmaj, Betty E. "Fry versus Dwight: American Music's Debate over Nationality." *American Music* 3, no. 1 (Spring 1985): 63–84.

Davis, Gerald H. "Orgelsdorf: A World War I Internment Camp in America." *Yearbook of German-American Studies* 26 (1991): 259–60.

DiMaggio, Paul. "Cultural Entrepreneurship in Nineteenth Century Boston: The Creation of an Organizational Base for High Culture in America." *Media Culture and Society* 4 (1982): 37–44.

Finck, Henry T. "German Opera in New York." *Cosmopolitan* 5 (March 1888): 3–23.

Freund, John Christian. *Musical America* 22 (1915): 64.

Freund, John Christian. *Musical America* 33 (1921): 43.

Gienow-Hecht, Jessica C. E. "Trumpeting Down the Walls of Jericho: The Politics of Art, Music and Emotion in German-American Relations, 1870–1920." *Journal of Social History* 36, no. 3 (Spring 2003): 585–613.

Gramophone (December 1972): 1107.

Gross, Daniel A. *Smithsonian* (July 2014).

Haag, Pamela S. "'In Search of 'The Real Thing': Ideologies of Love, Modern Romance, and Women's Subjectivity in the United States, 1920–1940." *Journal of the History of Sexuality* 2, no. 4 (April 1992): 547–77.

Hickey, Donald R. "The Prager Affair: A Study in Wartime Hysteria." *Journal of the Illinois State Historical Society* 62, no. 2 (Summer 1969): 117–34.

Horowitz, Joseph. "Reclaiming the Past: Musical Boston Reconsidered." *American Music* 19, no. 1 (Spring 2001) 18–38.

Jay, Lucie. "Intern All German Music!" *Musical Leader* 36 (July 1918): 213.

Lowens, Irving. "L'affaire Muck: A Study in War Hysteria (1917–1918)." *Musicology* I (1947): 265–74.

Lurie, Edward. "Louis Agassiz and the Races of Man." *Isis* 45, no. 3 (1954): 227–42.

Mugmon, Matthew. "Patriotism, Art, and 'The Star-Spangled Banner': A New Look at the Karl Muck Episode." *Journal of Musicological Research* 33 (2014): 4–26.

Music Magazine—Musical Courier 72 (June 15, 1916) and 75 (September 20, 1917).

Music News 11 (June 13, 1919): 2.

Nagler, Jorg. "Nationale Minoritaten im Krieg: 'Feindliche Auslander' und die amerikanische Heimatfront wahrend des Ersten Weltkriegs" ["National Minorities in War: "Enemy Foreigners" and the American Homefront during World War I]. *Journal of American History* 89, no. 2 (2002): 672–90.

Orgelsdorfer Eulenspiegel 1 (October 15, 1918) and 7 (January 7, 1919).

Posselt, Erich. "Prisoner of War Number 3598." *American Mercury Magazine* (May–August 1927).

Roberge, Marc-Andre. "Ferruccio Busoni in the United States." *American Music* 13, no. 3 (Fall 1995): 295–32.

Speier, Hans. "The Social Types of War." *American Journal of Sociology* 46, no. 1 (1941): 445–54.

Stansell, Christine. "Women, Children, and the Uses of the Streets: Class and Gender Conflict in New York City." *Feminist Studies* 8, no. 2 (Summer 1982): 309–35.

Steen, Ivan D. "Cleansing the Puritan City: The Reverend Henry Morgan's Anti-vice Crusade in Boston." *New England Quarterly* 54, no. 3 (September 1981): 385–411.

Sykley, Anatole. "Boston at War." *Over the Top Magazine of the World War I Centennial* (May 2009).

Tischler, Barbara. "One Hundred Percent Americanism and Music in Boston during World War I." *American Music* 4, no. 2 (Summer 1986) 164–76.

United States Investor 15 (1904): 29–101.

Lectures

Curtis, Liane. "Why Amy Beach Matters." Forest Hills Cemetery, Jamaica Plain, Massachusetts, March 25, 2018.

Horowitz, Joseph. "Rethinking What Orchestras Do: A Humanities Update." Harvard University, John Knowles Paine Hall, October 9, 2012.

Wallach, Alan. "The Battle of the Casts' Revisited." Association of Historians of American Art Symposium, Boston Athenaeum, October 11, 2012.

Zinn, Howard. Marge Piercy, et al., the American Civil Liberties Union of Massachusetts and PEN New England, "An Evening Without . . . Giving Voice to the Excluded," First Congregational Church, Wellfleet, Massachusetts, July 30, 2008.

Newspapers

American, 1918.

Associated Press, 2017, 2018.

Boston Daily Globe, 1879, 1907.

Boston Globe, 1917, 1940.

Boston Herald, 1878, 1915–18, 1940.

Boston Musical Intelligencer, 2017.

Boston Post, 1918, 1919, 1940.

Boston Transcript, 1916–19, 1926, 1931, 1940.

Chattanoogan, 2008.

Chattanooga News, 1919.

Chattanooga Times, 1918, 1920, 1945.

Chicago Daily Tribune, 1918.

Christian Science Monitor, 1918.

Constitution, 1906, 1912.

Daily Bulletin Supplement (San Francisco), 1890.

Fort Wayne Journal Gazette, 1919.

Galveston Daily News, 1886.

Guardian, 2011.

Huffington Post, 2012.

Independent, 1906.

Iowa City Citizen, 1916.

MetroWest (Framingham, MA) Daily News, 2014.

New York Evening Journal, 1918.

New York Evening Post, 1931.

New York Herald, 1918.

New York Review, 1918.

New York Sun, 1918.

New York Times, 1877, 1896, 1899, 1906, 1908, 1912, 1915919, 1921, 1940, 1941, 1984, 1985, 2018.

New York Transcript, 1931.

New York Tribune, 1918.

North American, 1918.

Philadelphia Evening Telegraph, 1917.

Philadelphia Inquirer, 1917.

Record, 1918.

Sandusky Star-Journal, 1908.

Seattle Post Intelligencer, 2014.

Traveler, 1918.

Traverse City Eagle Record, 1962.

Washington Post, 1907.

Washington Times, 1919.

World, 1918.

Online Sources

Allen Collection. *Anchor Line History*. Accessed November 21, 2013. http://www.benjidog.co.uk/allen/Anchor%20Line.html.

American Experience. "Influenza, 1918. City Snapshots: Boston." Accessed November 25, 2012. http://www.pbs.org/wgbh/americanexperience/features/influenza-boston/.

Axis History Forum. "Hitler's Dogs." Accessed November 25, 2012. http://forum.axishistory.com/viewtopic.php?f=45&t=86325.

Baer, John W. *The Pledge of Allegiance: A Revised History and Analysis* (2007). Accessed November 25, 2012. http://www.oldtimeislands.org/pledge/pdgech2.htm.

Bellamy, Edward. "Francis Bellamy, the Pledge of Allegiance, the Bellamy Salute, & Edward Bellamy" (2003). Accessed November 25, 2012. http://rexcurry.net.

Boston Musicians Association, "The Emergence of Classical Players in Local 9-535." Accessed November 25, 2012. http://www.bostonmusicians.org/history/the-emergence-of-classical-players-in-local-9-535.

Boston Musicians Association. "Oral History." Accessed November 25, 2012. http://www.bostonmusicians.org/history/.

Excerpt from the Comstock Law, 2012. Accessed November 25, 2012. http://law.jrank.org/pages/12349/Comstock-Law-Excerpt-from-Comstock-Law.html.

Darmstadt, Germany. The city's official website. Accessed November 25, 2012. www.darmstadt.de.

Domhoff, William G. *Who Rules America? Power in America.* Accessed November 25, 2012. http://sociology.ucsc.edu/whorulesamerica/methods/studying_power.html#axioms.

Dubois, Fletcher. "Celebrating Margaret Ruthven Lang's 150th Birthday." Accessed April 12, 2018. https://hampsongfoundation.org/resource/celebrating-margaret-ruthven-langs-150th-birthday/.

Fitzgerald, Brian. "General Pershing's Legacy Stands Tall in Memorabilia Collection." *B.U. Bridge,* November 23, 2001. Accessed November 25, 2012. http://www.bu.edu/bridge/archive/2001/11-23/pershing.htm.

Fleming, Thomas. "The Flames of Hatred, Then—and Now: The Illusion of Victory; America in World War I." *Once upon a Time . . .* (blog). May 13, 2004. Accessed November 25, 2012. http://powerofnarrative. blogspot.com/2004/05/flames-of-hatred-then-and-now.html.

Jamaica Plain Historical Society. *Boylston Schul-Verein and the German Saturday School.* Accessed November 25, 2012. https://www.jphs.org/victorian-era/boylston-schul-verein-and-the-german-saturday-school.html.

LaPlaca Cohen. "Reports." Accessed May 2018. https://culturetrack.com/wp-content/uploads/2017/03/Culture_Track_2011_Report.pdf.

Liszt Ferenc Memorial Museum and Research Center. *Exhibitions.* Accessed April 25, 2018. http://lisztmuseum.hu/.

Makow, Henry. "Did Hitler Betray Rudolf Hess (and Germany?)." Accessed November 25, 2012. https://www.henrymakow.com/hess_was_on_peace_mission_from.html.

Ochs, Michael. "Who Was M. D. Herter Norton?" *Musicology Now.* Accessed January 22, 2014. http://musicologynow.ams-net.org/2014/01/who-was-m-d-herter-norton.html.

Prochnik, George. *Our Viennese Friend.* Accessed November 25, 2012. http://www.boston.com/news/education/higher/articles/2006/08/20/our_viennese_friend/.

Shadle, Douglas. "Systemic Discrimination: The Burden of Sameness in American Orchestras." Accessed April 2, 2018. https://www.icareifyoulisten.com/2018/02/systemic-discrimination-burden-sameness-american-orchestras/.

St. Botolph Club. *History.* Accessed November 25, 2012. http://stbotolphclub.org/history.php.

Twain, Mark. *Travel Diary* as quoted in the *Chicago Daily Tribune*, December 6, 1891. Accessed November 25, 2012. http://www.twainquotes.com/ Travel1891/Dec1891.html.

US Department of Justice. "History: The U. S. Marshals during World War I; Protection of the Homefront." Accessed November 25, 2012. https://www.usmarshals.gov/history/ww1/ww1.htm.

Walsh, Colleen. "When the Genius Is Also a Symbol of Hate, Where Does That Leave Us?" *Harvard Gazette* April 23, 2018. Accessed April 23, 2018, https://news.harvard.edu/gazette/story/2018/04/ new-yorkers-alex-ross-speaks-at-harvard-on-wagner-and-nazism/.

Published Sources

Abbott, Karen. *Sin in the Second City*. New York: Random House, 2007.

Adam, Thomas, and Gisela Mettele. *Two Boston Brahmins in Goethe's Germany: The Travel Journals of Anna and George Ticknor*. Plymouth, UK: Rowman and Littlefield, 2009.

Adams, Russell B. *The Boston Money Tree*. Boston: Thomas Y. Crowell, 1977.

Alba, Richard D. *Ethnic Identity: The Transformation of White America*. New Haven, CT: Yale University Press, 1990.

Albert E. George and Captain Edwin H. Cooper, Pictorial History of the Twenty-Sixth Division United States Army: With Official Government Pictures Made by United States Signal Corps Unit Under Command of Captain Edwin H. Cooper. Boston: Ball, 1920.

Altman, Irwin, and Setha M. Low. *Place Attachment*. New York: Plenum Press, 1992.

Amory, Cleveland. *The Proper Bostonians*. Orleans, MA: Parnassus, 1947.

Anderson, Benedict R. *Imagined Communities: Reflections on the Origin and Spread of Nationalism*. New York: Verso, 2006.

Applegate, Celia. *Bach in Berlin: Nation and Culture in Mendelssohn's Revival of the "St. Matthew Passion."* Ithaca, NY: Cornell University Press, 2005.

Ayars, Christine Merrick. *Contributions to the Art of Music in America by the Music Industries of Boston 1640–1936*. New York: H. W. Wilson, 1937.

Ayer, Julie. *More Than Meets the Ear: How Symphony Musicians Made Labor History*. Minneapolis: Syren Book, 2005.

Bacon, Edwin Monroe. *Bacon's Dictionary of Boston*. Cambridge, MA: Riverside Press, 1886.

Bacon, John U. *The Great Halifax Explosion: A World War I Story of Treachery, Tragedy, and Extraordinary Heroism*. New York: Harper Collins, 2017.

Baer, John W. *The Pledge of Allegiance, a Centennial History, 1892–1992.* Annapolis, MD: Free State Press, 1992.

Baker, Kelly J. *Gospel according to the Klan: The KKK's Appeal to Protestant America, 1915–1930.* Lawrence: University of Kansas Press, 2017.

Baltzell, E. Digby. *The Protestant Establishment: Aristocracy and Caste in America.* New Haven, CT: Yale University Press, 1987.

Barclay, David E., and Elisabeth Glaser-Schmidt. *Transatlantic Images and Perceptions: Germany and America since 1776.* New York: Cambridge University Press, 1997.

Barrow, Clyde W. *Universities and the Capitalist State: Corporate Liberalism and the Reconstruction of American Higher Education, 1894–1928.* Madison: University of Wisconsin Press, 1990.

Barry, John M. *The Great Influenza: The Epic Story of the Deadliest Plague in History.* New York: Viking, 2004.

Bauer, Dale M. *Sex Expression and American Women Writers, 1860 to 1940.* Chapel Hill: University of North Carolina Press, 2009.

Beckert, Sven. *The Monied Metropolis: New York City and the Consolidation of the American Bourgeoisie, 1850–1896.* New York: Cambridge University Press, 2001.

Beckett, Lucy. *Richard Wagner: Parsifal.* Cambridge: Cambridge University Press, 1981.

Bederman, Gail. *Manliness and Civilization: A Cultural History of Gender and Race in the United States, 1880–1917.* Chicago: University of Chicago Press, 1995.

Bender, Thomas. *Rethinking American History in a Global Age.* Oakland: University of California Press, 2002.

Bernstein, Richard. *The East, the West, and Sex: A History of Erotic Encounters.* New York: Knopf, 2009.

Bessell, George. *Norddeutscher Lloyd, 1857–1957.* Bremen: Schunemann, 1957.

Blair, Karen J. *The Torchbearers: Women and Their Amateur Arts Associations in America, 1890–1930.* Bloomington: Indiana University Press, 1994.

Blake, Angela M. *How New York Became American: 1890–1924.* Baltimore: John Hopkins University Press, 2006.

Block, Adrienne Fried. *Amy Beach: Passionate Victorian; The Life and Work of an American Composer, 1867–1944.* New York: Oxford University Press, 1998.

Boston Herald. *Commercial and Financial New England Illustrated.* Boston: Boston Herald, 1906.

Brinkmann, Reinhard, and Christoph Wolff. *The Musical Migration from Nazi Germany to the United States: Driven into Paradise.* Oakland: University of California Press, 1999.

Brown, Jonathan. *Great Wagner Conductors: A Listener's Companion.* Canberra, Australia: Parrot Press, 2012.

Broyles, Michael. *"Music of the Highest Class": Elitism and Populism in Antebellum Boston.* New Haven, CT: Yale University Press, 1992.

Burton, Humphrey. *Leonard Bernstein.* New York: Doubleday, 1994.

Buzard, James. *The Beaten Track: European Tourism, Literature, and the Ways to "Culture" 1800–1918.* New York: Oxford University Press, 1993.

Byrnes, Garrett D., and Charles H. Spilman. *The Providence Journal 150 Years.* Providence, RI: Providence Journal, 1980.

Capozzola, Christopher. *Uncle Sam Wants You: World War I and the Making of the Modern American Citizen.* New York: Oxford University Press, 2008.

Carnegy, Patrick. *Wagner and the Art of the Theatre.* New Haven, CT: Yale University Press, 2013

Carr, Jonathan. *Wagner Clan: The Saga of Germany's Most Illustrious and Infamous Family.* New York: Atlantic Monthly Press, 2007.

Celello, Kristin. *Making Marriage Work: A History of Marriage and Divorce in the Twentieth Century United States.* Chapel Hill: University of North Carolina Press, 2009.

Cesare. *One Hundred Cartoons by Cesare.* Boston: Small, Maynard, 1916.

Clark, Christopher. *The Sleepwalkers: How Europe Went to War in 1914.* New York: Penguin, 2013.

Cole, David. *Enemy Aliens: Double Standards and Constitutional Freedoms in the War on Terrorism.* New York: New Press, 2003.

Conrad, Sebastian. *German Colonialism.* Cambridge: Cambridge University Press, 2011.

Conzen, Kathleen N. "Germans." In *Harvard Encyclopedia of American Ethnic Groups,* edited by Stephan Thernstrom, 409–22. Cambridge, MA: Harvard University Press, 1980.

Coontz, Stephanie. *Marriage: A History: From Obedience to Intimacy or How Love Conquered Marriage.* New York: Viking Press, 2005.

Cortner, Nancy Gailor. *Great German-American Feasts.* Dallas: Taylor, 1987.

Craven, Wayne. *Gilded Mansions: Grande Architecture and High Society.* New York: W. W. Norton, 2009.

Crawford, Richard. *American Musical Life: A History.* New York: W. W. Norton, 2001.

Creel, George. *How We Advertised America, the First Telling of the Amazing Story of the Committee on Public Information That Carried the Gospel of Americanism to Every Corner of the Globe.* New York: Harper and Brothers, 1920.

Crouthamel, James L. *Bennett's "New York Herald" and the Rise of the Popular Press*. New York: Syracuse University Press, 1989.

Crowl, Philip A. *Alfred Thayer Mahan: The Naval Historian in Makers of Modern Strategy from Machiavelli to the Nuclear Age*. Oxford: Clarendon Press, 1986.

Dalton, Kathleen. *Theodore Roosevelt: A Strenuous Life*. New York: Alfred A. Knopf, 2002.

Dalzell, Robert F., Jr. *Enterprising Elite: The Boston Associates and the World They Made*. Cambridge, MA: Harvard University Press, 1987.

Del Plato, Joan. *Multiple Wives, Multiple Pleasures: Representing the Harem, 1800–1875*. Madison, NJ: Fairleigh Dickinson University Press, 2002.

D'Emilio, John, and Estelle B. Freedman. *Intimate Matters: A History of Sexuality in America*. New York: Harper and Row, 1988.

Depken, Gerry, and Julie Powell. *Fort Oglethorpe*. Charleston, SC: Arcadia, 2009.

Doehl, Henry. *The Awards of the Greater German Reich: Orders, Decorations, Badges*. Berlin: Berlin Book and Magazine, 1943.

Doerries, Reinhard R. *Imperial Challenge: Ambassador Count Bernstorff and German-American Relations, 1908–1917*. Chapel Hill: University of North Carolina Press, 1989.

Dreyfus, Laurence. *Wagner and the Erotic Impulse*. Cambridge, MA: Harvard University Press, 2010.

Duncan, Isadora. *My Life*. New York: Boni and Liveright, 1927.

Duncan, James, and Derek Gregory, eds. *Writes of Passage: Reading Travel Writing*. London: Routledge, 1999.

Dyment, Christopher. *Conducting the Brahms Symphonies: From Brahms to Boult*. Suffolk, UK: Boydell and Brewer, 2016.

Dyment, Christopher. *Toscanini in Britain*. Suffolk, UK: Boydell and Brewer, 2012.

Evans, Richard J. *Coming of the Third Reich*. London: Allen Lane, 2003.

Evans, Richard J. *The Third Reich in Power, 1933–1939*. New York: Penguin, 2005.

Ewen, David. *Dictators of the Baton*. New York: Ziff-Davis, 1943.

Eyman, Scott. *Lion of Hollywood: The Life and Legend of Louis B. Mayer*. New York: Simon and Schuster, 2005.

Farrar, Geraldine. *Such Sweet Compulsion: The Autobiography of Geraldine Farrar*. New York: Greystone Press, 1938.

Farwell, Byron. *Over There: The United States in the Great War, 1917–1918*. New York: W. W. Norton, 1999.

Faucett, Bill. *George Whitefield Chadwick: The Life and Music of the Pride of New England*. Lebanon, NH: University of New England Press, 2012.

Ferguson, Niall. *The Pity of War: Explaining World War One.* New York: Basic Books, 1999.

Fiedler, Joanna. *Molto Agitato: The Mayhem behind the Music.* New York: Random House, 2001.

Flesch, Carl. *The Memoirs of Carl Flesch.* London: Bois de Boulogne, 1957.

Flood, Richard T. *The Story of Noble and Greenough School, 1866–1966.* Dedham, MA: Noble and Greenough, 1966.

Foster-Lussier, Danielle. *Music in America's Cold War Diplomacy.* Oakland: University of California Press, 2015.

Foucault, Michel. *Discipline and Punish: The Birth of the Prison.* New York: Pantheon, 1977.

Foucault, Michel. *History of Sexuality.* New York: Vintage Books, 1988.

Gal, Alton. *Brandeis of Boston.* Cambridge, MA: Harvard University Press, 1980.

Gan, Wendy. *Women, Privacy and Modernity in Early Twentieth Century British Writing.* New York: Palgrave Macmillan, 2009.

Garland, Joseph. *The Gold Coast: The North Shore, 1890–1929.* Manchester, MA: Commonwealth Editions, 1998.

Geiss, Imanuel. *German Foreign Policy, 1871–1914.* Boston: Routledge and Kegan Paul, 1976.

George, Albert E. *Pictorial History of the Twenty-Sixth Division United States Army.* Boston: Ball, 1920.

Gienow-Hecht, Jessica C. E. *Sound Diplomacy: Music and Emotions in Transatlantic Relations, 1850–1920.* Chicago: University of Chicago Press, 2009.

Glaze, Nancy, and Thomas Wolf. *And the Band Stopped Playing: The Rise and Fall of the San Jose Symphony Orchestra.* Cambridge, MA: Wolf, Keene, 2005.

Goethe Society of New England. *Germans in Boston.* Boston: Goethe Society of New England, 1981.

Goldschmidt, Richard B. *In and Out of the Ivory Tower: The Autobiography of Richard B. Goldschmidt.* Seattle: University of Washington Press, 1960.

Goldsmith, Martin. *The Inextinguishable Symphony—a True Story of Music and Love in Nazi Germany.* Somerset, NJ: John Wiley and Sons, 2000.

Green, James R., and Hugh Carter Donahue. *Boston's Workers: A Labor History.* Boston: Boston Public Library, 1979.

Green, Martin. *The Problem of Boston.* New York: W.W. Norton, 1966.

Haag, Pamela. *Consent: Sexual Rights and the Transformation of American Liberalism.* Ithaca, NY: Cornell University Press, 1999.

Haggin, B. H. *The Toscanini Musicians Knew.* New York: Horizon Press, 1967.

Handlin, Oscar. *Boston's Immigrants: 1790–1880.* Cambridge, MA: Harvard University Press, 1991.

Hansen, Eric. *A Horticultural Tale of Love, Lust and Lunacy.* New York: Random House, 2000.

Harris, James F. *German-American Interrelations, Heritage, and Challenge: Joint Conference Held at the University of Maryland, April 2–April 5, 1984.* Tübingen: Attempto Verlag, Tübingen University Press, 1985.

Haueisen, Alexandra. *Das Bostoner Intelligenz-Blatt: Kulturgeschichte der deutschen Immigration in Boston im 19. Jahrhundert Zur Biographie einer deutschen Kolonie.* Hamburg: Verlag Dr. Kovač, 2009.

Hawgood, John A. *The Tragedy of German-America: The Germans in the United States of America during the Nineteenth Century—and After.* New York: Putnam, 1940.

Hesse, Frank Pieter. *The Little Music Hall: A Contribution to the 100th Anniversary of the Laeiszhalle.* Hamburg: Conservation Hamburg, Ministry of Culture, Sports and Media, Heritage Institute, 2008.

Higham, John. *Strangers in the Land: Patterns of American Nativism, 1860–1925.* New Brunswick, NJ: Rutgers University Press, 2002.

Hitler, Adolf. *Mein Kampf.* Boston: Riverside Press, 1943.

Hobsbawm, Eric J. *The Age of Empire, 1875–1914.* Pantheon Books, 1987.

Hobsbawm, Eric, and Terence Ranger. *The Invention of Tradition.* Cambridge: Cambridge University Press, 2005.

Hofer, John. *The History of the Hutterites.* Altona, MB: D. W. Friesen and Sons, 1988.

Hoffman, Heinrich. *Hitler in Seinen Bergen.* Berlin: SS Totenkopf Library, 1935.

Hofstadter, Richard. *The Age of Reform.* New York: Knopf Doubleday, 1960.

Hofstadter, Richard. *The Paranoid Style in American Politics, and Other Essays.* New York: Knopf, 1965.

Holborn, Hajo. *A History of Modern Germany.* New York: Knopf, 1969.

Holoman, D. Kern. *Charles Munch.* New York: Oxford University Press, 2012.

Homberger, Eric. *Mrs. Astor's New York: Money and Social Power in a Gilded Age.* New Haven, CT: Yale University Press, 2009.

Hopkins, Michael F. *The Cold War.* New York: Thames and Hudson, 2011.

Horn, Stacy. *Imperfect Harmony: Finding Happiness Singing with Others.* Chapel Hill, NC: Algonquin Books, 2013.

Horowitz, Joseph. *Classical Music in America: A History of Its Rise and Fall.* New York: W. W. Norton, 2005.

Horowitz, Joseph. *Moral Fire: Musical Portraits from America's Fin De Siècle.* Oakland: University of California Press, 2012.

Horowitz, Joseph. *Understanding Toscanini: How He Became an American Culture-God and Helped Create a New Audience for Old Music.* New York: Knopf, 1987.

Horowitz, Joseph. *Wagner Nights: An American History.* Oakland: University of California Press, 1994.

Howard, Brett. *Boston—a Social History.* New York: Hawthorn Books, 1976.

Howe, M. A. DeWolfe. *The Boston Symphony Orchestra: An Historical Sketch.* Boston: Houghton Mifflin, 1914.

Hubbard, William Lines. *History of American Music.* New York: AMS Press, 1976.

Iversen, Joan Smyth. *The Antipolygamy Controversy in U.S. Women's Movements, 1880–1925.* London: Taylor and Francis, 1997.

Jackson, Kenneth T. *The Encyclopedia of New York City.* New Haven, CT: Yale University Press, 2010.

Jaher, Frederic Cople. *The Urban Establishment: Upper Strata in Boston, New York, Charleston, Chicago, and Los Angeles.* Urbana: University of Illinois Press, 1982.

Jenson, Joan M. *The Price of Vigilance.* Chicago: Rand McNally, 1969.

Jones, Heather. *Violence against Prisoners of War in the First World War: Britain, France and Germany, 1914–1920.* Cambridge: Cambridge University Press, 2011.

Katz, Merrill. *The Great Boston Trivia and Fact Book.* New York: Turner, 1999.

Kazal, Russell A. *Becoming Old Stock: The Paradox of German-American Identity.* Princeton, NJ: Princeton University Press, 2004.

Keene, Jennifer. *Doughboys, the Great War, and the Remaking of America.* Baltimore: Johns Hopkins University Press, 2001.

Kennedy, David M. *Over Here: The First World War and American Society.* New York: Oxford University Press, 2004.

Kirschbaum, Erik. *The Eradication of German Culture in the United States, 1917–1918.* Stuttgart: Hans-Dieter Heinz, 1986.

Klim, Jake. *Attack on Orleans: The World War I Submarine Raid on Cape Cod.* Gloucestershire, UK: History Press, 2014.

Koegel, John. *Music in German Immigrant Theater: New York City 1840–1940.* Rochester, NY: University of Rochester Press, 2009.

Kontje, Todd. *German Orientalism.* Ann Arbor: University of Michigan Press, 2004.

Knight, Ellen. *Charles Martin Loeffler: A Life Apart in American Music.* Chicago: University of Illinois Press, 1993.

Kruh, David. *Always Something Doing: A History of Boston's Infamous Scollay Square.* Boston: Northeastern University Press, 1999.

Lasswell, Harold. *Propaganda Technique in the World War.* Cambridge: Massachusetts Institute of Technology Press, 1971.

Lawton, Mary. *Schumann-Heink: The Last of the Titans.* New York: Macmillan, 1928.

Lears, T. J. Jackson. *Fables of Abundance: A Cultural History of Advertising in America.* New York: Basic Books, 1994.

Lears, T. J. Jackson. *No Place of Grace.* New York: Random House, 1981.

Lebrecht, Norman. *Great Conductors in Pursuit of Power.* New York: Birch Lane Press, 1991.

Lebrecht, Norman. *The Maestro Myth.* New York: Birch Lane Press, 1991.

Leighton, Alexander H. *The Governing of Men: General Principals and Recommendations Based on Experience at a Japanese Relocation Camp.* New York: Octagon Books, 1964.

Lentin, Anthony. *Banker, Traitor, Scapegoat, Spy? The Troublesome Case of Sir Edgar Speyer; An Episode of the Great War.* London: Haus, 2013.

Levi, Erik. *Music in the Third Reich.* London: Macmillan, 1994.

Levine, Lawrence W. *Highbrow / Lowbrow: The Emergence of Cultural Hierarchy in America.* Cambridge, MA: Harvard University Press, 1988.

Lewis, Reina. *Rethinking Orientalism: Women, Travel and the Ottoman Harem.* New Brunswick, NJ: Rutgers University Press, 2004.

Llosa, Alvaro Vargas. *Global Crossings: Immigration, Civilization, and America.* Oakland, CA: Independent Institute, 2013.

Locke, Ralph P., and Cyrilla Barr, *Cultivating Music in America: Women Patrons and Activists since 1860.* Oakland: University of California Press, 1997. https://publishing.cdlib.org/ucpressebooks/view?docId=ft838 nb58v;query=;brand=ucpress.

Lowenthal, Michael. *Charity Girls.* Boston: Houghton Mifflin, 2007.

Luebke, Frederick C. *Bonds of Loyalty: German Americans and World War I.* DeKalb: Northern Illinois University Press, 1974.

Luebke, Frederick C. *Germans in the New World: Essays in the History of Immigration.* Champaign: University of Illinois Press, 1999.

MacCannell, Dean. *The Tourist: A New Theory of the Leisure Class.* Oakland: University of California Press, 1999.

MacLeod, Beth Abelson. *Women Performing Music: The Emergence of American Women as Classical Instrumentalists and Conductors.* Jefferson, NC: McFarland, 2000.

MacMillan, Margaret. *The War That Ended Peace: The Road to 1914.* New York: Random House, 2013.

Martin, Benjamin G. *The Nazi-Fascist New Order for European Culture.* Cambridge, MA: Harvard University Press, 2016.

Martin, George. *The Damrosch Dynasty: America's First Family of Music.* Boston: Houghton Mifflin, 1983.

Massie, Robert K. *Castles of Steel: Britain, Germany, and the Winning of the Great War at Sea.* New York: Ballantine Books, 2004.

Mayer, Martin. *The Met: One Hundred Years of Grand Opera.* New York: Simon and Schuster, 1983.

McCarthy, Kevin F, Arthur Brooks, Julia Lowell, and Laura Zakarus. *The Performing Arts in a New Era.* Santa Monica, CA: Rand, 2001.

McCormick, Charles H. *Hopeless Cases: The Hunt for the Red Scare Terrorist Bombers.* Lanham, MD: University Press of America, 2005.

McLean, Jennifer P. *The Jays of Bedford.* New York: Friends of John Jay Homestead, 1984.

Mencken, Henry Louis. *Thirty-Five Years of Newspaper Work: A Memoir.* Baltimore: Johns Hopkins University Press, 1994.

Miller, John C. *Crisis in Freedom: The Alien and Sedition Acts.* Boston: Little, Brown, 1951.

Miller, Margarette S. *Twenty-Three Words: A Biography of Francis Bellamy; Author of the Pledge of Allegiance.* Idaho Falls, ID: Printcraft Press, 1976.

Miller, Margo. *Chateau Higginson: Social Life in Boston's Back Bay, 1870–1920.* Charleston, SC: Arcadia, 2017.

Miller, Neil. *Banned in Boston: The Watch and Ward Society's Crusade against Books, Burlesque, and the Social Evil.* Boston: Beacon Press, 2010.

Millman, Chad. *The Detonators: The Secret Plot to Destroy America and an Epic Hunt for Justice.* Boston: Little, Brown, 2006.

Mills, C. Wright. *The Power Elite.* Oxford: Oxford University Press, 2000.

Moore, MacDonald Smith. *Yankee Blues: Musical Culture and American Identity.* Bloomington: Indiana University Press, 1985.

Moore, Robin. *The Colorful Mr. Pops: The Man and His Music.* Boston: Little, Brown, 1968.

Moricz, Klara. *Jewish Identities: Nationalism, Racism and Utopianism in Twentieth Century Music.* Oakland: University of California Press, 2008.

Morton, Marcia, and Frederic Morton. *Chocolate: An Illustrated History.* New York: Crown, 1986.

Muck, Peter. *Dr. Karl Muck: Ein Dirigentenleben in Briefen und Dokumenten.* Tutzing: Verlegt Bei Hans Schneider, 2003.

Muina, Paula. *Remembering Fort Oglethorpe Post.* Fort Oglethorpe, GA: Post Community Association, 2008.

Münsterberg, Margareta Anna Adelheid. *Hugo Münsterberg: His Life and Work.* New York: D. Appleton, 1922.

Museum of Fine Arts, Boston School. *Thirty-Sixth Annual Report of the School of Drawing and Painting.* Boston: Museum of Fine Arts, 1913.

Nagler, Jorg. "Victims on the Home Front: Enemy Aliens in the United States during the First World War." In *Minorities in Wartime: National and Racial Groupings in Europe, North America and Australia during the Two World Wars.* Oxford: Berg, 1993.

Nast, T., and T. N. St. Hill. *Thomas Nast: Cartoons and Illustrations.* New York: Dover, 1974.

Nisbet, Peter, and Emilie Norris. *The Busch-Reisinger Museum: History and Holdings.* Cambridge, MA: Harvard University Press, 1991.

Nissenbaum, Stephen. *The Battle for Christmas.* New York: Knopf, 1997.

O'Brian, John Lord. *Reminiscences.* Glen Rock, NJ: Microfilming Corp of America, 1972.

O'Connor, Thomas H. *Boston A to Z.* Cambridge, MA: Harvard University Press, 2000.

Oja, Carol J. *Making Music Modern: New York in the 1920s.* New York: Oxford University Press, 2000.

Olge, Maureen. *Ambitious Brew: The Story of American Beer.* New York: Harvest-Harcourt, 2006.

Panayi, Panikos. *German Immigrants in Britain during the Nineteenth Century, 1815–1914.* Providence, RI: Berg, 1995.

Peiss, Kathy. *Hope in a Jar: The Making of American Beauty Culture.* New York: Henry Holt, 1999.

Perry, Bliss. *Life and Letters of Henry Lee Higginson.* Boston: Atlantic Monthly Press, 1921.

Pliley, Jessica R. *Policing Sexuality: The Mann Act and the Making of the FBI.* Cambridge, MA: Harvard University Press, 2014.

Post, Louis F. *The Deportation Delirium of Nineteenth Century: A Personal Narrative of an Historic Official Experience.* New York: Da Capo Press, 1923.

Rawls, Walton H. *Wake up, America! World War I and the American Poster.* New York: Abbeville Press, 1988.

Remy, Steven P. *The Heidelberg Myth: The Nazification and Denazification of a German University.* Cambridge, MA: Harvard University Press, 2002.

Rich, Burdett A., and M. Blair Wailes. *American Law Reports Annotated.* Vol. 12. Rochester, NY: Lawyers Cooperative, 1921.

Rieger, Eva. *Friedelind Wagner: Richard Wager's Rebellious Granddaughter.* Woodbridge, UK: Boydell Press, 2013.

Rippley, La Verne J. *The German-Americans: Immigrants in America.* Boston: Twayne, 1976.

Riis, Laurence. *Hitler's Charisma: Leading Millions into the Abyss.* New York: Pantheon, 2012.

Rosenbaum, Julia, and Sven Beckert. *The American Bourgeoisie: Distinction and Identity in the Nineteenth Century.* London: Palgrave Macmillan, 2010.

Ross, Alex. *The Rest Is Noise.* New York: Macmillan, 2007.

Rothman, Ellen K. *Hands and Hearts: A History of Courtship in America.* New York: Basic Books, 1984.

Ryan, Dennis P. *A Journey through Boston Irish History.* Charleston, SC: Arcadia, 1999.

Said, Edward W. *Orientalism.* New York: Vintage, 1993.

Sarcone, Anthony F., and Lawrence S. Rines. *A History of Shipbuilding at Fore River.* Quincy, MA: Thomas Crane Public Library, 1975.

Sarna, Jonathan D., and Ellen Smith. *The Jews of Boston.* New Haven, CT: Yale University Press, 2005.

Sauer, Robert J. *Holy Trinity German Catholic Church of Boston: A Way of Life.* Dallas, TX: Taylor, 1994.

Schonberg, Harold C. *The Great Conductors.* New York: Simon and Schuster, 1967.

Shand-Tucci, Douglass. *The Art of Scandal: The Life and Times of Isabella Stewart Gardner.* New York: Harper Collins, 1998.

Shanet, Howard. *Philharmonic: A History of New York's Orchestra.* New York: Doubleday, 1975.

Shaw, Albert. *The Messages and Papers of Woodrow Wilson.* Vol. 1. New York: George H. Doran, 1924.

Shirer, William. *The Rise and Fall of the Third Reich.* New York: Simon and Schuster, 1960.

Solomon, Barbara Miller. *Ancestors and Immigrants: A Changing New England Tradition.* New York: John Wiley, 1956.

Sonneborn, Liz. *German-Americans: Immigrants in America.* Philadelphia: Chelsea House, 2003.

Speed, Richard B., III. *Prisoners, Diplomats, and the Great War: A Study in the Diplomacy of Captivity.* New York: Praeger, 1990.

Spitzer, John. *American Orchestras in the Nineteenth Century.* Chicago: University of Chicago Press, 2012.

Spotts, Frederic. *Bayreuth: A History of the Wagner Festival.* New Haven, CT: Yale University Press, 1994.

Staiger, Janet. *Bad Women: Regulating Sexuality in Early American Cinema.* Minneapolis: University of Minnesota Press, 1995.

Stearns, Peter N. *Sexuality in World History.* New York: Routledge, 2009.

Stoltzfus, Duane C. S. *Pacifists in Chains: The Persecution of Hutterites in the Great War.* Baltimore: John Hopkins University Press, 2013.

Strath, Bo, and Nina Witoszek. *The Postmodern Challenge: Perspectives East and West*. Amsterdam: Rodopi, 1998.

Sullivan, Buddy, and the Richmond Historical Society. *Richmond Hill*. Charleston, SC: Arcadia, 2006.

Tager, Jack. *Boston Riots: Three Centuries of Social Violence*. Boston: Northeastern University, 2000.

Tannahill, Reay. *Sex in History*. Cardinal, UK: Sphere Books, 1990.

Tantillo, Maura Shaw. *American Sexual Politics: Sex, Gender and Race Since the Civil War*. Chicago: University of Chicago Press, 1993.

Tavern Club of Boston. *A Partial Semi-centennial History of the Tavern Club, 1884–1934*. Boston: Tavern Club of Boston, 1934.

Taylor, A. J. P. *The Struggle for the Mastery of Europe*. Oxford: Oxford University Press, 1971.

Thomas, Jerry. *How to Mix Drinks, or The Bon Vivant's Companion*. New York: Dick and Fitzgerald, 1876.

Tibbetts, John C. "The Missing Title Page: Dvorak and the American National Song." *Music and Culture in America, 1861–1918*. New York: Garland, 1998.

Tilchin, William N. *Artists in Power: Theodore Roosevelt, Woodrow Wilson and Their Enduring Impact on U.S. Foreign Policy*. Westport, CT: Praeger Security International, 2006.

Tipton, Frank B. *A History of Modern Germany since 1815*. Oakland: University of California Press, 2003.

Tischler, Barbara L. *An American Music: The Search for an American Musical Identity*. New York: Oxford University Press, 1986.

Tolzmann, Don H. *German-Americans in the World Wars*. Vol. 1, *The Anti-German Hysteria of World War One*. New Providence, NJ: KG Saur, 1995.

Toomey, Daniel P. *Massachusetts of Today: A Memorial of the State, Historical and Biographical, Issued for the World's Exposition at Chicago*. Boston: Columbia, 1892.

Tooze, Adam. *The Deluge: The Great War and the Remaking of Global Order 1916–1931*. London: Allen Lane, 2014.

Trommler, Frank, and Joseph McVeigh. *America and the Germans: An Assessment of a Three Hundred Year History*. Vol. 2, *The Relationship in the Twentieth Century*. Philadelphia: University of Pennsylvania Press, 1985.

Truxall, Aida Craig. *All Good Greetings: Letters from Geraldine Farrar to Ilka Marie Stotler*. Pittsburgh, PA: University of Pittsburgh Press, 1991.

Turner, Graeme. *Understanding Celebrity*. London: Sage, 2004.

US Alien Property Custodian. *Annual Report, Office of the Alien Property Custodian*. Washington, DC: US Printing Office, 1919.

Vischer, Adolf Lucas. *Barbed Wire Disease: A Psychological Study of the Prisoner of War.* London: Bale and Danielsson, 1919.

Weber, Thomas. *Our Friend "The Enemy": Elite Education in Britain and Germany before World War I.* Stanford, CA: Stanford University Press, 2008.

Wetzel, Richard. *The Globalization of Music in History.* New York: Routledge, 2012.

White, Edward. *The Tastemaker Carl Van Vechten and the Birth of Modern America.* New York: Farrar, Straus and Giroux, 2014.

Wilford, Hugh. *The Mighty Wurlitzer: How the CIA Played America.* Cambridge, MA: Harvard University Press, 2008.

Williams, Susan. *Food in the United States, 1820–1890.* Westport, CT: Greenwood Press, 2006.

Wittke, Carl. *The German Language Press in America.* Lexington: University of Kentucky Press, 1957.

Wolf Organization, Inc. *The Financial Condition of Symphony Orchestras.* Washington, DC: American Symphony Orchestra League, 1992.

Woodhull, Victoria C. *Steinway Speech.* New York: Woodhull and Claflin, 1871.

Vaughan, Elizabeth Head. *Community under Stress: An Internment Camp Culture.* Princeton, NJ: Princeton University Press, 1949.

Veblen, Thorstein. *The Theory of the Leisure Class.* New York: Dover, 1994.

Voluntary Committee of the Regiment. *History of the 101st United States Engineers American Expeditionary Forces, 1917–1918–1919.* Cambridge, MA: University Press, 1926.

Von Hoffman, Alexander. *Local Attachments: The Making of an American Urban Neighborhood, 1850–1920.* Baltimore: John Hopkins University Press, 1994.

Vonnegut, Kurt. *Palm Sunday.* New York: Delacorte Press, 1981.

Voss, Egon. *Die Dirigenten der Bayreuther Festspiele.* Regensburg: Gustav Boss Verlag, 1976.

Weber, Thomas. *Our Friend "the Enemy": Elite Education in Britain and Germany before World War I.* Stanford, CA: Stanford University Press, 2008.

Whitehill, Walter Muir. *A Seidel for Jake Wirth.* Lunenburg, VT: Stinehour Press, 1964.

Wiebe, Robert H. *The Search for Order, 1877–1920.* New York: Hill and Wang, 1967.

Wilson, Carol Green. *Arthur Fiedler: Music for the Millions; The Story of the Conductor of the Boston Pops Orchestra.* London: Evans, 1968.

Wokoeck, Ursula. *German Orientalism: The Study of the Middle East and Islam from 1800 to 1945.* New York: Routledge, 2009.

Zacks, Richard. *History Laid Bare: Love, Sex and Perversity from the Ancient Etruscans to Warren G. Harding.* New York: Harper Collins, 1994.

Zaitzevsky, Cynthia. *Frederick Law Olmsted and the Boston Park System.* Cambridge, MA: Harvard University Press, 1982.

Zimmermann, Warren. *First Great Triumph: How Five Americans Made Their Country a World Power.* New York: Farrar, Strauss and Giroux, 2002.

Zinn, Howard. "The Problem Is Civil Obedience." In *The Zinn Reader,* 403–11. New York: Seven Stories Press, 1970.

Unpublished Theses

Bomberger, Elam Douglas. "The German Musician Training of American Students, 1850–1900." PhD diss., University of Maryland, 1991.

Burrage, Melissa D. "Albert Cameron Burrage: An Allegiance to Boston's Elite through a Lifetime of Political, Business and Social Reform, 1859–1931." MA thesis, Harvard University, 2004.

Burrage, Melissa D. "Caught on the American Cultural Battleground: Dr. Karl Muck in World War I Boston." PhD diss., University of East Anglia, 2015.

Turk, Gayle K. "The Case of Dr. Karl Muck, Anti-German Hysteria and Enemy Alien Internment during World War I." BA thesis, Harvard University, 1994.

INDEX

Page numbers in *italics* indicate illustrations and photographs. BSO is an abbreviation for Boston Symphony Orchestra; BOI is an abbreviation for Bureau of Investigation.

Eastman Studies in Music

Ralph P. Locke, Senior Editor
Eastman School of Music

Additional Titles of Interest

American Popular Music in Britain's Raj
Bradley G. Shope

George Rochberg, American Composer:
Clues to a LifePersonal Trauma and Artistic Creativity
Amy Lynn Wlodarski

Good Music for a Free People:
The Germania Musical Society in Nineteenth-Century America
Nancy Newman

John Kirkpatrick, American Music, and the Printed Page
Drew Massey

Music and Musical Composition at the American Academy in Rome
Edited by Martin Brody

Music of the Moravian Church in America
Edited by Nola Reed Knouse

Reflections of an American Harpsichordist:
Unpublished Memoirs, Essays, and Lectures of Ralph Kirkpatrick
Edited by Meredith Kirkpatrick

Verdi in America:
"Oberto" through "Rigoletto"
George W. Martin

A complete list of titles in the Eastman Studies in Music series may be
found on the University of Rochester Press website, www.urpress.com

One of the cherished narratives of American history is that of the Statue of Liberty welcoming immigrants to its shores. Accounts of the exclusion and exploitation of Chinese immigrants in the late nineteenth century and Japanese internment during World War II tell a darker story of American immigration. Less well known, however, is the treatment of German-Americans and German nationals in the United States during World War I. Initially accepted and even welcomed into American society at the outbreak of war, this group would face rampant intolerance and anti-German hysteria.

Melissa D. Burrage's book illustrates this dramatic shift in attitude in her engrossing narrative of Dr. Karl Muck, the celebrated German conductor of the Boston Symphony Orchestra, who was targeted and ultimately disgraced by a New York Philharmonic board member and by capitalists from that city who used his private sexual life as a basis for having him arrested, interned, and deported from the United States. While the campaign against Muck made national headlines, and is the main focus of this book, Burrage also illuminates broader national topics such as: Total War; State power; vigilante justice; internment and deportation; irresponsible journalism; sexual surveillance; attitudes toward immigration; anti-Semitism; and the development of America's musical institutions. The mistreatment of Karl Muck in the United States provides a narrative thread that connects these various wartime and postwar themes.

MELISSA D. BURRAGE, a writing consultant at Harvard University Extension School, holds a master's degree in history from Harvard University and a PhD in American studies from University of East Anglia.

"In 1918, Karl Muck captured headlines, but *The Karl Muck Scandal* goes behind the front page to explain one of World War I's most remarkable events. Melissa Burrage draws on intensive research and careful listening while always keeping the human element in view. An immigrant in a new land; contests over loyalty and patriotism; fear, surveillance, and incarceration: this is not only the story of a single musician, but also a crucial chapter in the story of America itself."

—Christopher Capozzola professor of history at Massachusetts Institute of Technology and author of *Uncle Sam Wants You: World War I and the Making of the Modern American Citizen*

"I find Burrage's book to be a provocative, well-researched, and carefully argued contribution to the literature on American musical life, the impact of World War I on the American cultural scene, and issues of nationalism and identity in the early twentieth century. *The Karl Muck Scandal: Classical Music and Xenophobia in World War I America* is admirably evenhanded, presenting a complex portrait of Dr. Muck that stands as one of the book's best features. It will become a new point of departure for future scholars working on the Boston Symphony Orchestra and its conductor."

—S. Andrew Granade, is professor of musicology at the University of Missouri–Kansas and author of *Harry Partch, Hobo Composer*

"*The Karl Muck Scandal: Classical Music and Xenophobia in World War I America* is impressive, linking musical, historical, and cultural aspects in the career of Dr. Karl Muck as conductor of the Boston Symphony Orchestra. The author's narrative confronts effectively how Muck's career engaged with a variety of major issues—nationalism, anti- Semitism, sexual morality, and Nazism. Drawing on impressive archival and published sources, Burrage moves smoothly between the musical world and national politics, showing how deeply public opinion became inflamed in new ways in the early decades of the twentieth century."

—William A. Weber, professor emeritus of history at California State University, Long Beach, and author of *The Great Transformation of Musical Taste: Concert Programming from Haydn to Brahms*